Deep Learning at Scale
At the Intersection of Hardware, Software, and Data

Suneeta Mall

Beijing · Boston · Farnham · Sebastopol · Tokyo

Deep Learning at Scale

by Suneeta Mall

Published by O'Reilly Media, Inc., 1005 Gravenstein Highway North, Sebastopol, CA 95472.

O'Reilly books may be purchased for educational, business, or sales promotional use. Online editions are also available for most titles (*https://oreilly.com*). For more information, contact our corporate/institutional sales department: 800-998-9938 or *corporate@oreilly.com*.

Acquisition Editor: Nicole Butterfield	**Copyeditor:** Rachel Head
Development Editor: Sara Hunter	**Proofreader:** Kim Cofer
Production Editor: Aleeya Rahman	**Indexer:** Judith McConville
	Interior Designer: David Futato
	Cover Designer: Karen Montgomery
	Illustrator: Kate Dullea

June 2024:   First Edition

Revision History for the First Edition

2024-06-17:   First Release

See *http://oreilly.com/catalog/errata.csp?isbn=9781098145286* for release details.

978-1-098-14528-6

[LSI]

Table of Contents

Part I. Foundational Concepts of Deep Learning

Part II.   Distributed Training

Preface

I started my professional career as a software engineer. Over the course of my time in that role, I became deeply interested and involved in running software and systems at scale. I learned a lot about distributed systems, performance, optimizations, and running them reliably at scale. Subsequently, I went on to perform many other roles, from building systems at the intersection of software and operations (DevOps) and auxiliary systems to enable intelligent software (MLOps), to running deep learning inference at scale and developing data engines for deep learning (machine learning engineering), to developing multitasking, multiobjective models for critical functions such as healthcare and business decision workflows as a data scientist and machine learning specialist.

Since I've become involved in building intelligent systems, deep learning is a big part of what I do today. The wide adoption of deep learning–based intelligent (AI) systems is motivated by its ability to solve problems at scale with efficiency. However, building such systems is complex, because deep learning is not just about algorithms and mathematics. Much of the complexity lies at the intersection of hardware, software, data, and deep learning (the algorithms and techniques, specifically). I consider myself fortunate to have gained experience in a series of roles that forced me to rapidly develop a detailed understanding of building and managing deep learning–based AI systems at scale. The knowledge that I have acquired because of the opportunities presented to me is not so easily available and consumed, because each of these domains—hardware, software, and data—is as complex as deep learning itself.

The key motivation behind this book is to democratize this knowledge so that every machine learning practitioner, engineer or not, can navigate the deep learning landscape. I've always felt that this knowledge was somewhat fragmented, and saw an opportunity to pull it together to create a coherent knowledge base. This unified knowledge base will provide theoretical and practical guidance for developing deep learning engineering knowledge so you can easily scale out your deep learning workloads without needing to go through as many explorations as I did.

Why Scaling Matters

Deep learning and scaling are correlated. Deep learning is capable of scaling your objectives from single task to multitask, from one modality to multimodality, from one class to thousands of classes. Anything is possible, provided you have scalable hardware and a large volume of data and write software that can efficiently scale to utilize all the resources available to you.

Scaling is complex, and thus not free. Developing a deep learning–based system requires a large number of layers, a large volume of data, and hardware capable of handling computationally intensive workloads. Scaling requires understanding the elasticity of your entire system—not just your model but your entire deep learning stack—and adapting to situations where elasticity nears a breaking point. Therein lies the secondary motivation of this book: to enable you to gain a deeper understanding of your system and when it might break, and how you can avoid unnecessary breaks.

Who This Book Is For

This book aims to help you develop a deeper knowledge of the deep learning stack—specifically, how deep learning interfaces with hardware, software, and data. It will serve as a valuable resource when you want to scale your deep learning model, either by expanding the hardware resources or by adding larger volumes of data or increasing the capacity of the model itself. Efficiency is a key part of any scaling operation. For this reason, consideration of efficiency is weaved in throughout the book, to provide you with the knowledge and resources you need to scale effectively.

This book is written for machine learning practitioners from all walks of life: engineers, data engineers, MLOps, deep learning scientists, machine learning engineers, and others interested in learning about model development at scale. It assumes that the reader already has a fundamental knowledge of deep learning concepts such as optimizers, learning objectives and loss functions, and model assembly and compilation, as well as some experience with model development. Familiarity with Python and PyTorch is also essential for the practical sections of the book.

Given the complexity and scope, this book primarily focuses on scale-out of model development and training, with an extensive focus on distributed training. While the first few chapters may be useful for deployment and inference use cases, scaling inference is beyond the scope of this book. The topics we will cover include:

- How your model is decomposed into a computation graph and how your data flows through this graph during the training process.
- The less told but beautiful story of floating-point numbers and how these Higgs bosons of deep learning can be used to achieve memory efficiency.

- How accelerated computing speeds up your training and how you can best utilize the hardware resources at your disposal.
- How to train your model using distributed training paradigms (i.e., data, model, pipeline, and hybrid multidimensional parallelism). You will also learn about federated learning and its challenges.
- How to leverage the PyTorch ecosystem in conjunction with NVIDIA libraries and Triton to scale your model training.
- Debugging, monitoring, and investigating bottlenecks that undesirably slow down the scale-out of model training.
- How to expedite the training lifecycle and streamline your feedback loop to iterate model development and related best practices.
- A set of data tricks and techniques and how to apply them to scale your training over limited resources.
- How to select the right tools and techniques for your deep learning project.
- Options for managing compute infrastructure when running at scale.

How This Book Is Organized

This book consists of an introductory chapter followed by a dozen chapters divided into three parts covering foundational concepts, distributed training, and extreme scaling. Each chapter builds upon the concepts, fundamentals, and principles from the preceding chapters to provide a holistic knowledge of deep learning that will enable efficient and effective scale-out of training workloads.

Introduction

Chapter 1, "What Nature and History Have Taught Us About Scale", sets out the theoretical framework for deciding when to scale and explores the high-level challenges involved in scaling out. In this chapter, you will also read about the history of deep learning and how scaling has been a key driver of its success.

Part I: Foundational Concepts of Deep Learning

Chapter 2, "Deep Learning", introduces deep learning through the lens of computational graphs and data flow. Early-stage machine learning practitioners may find this chapter helpful as it explains the inner workings of deep learning through pure Python, no-frills exercises. More experienced deep learning practitioners may choose to skip this chapter.

Chapter 3, "The Computational Side of Deep Learning", dives into the inner workings of electronic computations and hardware, exploring how compute capabilities are achieved and scaled. It also provides detailed insights into the variety of accelerated hardware available today, to arm you with the knowledge required to choose the most suitable hardware for your project.

Chapter 4, "Putting It All Together: Efficient Deep Learning", brings the foundational knowledge of deep learning together to provide more practical guidance on how to build an efficient and effective intelligent system for your task and how to measure and monitor it. In this chapter, you will also learn about graph compilation and a series of memory tricks to provide you with the knowledge to build an efficient stack.

Part II: Distributed Training

Chapter 5, "Distributed Systems and Communications", introduces the foundations of distributed systems and provides detailed insights into the different types and the challenges associated with each one. Communication is a critical aspect of distributed systems that's explained in this chapter through the lens of deep learning. This chapter also provides insights into the options and tools that can be used to scale out your hardware resources to achieve distributed computing, along with what this means for hardware with acceleration.

Chapter 6, "Theoretical Foundations of Distributed Deep Learning", extends Chapter 5 to provide theoretical and foundational knowledge of distributed deep learning. In this chapter, you will learn about a variety of distributed deep learning training techniques and a framework for choosing one.

Chapter 7, "Data Parallelism", dives into the details of distributed data parallelism and provides a series of practical exercises demonstrating these techniques.

Chapter 8, "Scaling Beyond Data Parallelism: Model, Pipeline, Tensor, and Hybrid Parallelism", provides foundational and practical knowledge of scaling model training beyond data parallel. In this chapter, you will learn about model, pipeline, and multidimensional hybrid parallelism and experience the challenges and limitations of each of these techniques via practical exercises.

Chapter 9, "Gaining Practical Expertise with Scaling Across All Dimensions", brings all the learning of Part II together to provide knowledge and insights on how to realize multidimensional parallelism in a more effective manner.

Part III: Extreme Scaling

Chapter 10, "Data-Centric Scaling", provides a data-centric perspective and offers valuable information on assorted techniques to maximize the gain from your data. This chapter also provides useful insights on how to achieve efficiency in your data pipelines through sampling and selection techniques.

Chapter 11, "Scaling Experiments: Effective Planning and Management", focuses on scaling out of experiments and provides insights on experiment planning and management. This chapter provides useful information for when you're conducting multiple experiments and want to maximize your chances of finding the best-performing model; it covers techniques like fine tuning, mixture of experts (MoE), contrastive learning, etc.

Chapter 12, "Efficient Fine-Tuning of Large Models", explores low-rank fine tuning of large models with a practical example.

Chapter 13, "Foundation Models", lays out the conceptual framework of foundation models and provides a summary of this evolving landscape.

What You Need to Use This Book

To run the code samples in this book, you will need a working device with at least a 16-core CPU and 16 GB (ideally 32 GB) of RAM. Most of the exercises in Part II use accelerated hardware, so access to a system with more than one GPU—ideally NVIDIA—will be required for some of the exercises. Most exercises are written in a platform-agnostic way, and a Dockerfile with a list of runtime dependencies required to run the exercises is provided.

Setting Up Your Environment for Hands-on Exercises

Instructions to set up your environment for this book's practical exercises are included in the companion GitHub repository (*https://oreil.ly/deep-learning-at-scale*). This page includes specific guidelines to set up either a Python-based native environment or an emulated Docker environment. Instructions to set up the NVIDIA drivers and CUDA runtime are also provided, along with instructions on updating the versions and running the exercises.

Some exercises in Part II will come with special instructions that will be explained in the context of those exercises.

Using Code Examples

Supplemental material (code examples, exercises, etc.) is available for download at *https://github.com/suneeta-mall/deep_learning_at_scale*.

If you have a technical question or a problem using the code examples, please send an email to *bookquestions@oreilly.com*.

This book is here to help you get your job done. In general, if example code is offered with this book, you may use it in your programs and documentation. You do not need to contact us for permission unless you're reproducing a significant portion of the code. For example, writing a program that uses several chunks of code from this book does not require permission. Selling or distributing examples from O'Reilly books does require permission. Answering a question by citing this book and quoting example code does not require permission. Incorporating a significant amount of example code from this book into your product's documentation does require permission.

We appreciate, but generally do not require, attribution. An attribution usually includes the title, author, publisher, and ISBN. For example: "*Deep Learning at Scale* by Suneeta Mall (O'Reilly). Copyright 2024 Suneeta Mall, 978-1-098-14528-6."

If you feel your use of code examples falls outside fair use or the permission given above, feel free to contact us at *permissions@oreilly.com*.

Conventions Used in This Book

The following typographical conventions are used in this book:

Italic

> Indicates new terms, URLs, email addresses, filenames, and file extensions.

`Constant width`

> Used for program listings, as well as within paragraphs to refer to program elements such as variable or function names, databases, data types, environment variables, statements, and keywords.

`Constant width bold`

> Shows commands or other text that should be typed literally by the user.

`Constant width italic`

> Shows text that should be replaced with user-supplied values or by values determined by context.

> This element signifies a tip or suggestion.

> This element signifies a general note.

This element indicates a warning or caution.

O'Reilly Online Learning

 For more than 40 years, *O'Reilly Media* has provided technology and business training, knowledge, and insight to help companies succeed.

Our unique network of experts and innovators share their knowledge and expertise through books, articles, and our online learning platform. O'Reilly's online learning platform gives you on-demand access to live training courses, in-depth learning paths, interactive coding environments, and a vast collection of text and video from O'Reilly and 200+ other publishers. For more information, visit *https://oreilly.com*.

How to Contact Us

Please address comments and questions concerning this book to the publisher:

O'Reilly Media, Inc.
1005 Gravenstein Highway North
Sebastopol, CA 95472
800-889-8969 (in the United States or Canada)
707-827-7019 (international or local)
707-829-0104 (fax)
support@oreilly.com
https://www.oreilly.com/about/contact.html

We have a web page for this book, where we list errata, examples, and any additional information. You can access this page at *https://oreil.ly/DLAS*.

For news and information about our books and courses, visit *https://oreilly.com*.

Find us on LinkedIn: *https://linkedin.com/company/oreilly-media*.

Watch us on YouTube: *https://youtube.com/oreillymedia*.

Acknowledgments

To my beloved family: Your unwavering support and understanding during the creation of this book has been huge. My heartfelt thanks to my husband, whose patience and encouragement kept me going. To my incredible children, your curiosity and enthusiasm for learning inspire me every day. This book is as much yours as it is mine.

Mum, Dad, and parents in-law, your love, wisdom, unwavering belief in my abilities, and endless encouragement have been a guiding light throughout this journey. To my brother, your perseverance knows no bounds and keeps me inspired. This book is dedicated to all of you.

To the open source deep learning community: I have deepest gratitude for the open source communities around the world that have been forthcoming with their knowledge and work to collectively and collaboratively improve the posture of AI systems in production. Your commitment to innovation and accessibility in the field of deep learning has been revolutionary.

The knowledge, tools, and resources that these communities have built together have not only shaped this book, but have also transformed the landscape of machine learning. I'm deeply thankful for your contributions. This work would not have been possible without you. I take deep pleasure in dedicating this book to you!

To my dedicated tech reviewers and editorial team: I'm indebted to your valuable input and dedication to excellence. I would like to acknowledge and express my deepest gratitude to the technical reviewers, Tim Hauke Langer, Giovanni Alzetta, Satyarth Praveen, and Vishwesh Ravi Shrimali, and my editor, Sara Hunter, whose guidance and advice have greatly improved this book. I would also like to express my gratitude to Nicole Butterfield, my acquisitions editor, for her support and guidance in shaping the direction of the book.

## CHAPTER 1

What Nature and History Have Taught Us About Scale

What works at scale may be different from scaling what works.
—*Rohini Nilekani*

The main goal of this book is to present valuable information to allow you to efficiently and effectively scale your deep learning workload. In this introductory chapter, we'll consider what it means to scale and how to determine when to start scaling. We'll dive into the general law of scaling and draw some inspiration from "nature" as the most scalable system. We'll also look at evolving trends in deep learning and review how innovation across hardware, software, data, and algorithms is converging to power deep learning at scale. Finally, we'll explore the philosophy behind scaling and review what factors you should consider and what questions you should ask before beginning your scaling journey.

This chapter is front-loaded with philosophy and history. If you prefer technical material, please skip to "Artificial Intelligence: The Evolution of Learnable Systems" on page 7.

The Philosophy of Scaling

To *scale* a system is to grow its ability by adding more resources to it.[1] Increasing the capacity of a bridge by adding more lanes to accommodate more vehicles simultaneously is an example of scaling the bridge. Adding more replicas of a service to handle

---

[1] Bondi, André B. 2000. "Characteristics of Scalability and Their Impact on Performance." In *Proceedings of the Second International Workshop on Software and Performance (WOSP '00)*, 195–203. *https://doi.org/10.1145/350391.350432*.

additional simultaneous user requests and increase throughput is an example of scaling the service. Often when people talk about scaling, they start with a high-level goal, intending to scale a scenario or a capability of a higher order. Adding additional lanes to a bridge or adding more replicas of a service may seem like a straightforward goal, but when you start to dissect it and unravel its dependencies and the plan to execute it, you start to notice the challenges and complexities involved in meeting the original objective of scaling.

How can we assess these task- and domain-specific challenges? They're captured in the general law of scaling.

The General Law of Scaling

The general scaling law, given by $y \propto f(x)$, defines the scalability of y by its dependency on the variable x. The mathematical relationship given by $f(x)$ is assumed to hold only over a significant interval of x, to outline that scalability by definition is limited and there will be a value of x where the said (scaling) relationship between x and y will break. These values of x will define the limits of scalability of y. The generic expression $f(x)$ indicates the scaling law takes many forms and is very domain/task-specific. The general scaling law also states that two variables may not share any scaling relationship.

For example, the length of an elastic band is proportional to the applied pull and the elasticity of the material. The band's length grows as more force (pull) is applied. Yet, there comes a time when, upon application of further force, the material reaches its tensile strength and breaks. This is the limit of the material and defines how much the band can scale. Having said that, the band's elasticity does not share a scaling relationship with some other properties of the material, such as its color.

The history of scaling law is interesting and relevant even today, because it underscores the challenges and limitations that come with scaling.

History of Scaling Law

In the *Divine Comedy*, the 14th-century writer and philosopher Dante Alighieri gave a poetic depiction of his conception of Hell, describing it as an inverted cone descending in nine concentric rings to the center of the Earth. His description was accompanied by an illustration by Sandro Botticelli known as the *Map of Hell* (*https://oreil.ly/gzWZr*). This depiction was taken quite literally, leading to an investigation to measure the diameter of the cone (the so-called Hall of Hell). Galileo Galilei, a young mathematician, used Dante's poetic verse "Already the Sun was joined to the horizon / Whose meridian circle covers / Jerusalem with its highest point" as the basis for his conclusion that the diameter of the circle of the dome must be equal to the radius of the Earth and that the center of the roof would lie in Jerusalem. Attending to the term "meridian," Galileo also deduced that the boundary of the roof's dome would pass through France, at the point where the prime meridian cuts through. Mapping the dome's tip at Jerusalem and the edge in France, he concluded that the opposite edge would lie in Uzbekistan. Galileo's deduction of the size of the Hall of Hell resulted in a pretty big structure. He referenced the dome of Florence Cathedral, which is 45.5 meters (149 feet) wide and 1.5 meters (5 feet) thick, and *scaled its measurements linearly* to deduce that the roof of the hall would have to be 600 km (373 miles) thick in order to support its own weight. His work was well received, landing him a role as a lecturer in mathematics at the University of Pisa.

In an interesting twist, Galileo realized that the structure, at this thickness, would not be very stable. He pronounced that the thickness of the dome would have to increase much faster than the width to maintain the strength of the structure and keep it from collapsing. Galileo's conclusion was inspired by the study of animal bones, whose thickness, he observed, increases proportionally at a much faster rate than their length. For example, the longest and also strongest bone in humans, the femur, is on average 48 cm (18.9 in) in length and 2.34 cm (0.92 in) in diameter and can support up to 30 times the weight of an adult. The femur of a greyhound, however, measures on average just 19 cm (7.48 in) long and 0.13 cm (0.05 in) thick (see Figure 1-1).[2] Between the two species, this is a difference in length of just 2.5x, whereas the human femur is 18x thicker than that of a greyhound! Continuing the comparison, the second largest animal known to have existed in the world (second only to the blue whale), *Tyrannosaurus rex*, had a femur bone that measured as long as 133 cm (52.4 in), with an approximate thickness of 43 cm (16.9 in).[3]

Based on his studies, Galileo identified a limitation for the size of animals' bones, deducing that above a certain length the bones would have to be impossibly thick to maintain the strength needed to support the body. Of course, there are other practical challenges to life on Earth—for example, agility and mobility—that, together with Darwin's principles, limit the size of animals. I use this natural example to demonstrate the considerations involved in scaling, a topic that is central to this book. This historical context beautifully illustrates that *scaling is neither free nor unlimited*, and thus the extent of scaling should be considered thoroughly. "Why scale?" is an equally crucial question. Although a human femur bone can support 30 times the weight of an adult, an average human can barely lift weight twice their own. Tiny ants, on the other hand, are known to lift 50 times their weight!

2 Hutchinson, John R., Karl T. Bates, Julia Molnar, Vivian Allen, and Peter J. Makovicky. 2011. "A Computational Analysis of Limb and Body Dimensions in *Tyrannosaurus rex* with Implications for Locomotion, Ontogeny, and Growth." *PLoS One* 6, no. 10: e26037. *https://www.ncbi.nlm.nih.gov/pmc/articles/PMC3192160*.

3 Hutchinson et al., "A Computational Analysis," e26037; Persons, W. Scott IV, Philip J. Currie, and Gregory M. Erickson. 2019. "An Older and Exceptionally Large Adult Specimen of *Tyrannosaurus rex*." *The Anatomical Record* 303, no. 4: 656–72. *https://doi.org/10.1002/ar.24118*.

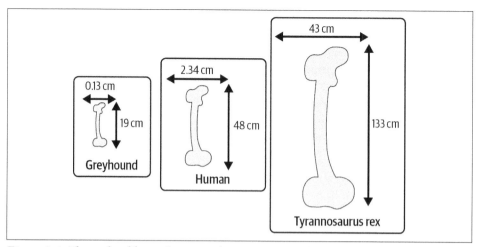

Figure 1-1. The scale of femur bones in three species: greyhound, human, and Tyrannosaurus rex

Ultimately, Galileo's research led to the general scaling law that forms the basis for many scaling theorems in modern science and engineering. You will read more about some of these laws that are applicable to deep learning scenarios, such as Moore's law, Dennard scaling, Amdahl's law, Gunther's universal scalability law, and the scaling law of language models, in Chapters 3, 5, 8, and 10, respectively.

Scalable Systems

The example discussed in the previous section demonstrates why scaling (increasing the size of an animal, for example) needs to be considered in the context of the entire system (looking at the quality of life of the animal, for example) and its desired abilities (say, to lift heavy weights). It also demonstrates that it is essential to build scalable systems.

Scaling in many ways is about understanding the constraints and dependencies of the system and proportionately scaling the dimensions to achieve the optimal state. Scaling with optimization is more effective than simply scaling. Indeed, *everything breaks at scale*. Later in this chapter, we'll talk about considerations for scaling effectively. For now, let's briefly review nature as a scalable system, and the natural tendency to scale.

Nature as a Scalable System

The surface area of planet Earth totals about 197 million square miles (510 million km^2), and it hosts at least 8.7 million unique living species.[4] The total population of just one of those 8.7 million species, humans, is estimated to be about 8 billion. As humans, we possess a spectacular ability to digest unlimited data through our visual and auditory senses. What is even more fascinating is that we don't put any conscious effort into doing so! All combined, we communicate in over 7,100 spoken languages.[5] If there is any testament to operating at scale, then the world that surrounds us has got to be it.

With our insatiable appetite for knowledge and exploration of our surroundings and beyond, we are certainly limited by the number of hours in a day. This limitation has resulted in an intense desire to automate the minutiae of our everyday lives and make time to do more within the limits of the day. The challenge with the automation of minutiae is that it's layered, it's recursive; once you automate the lowest layer and take it out of the picture, the next layer seemingly becomes the new lowest layer, and you find yourself striving to automate *everything*.

Let's take communication as an example. Historically, our ancestors would travel for days or even months to converse in person. The extensive efforts of travel were an obstacle to achieving the objective (conversation). Later, written forms of communication removed the dependency of the primary communicator traveling; messages could be delivered by an intermediary. Over time, the means of propagating written communications across channels also evolved, from carrier pigeons to postal services to Morse code and telegraph. This was followed by the digital era of messages, from faxes and emails to social communication and outreach through internet programs, with everything occurring on the order of milliseconds. We are now in a time of abundance of communication, so much so that we are looking at ways to automatically prioritize what we digest from the plethora of information out there and even considering stochastic approaches to summarizing content to optimize how we use our time. In our quest to eliminate the original obstacles to communication (time and space), we created a new obstacle that requires a new solution. We now find ourselves looking to scale how we communicate, actively exploring the avenues of brain–computer interface and going straight to mind reading.[6]

---

4 National Geographic. *n.d.* "Biodiversity." Accessed February 9, 2024. *https://education.nationalgeo graphic.org/resource/biodiversity.*

5 Ethnologue. *n.d.* Languages of the World. Accessed February 9, 2024. *https://www.ethnologue.com.*

6 Fields, R. Douglas. 2020. "Mind Reading and Mind Control Technologies Are Coming." *Observations* (blog), March 10, 2020. *https://blogs.scientificamerican.com/observations/mind-reading-and-mind-control-technologies-are-coming.*

Our Visual System: A Biological Inspiration

Scaling is complex. Your limits define how you scale to meet your ambitions. The human visual system is a beautiful example of a scalable system. It's capable of processing infinite visual signals—literally *everything*, from the surface of your eyeball to the horizon and everything in between—through a tiny lens with a focal length of about two-thirds of an inch (17 mm). It is simply magnificent that we can do all of that instantly, subconsciously, without any recognizable efforts. Scientists have been studying how the human visual system works for over a hundred years, and while important breakthroughs have been made by the likes of David Hubel and Torsten Weisel,[7] we are far from fully understanding the complex mechanism that allows us to perceive our surroundings.

Your brain has about 100 billion neurons. Each neuron is connected to up to 10,000 other neurons, and there are as many as 1,000 trillion synapses passing information between them. Such a complex and scalable system can only thrive if it's practical and efficient. Your visual system coordinates with about 10^{15} synapses, yet it consumes only about the amount of energy used by a single LED light bulb (12 watts or so).[8] Considering how implicit and subconscious this process is, it's a good example of minimal input and maximum output—but it does come at the cost of complexity.

As an adaptable information processing system, the level of sophistication the human visual system demonstrates is phenomenal. The cortical cells of the brain are *massively parallel*. Each cortical cell extracts different information from the same signals. This extracted information is then aggregated and processed, leading to decisions, actions, and experiences. The memories of your experiences are stored in extremely compressed form in the hippocampus. Our biological system is a great example of a parallelized, distributed system designed to handle information efficiently. Scientists and deep learning engineers have drawn a great deal of inspiration from nature and biology, which underscores the importance of efficiency and appreciating considerations of complexity when scaling. This will be the guiding principle through the course of this book as well: I will focus on the principles and techniques of building scalable deep learning systems while considering the complexity and efficiency of such systems.

Many of the advancements in building intelligent (AI) systems have been motivated by the inner workings of biological systems. The fundamental building block of deep learning, the neuron, was inspired by the excitation of biological nervous systems.

---

7 Wurtz, Robert H. 2009. "Recounting the Impact of Hubel and Wiesel." *The Journal of Physiology* 587: 2817–23. *https://doi.org/10.1113%2Fjphysiol.2009.170209.*

8 Jorgensen, Timothy J. 2022. "Is the Human Brain a Biological Computer?" Princeton University Press, March 14, 2022. *https://press.princeton.edu/ideas/is-the-human-brain-a-biological-computer.*

Similarly, the convolutional neural network (CNN), an efficient technique for intelligently processing computer vision content, was originally inspired by the human visual system. In the following section, you will read about the evolution of learnable systems and review evolving trends in deep learning.

Artificial Intelligence: The Evolution of Learnable Systems

In 1936, Alan Turing presented the theoretical formulation for an imaginary computing device capable of replicating the "states of mind" and symbol-manipulating abilities of a human computer.[9] This paper, "On Computable Numbers, with an Application to the Entscheidungsproblem" went on to shape the field of modern computing. Twelve years after Turing laid out his vision of "computing machines," he outlined many of the core concepts of "intelligent machines," or "[machines] that can learn from experience."[10] Turing illustrated that by memorizing the current state, considering all possible moves, and choosing the one with the greatest reward and least punishment, computers could play chess. His thoughts and theories were more advanced than the capacity of computational hardware at the time, however, severely limiting the realization of chess-playing computers. His vision of intelligent machines playing chess was not realized until 1997, some 50 years later, when IBM's Deep Blue beat Garry Kasparov, the then world champion, in a six-game match.

It Takes Four to Tango

In the last decade or so, the early 20th-century vision of realizing intelligent systems has suddenly started to seem much more realistic. This evolution is rooted in innovation in the realms of hardware, software, and data, just as much as learning algorithms. In this section, you will read about the collective progress across these four disciplines and how it has been shaping our progress toward building intelligent systems.

The hardware

IBM's Deep Blue computer boasted 256 parallel processors; it could examine 200 million possible chess moves per second and look ahead 14 moves. The success of Deep Blue was more attributed to hardware advances than AI techniques, as expressed by Noam Chomsky's observation that the event was "about as interesting as a bulldozer winning an Olympic weightlifting competition."

---

9 Turing, Alan. 1936. "On Computable Numbers, with an Application to the Entscheidungsproblem." In *Proceedings of the London Mathematical Society* s2-43, 544–46. *https://doi.org/10.1112/plms/s2-43.6.544*.

10 Turing, Alan. 1948. "Intelligent Machinery." Report for National Physical Laboratory. Reprinted in *Mechanical Intelligence: Collected Works of A. M. Turing*, vol. 1, edited by D.C. Ince, 107–27. Amsterdam: North Holland, 1992. *https://weightagnostic.github.io/papers/turing1948.pdf*.

This historical anecdote underlines the importance of computational power in the development of AI and machine learning (ML). Historical data, as shown in Figure 1-2, affirms the intensely growing demand for accelerated computation to power AI development. It is also testament to how the hardware and device industry has caught up to meet the demand for billions of floating-point computations per second.[11] This growth has largely been guided by Moore's law, discussed in Chapter 3, which projects a doubling of the number of transistors (on device) every two years. More transistors allows faster matrix multiplication at the level of electronic circuitry. The increasing complexity of building such powerful computers is evident, as the overcoming of Moore's law is being observed.[12]

NVIDIA has been the key organization powering the accelerated compute industry, reaching 1,979 trillion floating-point operations per second (1,979 teraFLOPs) for `bfloat16` data types with its Hopper chip. Google has also made significant contributions to powering AI computation with its Tensor Processing Unit (TPU), v4 of which is capable of reaching 275 teraFLOPs (`bfloat16`). Other AI chips, such as Intel's Habana, Graphcore's Intelligent Processing Units (IPUs), and Cerebras's Wafer Scale Engine (WSE), have also been under active development in the last few years.[13] The success (or failure) of many research ideas has been attributed to the availability of suitable hardware, popularly referred to as the *hardware lottery*.[14]

The limitations and constraints that come forth as a result of intensive energy use and emission are among key challenges for hardware. Some very interesting projects, like Microsoft's Natick (*https://oreil.ly/U5JdR*), are exploring sustainable ways to meet increasing intensive computation demands. You will read more about the hardware aspects of deep learning in Chapters 3 and 5.

---

11 Sevilla, Jaime, Lennart Heim, Anson Ho, Tamay Besiroglu, Marius Hobbhahn, and Pablo Villalobos. 2022. "Compute Trends Across Three Eras of Machine Learning." arXiv, March 9, 2022. *https://arxiv.org/abs/2202.05924.*

12 Heffernan, Virginia. 2022. "Is Moore's Law Really Dead?" WIRED, November 22, 2022. *https://www.wired.com/story/moores-law-really-dead.*

13 Heffernan, "Is Moore's Law Really Dead?" *https://www.wired.com/story/moores-law-really-dead.*

14 Hooker, Sara. 2020. "The Hardware Lottery." arXiv, September 21, 2020. *https://arxiv.org/abs/2009.06489.*

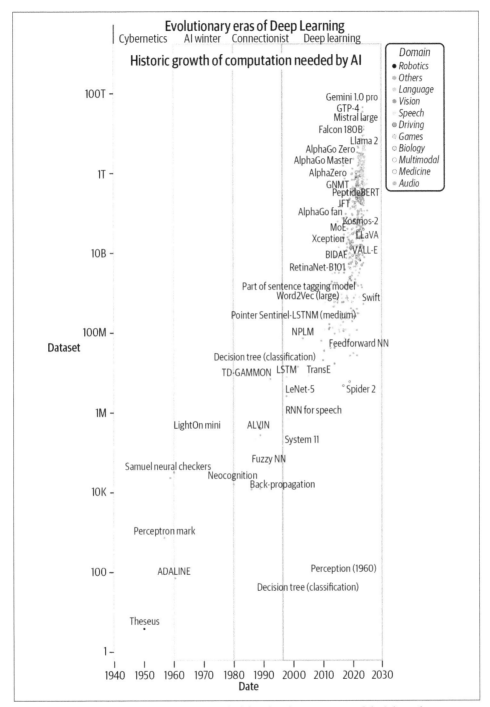

Figure 1-2. Growth of computation needed for developing AI models (plotted using data borrowed from Sevilla et al., 2022)

The data

After hardware, data is the second most critical fuel for deep learning. Tremendous growth in available data and the development of techniques to procure, create, manage, and use it effectively have shaped the success of learnable systems. Deep learning algorithms are data-hungry, but we have been successful in feeding this beast with increasing volumes of data to develop better systems (see Figure 1-3). This is possible because of the exponential growth in digitally created content. For example, in the year 2020 alone, an estimated 64.2e-9 TB (64.2 zettabytes) of data were created—32x more than the 2e-9 TB (2 ZB) created in 2010.[15]

We'll talk more about the role of data in deep learning in Chapter 2. A whole range of techniques have been innovated to leverage the volume, variety, veracity, and value of data to develop and scale deep learning models. These techniques are explored under "data-centric AI," which we'll discuss in Chapter 10.

Traditionally, the development of intelligent systems started with a highly curated and labeled dataset. More recently, innovative techniques like self-supervised learning have proven quite economical and effective at leveraging a very large corpus of already available unlabeled data—the free-form knowledge that we've created throughout history as news articles, books, and various other publications.[16] For example, CoCa, a contrastive self-supervised learning model, follows this principle and at the time of writing is the leader in top-1 ImageNet accuracy at 91% (see Figure 1-6 later in this section).[17] In addition, social media applications automatically curate vast amounts of labeled multimodal data (e.g., vision data in the form of images with captions/comments and videos with images and audio) that is powering more powerful generalist models (discussed further in Chapters 12 and 13).

Top-N accuracy is a measure of how often the correct label is among the model's top N predictions. For example, top-1 accuracy indicates how often the model's prediction exactly matched the expected answer, and top-5 accuracy indicates how often the expected answer was among the model's top 5 predictions.

---

15 Taylor, Petroc. 2023. "Volume of Data/Information Created, Captured, Copied, and Consumed Worldwide from 2010 to 2020, with Forecasts from 2021 to 2025." Statista, November 16, 2023. *https://www.statista.com/ statistics/871513/worldwide-data-created.*

16 Chen, Ting, Simon Kornblith, Mohammad Norouzi, and Geoffrey Hinton. 2020. "A Simple Framework for Contrastive Learning of Visual Representations." arXiv, July 1, 2020. *https://arxiv.org/abs/2002.05709.*

17 Yu, Jiahui, Zirui Wang, Vijay Vasudevan, Legg Yeung, Mojtaba Seyedhosseini, and Yonghui Wu. 2022. "CoCa: Contrastive Captioners Are Image-Text Foundation Models." arXiv, June 14, 2022. *https:// arxiv.org/abs/2205.01917.*

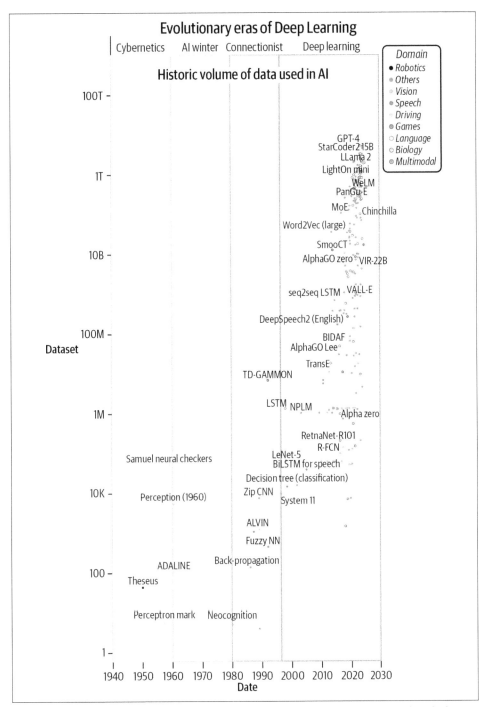

Figure 1-3. Growth in volumes of data used for training AI models (plotted with data from Sevilla et al., 2022)

The software

The software landscape supporting the development of AI solutions has been growing too. During the *inception* phase, from around the year 2000, only early-stage software frameworks such as MATLAB and the Lua-based Torch were available. This was followed by the *formation* phase that began around 2012, when machine learning frameworks like Caffe, Chainer, and Theano were developed (see Figure 1-4). It took another four years to reach the *maturity* phase, which saw stable frameworks like Apache MXNet, TensorFlow, and PyTorch providing more friendly APIs for model development. Attributed to open source communities around the world, working collaboratively to amplify the posture of software tooling for deep learning, we are now in an *expansion* phase. The expansion phase is defined by the growing ecosystem of software and tools to accelerate the development and productionization of AI software.

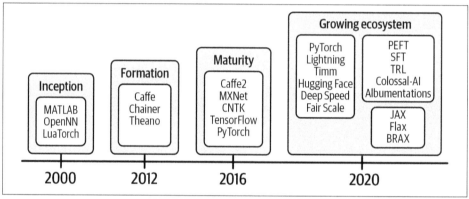

Figure 1-4. The evolutionary phases of software and tooling for deep learning

Community-driven open source development has been key in bringing together the software, algorithms, and people needed for exponential growth. Open source deep learning software development projects (such as PyTorch, JAX, and TensorFlow), foundations such as the Linux Foundation (responsible for PyTorch and its ecosystem), and research sharing forums such as arXiv and Papers with Code have encouraged and enabled contributions from people around the world. The role that open source communities have played in scaling the intelligent system efforts is nothing but heroic.

The (deep learning) algorithms

The vision of learnable intelligent systems started with heuristics-based, rules-driven solutions, which quickly evolved into data-driven stochastic systems. Figure 1-5 charts the evolution and corresponding rise in popularity of deep learning algorithms over time, capturing the progression from the birth of classical machine learning to perceptron-based shallow neural networks to the deeper and denser layers that shaped deep learning today. (For more detailed historical context, see the sidebar "History of Deep Learning" on page 13. Note that this is an indicative plot showing the popularity and growth of deep learning; it. It does not represent absolute popularity!) As you can see, the growth in popularity of deep learning has been exponential, but along the way there have been a few lulls—the so-called *AI winters*—as a result of constraints and limitations that needed to be overcome.

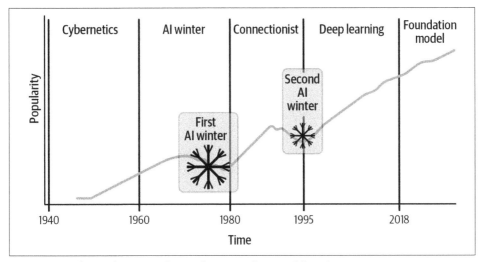

Figure 1-5. The evolution and growth in popularity of deep learning

History of Deep Learning

The exponential growth of deep learning began in the 1940s, and the landscape is still rapidly expanding. Here, I highlight the milestone years and some of the key research that shaped the direction of deep learning as we know it today. The timeline is typically divided into four eras:

Cybernetics (1940–1960)
    1943: Warren McCulloch and Walter Pitts's mathematical abstraction of a biological neuron, the *perceptron*

    1958: Frank Rosenblatt's Mark I Perceptron, which formed the basis for today's neural networks

    1960: Public reservations about AI lead to research funding drying up

AI Winter (1961–1980)
    Icy snow

Connectionist (1980–1995)
    1982: John Hopfield's neural network with bidirectional links

1975: Kunihiko Fukushima's Cognitron, a forward propagating neural network

1982: Douglas Reilly et al.'s multilayer hybrid network

1985: David Rumelhart et al.'s backpropagation algorithm to adjust neural network parameters

1985: Yann LeCun's three-layer network for character recognition

1989: Yann LeCun's convolutional network with backpropagation

1991–1994: Several challenges are noted with regard to scaling neural networks, such as the vanishing and exploding gradient problems described by Sepp Hochreiter (1991) and Yoshua Bengio et al. (1994), leading to a second brief AI winter

Deep Learning (1996–present)

2006: University of Toronto and Canadian Institute for Advanced Research revive AI as deep learning

2006: Geoffrey Hinton's deep belief network and Bengio's greedy layerwise training address some of the scaling challenges seen during the Connectionist era

2009: The ImageNet moment, led by Fei-Fei Li

2012: AlexNet wins ImageNet challenge with record margin and introduces distributed training

2017: Ashish Vaswani et al.'s Transformer architecture

2018: Transformers are applied in vision. Extreme scaling of deep learning models begins, enabling the progression discussed in "Evolving Deep Learning Trends" on page 16

The second AI winter persisted through 1995. By this point, researchers had realized that to achieve further success with neural networks they needed to find solutions to deal with the following three problems:

Scaling layers effectively

During the Connectionist era, deep learning researchers discovered that effective models for deep learning require a very large number of layers. Simply adding more layers to neural networks was not a viable option, due to overfitting (as outlined by Sepp Hochreiter and Yoshua Bengio et al.).[18]

---

18 Hochreiter, S. 1990. "Implementierung und Anwendung eines 'neuronalen' Echtzeit-Lernalgorithmus für reaktive Umgebungen." Institute of Computer Science, Technical University of Munich. *https:// www.bioinf.jku.at/publications/older/fopra.pdf*; Bengio, Y., P. Simard, and P. Frasconi. 1994. "Learning Long-Term Dependencies with Gradient Descent Is Difficult." *IEEE Transactions on Neural Networks* 5, no. 2: 157–66. *https://doi.org/10.1109/72.279181.*

Scaling computation efficiency

Unfortunately, the hardware lottery luck was out around this time! For instance, it took three days to train a 9,760-parameter model based on Yann LeCun's LeNet-5 architecture, proposed in 1989, which had five trainable layers.[19] The best computer available at the time was not efficient enough to provide fast feedback, and hardware constraints were throttling development.

Scaling the input

As shown in Figure 1-3, the volume of data used in deep learning experiments barely changed from the 1940s until about 1995. The ability to capture, store, and manage data was also still developing during this time.

Clearly, managing scale is a critical challenge in any deep learning system. The landmark research that accelerated the growth of deep learning was the deep, densely connected belief network developed by Hinton et al. in 2006,[20] which has as many parameters as 0.002 mm^3 of mouse cortex. This was the first time deep learning had come anywhere close to modeling a biological system, however small. As shown in Figures 1-2 and 1-3, this was also the landmark year when data and hardware gained momentum in their respective growth. Collaborative open source efforts have been drivers of growth too; this is evident from the evolution that followed the release of the ImageNet dataset in 2009, termed the "ImageNet moment." This dataset, containing over 14 million annotated images of everyday objects in about 20,000 categories, was made available for researchers to compete in the ImageNet Large Scale Visual Recognition Challenge (ILSVRC) and invent algorithms for the scaled-up task.[21]

Under Hinton's supervision, in 2017 Alex Krizhevsky produced a solution for the ILSVRC that outperformed the competition by a huge 10.8% margin (at 15.3% top-5 error).[22] This work, now popularly known as AlexNet, applied novel distributed training techniques to scale out the development of the solution on two GPUs with very limited memory. Figure 1-6 shows the success trajectory (increasing rate of the top-5 accuracy) of ImageNet since this groundbreaking development.

---

19 LeCun, Y., B. Boser, J.S. Denker, D. Henderson, R.E. Howard, W. Hubbard, and L.D. Jackel. 1989. "Backpropagation Applied to Handwritten Zip Code Recognition." *Neural Computation* 1, no. 4: 541–51. *https://doi.org/10.1162/neco.1989.1.4.541.*

20 Hinton, Geoffrey E., Simon Osindero, and Yee-Whye Teh. 2006. "A Fast Learning Algorithm for Deep Belief Nets." *Neural Computation* 18, no. 7: 1527–54. *https://doi.org/10.1162/neco.2006.18.7.1527.*

21 Deng, Jia, Wei Dong, Richard Socher, Li-Jia Li, Kai Li, and Fei-Fei Li. 2009. "ImageNet: A Large-Scale Hierarchical Image Database." In *Proceedings of IEEE Conference on Computer Vision and Pattern Recognition (CVPR)*, 248–55. *http://dx.doi.org/10.1109/CVPR.2009.5206848.*

22 Krizhevsky, Alex, Ilya Sutskever, and Geoffrey E. Hinton. 2012. "ImageNet Classification with Deep Convolutional Neural Networks." In *Advances in Neural Information Processing Systems (NIPS 2012)* 25, no. 2. *https://papers.nips.cc/paper_files/paper/2012/file/c399862d3b9d6b76c8436e924a68c45b-Paper.pdf.*

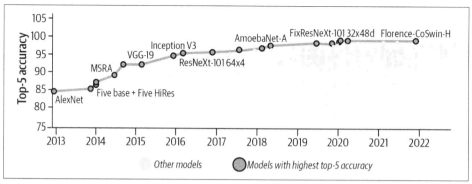

Figure 1-6. Top-5 accuracy of various deep learning models on the ImageNet dataset since the inception of AlexNet (plot based on data obtained from https://oreil.ly/mYfbq)

At around this time, the industry also started to take a serious interest in deep learning and its productionization; solid industry footings positioned it for a cash injection, and venture funding accelerated not just commercialization but also future research. Funds have been flowing into deep learning at a great rate since 2013, when Google's acquisition of Hinton's DNNresearch opened the floodgates, making it (as of 2023) a $27 billion industry.[23] The abundance of resourcing and support has supercharged the rise of deep learning over the past decade—and with industry support came the interdisciplinary growth that has driven the collective development of scientific aspects of deep learning and algorithms along with everything else that lies at the intersection of hardware, software, and data.

Now that you're familiar with a little of the history, in the next section we'll look at current trends in deep learning and see how the ability to scale is influencing ongoing research and industry adaptation.

Evolving Deep Learning Trends

Twenty years after Deep Blue's success, deep learning has evolved to entirely replace rules-based solutions and is increasingly superseding human-level performance in specific tasks. AlphaGo,[24] for instance, reached this level after about four hours of

---

23 Thomas, Owen. 2013. "Google Has Bought a Startup to Help It Recognize Voices and Objects." Business Insider, March 13, 2013. *https://www.businessinsider.com/google-buys-dnnresearch-2013-3*; Saha, Rachana. 2024. "Deep Learning Market Expected to Reach US$127 Billion by 2028." Analytics Insight, February 19, 2024. *https://www.analyticsinsight.net/deep-learning-market-expected-to-reach-us127-billion-by-2028.*

24 Silver, David, Thomas Hubert, Julian Schrittwieser, Ioannis Antonoglou, Matthew Lai, Arthur Guez, Marc Lanctot, et al. 2018. "A General Reinforcement Learning Algorithm That Masters Chess, Shogi, and Go Through Self-Play." *Science* 362, no. 6419: 1140–1144. *https://doi.org/10.1126/science.aar6404.*

training on a single 44-CPU-core machine with a TPU and can achieve approximate convergence in about nine hours through its novel algorithms and software implementations. It has defeated Stockfish, one of the world's top chess engines that has won various chess competitions. This enhanced ability to provide better solutions than rule/logic-based software is recognized by the Software 2.0 migration (discussed in more detail in Chapter 2), where traditional software is being made model-driven.

General evolution of deep learning

The application of deep learning in computer vision that began with Yann LeCun's digit recognition network[25] has today scaled to many vision tasks, such as image classification, object detection and segmentation, scene understanding, captioning, etc. These solutions are commonly developed and used around the world today. Efficiency was the key motivation behind the convolutional neural network architecture mentioned earlier in this chapter, and given the voluminous nature of vision data, that has remained a key consideration. CNN-based models like ResNet and EfficientNet have been very successful at vision tasks, reaching a top-1 accuracy of about 90% while carefully applying efficiency and scaling considerations. These models are great for small spatial contexts, but they don't scale for larger spatial contexts.

Google's Transformer architecture,[26] which pays attention to tokens in long sequences in a parallelized fashion, has been groundbreaking. Requirements to scale vision models for a global context have led to the exploration of the use of Transformer-based architectures. One such example is the Vision Transformer (ViT),[27] which tokenizes the images into small chunks and memorizes where these chunks lie in the global image space. For the last few years, most vision research has been driven by the Transformer architecture. CoAtNet, a combination of CNN and Transformer architectures, has 2.44 billion parameters and reaches 90.88% top-1 accuracy on ImageNet tasks. MaxViT, a ViT-based architecture, is close to CoAtNet on the accuracy benchmark but has about five times fewer parameters (475 million).[28] Still, scaling the context size of Transformers has remained a challenge due to memory and compute limitations. This has led to interesting and innovative techniques like MEG-

25 Turing, "Intelligent Machinery," 107–27.

26 Vaswani, Ashish, Noam Shazeer, Niki Parmar, Jakob Uszkoreit, Llion Jones, Aidan N. Gomez, Lukasz Kaiser, and Illia Polosukhin. 2017. "Attention Is All You Need." arXiv, December 6, 2017. *https://arxiv.org/abs/1706.03762.*

27 Dosovitskiy, Alexey, Lucas Beyer, Alexander Kolesnikov, Dirk Weissenborn, Xiaohua Zhai, Thomas Unterthiner, Mostafa Dehghani, et al. 2021. "An Image Is Worth 16x16 Words: Transformers for Image Recognition at Scale." arXiv, June 3, 2021. *https://arxiv.org/abs/2010.11929.*

28 Silver et al., "A General Reinforcement Learning Algorithm," 1140–1144; Tu, Zhengzhong, Hossein Talebi, Han Zhang, Feng Yang, Peyman Milanfar, Alan Bovik, and Yinxiao Li. 2022. MaxViT: Multi-Axis Vision Transformer. arXiv, September 9, 2022. *https://arxiv.org/abs/2204.01697.*

ABYTE and LongViT, which can process very large context sizes (e.g., million-byte sequences or the gigapixel images used in pathology).[29] Scaling is not just about parameter count, however; data, energy, and cost economies are critical too.

It was the Transformer architecture that revived innovation in the language processing domain, which had stagnated prior to 2017. Despite suffering from compute inefficiencies (due to quadratic computation in the attention module), this architecture completely revolutionized natural language processing. As shown in Figure 1-7, language models based on this architecture were able to scale their abilities by scaling the number of parameters—a trend referred to as the *scaling law of language models*.[30] OpenAI's Codex (*https://oreil.ly/TxDfT*) is one such scaled-up model; trained with open source code from GitHub, it is revolutionizing how developers code today. This trend continued until at least mid-2021. What followed in late 2021 was a serious reconsideration of scaling mainly by scaling the number of parameters, and a plateau ensued with a few significant dips caused by models that used considerably lower numbers of parameters but still outperformed their counterparts. Chinchilla is one such model that scales mainly on data volume; despite having 2.5 times fewer parameters, it still outperforms GPT-3. LLaMA (*https://oreil.ly/JDTPX*), another comparable model from Meta, has also gained popularity and is widely used. This trend can be seen in Figure 1-7, which highlights the model concentration zone around 7B-200B range even though >1T parameter models are being developed.

29 Yu, Lili, Dániel Simig, Colin Flaherty, Armen Aghajanyan, Luke Zettlemoyer, and Mike Lewis. 2023. "MEGA-BYTE: Predicting Million-Byte Sequences with Multiscale Transformers." arXiv, May 19, 2023. *https://arxiv.org/abs/2305.07185*; Wang, Wenhui, Shuming Ma, Hanwen Xu, Naoto Usuyama, Jiayu Ding, Hoifung Poon, and Furu Wei. 2023. "When an Image Is Worth 1,024 x 1,024 Words: A Case Study in Computational Pathology." arXiv, December 6, 2023. *https://arxiv.org/abs/2312.03558*.

30 Kaplan, Jared, Sam McCandlish, Tom Henighan, Tom B. Brown, Benjamin Chess, Rewon Child, Scott Gray, et al. 2020. "Scaling Laws for Neural Language Models." arXiv, January 23, 2020. *https://arxiv.org/abs/2001.08361*.

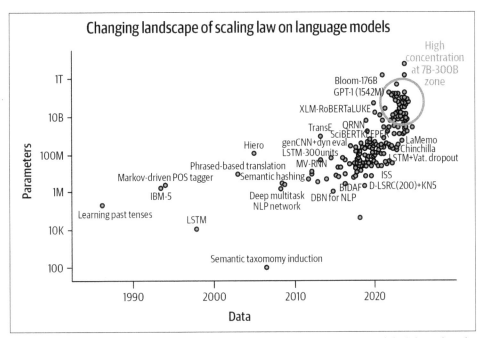

Figure 1-7. The changing landscape of the scaling law of language models (plotted with data from Sevilla et al., 2022)

The scaling law of deep learning models has been encouraging the development of overparameterized models and ever deeper and denser networks.[31] This trend is seen across all data modality vision, language, speech, etc. As mentioned earlier, an important innovation at the intersection of data and algorithms is self-supervised model development.[32] Together, these developments are supporting the creation of more general-purpose large models that exhibit emerging capabilities, enabling them to perform tasks without being explicitly trained for them. These large models, more commonly known as *foundation models*, leverage a suite of complex, well-engineered distributed training techniques to efficiently utilize the available resources to produce the best possible models. Another emerging trend is the development of large multimodal models (LMMs) that can work with data from different modalities (such as text, audio, and images), like CLIP (*https://oreil.ly/GPWnN*) and DALL-E (*https://oreil.ly/4ttDk*), GPT-4, Gemini, and Flamingo. This in turn has led to rapid growth in generative art, with models like Sora (*https://oreil.ly/otdWY*), GLIDE (*https://oreil.ly/*

---

31 Kaplan et al., "Scaling Laws for Neural Language Models," *https://arxiv.org/abs/2001.08361*

32 Gorton, Ian. 2022. *Foundations of Scalable Systems: Designing Distributed Architectures.* Sebastopol, CA: O'Reilly Media.

6L8Vu), Imagen (*https://oreil.ly/kkOul*), and Stability.ai's (*https://stability.ai*) Stable Diffusion creating a shakeup within the art industry.[33]

None of these developments would have been possible without advancements in algorithms, hardware, software, and data. You will read about these developments in Part I. In Part II we'll look at the details of distributed training, and in Part III we will dive deeper into the efficient and effective development of large-scale models, including foundation models.

Evolution in specialized domains

Aside from general-purpose progress, deep learning has also massively influenced processes and techniques in specialized domains such as the ones discussed in this section.

Math and compute. For centuries, mathematicians believed that the standard matrix multiplication algorithm was the most efficient one. Then, in 1969, Volker Strassen (*https://oreil.ly/MTvi4*) demonstrated another algorithm to be superior. The effort to optimize matrix computation has been ongoing. The overcoming of Moore's law necessitated exploration of alternative techniques to scale matrix multiplication, leading to *approximating multiplication*, which yields a 100x speedup but is less practical for scenarios where accuracy matters.[34] The most recent discovery, led by DeepMind, identified improvements to Strassen's algorithm for the first time since its discovery a half-century ago through the use of the deep learning system AlphaTensor.[35]

Protein folding. Another example of the success of open source and community-driven work is the effort to solve problems in protein folding research by automatically predicting evolutionary protein sequences end to end. AlphaFold, another deep learning system from DeepMind, scaled the protein dataset from 190K empirically derived structures to 0.2B AI-generated protein structures.[36] A great example of scale is ProGen2, a 6.4B-parameter model developed using distributed deep learning

33 Heikkilä, Melissa. 2022. "Inside a Radical New Project to Democratize AI." MIT Technology Review, July 12, 2022. *https://www.technologyreview.com/2022/07/12/1055817/inside-a-radical-new-project-to-democratize-ai/amp*.

34 Blalock, Davis, and John Guttag. 2021. "Multiplying Matrices Without Multiplying." arXiv, June 21, 2021. *https://arxiv.org/abs/2106.10860*.

35 Fawzi, Alhussein, Matej Balog, Aja Huang, Thomas Hubert, Bernardino Romera-Paredes, Mohammadamin Barekatain, Alexander Novikov, et al. 2022. "Discovering Faster Matrix Multiplication Algorithms with Reinforcement Learning." *Nature* 610: 47–53. *https://doi.org/10.1038/s41586-022-05172-4*.

36 Hassabis, Demis. 2022. AlphaFold Reveals the Structure of the Protein Universe. DeepMind blog, July 28, 2022. *https://deepmind.google/discover/blog/alphafold-reveals-the-structure-of-the-protein-universe*.

techniques to scale training across 256 nodes on TPUs.[37] The heated competition led to ESMFold, a 15B-parameter model requiring about 2,000 V100 NVIDIA GPUs to develop, that performs six times faster than AlphaFold2 at inference time.[38] With these innovations, the protein folding research community basically went from "the protein folding problem currently has no solution" to "deep learning solved it (mostly)."

Simulated world. Deep learning has made quite an impact on virtual reality and physics-guided simulation, even in designing and planning fabrics, and other related industries. The CVPR 2022 keynote "Understanding Visual Appearance from Micron to Global Scale" by Kavita Bala, Dean of Computing and Information Science at Cornell University, is an excellent talk highlighting how deep learning is changing industries all around.

You've read a lot about the history and evolution of deep learning in this chapter. In the following section, I will switch the focus to practical considerations and general principles that are essential to scaling. I believe an understanding of these issues is critical before I begin talking about how to scale your deep learning workload, although the guidance I provide here is so generic that it applies not only to deep learning but to scaling any task, engineering or otherwise.

Scale in the Context of Deep Learning

Scaling, in the context of deep learning, is multidimensional, broadly consisting of the following three aspects:

Generalizability
> Increasing the ability of models to generalize to diverse tasks or demographics

Training and development
> Scaling the model training technique to shorten development time while meeting resource requirements

Inference
> Increasing the serviceability of the developed model during serving

---

37 Nijkamp, Erik, Jeffrey Ruffolo, Eli N. Weinstein, Nikhil Naik, and Ali Madani. 2022. "ProGen2: Exploring the Boundaries of Protein Language Models." arXiv, June 27, 2022. *https://arxiv.org/abs/2206.13517*.

38 Lin, Zeming, Halil Akin, Roshan Rao, Brian Hie, Zhongkai Zhu, Wenting Lu, Nikita Smetanin, et al. 2023. "Evolutionary-Scale Prediction of Atomic-Level Protein Structure with a Language Model." *Science* 379, no. 6637: 1123–30. *https://doi.org/10.1126/science.ade2574*.

All of these are nuanced and require different strategies to scale. This book, however, will focus primarily on the first two; inference (deployment, serving, and servicing) is beyond the scope of the book.

Six Development Considerations

There are six considerations that are crucial to explore when developing a deep learning solution. Let's take a realistic use case as a basis to explore these considerations to decide when scaling might be necessary and how to prepare for it. I will be using this example throughout this section and often across the book.

Let's assume that you have built a system that analyzes satellite images to predict if there are any roofs present and, if so, what kinds of roof materials have been used. Let's also hypothesize that this system has originally been developed for Sydney, Australia. Your model is a vision-based supervised model. So, you have a ground truth dataset representative of roofs and roof materials used in Sydney, and the model has been trained with this dataset. Now, you want to scale your solution to work for *any roof in the world*!

When you start to decompose this mission, you soon realize that to be able to achieve this goal you'll need to consider the six aspects outlined in the following sections.

Well-defined problem

For data-driven solutions such as deep learning, it is really important to understand the exact problem one needs to solve and whether you have the right data for that problem.

So, to scale your solution to work for any roof in the world, the problem needs to be defined well. Consider questions like:

1. Are we still just detecting the presence of a roof and the materials used? Or are we expanding to determine the roof style as well (e.g., hip, gable, flat)?

2. How do the materials and shapes of roofs vary across geographies?

3. Are our success criteria uniform, or do we need to trade off sensitivity versus specificity given the circumstances (for certain roofs or specific geographies, for instance)?

4. How are the least and most acceptable error thresholds defined, and what are they? Are there any other success criteria?

These questions are crucial because, for example, if correctly detecting igloo roofs is equally as important as correctly detecting concrete roofs, you may have the added complexity of data imbalance given that concrete roofs are so common but igloos are likely to be underrepresented in your dataset. Geographical nuances, such as Canadian roofs that are often covered in snow, will need to be carefully managed too. This exercise of completely understanding your problem helps you extrapolate the limitations of your system and plan to effectively manage them with your constraints. Scaling is constrained, after all!

Domain knowledge (a.k.a. the constraints)

As discussed previously, scaling for detection of roofs and roof materials necessitates a very good understanding of factors like the following:

1. What defines a roof? Are there certain minimum dimensions? Are only certain shapes or materials recognized?

2. What is included and what is excluded, and why? Do we consider the roof of the shelter at a bus stop a roof? What about pergolas?

3. What are the domain-specific constraints that the solution must follow?

Mapping how roofs and roof materials relate to each other and how geographies constrain the types of roof materials is crucial. For example, rubber roofs have not yet penetrated the Australian market, but rubber is a popular material in Canada because of its ability to protect roofs from extreme weather conditions. Appearance- and material-wise, rubber and shingle roofs are much closer to each other than metal or color bond roofs, for instance. The domain knowledge derived from an extensive understanding of the problem space is often very helpful for building constraints and enforcing validation. For example, with domain knowledge, the model predicting relative probabilities of 0.5 and 0.5 respectively for shingle and rubber roof materials is understandable; however, predicting the same probabilities for tiles and concrete would be less understandable, as the appearance of these materials is quite distinct. Similarly, predicting rubber as the material for Australian roofs will likely be wrong. *A good system always understands the user's expectations*—but these can be hard to enforce in a data-driven system such as a deep learning solution. They can more easily be tested and enforced as domain adaptation strategies.

Ground truth

Your dataset is the basis of the knowledge base for your deep learning solution. When planning and building your dataset, you should ask questions like the following:

- How can we curate the dataset to be representative of roofs around the world?

- How do we ensure quality and generalization?

Your labeling and data procurement efforts will need to scale accordingly, and this can get really expensive very quickly. As you scale a deep learning system, the ability to quickly iterate on data becomes crucial. Andrej Karpathy (*https://oreil.ly/dhoOQ*), an independent researcher and previous director of AI at Tesla, talks about this in terms of a "data engine": "Competitive advantage in AI goes not so much to those with data but those with a data engine: iterated data acquisition, re-training, evaluation, deployment, telemetry. And whoever can spin it fastest."

As you scale, you also start to see interesting odd "real-world" scenarios. Scandinavian sod roofs, for instance, are a very interesting type of region-specific roof. Sod is a less common roof material for people living in many other parts of the world. In areas where it is used, you need to consider issues like how these roofs can be delineated from concrete roofs with artificial turf. How you identify and capture such outliers becomes an interesting challenge too. Having a clear understanding of where you draw the boundaries and what risks you accept is important in scaling your system. You will read more about techniques to handle these challenges in Chapter 10.

Model development

Your goal is to scale the model's ability to identify roofs and roof materials across the globe. Therefore, your scaling efforts may need to go beyond scaling the dataset (for better representation and generalization) into scaling the capacity of the model and the techniques involved. As discussed previously, if you globalize, your model will need to learn about an increased variety of roof styles and roof material types. If your model is not engineered for this scale, then there may be a risk of underfitting.

You may ask:

1. How do we plan the experiments to arrive at the optimal model for the scaled-up solution?

2. What approach should we adopt to rapidly develop to accelerate the buildup?

3. How can we improvise with our training methodologies so they are most optimal? When do we need distributed training? What efficient training strategies are relevant for our use case?

4. Should we develop with all the data, or use data-centric techniques like sampling and augmentations to accelerate development?

The plans for model evaluation require similar considerations as well, as do structuring the codebase and planning and writing automation tests around model development to support fast and reliable iteration. You will read about scaling model development and training techniques throughout the book, with an explicit focus on experiment planning in Chapter 11.

Deployment

Scaling a system to reach across the globe requires scale and sophistication in deployment strategies as well. While deployment is beyond the scope of this book, I recommend considering the deployment circumstances from the early development stages.

Here are some questions you should consider:

- What limitations will our deployable environment have?
- Can we get enough compute and provide the desired latency without compromising the serviceability of user requests for the techniques we're targeting?
- How do we get quality metrics from deployed environments for support purposes?
- How do we optimize the model for various hardware before it's deployed?
- Will our choice of tooling support this?

The speed of data processing and the forward pass of the model have direct implications on the serviceability of the system. The warmup and bootstrap lag in surfacing model services directly impacts the scalability strategies the services need to adopt for suitable uptime. This is important data to share as input to the planning of model development.

Feedback

Feedback is crucial for improvement, and there's no better feedback than direct real-time feedback, straight from your users. A great example of feedback collection is GitHub Copilot (*https://oreil.ly/63E8m*). Copilot collects feedback several times after code suggestions are made to gather accurate metrics on the usefulness of the provided suggestions, if the suggestions are still being used, and if so with what level of edits. This is a great opportunity to create a data engine.

As scale increases, the importance of feedback and support systems increases too. In essence, when thinking about feedback, the questions you should be asking are:

- How are we going to gather feedback from the users to continually improve our system?
- Can we automate the feedback collection? How can we integrate it with the model development workflow to realize a data engine–like setup?

The feedback needs actioning; otherwise, the feedback system is pointless. In the context of a data engine, measuring the gaps and continually iterating to close these gaps provides significant advantages when building any data-driven system, such as a deep learning solution. This is where the competitive advantage lies.

Scaling Considerations

Scaling is complicated. The mythical "embarrassingly parallel workload" where little or no effort is required to divide and parallelize tasks does not actually exist. For instance, graphics processing units (GPUs) are marketed as embarrassingly parallel devices for matrix computations, but their processing capacity is throttled by their memory bandwidth, limiting the practical computation throughput (see Chapter 3). As discussed earlier, the real challenge of scaling lies in understanding the limitations of subsystems and working with them to scale the entire system.

This section discusses the questions you should be asking before attempting to scale, and the framework for scaling.

Questions to ask before scaling

The proverbial saying "All roads lead to Rome" applies in scaling as well. Often, there may be many ways to achieve the desired scale. The goal should be taking the most optimal route.

For example, to halve the latency of your training process, you may need to scale. You could:

- *Scale your hardware* by getting beefier computing devices.
- *Scale your training process* by using distributed training.
- *Reduce the computation budget* of your process or program at the expense of accuracy/precision.
- *Optimize the input*, e.g., by compressing the dataset using data distillation (discussed in Chapter 10).

If you're financially constrained and unable to fund more or beefier devices, then the optimal route is likely to be option 3 or 4. If you can't compromise on precision, then by elimination option 4 is the most optimal one. Otherwise, option 3 may be the lowest-hanging fruit to shave the latency.

The topics discussed earlier in this chapter can be distilled into the following set of questions that it's critical to ask before commencing your scaling efforts. Answering these questions will help you define your options and allow you to scale more effectively:

- *What* are we scaling?
- How will we *measure success*?
- Do we really *need* to scale?
- What are the *ripple effects* (i.e., downstream implications)?

- What are the *constraints*?
- *How* will we scale?
- Is our scaling technique *optimal*?

Considering these questions will not only force you to ensure that the scope and limits of scaling are well understood, but also ensure that you have defined good metrics to measure your success. Cassie Kozyrkov, CEO at Data Scientific and previously the chief decision scientist at Google, has an excellent write-up titled "Metric Design for Data Scientists and Business Leaders"[39] that outlines the importance of defining metrics first before decisioning. Occam's razor, the principle of parsimony, highlights the importance of simplicity, but not at the expense of necessity. It is the rule #1 for efficient scaling that you are forced to consider when you ask, "Do we really need to scale?" The following chapters of this book are designed to dive deeply into the approaches and techniques for scaling and help you determine whether your chosen scaling technique is optimal for your use case.

Characteristics of scalable systems

Ian Gorton thoroughly covers the principles of a scalable system, the design patterns used in scaling systems, and the challenges associated with scaling in his book *Foundations of Scalable Systems: Designing Distributed Architectures*. Gorton's book is not a prerequisite for this book, but it's a recommended read if you have some background in software engineering. This section outlines four characteristics of a scalable system that are useful to keep in mind as you prepare to scale your workload.

Reliability.   The most important characteristic of a scalable system is reliability. A reliable system rarely fails. In the inopportune moments when it does, it fails predictably, allowing the dependent system and users to gracefully cope with said failure. In other words, a reliable system is capable of coping with (infrequent) failures and recovering from failure scenarios gracefully. Here's an example: all 224.641e+18 FLOPs that you have performed so far were lost when, due to a network fault, training came to a halt after running for two months using 500 A100 GPU nodes. When the system comes back up, are you able to resume from the last completed computed state and recover gracefully? A reliable system will be able to cope with this failure and gracefully recover.

The commonly known metrics to define a reliable system are as follows:

---

39 Kozyrkov, Cassie. 2022. "Metric Design for Data Scientists and Business Leaders." Towards Data Science, October 23, 2022. *https://towardsdatascience.com/metric-design-for-data-scientists-and-business-leaders-b8adaf46c00.*

Recovery point objective (RPO)

RPO is defined as how far back you can go to recover the data after a failure. For example, with checkpointing, the interval you decide on—the frequency with which you store the intermittent weights and training states (optimizers, etc.)—will define your RPO. This might be set in terms of the number of steps or epochs.

Recovery time objective (RTO)

RTO is defined as how long it takes to recover and get back to the state from right before the crash.

Downtime rate

Downtime rate is the percentage of time for which the system is observed to be unavailable or unresponsive.

Availability. Availability defines the likelihood that a system is operational and functional. The gold standard for highly available systems is *five nines*—i.e., the system is available and functional 99.999% of the time. Managing the availability of a deep learning–based system to five nines is an involved process. TikTok, the small-form video sharing procrastination service by ByteDance Ltd, has been internationally operational since 2017. In five years, it scaled its user content personalization services across 150 countries, hosting over 1 billion users. The system architecture, called Monolith,[40] combines online and offline learning to serve user-relevant content, creating sticky users by using click-through rate prediction techniques (DeepFM) and running at scale. While overall availability of TikTok is high, it has faced outage situations on occasions (up to five hours of outage).

Adaptability. Adaptability speaks to how resilient a system is in meeting the growing scaling demands. Are you able to scale the training over the number of available GPUs? How able is the training code to cope with failures like losing a node while training? These are some of the considerations that fall in the purview of adaptability. Some easily solved software engineering challenges surface as incredibly tough problems in the deep learning space.

Performance. Performance is defined in many ways, especially for deep learning–based systems. On the one hand, you have metrics that indicate how good the stochasticity of your deep learning system is and whether it meets the desired standard. On the other hand, you have technical metrics for how well the system is performing —these relate to how many resources it is consuming (RAM, CPU), what the

---

40 Liu, Zhuoran, Leqi Zou, Xuan Zou, Caihua Wang, Biao Zhang, Da Tang, Bolin Zhu, et al. 2022. "Monolith: Real Time Recommendation System With Collisionless Embedding Table." arXiv, September 27, 2022. *https://arxiv.org/abs/2209.07663*.

throughput rate is, and so on—that you can monitor when scaling is performed. Ideally, scaling is a favorable event for the stochastic metrics and metrics that drive the expectations and behavior of the system. You do not want the precision of roof detection to fall when you scale your roof detection system across geographies, for instance. Having said that, the technical metrics are expected to align following their respective scaling laws. If you scale the API serving the model to have twice the throughput rate, then you would expect to have the memory requirements change, although you would expect this to have a minimal impact on latency.

Considerations of scalable systems

In a stark reminder of Murphy's law, the famous saying "Everything breaks at scale!" almost always holds. This should not come as a surprise, because scaling is all about working with the limitations—either to resolve them or to circumvent them. Doing this effectively requires a high level of care and consideration. The following sections touch on some of the factors to keep in mind when designing scalable systems and some commonly useful design patterns for scaling.

Avoiding single points of failure.   A single point of failure (SPOF) is a component whose failure can bring the entire system to a halt. Let's say a model is being trained at scale, across 1,000 A100 GPUs. All these machines are communicating with a distributed data store to read the data needed for training. If this data store fails, it will bring the training to halt; thus, the data store is a single point of failure. Clearly, it's important to minimize the presence of SPOFs if they can be eradicated.

Designing for high availability.   In the previous section, we talked about why availability is an important characteristic of a scalable system. Extending that discussion, all components of a scalable system must be designed to be highly available. High availability is realized through the three Rs: *reliability*, *resilience*, and *redundancy*. This is to say that the components of the system must be designed to be reliable (i.e., to rarely fail and, if they do fail, to do so predictably), resilient (i.e., to gracefully cope with downstream failures without bringing the entire system to halt), and redundant (i.e., to have redundancy baked in so that, in case of a failure, a redundant component can take over without impacting the entire system).

Scaling paradigms.   The following three scaling paradigms are commonly used today:

Horizontal
   In horizontal scaling, the same system is replicated several times. The replicas are then required to coordinate amongst themselves to provide the same service at scale. Distributed training, in which multiple nodes are added with each node only looking at specific independent parts of a larger dataset, is a very good example of horizontal scaling. This type of scaled training is known as distributed data parallelism; we'll discuss it further in Chapters 6 and 7.

Vertical

In vertical scaling, the capabilities of the system are scaled by adding more resources to an existing component. Adding more memory cards to increase RAM by 50% is an example of vertical scaling from the node viewpoint. This type of scaled training will be discussed further in Chapters 8 and 9.

Hybrid

In hybrid scaling, both horizontal and vertical scaling techniques are applied to scale across both dimensions. This type of scaled training will be discussed further in Chapters 8 and 9.

Coordination and communication.   Coordination and communication are at the heart of any system. Scaling any system creates pressure on the communication backbone used by the system. There are two main communication paradigms:

Synchronous

Synchronous communication occurs in real time, with two or more components sharing information simultaneously. This type of communication is throughput-intensive. As scale (e.g., the number of components) increases, this paradigm of communication very quickly becomes a bottleneck.

Asynchronous

In asynchronous communication, two or more components share information over time. Asynchronous communication provides flexibility and relaxes the communication burden, but it comes at the expense of discontinuity.

Communication and coordination are critical in scaling deep learning systems as well. As an example, stochastic gradient descent (SGD), a technique applied to find the optimal model weights, was originally synchronous. This technique very quickly became a bottleneck in scaling training, leading to the proposal of its asynchronous counterpart, asynchronous SGD (ASGD).[41] You will read more about coordination and communication challenges in Chapters 5 and 6.

Caching and intermittent storage.   Information retrieval necessitates communication in any system, but the trips to access information from storage are often expensive. This is intensified in deep learning scenarios because the information is spread across compute nodes and GPU devices, making information retrieval involved and expensive. Caching is a very popular technique used to store frequently needed information in inefficient storage to eliminate bottlenecking on this piece of information. Current

---

41 Dean, Jeffrey, and Luiz André Barroso. 2013. "The Tail at Scale." *Communications of the ACM* 56, no. 2: 74–80. *https://doi.org/10.1145/2408776.2408794*; Chen, Jianmin, Xinghao Pan, Rajat Monga, Samy Bengio, and Rafal Jozefowicz. 2017. "Revisiting Distributed Synchronous SGD." arXiv, March 21, 2017. *https://arxiv.org/abs/1604.00981*.

systems are more limited by memory and communication than by compute power; this is why caching can also be helpful in achieving lower latency.

Process state.   Knowing the current state of a process or system is critical to progress to the next stage. How much contextual information a component needs defines whether or not it is stateful: stateless processes and operations don't require any contextual information at all, whereas stateful processes do. Statelessness simplifies scaling. For example, calculating the dot product of two matrices is a completely stateless operation, as it only requires element-wise operation on indices of the matrix. The statelessness of matrix multiplication enables the so-called embarrassing parallelization of tensor computations. Conversely, gradient accumulation, a deep learning technique used to scale batch size under tight memory constraints, is highly stateful. Using components and techniques that are as stateless as possible reduces complexity of the system and minimizes bottlenecks in scaling.

Graceful recovery and checkpointing.   Failures do occur, as is evident from the fact that the gold standard of service availability is five nines (i.e., 99.999% uptime). This acknowledges that even in the most highly available systems, some type of failure will always happen eventually. The sophistication of a scalable system lies in having an efficient pathway to recovery when failure arises, as discussed earlier. Checkpointing is a commonly used technique to preserve intermittent state, storing it as a checkpoint to allow for recovery from the last known good state and maximizing the RPO.

Maintainability and observability.   The maintainability of any system is important, because it is directly associated with its continuation. As the complexity of a system increases, as is to be expected when scaling, the cost of maintaining it increases as well. Observability, achieved through monitoring and notification tooling significantly, increases the comfort of working with and maintaining complex systems. Moreover, when failures do occur, identifying and remedying them becomes a much simpler operation, resulting in a shorter RTO.

Scaling effectively

Throughout this chapter, you have gained insight on the importance of scaling effectively. As you have seen, it's critical to understand what your scale target is, what your limitations are, and what your bottlenecks will be, and to carefully work within your scaling framework to achieve that target.

The old carpentry proverb "measure twice, cut once" has been widely adopted in many domains and has proven its mettle in software development practices. If you're looking to build quality systems while minimizing the risk of errors and catastrophic failures, it's very useful to keep this in mind! The same principle applies to deep learning–based systems as well. "Measuring twice and cutting once" is an important strategy for scaling effectively. It provides a much-needed framework to:

- Know the current benchmarks and highlight known limitations.
- Test ideas and theories about the solution in a simulated environment and provide fast feedback.
- Gain confidence in the solution, reducing the risk of errors/accidental gains.
- Identify subtle, nonobvious bottlenecks early on.
- Quantify the revised benchmarks with the solution in place.
- Quickly iterate on strategies for improvement by applying them incrementally.

Efficiency is also about the effective use of available resources. The cost of ineffective deep learning practices is too high, even though letting GPUs "go burrr" has a power law associated with the adrenaline spike it causes in any deep learning practitioner. And that cost is not just limited to money and time; there are environmental and societal effects to consider as well, due to the sheer amount of carbon emissions associated with the energy consumption of these operations and the resulting adverse irreversible climate change impact. Training a large language model such as GPT3 can produce 500 metric tons of carbon dioxide emissions—the equivalent of around 600 flights between London and New York. More carbon-friendly computers like the French supercomputer used for training BLOOM, which is mostly powered by nuclear energy, emit less carbon than traditional GPUs; still, BLOOM is estimated to produce 25 metric tons of carbon dioxide emissions (the equivalent of 30 London–New York flights) during training.[42] Techniques like pretraining, few-shot learning, and transfer learning emphasize reducing the training time and repurposing the model's learnings for other tasks. Pretraining, in particular, lays the foundations for improvements in efficiency through reusability. Contrastive learning implementations such as CoCa, CLIP, and SigLIP are great examples of pretraining at scale achieved via self-supervision.[43] Model benchmarks from training with fixed GPU budgets can provide very useful insights for model selection, enabling you to scale efficiently.[44]

42 Heikkilä, Melissa. 2022. "Why We Need to Do a Better Job of Measuring AI's Carbon Footprint." MIT Technology Review, November 15, 2022. *https://www.technologyreview.com/2022/11/15/1063202/why-we-need-to-do-a-better-job-of-measuring-ais-carbon-footprint.*

43 Radford, Alec, Jong Wook Kim, Chris Hallacy, Aditya Ramesh, Gabriel Goh, Sandhini Agarwal, Girish Sastry, et al. 2021. "Learning Transferable Visual Models from Natural Language Supervision." arXiv, February 26, 2021. *https://arxiv.org/abs/2103.00020*; Zhai, Xiaohua, Basil Mustafa, Alexander Kolesnikov, and Lucas Beyer. 2023. Sigmoid Loss for Language Image Pre-Training. arXiv, September 27, 2023. *https://arxiv.org/abs/2303.15343.*

44 Geiping, Jonas, and Tom Goldstein. 2022. "Cramming: Training a Language Model on a Single GPU in One Day." arXiv, December 28, 2022. *https://arxiv.org/abs/2212.14034.*

When it comes to climate change, however, limiting carbon emissions at training time is just a feel-good measure—it's large, but it's only a one-time expense. Hugging Face estimated that while performing inference, BLOOM emits around 42 lbs (19 kg) of carbon dioxide per day. This is an ongoing expense that will accumulate, amounting to more than the training expenses in about three and a half years.[45] These are serious concerns, and the least we can do is make sure we use the resources available to us as efficiently as possible, planning experiments in such a way as to minimize wasted training cycles and using the full capacity of GPUs and CPUs. Through the course of this book, we will explore these concepts and various techniques for developing deep learning models effectively and efficiently.

Summary

According to Forbes, in 2021 76% of enterprises were prioritizing AI.[46] McKinsey reports that deep learning accounts for as much as 40% of annual revenue created by analytics and predicts that AI could deliver $13 trillion of additional economic output by 2030.[47] Through open sourcing and community participation, AI and deep learning are increasingly being democratized. However, when it comes to scaling, due to the expenses involved, the leverage primarily stays with MAANG (previously FAANG) and organizations with massive funding. Scaling up is one of the biggest challenges ML practitioners.[48] This should not come as a surprise, because scaling up any deep learning solution requires not only a thorough understanding of machine learning and software engineering, but also data expertise and hardware knowledge. Building industry-standard scaled-up solutions lies at the intersection of hardware, software, algorithms, and data.

To get you oriented for the rest of the book, this chapter discussed the history and origins of scaling law and the evolution of deep learning. You read about current trends and explored how the growth of deep learning has been driven by advancements in hardware, software, and data as much as the algorithms themselves. You

---

45 Heikkilä, "Why We Need to Do a Better Job of Measuring AI's Carbon Footprint," *https://www.technologyre view.com/2022/11/15/1063202/why-we-need-to-do-a-better-job-of-measuring-ais-carbon-footprint.*

46 Columbus, Louis. 2021. "76% of Enterprises Prioritize AI & Machine Learning in 2021 IT Budgets." Forbes, January 17, 2021. *https://www.forbes.com/sites/louiscolumbus/2021/01/17/76-of-enterprises-prioritize-ai--machine-learning-in-2021-it-budgets.*

47 Bughin, Jacques, Jeongmin Seong, James Manyika, Michael Chui, and Raoul Joshi. 2018. "Notes from the AI Frontier: Modeling the Impact of AI on the World Economy." McKinsey Global Institute discussion paper. *https://www.mckinsey.com/featured-insights/artificial-intelligence/notes-from-the-ai-frontier-modeling-the-impact-of-ai-on-the-world-economy.*

48 Thormundsson, Bergur. 2022. "Challenges Companies Are Facing When Deploying and Using Machine Learning from 2018, 2020 and 2021." Statista, April 6, 2022. *https://www.statista.com/statistics/1111249/machine-learning-challenges.*

also learned about key considerations to keep in mind when scaling your deep learning solutions and explored the implications of scale in the context of deep learning development. The complexity that comes with scaling is huge and the cost it carries is not inconsequential. One thing that's certain is that scaling is an adventure, and it's a lot of fun! I'm looking forward to helping you gain a deeper understanding of scaling deep learning in this book. In the following three chapters, you'll start by covering the foundational concepts of deep learning and gaining practical insights into the inner workings of the deep learning stack.

## PART I

Foundational Concepts of Deep Learning

The following chapters delve into foundational concepts that are essential for understanding and implementing deep learning. It begins by introducing deep learning principles through computational graphs and data flow, offering clarity through Python exercises. The section further explores the computational aspects of deep learning, including electronic computations and hardware considerations crucial for achieving and scaling compute capabilities. Additionally, it provides insights into accelerated hardware options available today, aiding in informed hardware selection for deep learning projects. Finally, the section synthesizes this knowledge to provide practical guidance on building efficient and effective intelligent systems, emphasizing strategies for optimization and performance measurement through graph compilation and memory management techniques.

## CHAPTER 2

Deep Learning

Chapter 1 covered the impact of scale on the history and evolution of deep learning. This chapter dives into the internal mechanics of deep learning and includes two practical Hands-On Exercises to warm up your deep learning skills. You will investigate the role of data in deep learning and explore several concepts involved in model development, using a minimalistic Python implementation of deep learning. You'll get the opportunity to apply these learnings by building a PyTorch-based model and exploring some important and interesting auxiliary utilities that are needed for all scaling efforts. This chapter is very practice-oriented and does not dive deeply into the theoretical foundations of deep learning. Please refer to *Deep Learning* by Aaron Courville, Ian Goodfellow, and Yoshua Bengio if you are seeking theoretical foundational knowledge.[1]

The Role of Data in Deep Learning

> All models are wrong, but some are useful.
>
> —George Box

Deep learning is a data programming technique that uses algorithmic approaches to obtain results given the input variable(s). Deep learning relies heavily on mathematics and statistics to obtain a model M such that result y can be obtained by applying $y \leftarrow M(x)$ to the given input x. The methodology for obtaining the model M in deep learning differs from the traditional stochastic data modeling techniques, such as linear or logistic regression. Traditional data modeling techniques heavily emphasize the goodness of fit. In contrast, deep learning treats the true data model of expected

---

1 Goodfellow, Ian, Yoshua Bengio, and Aaron Courville. 2016. *Deep Learning*. Cambridge, MA: MIT Press. *https://www.deeplearningbook.org*.

inputs—both the given (ground truth) and the future inputs—as unknown and optimizes for the best outcome using approximation strategies, caring less about the goodness of fit.[2]

While this approach of approximation and opaque data modeling may seem dangerous at first, empirically speaking, it is more feasible and adaptable. The practical applications of deep learning have been recognized since the early 1990s, based on predictive abilities (e.g., accuracy) and spontaneous feedback through more empirical evaluation techniques (e.g., using training, validation, and test sets). The usefulness of deep learning is also evident in the fact that hard-to-maintain, complex software built using deterministic programming approaches such as control flow or rule-based systems is increasingly being rewritten to be data-driven (rather than logic-driven) through "Software 2.0" strategies.[3]

The Software 2.0 approach holds that instead of compiling instructions to solve a complex problem, you should infer the most optimal, albeit approximate, representation of the solution through data, neural networks, and their weights and biases. Taking the example of the roof detection system discussed in Chapter 1, if you wanted to extend the abilities of that system to also produce roof outlines, then using classical image processing techniques could be a potential answer—identify the edges of predictions, and refine and optimize the output to create sharp outlines.

Considering the variations in shapes, sizes, and architectural designs of roofs across the globe, building a logic-driven roof outline solution would be incredibly complex, and the result would be fragile. The Software 2.0 solution to this problem might instead be to extend the roof detection model to produce a sequence of key corner points in addition to a pixel-wise segmentation.

Database indexes are another interesting example of Software 2.0 migration. For years, relational databases have used traditional data structures like BTree to store and look up indexes and applied traditional software engineering techniques like Bloom filters to speed up searching for specific data. Scaling these techniques to keep up with growing data volume needs has been a challenge. Deep learning techniques such as neural networks and reinforcement learning have achieved better performance and scalability in indexing algorithms, demonstrating a 44% increase in speed and a 3x reduction in memory requirements.[4]

2 Breiman, Leo 2001. "Statistical Modeling: The Two Cultures." *Statistical Science* 16, no. 3: 199–215. *http:// www.jstor.org/stable/2676681*.

3 Karpathy, Andrej. 2017. "Software 2.0." Medium, November 11, 2017. *https://karpathy.medium.com/ software-2-0-a64152b37c35*.

4 Beutel, Alex, Tim Kraska, Ed H. Chi, Jeffrey Dean, and Neoklis Polyzotis. 2017. "A Machine Learning Approach to Databases Indexes." ML Systems Workshop at NIPS 2017. *http://learningsys.org/nips17/assets/ papers/paper_22.pdf*.

So far, we've been considering deep learning as a data programming technique and its usefulness in tandem with traditional programming. In the following section, we'll look at how the data flows through a deep network to perform the deep magic.

Data Flow in Deep Learning

Deep learning models deduce a lossy compressed representation of the data they have been trained with. This section details how this compressed representation materializes and visualizes some of these latent learnings.

Figure 2-1 provides an overview of the typical data flow in building a deep learning model. As shown in the figure, at a high level, this is an eight-step process.

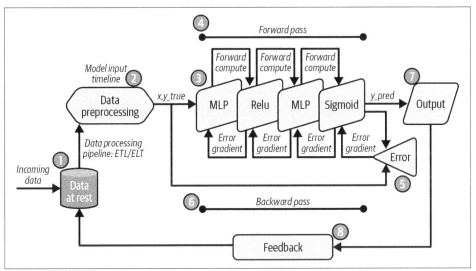

Figure 2-1. The flow of data in deep learning

Let's look at the eight stages the data goes through in a bit more detail:

1. *Incoming data and data at rest*: Data forms the foundation of the knowledge you want the model to learn. This phase encompasses the programs and processes associated with data collection, governance, labeling, and management. The data acquisition part of this process tends to be much more human-centric than the rest of the steps in the workflow. This is because humans are often heavily involved in data generation, be it the raw data or ground truth labels (where applicable). The more frictionless and fluid you can make this step, the more scalable and efficient your entire model development regime will be. This is the concept of the data engine that we discussed briefly in Chapter 1 and will consider further in Chapter 10.

2. *Data preprocessing*: This step encompasses extracting data for use in model train‐
   ing, validation, and testing; transforming and massaging these data points; and
   loading them for computation and model development. In data engineering ter‐
   minology, this is referred to as ETL (extract, transform, and load). This step per‐
   tains to the pipeline that feeds input data to the model.

3. *The model*: The model is defined by a series of mathematical operations where
   the output of the preceding operation is used as input to the following operation.
   These chains of operations are stacked together, effectively forming a mathemati‐
   cal formula, M, representing the model. This formula defines the compression
   algorithm that will be applied to extract the latent knowledge, or internal repre‐
   sentation of the learning. The following three steps—the forward pass, error cal‐
   culation, and backpropagation—will guide the actual compression process.

4. *Forward pass*: This step is simply about applying the chain of operations on the
   given data to achieve the model's prediction (the output). The example model in
   Figure 2-1 consists of four layers, linear (MLP)→ReLU→linear→sigmoid, so the
   output is defined by Equation 2-1.

> *Equation 2-1. Chain of (math) operations representing the computational
> graph of the model*
>
> $$y_{pred} = sigmoid(linear(relu(linear(x))))$$

   At the inception of training, the initial parameters (weights and biases) are ini‐
   tialized randomly through an initialization algorithm like Kaiming/He or Xavier/
   Glorot. (For an accessible introduction to initialization algorithms, see James
   Dellinger's article on weight initialization in neural networks.[5]) Another initiali‐
   zation technique, transfer learning with pretraining, involves copying over
   weights from a previously trained model. We'll talk more about this technique in
   Chapter 11.

5. *Error*: You now have the model's prediction and the ground truth, which can be
   used to calculate the extent to which the model was wrong (or right) in predict‐
   ing the output for that sample x. This feedback—i.e., how wrong the model was
   in a given prediction—is very useful in adjusting the parameters of the model so
   it can correct its course and align in a direction (positive or negative) and magni‐
   tude that provide better results. The error is defined by a mathematical function
   termed the *loss function* (also known as the *objective function* or *criterion*).
   Appropriate selection of the objective function (see Equation 2-2) is crucial in

---

5 Dellinger, James. 2019. "Weight Initialization in Neural Networks: A Journey from the Basics to Kaiming."
   Towards Data Science, April 3, 2019. *https://towardsdatascience.com/weight-initialization-in-neural-networks-
   a-journey-from-the-basics-to-kaiming-954fb9b47c79*.

approximating the data model for all x, known (training set) or expected (test data and data provided at an inference or use/runtime), as this function guides the learning. Mean squared error, cross-entropy loss, and contrastive loss are commonly used loss functions for tasks specific to regression, classification, and unsupervised learning, respectively.

Equation 2-2. Formula to calculate error from predicted outcome using objective/loss function

$$error = loss_{fn}(y_{pred}, y_{true})$$

6. *Backward pass*: So far, you have performed a forward pass on the model and calculated the error. You now need to adjust the parameters (weights and biases) of the model based on the error feedback you received in the previous step. If you can estimate the change in error for each change in the parameters of the model, then you can update the parameters appropriately to minimize the error. Differential calculus is useful here: you calculate the derivative of the loss function with respect to the parameters of the model (see Equation 2-3) and apply that to the actual parameter values to deduce approximately better parameters than before (see Equation 2-4).

Equation 2-3. Formula to obtain error gradients using differential mathematics

$$error' = error\_gradients = \frac{\delta error}{\delta parameters} = \frac{\delta error}{\delta y_{pred}} \times \frac{\delta y_{pred}}{\delta parameters}$$

Equation 2-4. Formula for parameter (weight) adjustment to account for error in prediction

$$parameter - = error\_gradient \times learning\_rate$$

The parameters are spread across the chained operations of the model. So, when you apply $\partial y_{pred} / \partial parameters$ across the model, following the differential rules for chained operation, the *error_gradient* is propagated through the network in reverse order: i.e., *linear'(relu'(linear'(sigmoid'(∂error/∂y_{pred})))).* In each call, the respective operation's parameters are adjusted based on the magnitude and direction of errors (Equation 2-4).

During training, you perform steps 4, 5, and 6 in a loop several times to iteratively approximate better parameters. You stop when the loss no longer changes, indicating that the current parameters are likely the most optimal ones (i.e., convergence has been reached and further training in this loop will not provide any additional return on compute and time investment). This loop encompasses two types of data flow:

- *Gradient computation flow*, defined by the computation of Equation 2-1, Equation 2-2, and Equation 2-3 that takes place during the forward pass, error computation, and backward pass.

- *Parameter update flow*, defined by the computation of Equation 2-4 that takes place during the backward pass.

In Part II of this book, you will see that these two flows are central to scaling out.

7. *Output*: The optimal parameters achieved through this iterative process represent the "compressed" knowledge learned from the training dataset. Once these parameters are known, together with chained operations they form the model that's ready for use in relevant applications. Inference—the forward pass on the learned model M, which is equivalent to *sigmoid(linear(relu(linear(x))))* (i.e., Equation 2-1) in this example case—leads to the prediction y_{pred} on the unknown/expected data x.

8. *Feedback*: The last, crucial step in the data flow for deep learning is learning at inference time and continually updating the model to ensure its relevance. There are various approaches to building a feedback channel, depending on how much control and access you have to data used for inference. These range from model monitoring, drift analysis, continual learning, and using end users' direct feedback to even more advanced implementations using various signals at inference time to deduce feedback. For instance, as discussed in Chapter 1, GitHub's Copilot gathers feedback by checking if model suggestions are actively used for a prolonged time to decide if the model's prediction was of the appropriate standard.

In this section, we looked at the data flows in deep learning. Next, we'll apply this concept in a toy setting and explore a practical minimalist implementation of deep learning.

Hands-On Exercise #1: Implementing Minimalistic Deep Learning

In this section we'll consider a practical example and walk through the network to see what happens behind the scenes. Let's say that you have to build a model that can classify whether the provided grayscale image contains a 3x3 black square patches anywhere in the middle half of the image. For simplicity, we will limit the size of the image to 9x9 pixels. In grayscale images, the pixel values are in the range of 0 to 255: 0 for black, 255 for white, with values in between representing different shades of gray.

You are really after the model deducing the logic rule to indicate whether the pixel values of any of these patches sum to 0. This logic rule is as follows:

```
for i in range(h//4 -1, (h - h //4) -1):
    for j in range(w//4 -1, (w - w //4) - 1):
        if sum(image[j:j+3, i:i+3]) == 0:
            return True
return False
```

Developing the Model

In this section, we'll walk through how to develop and train a model for this toy problem. The Python code for this example is located in the book's GitHub repository, in the script *has_black_patches_or_not.py* (*https://oreil.ly/3Qtz4*). In the following subsections, snippets of this script will be discussed. Please refer to "Setting Up Your Environment for Hands-on Exercises" on page xv for more information on creating the execution environment, setting up dependencies, and navigating the code repository.

Complete code for the book's hands-on examples and instructions for running them are provided in the companion GitHub repository. Because of space constraints, the full code for the examples is not reproduced in the book. Readers are invited to explore the code themselves, and instructions for running the examples are provided, along with discussion of certain relevant details.

Model input data and pipeline

First, let's generate the data for the toy problem, which consists of 9x9 white squares containing at most one randomly positioned 3x3 black patch in the middle half of the image. Then we'll apply the logic to preprocess this synthetically derived dataset of images (the source) with a Boolean flag (the label) to indicate whether they contain a black patch or not.

Figure 2-2(a) shows a randomly generated image with fractional bits of white noise. Figure 2-2(b) shows examples of randomly generated sample images (like the one in Figure 2-2(a) with and without a 3x3 black square patch injected in a random location anywhere in the middle half of the image, corresponding to the positive and negative classes, respectively. Because of the scale and the resulting rounding, the images on the right do not provide as effective a visualization of the white noise as the image on the left.

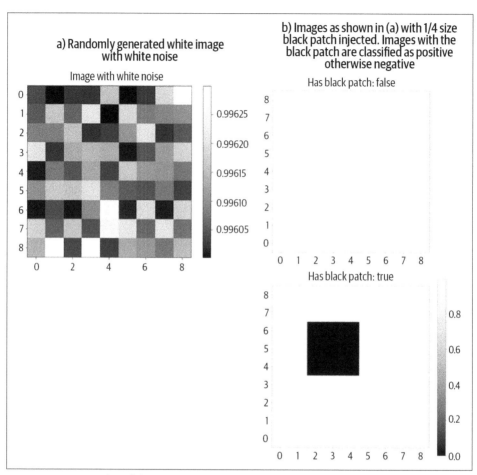

Figure 2-2. Examples of the normalized source data and ground truth labels

The following snippet defines the function, random_x_y, that is used to generate the samples of this dataset. First, you create a size * size array for a grayscale image. The image is represented as a floating-point (instead of integer) value type, so the pixel value range of [0, 255] will be represented by its normalized counterpart, [0, 1], where 0 is black and 1 is white. Then, using 50% likelihood, you add a black patch randomly in the middle half of the image. Finally, you add some fractional white noise to create some more variety in your input dataset. Here's the function definition:

```python
def random_x_y(size: int):
    x = np.full((size * size), 0.996, dtype=np.float32)
    x = x.reshape((size, size))
    y = np.zeros((1), dtype=np.float32)
    if np.random.uniform() < 0.5:
```

```
        idx = np.random.randint(size // 4, size - size // 4)
        x[idx - 1 : idx + 1, idx - 1 : idx + 1] = 0
        y[0] = 1
    x = x.reshape((1, size * size))
    x += np.abs(np.random.normal(-1e-4, 1e-4, (size * size)))
    yield x, y
```

Using the `random_x_y` function, you can generate input data on the fly so it does not require persistence (i.e., storing on disk). Moreover, with `size = 9` and using `float32` NumPy data containers, the image and ground truth label for each sample require a total of only 436 and 116 bytes of memory, respectively. Some memory overhead is generated by the NumPy array representation, as the actual byte size for the data is 324 bytes for the image and 4 bytes for the label, respectively. You can explore this using the following snippet:

```
import numpy as np
import sys

size = 9

x=np.full((size * size), 0.996, dtype=np.float32)
sys.getsizeof(x) # results in 436 bytes
x.nbytes # results in 324

y = np.zeros((1), dtype=np.float32)
sys.getsizeof(y) # results in 116

y.nbytes # results in 4
```

Generating samples with `random_x_y` results in a very simple model input pipeline. Typically, a model input pipeline will consist of several preprocessing and data augmentation steps in addition to a mechanism to provide an input stream of samples. However, in this toy problem, we will skip the preprocessing and just create an iterator for input data consisting of a total of `input_size` samples:

```
def generate_data(sample_size: int, input_size: int):
    for _ in range(sample_size):
        yield from random_x_y(input_size)
```

Let's walk through how to develop and train a model for this toy problem.

Model

As shown in Figure 2-1, you are building a model *M = sigmoid(linear(relu(linear(x))))* that has a shallow network. This network is based on a multilayer perceptron (MLP) consisting of a stack of linear layers, followed by nonlinear rectified linear unit (ReLU) activation function and a second MLP layer. The last layer, a sigmoid activation function, provides the ability to constrain the output into a 0–1 probability range suitable for binary classification.

The minimalistic implementation for each of these layers is available in the example script *has_black_patches_or_not.py* (*https://oreil.ly/Z2uUI*). The implementation for each layer contains `forward(self, x)` and `backward(self, error, learning_rate)` methods representative of the operations required for the forward and backward pass, respectively. Here are the key points:

Linear layer
> Implemented by the class `LinearLayer`, where `forward` computes the operation $y \leftarrow weights \times x + bias$ and `backward` computes the differential of the forward equation and applies the parameter update as described by Examples Equation 2-3 and Equation 2-4.

Activation layer
> Implemented by the class `ReluActivationLayer`, where `forward` computes the operation $y \leftarrow max(x, 0)$ and `backward` propagates the error if $x > 0$. ReLU does not have parameters; this is why there are no weight updates required at this stage.

Sigmoid layer
> Implemented by the class `SigmoidLayer`, where `forward` applies the sigmoid operation, $y \leftarrow \frac{1}{(1 + e^{-x})}$, and `backward` computes the differential of the sigmoid, $\frac{\delta sigmoid(x)}{\delta x} = \frac{e^{-x}}{(1 + e^{-x})^2}$ (also represented as $sigmoid(x) \times (1 - sigmoid(x))$).

In this example, the linear layers are the only layers with learnable parameters. The other layers are non-learnable layers. The first linear layer takes a flattened 9x9 (i.e., 1x81) array and outputs a 1x56 array. The total number of parameters of this layer thus is 4,592, determined by multiplying the number of weights (81) by the number of biases (56). The second linear layer takes in a 1x56 array and outputs a unit size array; thus, it has 57 additional parameters (56 for weights and 1 for bias).

A good test prior to scaling the network capacity is to confirm that your current network is insufficient for your task and/or possibly underfitting your training set. For such exploration, it's common to use a portion of the dataset that is held out and not used for training (known as a *validation set*). This allows you to validate and inform the design and configuration of your network. This exercise skips the use of validation, for the sake of simplicity; however, in this chapter's second Hands-On Exercise ("Hands-On Exercise #2: Getting Complex with PyTorch" on page 57) we will use a validation set. Exploring the embedded space and the features of your data is also a very good exercise to inform the model choices. We'll look at how to do this in the following section.

Training loop

In the training loop, you iterate on generated training samples, compute the model *M*'s output via the forward pass, deduce the error/loss and compute the error gradient, and propagate it back, as defined in the data flow in Figure 2-1 (discussed earlier in the chapter).

Loss. In this example, you will use *binary cross entropy* (BCE) as your loss function. This is a suitable loss function for binary classification tasks such as ours (whether an image contains a black patch or not). The formula for BCE loss is given by Equation 2-5.

Equation 2-5. Formula for binary cross entropy loss

$$bce = \tfrac{-1}{N} \Sigma_{i=1}^{N} \left(y_i \times log(p(y_i)) + (1 - y_i) \times log(1 - p(y_i)) \right)$$

The differential (derivative) for BCE is given by Equation 2-6.

Equation 2-6. Derivative of binary cross entropy loss

$$bce' = \tfrac{1}{N} \Sigma_{i=1}^{N} \left(- y_i / (p(y_i) + (1 - y_i) / (1 - p(y_i)) \right)$$

These are implemented as the `bce` and `bce_prime` methods in the example script *has_black_patches_or_not.py* (*https://oreil.ly/t-qhM*). In the training loop, you calculate the error and error gradient and propagate the error gradient backward through each layer by invoking its `backward` method.

Metrics. You will need metrics to compute your model's performance. In this example, using the numbers of true positives (TP), false positives (FP), true negatives (TN), and false negatives (FN), we'll compute the following metrics:

Accuracy
Given by the ratio of the number of correct classifications to all classifications:

$$accuracy = (TP + TN) / (TP + TN + FN + FP)$$

Precision
Measures the accuracy of positive predictions and is given by:

$$precision = \frac{TP}{(TP + FP)}$$

Recall

Measures the completeness of positive predictions and is given by:

$$recall = \frac{TP}{(TP + FN)}$$

F1 score

Defined as the harmonic mean of precision and recall and is given by:

$$recall = \frac{(2 \times precision \times recall)}{(precision + recall)}$$

Figure 2-3 plots the loss and performance metrics over several iterations (epochs) of training data. You can run this sample from the code repository by executing the following command:

```
deep-learning-at-scale chapter_2 has_black_patch train
```

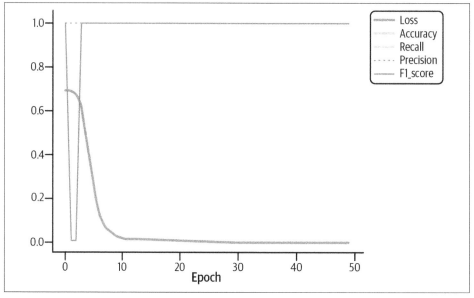

Figure 2-3. A plot of the loss and performance metrics of the model over 50 epochs

As you can see, the model is converging by the fifth epoch, and the loss plateaus at about the tenth epoch. After this point, the loss on the test set is 0.001, and all the metrics are 1. You have built and trained a simple network and achieved good performance on this data. In the next section, we'll explore further to understand what's happening behind the scenes.

The Embedded/Latent Space

As you may have noticed, the input data has a pattern where images with no patches have a mean pixel value of about 1 (as they are all-white images with slight white noise) and images with a 3x3 black patch somewhere in the inner half have a mean pixel value of about 0.89. Given that only the inner half of the image has the signals to deduce whether it contains a black patch or not, it's probably an effective technique to not give weights to every pixel in the images. You can safely ignore pixels in the outer 1/4 periphery. Given that the black patches are 3x3, it is probably also an effective strategy to not give weights to every pixel, but instead to sample a few pixels at an interval. You just need to make sure the intervals are less than 3 in stride so you don't miss any black patches.

Figure 2-4 visualizes the weights of the model trained using the hands-on sample. You can see that most of the weights are leaning toward 0, so they will effectively be masking the contributions from pixel value.

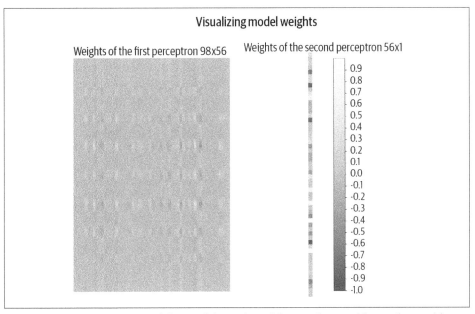

Figure 2-4. A visualization of the model weights of first and second linear layers (the layers with learnable parameters)

Since the patch generation is centered at a random p * p where p = np.random. randint(size // 4, size - size // 4), the value of p will be in the range [2, 6] for a 9x9 image. The 9x9 image is reshaped to a vector of length 81, meaning the first 10 indices (9 for the first row of the image and 1 for the first pixel of the second row) in this vector do not contain any signals to determine whether the image contains a patch in the middle half or not. Looking at the weights of the first perceptron, as shown in Figure 2-4, you can see the first 10 indices tending to zero. Likewise, you may note that the tail end of the weight matrix is tending to zero as well. At the same time, you can see an interesting pattern in the weights that have higher values of ~0.9. On the right side of the weight matrix, there are three consecutive positions across rows with weights tending to 1. You may also note the spacing of these higher-weighted positions, representing the sparse selection of signals to determine whether patches are present or not. This pattern is also present in the weights of the second perceptron, which operates on a feature vector of length 56 obtained from the preceding layer.

To visualize the feature embedding and explore the latent space, we'll use the Uniform Manifold Approximation and Projection (UMAP)[6] algorithm that reprojects high-dimensional vectors onto a lower-dimensional embedded space and teases out the pattern in data based on neighborhood statistics.

You can run the following command to visualize the results and explore the specifics:

```
deep-learning-at-scale chapter_2 has_black_patch feature-embedding
```

The results of this UMAP analysis, as shown in Figure 2-5, confirm that the dataset is clearly separable. You may note that the images without patches in reduced dimensions are well clustered into a blob. The other five clusters represent five unique groups of samples with patches. The second and third subplots in this figure also show how there is a clear linear separation boundary forming, starting from the first layer's output. These boundaries become more refined in the subsequent second linear layer.

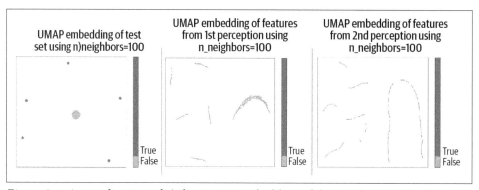

Figure 2-5. A visualization of a) the UMAP embedding of the test dataset, b) a feature map of the first layer linear, and c) a feature map of the second layer linear

---

6 Mall, Suneeta. 2022. "Review and Comparison of Two Manifold Learning Algorithms: t-SNE and UMAP." Suneeta Mall's blog, June 9, 2022. *https://suneeta-mall.github.io/2022/06/09/feature_analysis_tsne_vs_umap.html*.

Because of this clear separation, you get optimal test measures of accuracy, precision, recall, and F1 score, all of which (as shown in Figure 2-3) are equal to 1 after just a few epochs of training. In light of the Software 2.0 discussion at the start of this chapter, it's worth drawing attention to the fact that you have just explored how deep learning solved a simple challenge. In this case, a solution could have been easily implemented using a logic-driven program following the logic rule defined earlier. Still, this toy example hints at how stochastic approaches such as deep learning can be used to solve challenges that are not easily solved by traditional programming, which is the main motivation behind these approaches.

A Word of Caution

You have just gone through a data modeling exercise to fit a model on your black patch dataset. However, your data is biased. While the intention is to model `sum(image[j:j+3, i:i+3]) == 0`, there are no negative samples for when 0 < `sum(image[j:j+3, i:i+3]) &lt; ~9`) (see Figure 2-6). This may mean that when it encounters such samples, the model will either spew out random outputs or show inherent bias, depending on the input x.

Based on the logic rule set out earlier in the chapter, the examples shown in Figure 2-6 should be classified as negative samples and should ideally lead to $y =$ False. However, each of these input xs will result in a false positive. If you investigate further, you will note that this model detects positive signals even for images with a single pixel with a value of 0.

This gap in the model's knowledge stems from the skewed representation of the problem domain as presented by the training data. So far, you have looked at the source input, layer parameters, all the intermediate layers' input and output, and the final model predictions. You have also seen a reduction in loss per epoch over the course of training (Figure 2-3). In the following section, we'll explore the learning rate and loss landscape.

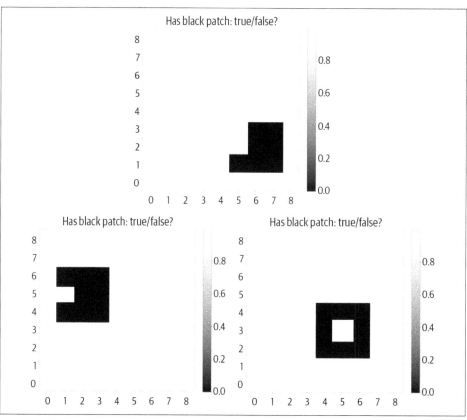

Figure 2-6. Possible negative samples for "has 3x3 black patch" that are not represented in the dataset generated by the `random_x_y` method

The Learning Rate and Loss Landscape

The *loss landscape*, also known as *loss curvature*, is defined by the surface plot of the loss function $loss_{fn}(y_{pred}, y_{true})$. This is the surface that the model algorithm should navigate to attain, ideally, the global minima (i.e., the points in parameter space where loss on the dataset is lowest). An example of a model's loss landscape is shown in Figure 2-7, to illustrate the regions of the curve with varying loss intensities (ranging from maxima to minima).

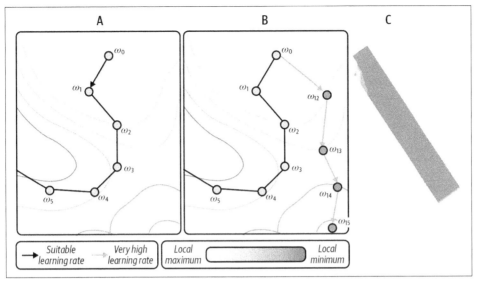

Figure 2-7. A depiction of a model's loss landscape, showing: a) a simulated loss curve to illustrate how incremental versions of models navigate the curvature to arrive at local minima; b) extension of the loss curvature navigation when the learning rate is too high; and c) the curvature obtained from this section's Hands-On Exercise

Hao Li et al.'s 2017 paper, "Visualizing the Loss Landscape of Neural Nets,"[7] presents a linear interpolation algorithm with normalization techniques that is useful in visualizing the loss curvatures of deep networks. You can explore this algorithm through a hands-on example, *loss_landscape.py* (*https://oreil.ly/sDZEq*), by executing the following command:

```
deep-learning-at-scale chapter_2 simulate-loss-curve
```

The learning rate as employed in this example is a simplistic implementation of the optimization algorithm. The role of the optimization algorithm is to guide the parameter adjustment through backpropagation such that you can maximize the objective function (i.e., minimize the loss). As shown in Figure 2-7(a), the initial version of the model (version w_0) starts from local maxima, and as the training progresses each subsequent version of the model converges to minima. Most deep learning optimization algorithms stem from optimization theory describing convex and nonconvex optimization techniques. Deep learning is nonconvex, as there can be many local minima. Generally, gradient descent–based techniques are sufficient in deep learning.

---

7 Li, Hao, Zheng Xu, Gavin Taylor, Christoph Studer, and Tom Goldstein. 2018. "Visualizing the Loss Landscape of Neural Nets." arXiv, November 7, 2018. *https://arxiv.org/abs/1712.09913*.

In this example, a gradient descent–based technique is used to navigate the loss landscape. As shown in the `Linear.backward` implementation, the proportion of error applied to weight adjustment depends on the learning rate. If you play with the learning rate parameter, you will notice that as you increase the learning rate the convergence happens faster, and vice versa. For instance, if you change the learning rate to 0.1 then the convergence is achieved right after the first epoch, whereas if you increase it to 1e-4 you will need at least 150 epochs for convergence to commence and about 400 epochs to achieve a plateau.

You can explore the learning rate behavior through this example using the following commands:

```
deep-learning-at-scale chapter_2 has_black_patch train --learning-rate 1e-1
```

```
deep-learning-at-scale chapter_2 has_black_patch train --learning-rate 1e-4
--epochs 500
```

This is not to say that the learning rate should always be higher for efficient learning. A high learning rate could mean too much bouncing around the loss landscape and an increased risk of getting stuck in local minima (see Figure 2-7(b), where a high learning rate led the model to suboptimal minima). A very slow learning rate can also be suboptimal, though, as it can significantly slow down training/convergence time. This is why the learning rate is a tunable hypermeter of the network, and its effectiveness depends on the loss landscape.

Let's now consider the minimalist toy solution you have built and explore the implications of scaling it.

Scaling Consideration

As the complexity of the data and the task increases, the gap in the decision boundary between True/False, as shown in Figure 2-5, will start to narrow, requiring more layers representing even more complex mathematical operations. This is primarily how scaling deep learning by scaling the network works. An example of a complexity increase in the "has a 3x3 square black patch" problem you tackled in this section could be the introduction of other geometric shapes (triangles, circles, etc.). For further complexity, there might be multiple such shapes in an image, which might even overlap; or your requirements might change so that you now need to not only tell if there is a black patch of some shape in the images but also identify the shapes of the patches.

In such cases, your model needs to learn a lot more features and capture the nuances of all the possible shapes. As a result, scaling the capacity of your network may be needed. To scale the capacity of the network, you might want to add more parameterized layers. One example of scaling could be $M = sigmoid(linear(relu(linear(relu(linear(x))))))$, where an additional `LinearLayer`

layer followed by a `ReluActivationLayer` is added. By doing this, you would be adding 2,726 additional parameters. You would also be accumulating the additional computational burden (FLOPs) from these two layers.

The following snippet can be used to extend the existing example to leverage a scaled-up version of this network:

```
model = [
    LinearLayer(input_size=input_size * input_size, output_size=56),
    ReluActivationLayer(),
    LinearLayer(input_size=56, output_size=48),
    ReluActivationLayer(),
    LinearLayer(input_size=48, output_size=output_size),
    SigmoidLayer(input_size=output_size),
]
```

In this example, however, there is an optimization opportunity of dropping the second layer and reducing the memory requirements.

Profiling

Chapter 1 discussed how the extensive scaling of computing infrastructure has facilitated the growth of deep learning. Let's explore the computing and memory requirements of your toy model training exercise.

As shown in Figure 2-8, most of the compute burden is coming from the loss calculation arithmetic, error gradient computation, and backward propagation. While other operations are consuming compute and memory resources, their requirements are substantially lower than the aforementioned computations.

To generate these profiles yourself, run the following commands over the example repository:

1. For the memory profile, use:

    ```
    mprof run deep-learning-at-scale chapter_2 has_black_patch train
    ```

    ```
    mprof plot
    ```

2. For the compute profile, use:

    ```
    python -m cProfile -o output.pstats \
        deep_learning_at_scale/chapter_2/has_black_patches_or_not.py train
    ```

    ```
    gprof2dot --colour-nodes-by-selftime -f pstats output.pstats |
    dot -Tpng -o output.png
    ```

    You might have to install `gprof2dot` to visualize the profilers' output.

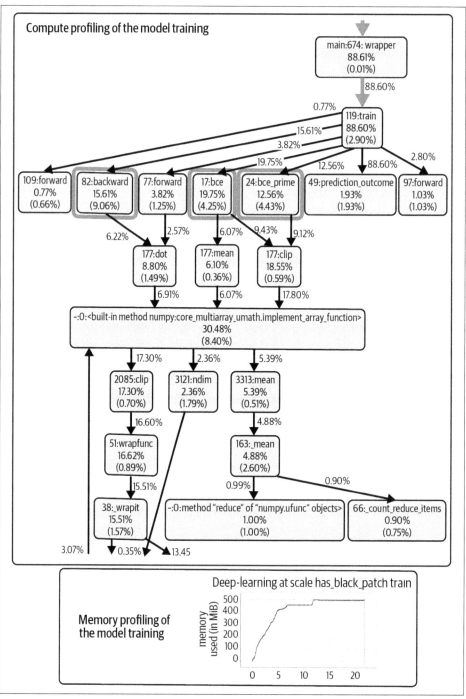

Figure 2-8. Memory and compute profiles generated for the example model using mprof and cProfile (extensive computation steps are circled)

As discussed earlier, this model consists of 4,592 parameters, and it occupies a total of about 520 MB in memory.

In this section, you built a minimalist deep learning network purely in Python. You worked through several nuances of the network, exploring how data flows through it, how deep learning models the input data and learns the latent representation, and how the model is built, trained, and profiled. As the complexities grow, for scalability and reusability reasons, the use of deep learning frameworks such as PyTorch, TensorFlow, and JAX may be required. In this book, I will predominantly use PyTorch (and its ecosystem) for Hands-On Exercises going forward.

Hands-On Exercise #2: Getting Complex with PyTorch

PyTorch (*https://pytorch.org*) provides both functional and objective interfaces to develop deep learning solutions in a very Pythonic way. It offers the ability to easily execute your operations across various compute types, including accelerated devices. One of the great advantages of using a deep learning framework such as PyTorch is that it uses automatic differentiation algorithms,[8] meaning that the backward pass (like the one you implemented in the previous toy problem) is automatically deduced and executed. Because of this automation and the effective engineering behind it, integrations of layers and the development of models are a lot faster. PyTorch has wide community support with its open source strategies and association with the Linux Foundation (*https://oreil.ly/3YS2H*). This is also the reason why PyTorch has a large ecosystem growing up around it.

PyTorch Lightning (*https://oreil.ly/mYN91*) is a library in the PyTorch ecosystem that aims to simplify PyTorch-based model development by removing boilerplate code and providing easy-to-use application programming interfaces (APIs). PyTorch Lightning is also actively used for Hands-On Exercises throughout this book.

In this section, we're going to dive into PyTorch through a slightly more complex Hands-On Exercise than the one you worked through in the previous section. The purpose of the earlier exercise was to understand the data flow, dissect the process of learning, and explore the learned representation. In this exercise, the focus will be on assembling somewhat more complex model training code that can run seamlessly across various computing devices and has utilities to effectively train the model. In summary, this section's components focus more on efficiency.

Let's walk through the eight-step workflow from Figure 2-1 and explore what this would look like in the PyTorch ecosystem. This example makes heavy use of both

---

8 Preferred Networks. 2021. "Overview of PyTorch Autograd Engine." PyTorch blog, June 8, 2021. *https://pytorch.org/blog/overview-of-pytorch-autograd-engine*.

PyTorch and Lightning APIs and implementations. The complete code can be found in the book's code repository, in the *app.py* (*https://oreil.ly/qlPSR*) script.

Model Input Data and Pipeline

For this exercise, you'll use one of the most popular and oldest open source deep learning datasets: the MNIST (Modified National Institute of Standards and Technology) dataset of images of handwritten digits for digit classification. The dataset consists of 60,000 training samples and 10,000 test samples.

The MNIST images are 28x28-pixel grayscale images. You may have noticed that this dataset is substantially larger than the one you created on the fly in the previous example. Also noteworthy is that this dataset will require persistence: it's distributed in a compressed format, and you'll need to download and decompress the file.

The MNISTDataModule defined in the example script is an implementation of the model input pipeline that extends Lightning's LightningDataModule. The pre pare_data call addresses the downloading and unpacking of the training and test samples, while setup handles slicing the data into training, validation, and test sets and defining an MNIST dataset interface that knows how to convert the MNIST images and labels from their compressed format into uncompressed image array and classification output. Following that, four different DataLoaders are defined for training, validation, testing, and prediction. The role of a DataLoader (*https://oreil.ly/-sIta*) is to provide map-style access to samples such that customized sampling of the dataset—for example, random access—is possible.

This example also uses the *data batching* concept, where instead of passing a single sample per forward pass, a bundle of samples are passed through. One advantage of batching is efficient computing, as some devices (e.g., GPUs) can efficiently compute multidimensional operations. The other advantages of batching relate to optimization techniques: for instance, gradient descent, where batching makes the gradients less noisy, and regularization techniques like batch normalization that allow for building more generalized networks.

More interesting sampling strategies, such as weighted sampling, can be implemented using the Sampler interface of the DataLoader API. Data mining techniques for efficient training (discussed in Chapter 10) are built on this sampling interface. For this example, however, you will just use shuffle = True for training for random access and keep the validation and test sets sequential.

In this data pipeline, a couple of transformation requests are issued via self.trans form to convert the array object to a Tensor (PyTorch's abstraction to represent a matrix) and to normalize the images with a mean and standard error. In this case, the chain of transform requests is consistent across training/validation/testing; however, in general you may need variations between transforms for training versus validation/testing. In particular, if you want to build a more robust, generalized model, you may want to use augmentations to create a richer dataset by performing affine transformations, injecting noise, making color adjustments, etc. Albumentations (*https://oreil.ly/xnTtt*) and Kornia (*https://oreil.ly/T4O8T*) are two great libraries for various augmentation and transformation operations.

The `teardown` method is generally used for cleanup, such as removing the cache, clearing out files, etc. for manageability.

Model

Similar to the previous Hands-On Exercise, this problem is also a classification challenge. But instead of binary classification (yes/no), this is a multiclass classification problem where the output needs to be one of the 10 class outputs from the range 0–9 for the digits.

The `MNISTModel` defined in the example script is an implementation of `LightningModule` that clearly separates the training/validation/testing and prediction stages, providing clearer and more manageable abstractions for these operation flows.

Looking more specifically at `self.model` and comparing it with the earlier implementation, you'll see that in this approach you are flattening the input as a part of the model, whereas earlier you did this as part of the data pipeline. This is a non-learnable layer, so the decision of where to flatten is up to you. The choice might depend on whether you want to execute this operation on the same device as the model, especially if, for example, you want to leverage accelerated computing for efficiency reasons. Chapter 3 covers more specific details and nuances of accelerated computing and addresses this topic.

The stack of linear and ReLU layers used in this chained `Sequential` stack is in line with the previous implementation. However, this sample is using the regularization technique *dropout*, which randomly drops some neurons' signals to mitigate overfitting. The last interesting difference between this example and the previous one is the use of $LogSoftmax(x_i) = log(exp(x_i)) / \Sigma_j exp(x_j)$ instead of $Sigmoid(x) = \frac{1}{(1 + e^{-x})}$. This is to support the multiclass nature of the problem in comparison to the binary classification performed earlier.

You may have noted already that the `forward` call is simply calling the built-in `__call__` function of the PyTorch module, which implicitly executes all the mathematical operations stacked in the sequence chain. If you look at the `training_step`, you may note that there is no call, handle, or hook for backward propagation; this is because the backpropagation is dealt with by PyTorch's `autograd` module, which handles automatic differentiation. However, the `training_step` does calculate the loss and log metrics. If you're wondering what happens to the learning rate and how optimizers are applied in `autograd` (automatic differentiation), the implementation of the `configure_optimizers` method is worth looking into. PyTorch Lightning uses this method to simulate Equation 2-4, discussed previously.

This example uses Adam, an adaptive optimization technique that can better cope with noisy gradients using moment statistics.[9] The configuration provided by `config ure_optimizers` thus guides the learning and loss curve navigation during training and gradient descent.

This model has a total of 55,050 trainable parameters. It requires 1.76 million multiply–accumulate (MAC) operations on an input size of 0.1 MB, with parameter memory requirements of 0.22 MB and forward and backward pass memory requirements of 0.04 MB, for a total memory use of less than 1 MB. These details have been generated using the `torchinfo` library and can be reproduced using the example repository as follows:

```
deep-learning-at-scale chapter_2 inspect-model
```

Auxiliary Utilities

As discussed in Chapter 1, monitoring, observability, and criteria to manage training as efficiently as possible are prerequisites to scaling. Callbacks, loggers, and profilers are three hooks available to build more observable and manageable deep learning training applications.

Callbacks

Callbacks are hooks that are registered with training code that is called at an agreed-upon interval, such as at the beginning or end of the epoch, step, or batch. You can use callbacks, for example, to capture monitoring data via `DeviceStatsMonitor` or `TQDMProgressBar`, to persist intermediate model computation state (checkpoints or model snapshots) using `ModelCheckpoint`, or even to control the lifecycle of training (e.g., by using `EarlyStopping` to stop the training if the loss is not reducing further).

Loggers

Loggers, as the name implies, are used for logging metadata about the training run, with the data scope ranging from run logs to metric logging to capturing sample data and outcomes, etc. These tools are primarily designed for observability and monitoring purposes.

---

9 Kingma, Diederik P., and Jimmy Ba. 2014. "Adam: A Method for Stochastic Optimization." arXiv, December 22, 2014. *https://arxiv.org/abs/1412.6980*.

This book actively uses the open source version of Aim (*https://aimstack.io*) for run logs and metrics visualization, and occasionally uses `TensorBoardLogger` for profiling. The following snippet shows how these are integrated (for the full code, see the `train` method in the *app.py* (*https://oreil.ly/pMdWw*) script in the example repository):

```
aim = AimLogger(
    experiment=exp_name,
    train_metric_prefix="train/",
    val_metric_prefix="val/",
    test_metric_prefix="test/",
)
trainer = Trainer(
    ...,
    logger=[
        aim,
        TensorBoardLogger(save_dir=result_dir / "logs"),
    ],
    ...,
)
```

Profilers

Profilers are designed to measure the performance of training and to provide details of where computational bottlenecks are coming from and what the resource requirements for the training may be. These details are crucial for determining if and when you need to scale, and how.

In the previous hands-on example, you used `cProfile` and `mprof` to generate compute and memory profiles for your model. In this example (and throughout the rest of the book), you will use `PyTorchProfiler` instead. `PyTorchProfiler` not only enables profiling of CPU/memory, but also of accelerated computing devices. Another advantage of using `PyTorchProfiler` is that it comes with a `schedule` API to limit the profiling session. Profiling can be an expensive effort to run for the course of training, so schedules are very helpful.

The profiler code from *app.py* is shown here:

```
torch_profiler=PyTorchProfiler(
    dirpath=perf_dir,
    filename="perf_logs_pytorch",
    group_by_input_shapes=True,
    activities=[
        torch.profiler.ProfilerActivity.CPU,
    ],
    schedule=torch.profiler.schedule(wait=1, warmup=1, active=5,
                                      repeat=10, skip_first=True),
    profile_memory=True,
    with_stack=True,
    with_flops=True,
```

```
            with_modules=True,
            on_trace_ready=torch.profiler.tensorboard_trace_handler(
                                    str(perf_dir / "trace")),
    )
```

Putting It All Together

Lightning's Trainer API glues everything together—the model, data module, callbacks, loggers, computational devices, and profilers—to provide train and test interfaces. The trainer code for this example is shown here:

```
model = MNISTModel()
datamodule = MNISTDataModule(data_dir, num_workers=num_workers)
trainer = Trainer(
    accelerator="auto",
    devices="auto",
    max_epochs=max_epochs,
    callbacks=[
        TQDMProgressBar(refresh_rate=refresh_rate),
        checkpoint_callback,
        DeviceStatsMonitor(cpu_stats=True),
        EarlyStopping(monitor="val/loss", mode="min"),
    ],
    logger=[
        aim,
        TensorBoardLogger(save_dir=result_dir / "logs"),
    ],
    profiler=torch_profiler,
)
trainer.fit(model, datamodule)
trainer.save_checkpoint(result_dir / "model.bin")

if include_test:
    trainer.test(model, datamodule)
```

Figure 2-9 shows low-level observability controls covering the time required to perform computations and operations. These low-level details are provided by the profiler, along with finer details about how threads and processes from the operating system are interleaved and traces of the computations, to capture the amount of resources these computations are using on the system and on accelerated devices (whenever used). The figure also shows some high-level training-specific observability options to monitor metrics and loss and to observe and explore feature embeddings and the model's predictability during a training run through visualization tools (e.g., images, plots, charts). Chapter 4 dives into the details of profiling with accelerated computing using these tools.

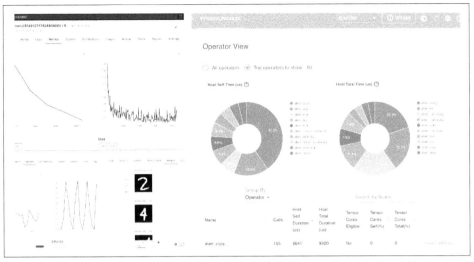

Figure 2-9. The experiment tracking (AIM) visualizations and PyTorch profiler's output. Running this example will produce profile and run logs that you can visualize in color and full resolution using tensorboard and aimhub.

> You can run this exercise using command `deep-learning-at-scale chapter_2 train` and visualize the profile logs using `tensorboard ("tensorboard --log-dir <>")` and run logs using aimhub local server ("aim up").

Through two hands-on examples, this chapter has covered various aspects of developing models. Underneath the Python/NumPy and PyTorch/Lightning APIs, the model is, in effect, a computation graph. Each node of the graph indicates what operations are applied, while the edges represent how the data flows through the graph. To clarify this concept, the next section will provide some fundamentals on computation graphs.

Computation Graphs

Directed acyclic graphs (DAGs) are a special type of graph composed of vertices and edges where each edge connects one vertex to another in a certain direction, ensuring the graph does not form any directed cycles (i.e., closed loops). The computation graphs used in deep learning are actually DAGs represented by abstract syntax trees (ASTs) (*https://oreil.ly/0DUa0*). Figure 2-10 shows two DAG representations of the model used in this example: the graph on the left was generated using PyTorchViz (*https://oreil.ly/-fVyV*), which produces module-level DAGs; the graph on the right, generated using `functorch` (*https://oreil.ly/gBHOz*), shows a low-level AST of computational operations.

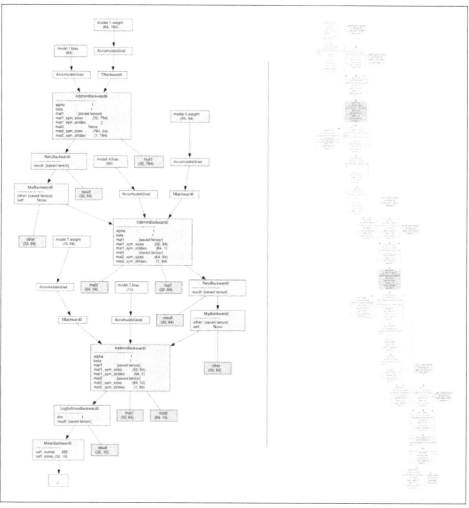

Figure 2-10. Visualizations of the high-level computation graph of the model from the PyTorch Hands-On Exercise

The visualizations shown in Figure 2-10 can be generated using the following script in the example repository:

```
deep-learning-at-scale chapter_2 viz-model
```

These computational DAGs represent the chain of operations applied to the data as it flows through them. While the higher-level API wiring of the deep learning code is more human-friendly and readable, prior to execution this code is compiled into an internal representation (IR) before being translated to optimized machine code. If you are interested in diving into the details of this common three-step process that converts the high-level code to low-level machine code, then check out Chris Lattner's "LLVM" chapter in *The Architecture of Open Source Applications* and Victor Skvortsov's blog post on how the CPython compiler works.[10]

From a Python-based deep learning framework viewpoint, this conversion of high-level code to computation graphs can be achieved in two ways:

Static computation graphs

In static computation graphs, once the model is built, it is explicitly compiled, creating a fixed computation graph. This is expected to be more efficient, because the graph does not need rebuilding on every iteration. This efficiency, however, comes at the expense of flexibility, ease of use, and development experience. TensorFlow follows a static graph computation approach but also supports an "eager mode" configuration to provide a better development experience.

Dynamic computation graphs

Dynamic computation graphs are rebuilt on every iteration, as operations and inputs are defined. This approach allows greater flexibility and ease of use and provides a superior development experience, but at the expense of the overhead of graph rebuilding. PyTorch uses dynamic computation graphs. The post "How Computational Graphs Are Constructed in PyTorch" on the PyTorch blog[11] provides a good overview of how computation graphs are created in PyTorch. Using scripting techniques like TorchScript, static AST-based computation graphs can be obtained in torch; however, TorchScript is still evolving.

In PyTorch 2.0 (*https://oreil.ly/tNUzM*), the computation graph handling has been massively revamped, with the introduction of a single call to torch.compile providing up to a 75% gain in performance. This was made possible via PEP 523 (*https://oreil.ly/ZO7vd*), which allowed adding arbitrary data for use during Python's frame evaluation at CPython level, enabling define-by-run loop-level execution at IR conversion. Chapter 3 revisits this topic to explore how the computation graphs are made compatible with accelerated devices such as GPUs.

I have touched on several aspects of model building so far. There are a few ways inference can be conducted on the trained model. The following section compares the differences among these modes.

---

10 Lattner, Chris. 2011. "LLVM." Chapter 11 in *The Architecture of Open Source Applications*, edited by Amy Brown and Greg Wilson. *http://aosabook.org/en/llvm.html*; Skvortsov, Victor. 2020. "Python Behind the Scenes #2: How the CPython Compiler Works." *Ten Thousand Meters* (blog), September 20, 2020. *https://tenthousandmeters.com/blog/python-behind-the-scenes-2-how-the-cpython-compiler-works*.

11 Preferred Networks. 2021. "How Computational Graphs Are Constructed in PyTorch." PyTorch blog. August 31, 2021. *https://pytorch.org/blog/computational-graphs-constructed-in-pytorch*.

Inference

As discussed earlier, model inference is simply a forward pass over the model. In this flow, backpropagation is not needed, which means all the computation done in automatic differentiation is also not needed. Some regularization techniques, often applied during training to avoid overfitting or to mitigate exploding gradients, either do not play any role during inference or behave differently upon inference than in training. Dropout, for instance, is simply turned off during inference, and batch normalization simply applies normalizations and skips capturing running statistics for mean, variance, and other learnable parameters (i.e., the shift and scale). This change in the behavior of batch normalization can be leveraged to speed up inference by fusing the normalization operation with another preceding linear operation like convolution (see Nenad Markuš's blog post "Fusing Batch Normalization and Convolution in Runtime" for more information).[12]

For these reasons, while inference can simply be performed by calling $M(x)$, that's not the most effective approach. The PyTorch `model.eval` call can be used to signal to the model that regularization operations like dropout should be skipped and operations like batch normalization should be altered in inference mode. Using this call before inference leads to better turnaround times and avoids unnecessary computations. The disadvantage of this call, however, is that automatic differentiation still occurs. If you recall the discussion of the toy example from earlier in this chapter, a significant compute expense came from backpropagation. In addition to compute, automatic differentiation can incur memory expenditure, especially if complex optimizers are used that store intermediate representations in memory for the backward pass. To improve on these inference inefficiencies, you can use `torch.no_grad`, which effectively turns off automatic differentiation, ceasing the backward pass computation. The implications of these inference techniques are detailed in Figure 2-11.

As discussed in the previous section, statically compiled graph computations offer better performance than their dynamic graph counterparts, albeit at the expense of inconvenience. The difference in inference time performance for the just-in-time (JIT) compiled graph can be seen in the lower-right plot in Figure 2-11. Although the network used in this example is very small and does not include regularization techniques as such, you can see that the compute requirement (i.e., the inference time) reduces with `model.eval`, and a further reduction in compute and memory requirements is seen with `torch.no_grad`. Pytorch has also recently released a new context manager for inference mode `torch.inference_mode` (*https://oreil.ly/2-xFO*) which is

---

12 Markuš, Nenad. 2018. "Fusing Batch Normalization and Convolution in Runtime." Nenand Markuš's blog, May 25, 2018. *https://nenadmarkus.com/p/fusing-batchnorm-and-conv*.

analogous to no_grad. A still greater reduction is seen with a statically compiled graph using TorchScript.

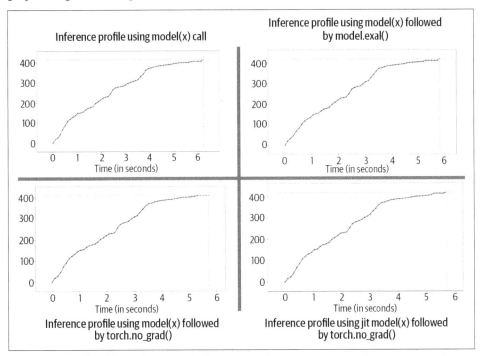

Figure 2-11. The effects of various inference modes on compute and memory requirements (these profile results are obtained from the PyTorch MNIST example)

Summary

In this chapter, you learned about deep learning as a data flow system and practiced building a minimalistic deep learning network in pure Python. You scaled your approach by increasing the complexity of your task and built a simpler, more reusable and well-observed model training application using PyTorch and PyTorch Lightning. You also learned about the different types of computation graphs used in deep learning and explored various modes of inference and how to choose one over the other.

The next chapter focuses on the computational aspects of deep learning, diving into the details of scaling processes, accelerated devices and how they interface with the operating system, and how to develop and profile custom operators for accelerating devices.

## CHAPTER 3

The Computational Side of Deep Learning

This chapter explores how computations are performed on the hardware and how acceleration is achieved through hardware advancements. As discussed in Chapter 1, the power of having a clear understanding of what is happening across the stack of your application, spanning the algorithm, software, hardware, and data, is profound. Limitations and trade-offs could surface from anywhere in your stack, and such an understanding empowers you to make careful, optimal decisions and find the right balance while working within your limitations, especially when scaling.

In Chapter 2, you learned about the foundational concepts of deep learning and worked through the software implementations of a couple of basic problems. In this chapter, you will dive into the details of how that software interacts with hardware. We'll cover the fundamentals of computation units and specialized hardware for accelerated computing, looking at their inner workings and considerations on how to get the best out of these silicon powerhouses. As well as delving into the foundational concepts of computer architecture and the accelerated computing landscape, we'll examine the implications of scaling on hardware devices.

The field of artificial intelligence, widely recognized as being established in 1956 during a workshop held at Dartmouth College, requires specialized scaled-up computing infrastructure. Up until the turn of the century, extensive research and development efforts focused on improving computing infrastructure, taking it from small-scale computers to much beefier supercomputers like CRAY. Around 2000, the exploration of using devices designed for graphics rendering (GPUs) for general-purpose computing began, with the first success being a 20x speedup in training a neural network using a GPU (compared to the best CPU available at that time).[1] This

---

1 Oh, Kyoung-Su, and Keechul Jung. 2004. "GPU Implementation of Neural Networks." *Pattern Recognition* 37, no. 6: 1311–1314. *https://doi.org/10.1016/j.patcog.2004.01.013*.

benchmark was quickly superseded, with about a 72x speedup.[2] Recognition of the advantages and feasibility of using GPUs for deep learning grew quickly from that point, leading to rapid progress in the development of specialized processing units focusing primarily on AI/ML use cases. There are some excellent resources that provide detailed insights into the evolution of hardware for deep learning.[3] This chapter will take a bottom-up approach, diving into the foundations of computation and how deep learning leverages it.

The Higgs Boson of the Digital World

The entirety of the digital world is based on two discrete values, 0 and 1, representing the high and low voltages in the circuitry, respectively. It's fascinating how these two simple "power on" and "power off" signals—the binary digits, or bits—can be used so efficiently to represent complex real-world signals ranging from audio in continuous wavelengths to images in limited raster space to express thoughts and emotions in alphanumeric textual format.

Combinations of these two 0 and 1 values (bits) are stored in various standardized data containers used to represent data types like int, float, bool, char, etc. The total allowable length of the bit sequence for a data type is given by *number_of_bits*, enabling the representation of a total of $2^{number\_of\_bits}$ possible unique values. A byte is a composition of 8 bits, providing the ability to represent $2^8 = 256$ unique values. The types int, float, and bool are able to accommodate 4, 4, and 1 byte, respectively.

Floating-Point Numbers: The Faux Continuous Numbers

The real numbers of mathematics are radix-separated sequences of integers and can carry infinite precision between any two integer numbers (e.g., 10.3433859345...). Presenting precision at this scale with inherently discrete bits, in digital space, has been a challenge. To resolve this scaling challenge, the Institute of Electrical and Electronics Engineers (IEEE) has defined a standard outlining the group of floating-point (FP) numbers. The latest revision of this standard, established in 2019, is IEEE 754-2019.[4] The real numbers represented in base 10, in FP, are given by

---

2 Raina, Rajat, Anand Madhavan, and Andrew Y. Ng. 2009. "Large-Scale Deep Unsupervised Learning Using Graphics Processors." In *Proceedings of the 26th International Conference on Machine Learning*, 873–880. *http://dx.doi.org/10.1145/1553374.1553486*.

3 Fuchs, Adi. 2021. "AI Accelerators—Part II: Transistors and Pizza (Or: Why Do We Need Accelerators)?" Medium, December 5, 2021. *https://medium.com/@adi.fu7/ai-accelerators-part-ii-transistors-and-pizza-or-why-do-we-need-accelerators-75738642fdaa*; Hooker, Sara. 2020. "The Hardware Lottery." arXiv. September 21, 2020. *https://arxiv.org/abs/2009.06489*.

4 IEEE. 2019. "754-2019 - IEEE Standard for Floating-Point Arithmetic." *https://ieeexplore.ieee.org/document/8766229*.

whole_part.fractional_part = number_in_integer * $10^{-precision}$, wherein both the *whole_part* and the *fractional_part* are discrete integer values. To represent a real number as a floating-point number, one needs to trade off between the range of the whole bit and the fractional bit. This section will discuss how these trade-offs are made.

Given the discrete nature of the digital world, the infinitely precise number 10.3433859345… will need to be presented with limited precision at the expense of a precision error. Let's cap the max precision to 10 decimal places to arrive at exactly 10.3433859345, i.e., 10.3433859345 = 103433859345 * 10^{-10}, with *whole_part* = 10 and *fractional_part* = 3433859345 (see Figure 3-1, in the next section). These two discrete integers, the whole part 10 and the fractional part 3433859345, are represented as bits in floating-point digital formats. If only 2 decimal places of precision were required, then with *whole_part* = 10 and *fractional_part* = 34 an even smaller number of bits would suffice. Having said that, if the requirement was to present a larger number— say, 100000010.3433859345—then the trade-off between *whole_part* and *fractional_part* would become obvious: the more bits you allocate for the whole part, the less are available for the fractional part, so for larger numbers the precision will be poorer.

A more generalized formula to represent floating-point numbers is given by $(-1)^{sign}$ * *mantissa* * $base^{exponent}$. Here, *sign* is a single bit with possible values of either 0 or 1 to appropriately represent negative or positive numbers, whereas *base* varies on a case-by-case basis; e.g., decimal (base 10) for real numbers, binary (base 2) for digital numbers, etc. To standardize the floating-point number representation, instead of floating the radix placement, which can produce various representations of the same number with varying exponents (e.g., 10.3433859345 = 103433859345 * 10^{-10} = 1.03433859345 * 10^{1}), some implementations fix the placement of the radix in the mantissa. Just after the most significant bit (i.e., 1.03433859345 * 10^{1}) or just before the least significant bit (i.e., 10343385934.5 * 10^{-9}) is a common approach for this standardization.

IEEE 754 defines an encoding to transform decimal numbers to digital (binary) format using base 2. The following section dives into the details of how this encoding aids scaling of representation of numbers with limited bits.

Floating-point encoding

Let's assume a format X that uses 8 bits to represent the exponent, 23 bits to represent the mantissa, and 1 bit for the sign. This translates to 31 bits for number representation with 1 bit reserved for the sign. A simple 32-bit signed representation could hold the maximum value of 214,748,3647 according to the formula $\mp[0, 2^{number\_of\_bits} - 1]$. However, this simple representation does not scale well for the number of bits. To address this challenge, the IEEE 754 encoding scheme derives a mantissa and uses the exponent to scale the value.

The schematic of this encoding workflow is shown in Figure 3-1. The whole and fractional parts of the real number (e.g., 10.3433859345) are binary-encoded separately ($10 = (1010)_2$ and $3433859345 = (11001100101011001000100100010001)_2$) to derive the binary equivalent of the radix-separated number (i.e., 1010.11001100101011001000100100010001). The radix is shifted to be right after the most significant bit, creating a value known as the *normalized mantissa*. The total shift of the radix (3 in this example) is used to derive the exponent. This final exponent is the sum of the shift and exponent bias, which is given by $2^{number\_of\_exponent\_bits} - 1$ (= 127 for this example), resulting in an effective exponent value of 130 (= 127 + 3), represented in binary as $(10000010)_2$. With this encoding scheme, the maximum number represented by this format X is $\left(2 - 2^{-number\_of\_mantissa\_bits}\right) \times 2^{\left(2^{(number\_of\_exponent\_bits-1)}-1\right)}$; i.e., $3.4028235 * 10^{38}$, a significantly higher number than $2.147483647 * 10^9$.

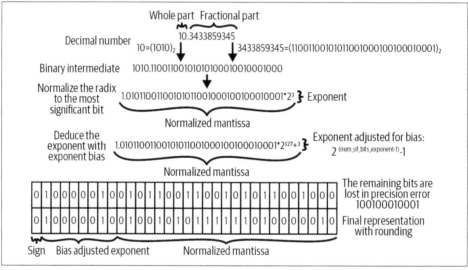

Figure 3-1. Floating-point encoding and the error incurred

This format X used in this example is a common floating-point format known as *single-precision floating point* that uses 32 bits to represent the number. This example shows how floating-point encoding uses the mantissa to represent the number and the exponent to scale it. Because of this exponent-based scaling, floating-point numbers are not equidistant (you can find a helpful visualization of this scaling in Volker Schatz's blog post, "What You Never Wanted to Know About Floating Point but Will

Be Forced to Find Out").[5] The example number 10.3433859345, however, is too precise to be represented by 32 bits, so there is a rounding error incurred in the process shown in Figure 3-1. Consequently, the actual rounded number to be represented is 10.343386. In essence, even though digital floating point numbers seeks to represent continuous real numbers, they are themselves discrete.

Floating-point standards

The numbers of bits allocated for the mantissa and exponent are not dynamic (i.e., varying per number) because of the exponential complexity and implications for hardware that this would entail (you will read more about this in the following section). These are standardized as types of data containers for interoperability. Given the varying degree of precision requirements, an assorted range of FP data types are defined. These are shown in Table 3-1.

Table 3-1. Floating-point formats commonly used in deep learning

Type	Mantissa (no. of bits)	Exponent (no. of bits)	Source
Single precision (fp32)	23	8	IEEE standard
Half precision (fp16)	10	5	IEEE standard
Double precision (fp64)	52	11	IEEE standard
Brain floating point (bfloat16)	8	8	Google (optimized for precision and memory, suitable for precision-intensive workloads such as machine learning/deep learning)
TensorFloat (tf32)	10	8	NVIDIA (hybrid float giving range of fp32 but precision of fp16)
Hopper E4M3 (fp8)	3	4	NVIDIA (optimized for memory and throughput)
Hopper E5M2 (fp8)	2	5	NVIDIA (optimized for memory and throughput)

For all these data types, 1 bit is reserved for the sign. The range of these numbers is thus $\mp[0, 2^{number\_of\_bits} - 1]$—i.e., defined by the number of bits of their respective mantissa. Attempting to store a value beyond this range for a given type results in underflow (flowing over the negative side) or overflow (flowing over the positive side). David Goldberg's "What Every Computer Scientist Should Know About

5 Schatz, Volker. *n.d.* "What You Never Wanted to Know About Floating Point but Will Be Forced to Find Out." *https://www.volkerschatz.com/science/float.html.*

Floating-Point Arithmetic" is a good article covering the details of the various error scenarios of FP numbers, a discussion of which is beyond the scope of this book.[6]

Understanding the data types and their storage sizes in terms of bits is advantageous in selecting suitable data formats for computation and storage in order to build efficient and scalable solutions.

Units of Data Measurement

There are two types of units of measurement for data: binary and decimal. Table 3-2 lists the equivalent types, along with an indication of the difference in accuracy between the binary and decimal variants. As you can see, the binary units provide a more accurate representation of the data size than the more popular decimal units, with the error increasing as the size increases. I generally use decimal units in this book, but in specific scenarios where accuracy of data measurements becomes really important, you will see references to binary units.

Table 3-2. Binary and decimal units of measure for data in the digital world

Binary (represented as base 2, i.e., 2^n)			Decimal (represented as base 10, i.e., 10^n)			Difference in precision between binary and decimal units
Name	Symbol	Size	Name	Symbol	Size	%
Kibibyte	KiB	2^{10}	Kilobyte	KB	10^3	2.4
Mebibyte	MiB	2^{20}	Megabyte	MB	10^6	4.86
Gibibyte	GiB	2^{30}	Gigabyte	GB	10^9	7.37
Tebibyte	TiB	2^{40}	Terabyte	TB	10^{12}	9.95
Pebibyte	PiB	2^{50}	Petabyte	PB	10^{15}	12.59
Exbibyte	EiB	2^{60}	Exabyte	EB	10^{18}	15.29
Zebibyte	ZiB	2^{70}	Zettabyte	ZB	10^{21}	18.06
Yobibyte	YiB	2^{80}	Yottabyte	YB	10^{24}	20.89
Robibyte	RiB	2^{90}	Ronnabyte	RB	10^{27}	23.79
Quebibyte	QiB	2^{100}	Queccabyte	QB	10^{30}	26.77

---

6 Goldberg, David. 1991. "What Every Computer Scientist Should Know about Floating-Point Arithmetic." *ACM Computing Surveys* 23, no. 1: 5–48. *https://doi.org/10.1145/103162.103163*. Edited reprint included as Appendix D of *Numerical Computation Guide*. Palo Alto: Sun Microsystems, 2000. *https://docs.oracle.com/cd/E19957-01/806-3568/ncg_goldberg.html*.

Data Storage Formats: The Trade-off of Latency and Throughput

Digital data is persisted in various formats suitable for its use and the data it represents. While an in-depth review of these formats is beyond the scope of the book, here are some of the ones you're likely to encounter for different purposes in machine learning workloads:

- Structured tabular/series data: Parquet, CSV, TSV, JSON, etc.
- Multimedia: *.jpg*, *.mov*, *.png*, *.tiff*, *.wav*, etc.
- Binary: pickle, *.gzip*, *tar.gz*, etc.
- Numerical: *.npz*, etc.
- Unstructured/text: HTML, *.txt*, BLOB, etc.

The sizes of these persisted files are typically measured in decimal units, but occasionally they are misrepresented (e.g., on Windows platforms files are measured in binary units but misrepresented as decimal units). This is something you'll need to navigate carefully, as using the right units provides better accuracy. To optimize use of storage space, data compression algorithms like ZIP, zstd, JPEG, etc. are applied to the raw data. These techniques leverage redundancies in data to minimize storage requirements.

However, the trade-off with compression is increased latency for reading and writing. These latency spikes are due to the additional computation required for converting the data between its compressed format and the native format used by the application. This is a very important consideration to keep in mind when building the model input pipeline that loads the raw data and performs preprocessing before handing it over to the model for training or inference. The slower this data flow is, the slower training will be, however performant the computation device used in training is. In Chapter 7, you'll work through a hands-on exercise to investigate this exact challenge.

So far, you have read about data types, sizes, and formats. Let's now dive into the details of computer architecture to explore how computers crunch this data today.

Computer Architecture

The digital world is underpinned by electronic circuitry utilizing Boolean algebra. George Boole first introduced Boolean algebra around 1850, through his works *The Mathematical Analysis of Logic* and *An Investigation of the Laws of Thought*. Alongside the primary Boolean operators AND, OR, and NOT, several other secondary operators, such as XOR, have been defined to present information flow in Boolean algebra.

The Birth of the Electromechanical Engine

In the 1830s, mechanical engineer and polymathematician Charles Babbage designed a mechanical computer dubbed the "analytical engine" that formed the basis of the electromechanical engine used today. It wasn't until about a century later, though, that Boolean algebra made its way into electromechanical engineering, when Claude Shannon recognized the relevance of Boole's symbolic logic and published his thoughts in *A Symbolic Analysis of Relay and Switching Circuits*, demonstrating how decision circuits can be built from electromechanical relay switches.[7] Shannon's work laid the foundations for digital circuit design; he not only explained how to implement basic logic gates like AND, OR, NOT, and XOR but also how to represent more complex combinational logic circuits such as adders, subtractors, and multipliers (see Figure 3-2).

To scale the build-out of electronic circuits, more integrated logic units combining several gates into one unit, known as *integrated circuits* (ICs) or *chips*, were made. Most commonly used CPUs and accelerated computing devices today have millions of gates, making very large-scale integrated circuits (VLSICs) a common commodity. Transistors facilitate the flow of current through the electronic circuitry used to turn the voltage on and off to simulate the bits. As the number of gates on an IC increases, the number of transistors used also rapidly increases. For energy efficiency reasons, the transistors are required to run at a very low voltage with minimum heat implications. The first transistor was built in 1947, by Nobel Prize winners William Shockley, John Bardeen, and Walter Brattain. The issue with voltage and heat quickly resulted in the exploration of the use of silicon, a highly effective semiconductor with a unique ability to both conduct and block electricity. The first silicon-based transistors were developed at Bell Labs in 1954. Since then, rapid growth has been seen in the semiconductor and electronic circuits industry.

Now that you have seen how the logic gates of computers use electronic circuits and electric currents to perform algebraic operations on binary inputs to produce an output, in the next section we'll look at how memory is represented in electronic circuitry.

---

7 Shannon, Claude Elwood. 1938. "A Symbolic Analysis of Relay and Switching Circuits." Transactions of the American Institute of Electrical Engineers 57, no. 12: 713–23. *https://doi.org/10.1109/T-AIEE.1938.5057767*.

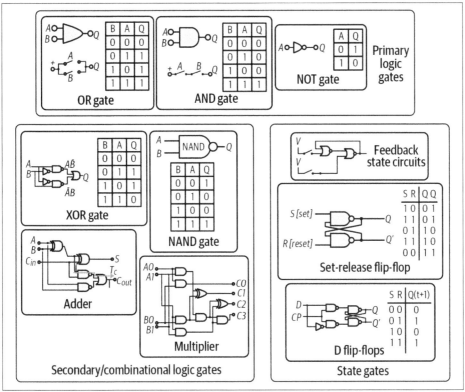

Figure 3-2. Some of the fundamental logic gates used to perform algebra on binary values (bits), indicating how electronic circuits are designed to perform matrix computations today

Memory and Persistence

All the computational logic gates are stateless. However, to be able to store binary data, the circuits need to be able to hold state. In electronics, this is achieved through a feedback signal that allows the output to be dependent on the value of the previous output, or state. The most basic form of circuit is the feedback state circuit shown in Figure 3-2. Here, if the top circuit switch is closed, current flows through the circuit. Because of the feedback, once the loop is activated the output value will be held until the inputs are changed. Flip flop circuits and their variants (e.g., set-reset flip-flops and D flip-flops, as shown in Figure 3-2) are some of the basic state gates commonly used today. These state gates form the basis of complex circuits used in high-performance memory chips, registers, etc. The limitation with these circuitry-based memory units, however, is that they are volatile state storage; that is, the stored state will be lost if power is lost.

To allow a more efficient random access pattern by removing the limitation of accessing the bit state in a predefined sequential order, state gates are combined with another logic gate unit called a *multiplexer*. These units are used to make random access memory (RAM). There are two variants of RAM:

Static RAM (SRAM)
> These pure circuitry-based memory units are the fastest but also most expensive and thus generally available in smaller storage capacities, ranging on the order of KB.

Dynamic RAM (DRAM)
> These memory units use capacitors in their circuitry. The nature of capacitors is such that they don't need constant power but only a periodic injection of charge to retain the state. DRAM is less performant and energy efficient[8] than SRAM but can provide more scaled memory storage.

> The main memory and caching units of the computer are based on DRAM and have a storage capacity ranging on the order of MB/GB.

> Synchronous dynamic random access memory (SDRAM) is a more recent (1990s) variant of DRAM that is more scalable in terms of data transfer rates.

The primary memory circuits you've learned about so far are volatile in nature. *Secondary storage* is the class of persistent storage units. Secondary storage is based on spinning disks, magnetic tapes, optics, and more recently solid state devices (SSDs). These storage units are more cost-effective and have higher storage capacity but are less performant than their primary counterparts (such as SRAM/DRAM, registers, or caches), because their throughput and memory bandwidth are lower and their latency is higher. To put things into context, Figure 3-3 gives a comparison of primary and secondary storage types in terms of latency, memory bandwidth, cost, and capacity.

Knowledge of these factors helps you make informed choices when scaling an application. When the requirement of running an intensive computation on a large corpus of data arises, navigating the trade-offs between storage capacity, I/O latency, throughput, and data co-locality concerning the computation unit becomes difficult. While some of the primary memory units, such as registers, are implicitly managed

---

8 Horowitz, Mike. 2014. "Computing's Energy Problem (And What We Can Do About It)." In *2014 IEEE International Solid-State Circuits Conference Digest of Technical Papers (ISSCC)*, 10-14. *http://dx.doi.org/10.1109/ISSCC.2014.6757323*.

by the application runtime and not in direct control of high-level application code, others, such as caches and RAM, can be carefully leveraged at the application level.

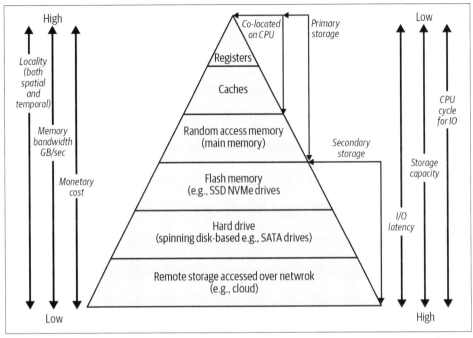

Figure 3-3. *The memory hierarchy of primary and secondary storage options, with performance indicators for capacity, bandwidth, and latency*

The role of the cache in increasing temporal locality by preloading the required data into a faster storage type is hugely beneficial. However, the maximum practical cache size ranges on the order of MB, up to about 32 MB. Likewise, RAM sizes available today typically range on the order of GB, scaling up to 2–8 TB depending on the chipset. These numbers underscore the importance of the role secondary storage plays in a scaled-up setting with high data storage requirements. However, the higher I/O latency and throttling it may cause can become a challenge for compute-intensive applications such as model training. Amongst all secondary flash memory storage types, SSD-based nonvolatile memory express (NVMe) drives offer the lowest latency. On average, SSD-based NVMe drives provide a latency of milliseconds and throughput of the order of GB/sec, whereas for hard disk drives (HDDs) these range on the order of milliseconds and MB/sec, respectively.

Virtual memory

Virtual memory is an interesting implementation at the software level to artificially extend primary memory's storage capacity by storing blocks of memory that are not immediately useful into a portion of secondary storage. Thereby, by design, virtual memory aims to mask the latency algorithmically, while virtually extending the main memory capacity. There is a divide in the kernel developer community on whether the virtual memory implementation is a feature or a bug because of the complexity and challenges it brings to provide this flexibility. Many think it is not performant because it slows effective RAM performance.

Input/output

Figure 3-3 showed the respective I/O latency (read/write rate) of the different primary and secondary storage units. The lower this rate is for your system, the more time for computation you will have. With that in mind, specialized hardware is designed to accelerate the access rate through the use of techniques such as the following:

Direct memory access (DMA)
> DMA enables the transfer of data between an I/O device and DRAM. The advantage of DMA is that the CPU can offload the copying instruction to the DMA controller and can focus on executing the compute instructions—that is, DMA decouples the memory access from the CPU, allowing data movement to happen in parallel to "on the CPU" data processing. Given that DMA is mainly designed for data movement, it can perform the transfer with encoding/decoding overhead more efficiently.

Remote direct memory access (RDMA)
> RDMA is an extension of DMA principles to networked computers. It has a remote memory management capability that allows data movement directly to and from a GPU's memory without any CPU involvement. (We'll talk more about these GPUDirect techniques in Chapter 5.) InfiniBand (IB) is more popularly used for massively parallel cluster computing than Ethernet or Fibre Channel, although the more recent RDMA over Converged Ethernet (RoCE) allows efficient data transfer with very low latencies on lossless Ethernet networks.

Memory and Moore's law

Unfortunately, Moore's law (discussed in Chapter 1 and "The Scaling Laws of Electronics" on page 83) does not hold as well for memory as it does for computation. As shown in Figure 3-4, the gap between the performance of computation and memory has grown significantly over time, resulting in memory being slower than computation. Besides, transferring and storing data requires more energy than computation, which collectively creates a progress blockage referred to as the "memory wall."

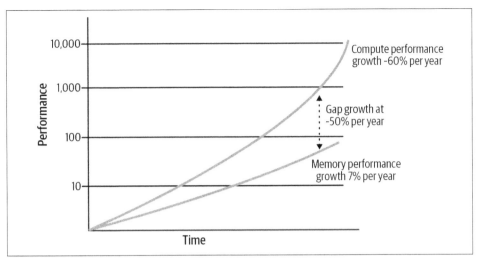

Figure 3-4. Growth of memory and compute performance with respect to time to show why Moore's law does not hold for memory[9]

Computation and Memory Combined

As discussed in Chapter 2, when an application's code is compiled, the interpreter internally generates its equivalent machine-level AST code. The conversion of high-level application code to low-level machine code is seamlessly taken care of by the underlying runtime, which in the case of PyTorch will be Python—in other words, it will be CPython that executes the program instructions FrameSet by FrameSet. The program instructions and data are stored in RAM. The processing unit of the computational device loads the instruction sets and data and executes the machine-level instruction set, triggering the electricity flow across the circuitry as per its relevant logic gate implementations.

A computer's instruction set architecture (ISA) is equivalent to a hardware device's API interface, setting out the operations supported by the device and how to invoke them. The ISA is a device specification that defines a set of instructions and their binary encoding, the CPU registers, and the effects of executing instructions on the state of the processor. Intel's x86, ARM, IBM Power, MIPS, and RISC-V are some ISA examples. Reduced Instruction Set Computer (RISC) and Complex Instruction Set Computer (CISC) are two broad types of architectures, with the former optimizing on a minimum required instruction set while the latter focuses on compute efficiency and packs complex circuits to enable complex operations to be carried out in

---

9 Chauan, Praveena, Gagandeep Singh, and Gurmohan Singh. 2015. "Cache Controller for 4-Way Set-Associative Cache Memory." *International Journal of Computer Applications* 129, no. 1: 1–8. *http://dx.doi.org/10.5120/ijca2015906787.*

single instructions. RISC by definition is memory-efficient, and it's widely used in mobile and Internet of Things (IoT) devices.

The *von Neumann architecture* is one of the most common design models for computers. It uses shared memory for instructions and data (as opposed to the Harvard architecture, which uses separate memory spaces for program code and data. In the von Neumann architecture, shown in Figure 3-5, the processing unit—the core—has a logic unit, a control unit, and a memory unit. The logic unit is for arithmetic operation and leverages circuitry-based registers for storing instructions and data required in the scope of those specific instructions. The control unit, on the other hand, controls the loading and storing of values in different levels of storage (registers, cache, and RAM) and directs the control flow. Multiplexers and demultiplexers are crucial logic gates in building control unit circuitry.

The cores, as shown in Figure 3-5, execute the instructions, with each core capable of executing one instruction at a time. To run multiple instructions simultaneously (to support horizontal scaling), more cores are added to the computer. Figure 3-5 depicts a CPU with N cores.

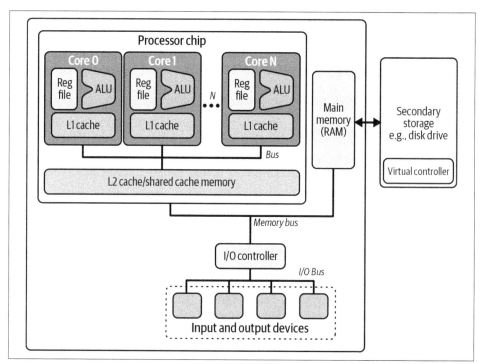

Figure 3-5. The von Neumann architecture for standard computers

You already read about memory units in detail in the previous section. CPUs, and computation devices in general, incorporate a tiered cache structure (see Figure 3-5) consisting of a very small but very fast level-one (L1) cache, which sits relatively close to the arithmetic logic units (ALUs) and control units, and a larger but slower level-two (L2) cache that resides farther away. An even larger and slower level-three (L3) cache is also present (not shown in the figure) to share data between the cores of multicore CPUs. The interaction with L2 and other higher storage units from the memory hierarchy is via I/O interconnect, which is handled by the I/O bus for the local machine and an I/O connection over the network interface for remote storage. As the locality decreases, the latency increases, with the highest latency in loading data from remote storage.

 NVMe over Fabrics (NVMe-oF), an extension of the NVMe protocol, provides faster and more efficient storage access over Ethernet and fiber network channels, ranging up to 128 GB/s.

Non-Uniform Memory Access (NUMA)

As discussed previously, the co-location of the memory unit with the compute unit is an important consideration for efficient computing. NUMA is a hardware design where each processor has a local memory that only it can access, which is faster than accessing the local memory of another processor/core. Most multicore computers today are NUMA-based.

As a programmer, generally you don't have to do anything specific to use NUMA, and the underlying runtime takes care of generating the right instructions for the memory and processor. However, as Ulrich Drepper discusses at length in his interesting article on the topic,[10] there are some considerations that every programmer should know about memory.

The following section covers the challenges encountered in scaling electronics to meet the massive scale requirements of modern computing.

The Scaling Laws of Electronics

In 1965, the first scaling law of electronics was observed by Gordon Moore, the co-founder of Intel, when he observed that the number of transistors in a dense integrated circuit doubled every 18–24 months and postulated that the trend would likely

---

10 Drepper, Ulrich. 2007. "What Every Programmer Should Know About Memory." *https://people.freebsd.org/ ~lstewart/articles/cpumemory.pdf.*

continue for another decade.[11] Observing the effects of the increase in the number of transistors on circuits, in 1974 Robert Dennard, a researcher at IBM, hypothesized that the circuit's power consumption would remain the same even if transistor numbers were scaled by a power law of second order (i.e., k^2). His theory was based on the fact that charges would have to travel shorter distances, so the smaller transistors would be more energy-efficient. This became another scaling law of electronics, until it hit a wall in 2005 when transistors reached the maximum power per transistor. This limitation is more popularly known as the "power wall," underscoring the fact that further reducing their size would result in overheating of circuits through heat dissipation and current leakage.

Until 2005, most hardware scaling was focused on increasing the number of instructions per second (clock cycle) of the computer. However, due to the power wall, scaling by adding more complex and beefier circuitry plateaued. This led to the introduction of multicore computing devices like the one shown in Figure 3-5 that scale the computational power by horizontally scaling the number of processing units as well, instead of simply scaling the number of transistors in a single processing unit/core. Multicore processors meant that more than one application could now execute in parallel without bottlenecking on the single core. The following sections will delve into the use of processes and threads to efficiently leverage multicore computers for your needs.

Scaling out by increasing the number of cores enabled another decade of scaling computational capabilities. However, managing heat remained a constant challenge,[12] as evidenced by the fact that the maximum number of cores available today is typically in the range of 24 for common desktop computers and 256 for server workstations. Due to heat dissipation and the power wall, as the circuitry gets more complex, parts of it need to be partially turned off to manage the heat. This led to the dark silicon era and the second AI winter, when, as you read in Chapter 1, these limitations on scaling computational capabilities throttled the progress of deep learning.

The dark silicon era inspired the new generation of computational devices that are used today in conjunction with traditional computers. We'll dive into the details of accelerated computing later in this chapter. First, however, let's review Amdahl's law and how to effectively utilize available computational resources during scale-out efforts.

---

11 Moore, Gordon E. 1965. "Cramming More Components onto Integrated Circuits." *Electronics* 38, no. 8: 114–17. Available at *https://www.computerhistory.org/collections/catalog/102770822*.

12 Fuchs, Adi. 2019. "Overcoming the Limitations of Accelerator-Centric Architectures with Memoization-Driven Specialization." PhD diss., Princeton University. *https://dataspace.princeton.edu/handle/88435/dsp01qf85nf16z*.

Scaling Out Computation with Parallelization

Gene Amdahl, in 1967, proposed a formulation to explain the speedup that can be achieved by scaling a workload through parallelization. According to Amdahl's law, when parallelizing, if F is the fraction of a system or program that can be made parallel and $1 - F$ is the fraction that remains serial, then the maximum speedup $S(N)$ that can be achieved using N processors is given by $S(N) = 1/((1 - F) + (F/N))$.

As N tends to infinity, the speedup tends to be $(1 - F)^{-1}$, which is inversely proportional to the part of the program or system that cannot be made parallel (i.e., is serial). As discussed in Chapter 1, scaling is defined by the limits of the system or program, and this formula reinforces the same principle, underlining that to create an embarrassingly parallel program we need the serial parts of the program to be nonexistent (or at least tending to 0). When this is achieved, the speedup tends to be infinite; i.e., $1/(1 - P)$.

The evolution of computational devices so far has been accomplished by both vertical scaling (increasing the computational capacity—i.e., the clock cycles of the devices—by packing in more complex electronic circuitry) and horizontal scaling (adding more cores to the computing system and/or interconnecting multiple computing systems over a network to form a computation cluster). Expanding the resources in either direction allows you to parallelize your task accordingly.

Let's first look at the parallelization technique used to efficiently scale out on a single computer. Then we'll explore how scaling out over a network is achieved.

Threads Versus Processes: The Unit of Parallelization

A *process* is a logical (software) representation of a computational task/unit that has a context comprising memory, data, and compiled instruction sets (code). The process can have one or more threads that execute the instructions in the scope of the processor (see Figure 3-6). As discussed earlier, a process can run over one or more cores; however, each core can run only one instruction at a time. A processor's clock speed (cycles per second) indicates the number of instructions it can execute per second. To work with this limitation, whenever a process/thread is not ready for computation (e.g., if it's waiting on input, data, or other resources), that process/thread is taken out of execution and the core is made available for other processes/threads. This trick allows for pseudo parallelism, wherein on the surface it may seem multiple tasks are in execution but in truth one task is run at a time, in a more efficient manner.

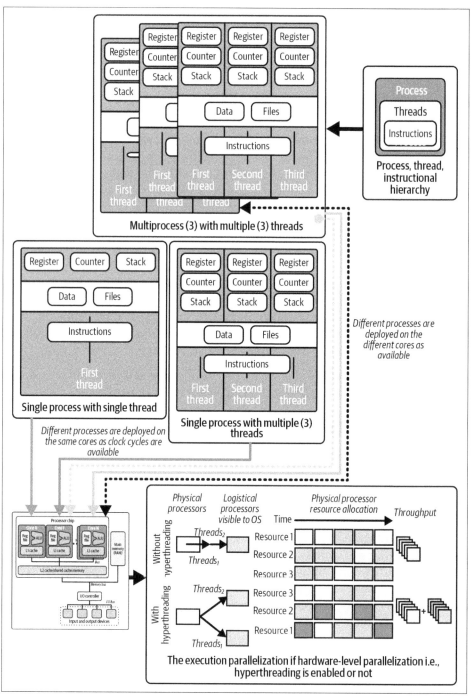

Figure 3-6. Instruction execution with processes and threads over single-core and multi-ticore systems with and without hyperthreading

Having multiple threads in a process is a great technique to deal with the computational inefficiency of a task (I/O wait, for example). Multithreading is also useful in scaling the workload so all cores allocated to the process are effectively utilized, reducing the potential idle compute cycles to a bare minimum. That said, nowadays a CPU cycle can involve many different operations, so there will be circumstances where some cycles won't be used to their full capacity.

Writing code to be multiprocess allows you to expand the workload across all the cores of the computing device. This paradigm is analogous to horizontal scaling until all of the device's cores have been exhausted. As shown in Figure 3-6, the fleet of processes of the multiprocess task each have their context and latch on to different cores. This allows multiprocess tasks to not be throttled by the compute cycles of a core and to achieve parallelism (until all the computer's cores are running at full capacity). See Table 3-3 for a more detailed comparison of the pros and cons of using multithreading and multiprocessing for scaling.

Table 3-3. Comparison of threads and processes across various categories

	Processes	Threads
Heavy or lightweight	Heavyweight	Lightweight
Process context	Separate	Shared
Memory space	Separate	Shared
Compute units (cores)	Separate	Shared
Memory footprint	Larger because each process requires its own context and resources	Relatively lightweight due to sharing of resources
Warmup	Slow	Fast
Impacted by Global Interpreter Lock (GIL)	No	Yes
Effective for	CPU-bound tasks	I/O- or resource-bound tasks
Communication	Via interprocess communication (IPC), complex and difficult to implement	Via interthread communication (ITC), easy to implement
Context switching	Slower	Faster
Object sharing	Object sharing across processes is achieved via pickling (with Python's `pickle` module) in memory. Relies on `pickle` to send to other processes.	Because threads share memory, data can be made accessible across threads but requires careful synchronization for thread safety. Pickling is thus avoided.

Simultaneous multithreading

The throttle point in scaling out computation on a single device is the computational cycles of the core. To mitigate this limitation (the reasons for which we explored in "The Scaling Laws of Electronics" on page 83), a technique called *simultaneous multithreading* (SMT) is employed. SMT is analogous to true multithreading but is achieved through virtualizing the core into smaller cores through hardware-level threading. Most processors today are powered by SMT (Intel calls this hyperthreading) and offer up to eight hardware-level threads. The advantages and implications of this technique are shown in Figure 3-6.

In the following section, we'll explore how you can apply these parallelization techniques to scale your solution.

Scenario walkthrough: A web crawler to curate a links dataset

In practice, you can combine both paradigms in your deep learning application to achieve scale and efficiency. Suppose you want to develop a dataset from arXiv (*https://arxiv.org*) by crawling through a list of submissions to extract sentences that mention "deep learning" along with a list of full names mentioned in the entries. For this challenge, first, you want to exhaustively crawl arXiv for all the unique submissions/abstracts to build this "links" dataset. Second, you want to build an analytics component that downloads the abstracts and analyzes them to extract the sentences containing "deep learning" along with any full names that are mentioned. Let's take a look at some of the design considerations you'll need to keep in mind to utilize multithreading and multiprocessing in this scenario:

Consideration 1: Design
> In this scenario, the opportunity of scale is in the design of the workers. The workers are doing two things here:
>
> - Performing the I/O operation to download the web page over the network
> - Processing the page content to filter out links to crawl, extract sentences and names, and persist them to create your dataset
>
> Let's say you create LinkFinder and TextMatcher modules to handle these tasks. For every link, you can independently run TextMatcher and scale it out in embarrassingly parallel fashion, as this part of the flow does not have serial dependencies. However, LinkFinder is stateful: for every link it grabs it needs to make sure it crawls it if and only if it has not been crawled already. LinkFinder is more challenging to scale out, but it can be scaled by trading off redundancy (i.e., allowing it to do a degree of redundant work and performing deduplication at a central store).

Consideration 2: Scale-out
> LinkFinder is I/O-heavy and compute-light. It's a great candidate for a multithreaded paradigm, so that while one thread is busy "fetching" (i.e., consuming network bandwidth), others can occupy CPU cycles. TextMatcher, on the other hand, is compute-heavy due to all the required text analytics, as well as having I/O needs for content download, saving files, etc. Multiprocessing is more suitable to scale out TextMatcher due to its intensive operations occupying large blocks of CPU cycles. Profiling the resource requirements to decide on a suitable scaling configuration is always a helpful exercise, as discussed in Chapter 1.

A sample implementation of TextMatcher and LinkFinder is located in the *crawler.py* script (*https://oreil.ly/vAI1a*) in the book's code repository. You can run the link generation and text analytics processes by executing the following commands:

```
deep-learning-at-scale chapter_3 crawler get-links
```

```
deep-learning-at-scale chapter_3 crawler extract-sentences
--mode [process|thread|serial]
```

When I ran these commands on my machine, I found that when LinkFinder was scaled out with multiple processes CPU utilization increased to 368% and the time to complete was shortest (about 49 s, with --max-workers 8). With multithreading, the CPU utilization was 105% and the time to complete was half that of serial CPU computation, which exhibited utilization at 23%. Your observations will likely vary depending on your system's configuration; however, at a high level you may note similar trends.

Consideration 3: Resiliency

As discussed in Chapter 1, resiliency is an important consideration for efficient engineering. Building a web crawler is a complex task, and there are several considerations to account for in building a resilient crawler that would be beyond the scope of this book. However, simple measures like the following can greatly improve resiliency:

- Save checkpoint states so that in case of failure when the worker is resumed, it starts crawling from the last successful crawl.

- Add robustness in LinkFinder to deduplicate asymmetric URLs (i.e., distinct URLs that redirect to the same URL).

Consideration 4: Limits of scale and efficiency

To understand the limits of scale, you need to calibrate the compute and memory requirements of your program (the get-links and extract-sentences processes) and the service that's distributing the URLs for crawling. Extrapolating this information over available resources in terms of your system's compute capacity, memory and storage availability, and network bandwidth to crawl the web will guide the maximum possible scale-up of your crawler.

For instance, when I ran this example with parallelism of 30 (--max-workers 30), I noted that even though peak CPU utilization spiked to about 476%, the total time to complete was similar to that with 10 multithreaded workers. In this case, this is due to the overhead of spinning up 30 processes, which dwarfs the gains made by scaling the TextMatcher. The limitation of bandwidth could be another consideration that can be monitored using network statistics. You can try this yourself using the following command:

```
deep-learning-at-scale chapter_3 crawler extract-sentences --mode process
--max-workers 30
```

Your results may vary, as these numbers are hardware- and I/O-dependent.

 Using multithreading in pure Python functions cannot effectively scale compute-intensive workloads, as Python's Global Interpreter Lock (GIL) limits the parallelization by enforcing sequential behavior. With Sam Gross's initial work (*https://oreil.ly/iGiHJ*), future versions of Python might make the GIL optional.

Hardware-Optimized Libraries for Acceleration

For pure numeric and scientific computing, hardware-optimized libraries also exist. One good example of this is Intel's oneAPI Math Kernel Library (oneMKL), which defines multiple versions of hardware-specific implementations for a given function. At execution time, the most optimal implantation is chosen. OneMKL's implementation is based on Basic Linear Algebra Subprograms (BLAS) specifications. AMD offers a similar library based on BLAS, AMD Optimizing CPU Libraries (AOCL). Per the benchmarks run by Apache, on an Intel CPU oneMKL-based libraries provided up to a 35x efficiency gain both in latency and throughput for convolution-based deep learning operations.[13] The rate of gain for a more popular ResNet-based network stood at around 7x and 15x for latency and throughput, respectively. These are significant advantages that you can realize on already available resources by carefully considering the library and runtime in your stack.

Parallel Computer Architectures: Flynn's and Duncan's Taxonomies

A classification of computer architecture exists that guides parallelization by multiplying data, instructions, or both. It was originally proposed by Michael J. Flynn in 1966, and revised in 1972. Flynn's classification divides computers into four categories, based on the number of instruction and data streams available in the architecture:

Single instruction, single data (SISD)
    Represents a serial device.

---

13 Lupesko, Hagay. 2018. "MXNet with Intel MKL-DNN - Performance Benchmarking." Apache MXNet wiki, December 23, 2018. *https://cwiki.apache.org/confluence/display/MXNET/MXNet+with+Intel+MKL-DNN+-+Performance+Benchmarking.*

Multiple instruction, single data (MISD)
> Represents devices that can apply multiple instructions on the same data. This is very hard to achieve at the hardware layer and thus remains impractical.

Single instruction, multiple data (SIMD)
> Represents devices where a single instruction is applied simultaneously across multiple data elements. Flynn's revised taxonomy subclassified SIMD into three subcategories: array, pipeline, and associative processors.

Multiple instruction, multiple data (MIMD)
> Represents devices where multiple processors autonomously execute different instructions on different data elements.

In 1990, Ralph Duncan revised Flynn's taxonomy to include new classes of parallel computing paradigms (vector and systolic array processing) while also expanding on the MIMD paradigm and its memory considerations.[14] Duncan's distributed memory architecture proposed message passing across processes as a means of information sharing across processors during scale-out. Part II of this book, specifically Chapter 5, addresses these amendments and starts to get into distributed systems and the distributed training paradigm.

So far in this book, you have learned about bits and bytes and how these are computed over electronic circuits. You have also learned about how computer architecture is realized and how you can write an efficient, scalable program for a given computer. In the following section, we'll explore the specialized hardware that's available for accelerated computing today.

Accelerated Computing

In a thought-provoking article titled "The Hardware Lottery," Sara Hooker connects the dots between the AI winter of deep learning described in Chapter 1 and the dull phase in hardware growth.[15] She calls out Maslow's famous observation "I suppose it is tempting, if the only tool you have is a hammer, to treat everything as if it were a nail," indicating that deep learning required a different set of tools (more specialized hardware) than what was available prior to 1995 (the deep learning era) and that the lack thereof resulted in a significant slowdown of research and advancements.

---

14 Duncan, Ralph. 1990. "A Survey of Parallel Computer Architectures." *Computer* 23, no. 2: 5–16. *https://doi.org/10.1109/2.44900*.

15 Hooker, Sara. 2020. "The Hardware Lottery." arXiv. September 21, 2020. *https://arxiv.org/abs/2009.06489*; Y. LeCun, "1.1 Deep Learning Hardware: Past, Present, and Future," 2019 IEEE International Solid-State Circuits Conference (ISSCC), San Francisco, CA, USA, 2019, pp. 12-19, doi: 10.1109/ISSCC.2019.8662396.

CPUs are designed for multitasking and user interactions (I/O). Even though most CPUs today implement some SIMD instructions, they are built primarily to execute a series of instructions in sequential order. The control unit of the CPU plays a critical role in the instruction ordering, encoding, and decoding, ensuring the instructions are executed in that order. To execute instructions on a large volume of data in a massively parallel fashion, the chipset must be able to host multiple cores and run the same instructions on chunks of data in an implementation that capitalizes on SIMD architecture. This implies that the number of control units per core can be many times less than in the multitasking, interrupt-based processor designs used in CPUs today (see Figure 3-7; we'll discuss the architecture of GPUs in the following section).

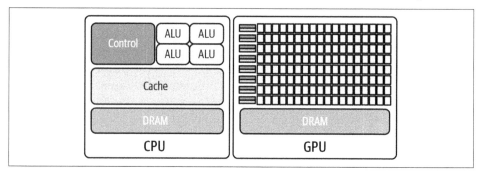

Figure 3-7. The difference between CPUs and the GPUs that power massive-scale matrix computation today

This is the main reason why, today, there are classes of specialized accelerated computing devices used in conjunction with a CPU (hereafter referred to as the *host*), in a heterogeneous manner. To realize massive-scale data crunching, especially in deep learning, where sporadic arithmetic operations on high-dimensional matrices are desired, a multicore architecture is often needed. How the host and the accelerating device (hereafter referred to simply as the *device*) interact to scale the program is shown in Figure 3-8, which puts Amdahl's law into context. This figure uses the analogy of a peach, from Wen-mei Hwu et al.'s *Programming Massively Parallel Processors*,[16] where the pit of the peach represents the serial part of the program that requires sequential execution (this portion is thus more suitable for the CPU and relates to the serial portion of Amdhal's law) and the "meaty" part of the peach is parallelizable. This part of the process becomes a great candidate for execution by devices such as a GPU when the parallelism it requires is SIMD-like. In this case, a scale-out by N workers can be easily achieved.

---

16 Hwu, Wen-mei, David Kirk, and Izzat El Hajj. 2022. *Programming Massively Parallel Processors: A Hands-on Approach*, 4th ed. Waltham, MA: Morgan Kaufmann.

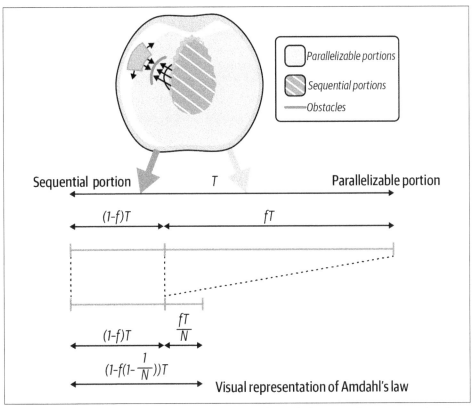

Figure 3-8. A user's program visualized as a peach, with the pit indicating serial code and the meat indicating parallelizable parts of the code, overlaid on a visual representation of Amdahl's law to indicate the implications of program structure on its scalability

SIMD architectures and systolic arrays (as given by Flynn's taxonomy, discussed in the previous section) are currently the most relevant architectures for deep learning accelerators. Single instruction, multiple threads (SIMT) is currently the most popular array processor implementation across accelerating devices. Next, we'll take a look at some of the devices commonly used today.

Popular Accelerated Devices for Deep Learning

As of early 2024, the devices most commonly used to accelerate compute-intensive deep learning workloads include graphics processing units (GPUs), application-specific integrated circuits (ASICs), field-programmable gate arrays (FPGAs), and Wafer Scale Engines (WSEs). Tensor Processing Units (TPU) and Intelligence Processing Units (IPUs) are two specialized implementations of ASICs that are widely used in deep learning acceleration.

Acceleration for deep learning became mainstream in 2007, when NVIDIA's GPUs demonstrated scale in computation with specialized hardware. Although FPGAs have existed since 1984, their use in deep learning only began in 2010. The introduction of the TPU in 2013 made ASICs mainstream, and this was followed by the IPU in 2018. WSEs started to evolve around 2016, and their use has been gaining momentum since 2021. We'll look more closely at all of these devices in the following sections.

 Adi Fuchs has written a brilliant article covering these hardware variations in extensive detail.[17] There are also significant efforts ongoing in alternative forms of compute acceleration through techniques like neuromorphic hardware and quantum computing. These techniques are, however, in the very early stages of research and development and have not yet proven their mettle for use in scaled-up deep learning.

Graphics processing units (GPUs)

Specialized graphics chips to handle displaying and rendering large arrays of pixel data have existed since the 1970s. Graphics rendering is a SIMD operation that applies the same transformation to objects for pixel-wise rendering. The 3D graphics and video game industries needed this to be really fast, so they poured a lot of money into solving this challenge.

In the 1990s, OpenGL brought out fixed APIs for graphics, enabling graphics programming. This development was soon followed by rapid advancements in programming for graphics shaders, renderers, and frameworks based on Microsoft's Direct3D APIs. Intel, AMD, and NVIDIA were actively involved in the development of the graphics chipset landscape, with a main focus on high-definition rendering of 3D objects. NVIDIA was the first to come up with more flexible programmable shaders with floating-point support, raising excitement about how these graphics cards can be used in general-purpose high-dimensional array processing. These developments led to the creation of the *general-purpose graphics processing unit* (GPGPU), more commonly referred to as a GPU.

In 2007, NVIDIA proposed the Compute Unified Device Architecture (CUDA), a programming interface for general-purpose computation that exploits graphics cards as massively parallel SIMT processors. The CUDA interface was released with the NVIDIA GeForce 8 series GPU (Tesla microarchitecture). In the following subsections, we'll first take a high-level look at the microarchitecture for GPUs in the context of how SIMT is realized, taking into account the performance characteristics and

---

17 Fuchs, Adi. 2021. "AI Accelerators—Part IV: The Very Rich Landscape." Medium, December 5, 2021. *https:// medium.com/@adi.fu7/ai-accelerators-part-iv-the-very-rich-landscape-17481be80917*.

considerations. Then we'll briefly explore how CUDA wraps the graphics device, providing an easily programmable interface.

GPU microarchitecture. Although there are some CPU ICs where graphics chips are integrated into the same chip to allow for more homogeneous computing, due to the power wall, the computational capabilities of such devices are very limited. This limit comes from having a very small number of cores fitted in the IC. In heterogeneous computing, the host and devices from separate chips are interconnected, allowing the devices to accommodate a lot more cores than the host (as shown in Figure 3-7).

The architecture of a GPU comprises an array of highly threaded streaming multiprocessors (SMs) with a shared control and instruction cache and Graphics Double Data Rate (GDDR) SDRAM (also known as VRAM). This is very similar to the DRAM of the CPU except that it's made with frame buffers designed for graphics, so these memory chips have higher bandwidth than standard DRAM. This is also why GPUs' memory bandwidth is high, and it's the source of the leverage GPUs have to mask memory latency (by parallelizing the reads). The bottleneck in the case of heterogeneous computing comes from the host's memory bandwidth and the interconnect that needs to keep up with the GPU's memory bandwidth, resulting in throttling. Traditionally, the communication between CPUs and GPUs happens over PCIe, but more recently NVIDIA has introduced an alternative, SXM (Server PCI Express Module), that can offer higher-bandwidth transfer rates (we'll discuss this more in the following sections). Memory copy from CPU to GPU can be more efficient through direct memory access, realized by using memory pinning, which allocates memory in RAM for quick transfer. Memory pinning is realized by creating mapped memory on the host for device-related memory operations; Mark Harris discusses it in detail in a post on the NVIDIA Technical Blog.[18]

The microarchitecture of the NVIDIA Hopper series H100 GPU is shown in Figure 3-9. This architecture hosts 144 SMs per GPU, organized in a hierarchy where the GPU consists of eight graphics processing clusters (GPCs), with each GPC containing about nine texture processing clusters (TPCs) and every TPC containing two SMs. This processor hierarchy is supported by a memory hierarchy given by registers, L0, L1, and L2 caches, and high-bandwidth memory (HBM). As with the CPU, the register is co-located with the processor and the L0 and L1 caches sit with the SMs, whereas the L2 cache acts as a global cache for the chip, supported by HBM (based on DRAM) as the main memory of the device. The main memory of the H100 is 80 GB, with a bandwidth capability of 3 TB/sec for the SXM variant and 2 TB/sec for the PCIe variant, respectively.

---

18 Harris, Mark. 2012. "How to Optimize Data Transfers in CUDA C/C++." NVIDIA Technical Blog, December 4, 2012. *https://developer.nvidia.com/blog/how-optimize-data-transfers-cuda-cc*.

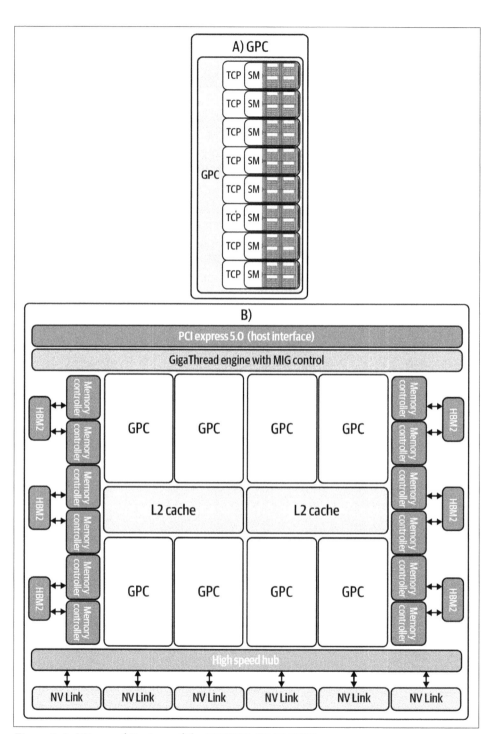

Figure 3-9. Microarchitecture of the NVIDIA H100 GPU

Analogous to the DMA used in CPUs, recent GPUs (Hoppers) use a *Tensor Memory Accelerator* (TMA) that can accelerate the transfer of large blocks of data and multi-dimensional tensors from main memory to the shared memory of the SM.

The architecture of the SM used in the H100 GPU is shown in Figure 3-10. This is the unit that hosts the graphics processing cores. The architecture is similar to a CPU in terms of arithmetic units and memory organization. Notice the specialized hardware dedicated to the computation of specialized data types. The tensor core block shown in this figure is a specialized half-precision MAC chip that runs faster than other ALU units featuring higher precision (`fp32`, `fp64`, etc.).

The Hopper series also features specialized hardware for speeding up training and inference of models based on the Transformer architecture. These models can have trillions of parameters and take an enormous amount of time to train—for instance, it takes eight weeks to train the Megatron Turing Natural Language Generation (MT-NLG) model on 2,048 NVIDIA A100 GPUs.[19] The efficiency of the transformer engine stems from a combination of leveraging the Tensor Core efficiently and effectively right-sizing the precision (floating-point data type) of the matrix, allowing MAC operations to be performed faster.

To scale computations horizontally, more GPUs are needed. NVIDIA's H100 GPU boasts 80 billion transistors. Given that, the power wall, and the cap on the number of PCIe slots available to connect to the CPU, very few GPUs (up to eight) can be hosted on the motherboard. On each GPU, there are 144 SMs performing computations that need to communicate and synchronize with each other. When the communication requires the exchange of large volumes of data (e.g., full-precision high-dimensional tensors that range in GB), efficient peer-to-peer communication across GPUs becomes critical, otherwise you risk throttling on the PCIe-CPU interface.

To address this, most modern NVIDIA GPUs utilize NVIDIA Link (NVLink) as the interconnect, offering higher network bandwidth than a PCIe interconnect. To quantify this, the H100 SXM supports up to 18 NVLink connections, for a total bandwidth of 900 GB/sec—over 7x the bandwidth of the H100 PCIe equivalent GPU. NVLink can only connect 4 GPUs, so the interconnect is beefed up by using a switch (called the NVSwitch) that supports 64 NVLink ports with hardware components to provide efficient networking via the Scalable Hierarchical Aggregation Reduction Protocol (SHARP) for latency reduction (achieved via in-network reduction operations and multicast acceleration). Figure 3-11 shows an example layout of eight GPUs connected with high-speed NVLink interfaces and NVMe storage devices (through PCIe interfaces, but also configured for InfiniBand for remote access).

---

19 Andersch, Michael, Greg Palmer, Ronny Krashinsky, Nick Stam, Vishal Mehta, Gonzalo Brito, and Sridhar Ramaswamy. 2022. "NVIDIA Hopper Architecture In-Depth." NVIDIA Technical Blog, March 22, 2022. *https://developer.nvidia.com/blog/nvidia-hopper-architecture-in-depth.*

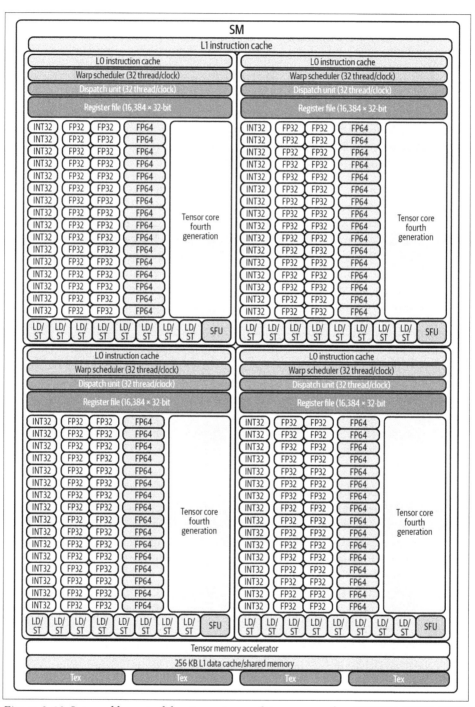

Figure 3-10. Internal layout of the streaming multiprocessor of an NVIDIA H100 GPU

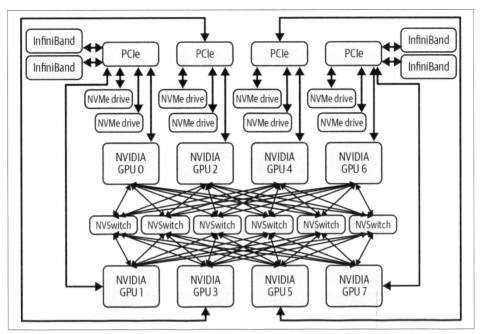

Figure 3-11. An example of GPU interconnect

Scaling beyond eight GPUs requires a cluster of nodes connected with a high-bandwidth, low-latency network interconnect. These are utilized via NVSwitches and NVLinks, which can surface GPUs interconnected over a remote network provider's horizontally scalable compute clusters. NVIDIA's SuperPOD, for example, features 160–1,120 nodes with additional cluster management capabilities.

You'll learn more about scaling infrastructure in a more cost-efficient manner in Chapter 5.

Myth: GPUs Are Embarrassingly Parallel

The fundamental design goal of the GPU was to allow for embarrassingly parallel computing. GPUs have extensive compute capabilities and memory bandwidth. However, there is a limitation lurking here that requires consideration in scaling appropriately. Performing a simple matrix multiplication operation—i.e., taking two matrices A and B, multiplying them, and obtaining the result in another matrix, C—requires two memory load operations for read, one memory operation for write, and a single compute operation (for multiply).

Taking the H100 SXM GPU as an example, multiplying two infinitely large matrices of half-precision (fp16) floating-point numbers and keeping the GPU completely occupied at 100% efficiency at the 120 TFLOPs performance benchmark would

---

require 720 TB/sec of memory bandwidth. However, the memory bandwidth of this card is just 3,000 GB/sec.

This is why the data type, format, and precision are important considerations in achieving efficiency. The right balance for you and your application/algorithm in terms of numeric precision and compute performance will depend on your requirements and objective. As discussed in Chapter 1, identifying your limits and the acceptable trade-offs is a crucial step in the development process.

CUDA

CUDA is NVIDIA's proprietary interface to enable general-purpose programming for massive-scale computing. Table 3-4 lists the abstractions used in CUDA and how they map to the hardware components in the GPU microarchitecture.

Table 3-4. GPU microarchitecture components and their comparable abstractions for the programming interface defined by CUDA

Component	Definition	Parallel CUDA programming construct	Other contemporary terminology for vectorized operations
GPU	The chip representing a single GPU.	Grid	Vectorized loop
Graphics processing cluster (GPC)	A cluster of physically packed together streaming multiprocessors that can communicate and cooperate with each other much more efficiently using faster and direct SM-to-SM communications without involving a cache or memory hierarchies at all. This capability is available in Hopper series GPUs and is optional at the software level.	Thread block cluster (TBC)	
Texture processing cluster (TPC)	A group of physically packed together SMs that share texture memory, mainly designed for graphics.		
Streaming multiprocessor (SM)	The specialized processor capable of SIMD, hosting a large number of cores (as shown in Figure 3-10).	Block	Vector processor
Streaming processor core	A single core of the GPU.	Thread	
Set of instructions	The software function that should run on the array in a parallel fashion.	Kernel	
Instruction set architecture (ISA)	The interface between the software and the hardware.	Parallel Thread Execution (PTX)	Vector instruction

The threads are executed in a block of 32 warps (warps are hardware implementation details and are not directly utilized in the CUDA programming model). It's interesting to note that whenever the number of threads is not a multiple of 32—e.g., when performing a matrix multiplication of two vectors of length 24—then padding is applied to make it a multiple of 32. In other words, for this example, eight processors will be wasted for that cycle, doing nothing useful.

This hierarchical GPU organization is leveraged in managing a large number of threads cooperatively executing on the cores. It allows for indexing each thread in tiles in a mosaic manner given by row and column order, with the top-left core indexed at (0,0) and the bottom-right core, for an N-core SM, indexed at (N, N). Note that even though an SM consists of heterogeneous cores (as shown in Figure 3-10) for various data types and specialized hardware for each type, for a given instruction only the relevant processors are activated.

Figure 3-12 demonstrates the core activation and indexing for a given computation. This pattern of indexing is applied at each level in the grid hierarchy.

The programming model of CUDA is demonstrated in Figure 3-13. CUDA is natively written in C++, which libraries such as PyTorch use to execute the parallelizable parts of their serial programs through functions that compile into CUDA kernels. The kernel is sent off to graphics cores for processing in parallel in a threaded fashion. The kernels are compiled using the NVIDIA compiler, NVCC, which translates them into hardware-specific instruction sets (PTX). This is the SIMT programming that you read about earlier; it's explained in greater detail in the NVIDIA documentation (*https://oreil.ly/Kbmes*).

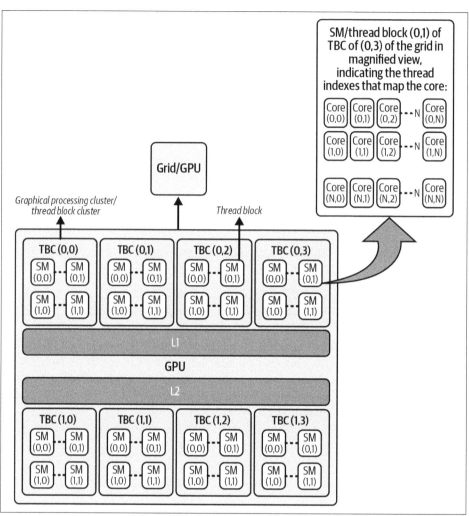

Figure 3-12. A GPU's compositional hierarchy leveraged in CUDA programming is shown here; the indexing is achieved through row, column (x, y) format at each level in the hierarchy

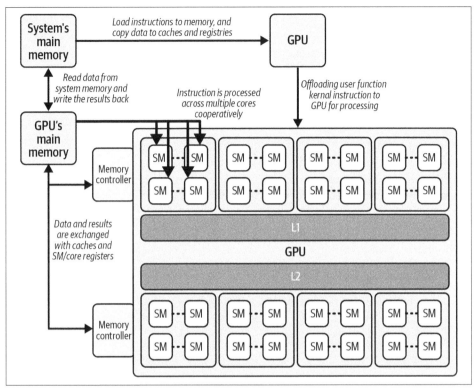

Figure 3-13. The programming model for CUDA and its interaction with the GPU and CPU

The SIMT execution model is asynchronous, to the extent that even the copy operation to move data from the system to GPU memory is executed asynchronously. Whenever synchronization across a block of threads is needed, the asynchronous barrier API of CUDA is leveraged.

Let's go back to the matrix multiplication example from the sidebar "Myth: GPUs Are Embarrassingly Parallel" on page 99 and look at a CUDA implementation for it. The following snippet shows a kernel function written in C++ that simply multiplies the values from matrices A and B at the respective indices and stores the results in matrix C. Here, you may note kernels are written in conjunction with blocks that map to SMs. You can find the full example in the NVIDIA docs (*https://oreil.ly/OnSmM*).

The host code for the matrix multiplication operation that takes A and B, multiplies them, and writes the results into C is as follows. This code represents the serial code that invokes the kernel, where wA and wB are the widths of the two matrices A and B:

```
void matrixMul(float* C, float* A, float* B, int wA, int wB)
{
    // Set up execution parameters
    dim3 threadsPerBlock(BLOCK_SIZE, BLOCK_SIZE);
    dim3 blockPerGrid(WC / threads.x, HC / threads.y);

    // Execute the kernel
    matrixMul<<< blockPerGrid, threadsPerBlock >>>(C, A, B, wA, wB);
}
```

The kernel function `matrixMulKernel` for the device is shown next. The reference of
`__global__` indicates it is aimed to be run on the device. Notice how the matrices are
subdivided to be run cooperatively over the block (i.e., the processor) in a threaded
manner. The shared memory of the SM is used and synchronization is performed
before proceeding to the next iteration:

```
__global__ void matrixMulKernel(float* C, float* A, float* B, int wA, int wB)
{
    // Block index
    int bx = blockIdx.x;
    int by = blockIdx.y;

    // Thread index
    int tx = threadIdx.x;
    int ty = threadIdx.y;

    // Start and end index of the submatrix of A processed by the block
    int aBegin = wA * BLOCK_SIZE * by;
    int aEnd = aBegin + wA - 1;

    // Step size used to iterate through the submatrices of A Stepped in
    // the size of the block to achieve cooperation
    int aStep = BLOCK_SIZE;

    // Start and step index of the submatrix of B processed by the block
    int bBegin = BLOCK_SIZE * bx;
    int bStep = BLOCK_SIZE * wB;

    // Csub is used to store the element of the block submatrix
    // that is computed by the thread
    float Csub = 0;

    // Loop over all the submatrices of A and B
    // required to compute the block submatrix
    for (int a = aBegin, b = bBegin;
            a <= aEnd;
            a += aStep, b += bStep) {

        // Declaration of the shared memory array As used to
        // store the submatrix of A
        __shared__ float As[BLOCK_SIZE][BLOCK_SIZE];
```

```
// Declaration of the shared memory array Bs used to
// store the submatrix of B
__shared__ float Bs[BLOCK_SIZE][BLOCK_SIZE];

// Load the matrices from device memory to shared memory;
// each thread loads one element of each matrix
AS(ty, tx) = A[a + wA * ty + tx];
BS(ty, tx) = B[b + wB * ty + tx];

// Synchronize to make sure the matrices are loaded
__syncthreads();

// Multiply the two matrices together;
// each thread computes one element of the block submatrix
for (int k = 0; k < BLOCK_SIZE; ++k)
    Csub += AS(ty, k) * BS(k, tx);

// Synchronize to make sure that the preceding
// computation is done before loading two new
// submatrices of A and B in the next iteration
__syncthreads();
}

// Write the block submatrix to device memory;
// each thread writes one element
int c = wB * BLOCK_SIZE * by + BLOCK_SIZE * bx;
C[c + wB * ty + tx] = Csub;
}
```

NVIDIA's dominance: The competition landscape

NVIDIA currently dominates the GPU market for deep learning. If you're interested, you can explore the evolution of the NVIDIA architecture in the technical white papers available on the NVIDIA website (*https://oreil.ly/LmKU_*). These include some well-known names, including Fermi, Maxwell, Kepler, Pascal, Volta, Turing, Ada Lovelace, and Ampere, and the more recent Hopper. NVIDIA has been very methodical in pushing backward compatible, incremental changes through its evolution, which has helped gain the confidence of the developer community.

NVIDIA does have some competitors. In 2006, following the acquisition of ATI for a hefty $5.4 billion, AMD aimed to gain market capital for GPU development. However, following the less-than-impressive release of its GPU, it struggled to achieve market capitalization. More recently, with the Radeon Instinct series, AMD is gaining traction by providing comparable GPUs at a much lower cost than NVIDIA. The biggest challenge with AMD has been the lack of integration support through software, libraries, and high-level programming interfaces. NGO Khronos Group launched a dedicated effort to create a unified GPU programming language called Open Computing Language (OpenCL) back in 2008 and has been actively working toward this goal. Supporting OpenCL has been helpful for AMD, and more recently it has been bridging this gap (albeit slowly) with ROCm, a collection of drivers, development tools, and APIs for GPU programming.

CUDA, the proprietary software specifically for NVIDIA's GPUs, remains incompatible with AMD's, and the maturity of CUDA and its off-the-shelf support by many deep learning libraries (such as PyTorch and TensorFlow) provide NVIDIA with significant leverage over AMD. As of March 2021, ROCm support for PyTorch has become mainstream (*https://oreil.ly/dJ7fN*), but it's still relatively immature.

In 2014, Intel introduced the Core i5, a homogeneous processor with more GPU than CPU execution units. Intel largely remained in homogeneous computing until 2019, when it acquired Habana and re-entered the realm of heterogeneous computing. The key difference with Habana accelerators is that they have faster (flash-based) memory and are more power-efficient. Per a benchmark by Hugging Face, the Gaudi2 offered a 1.8x speedup over the NVIDIA A100 in training the BERT model (consistent with the results reported by Intel).[20]

Competition is certainly a good thing for the consumer base, and it's great to see AMD and Intel catching up. NVIDIA still dominates the GPU market, however, with an estimated 88% share as of early 2023,[21] and major companies like OpenAI using its GPUs to train models like ChatGPT (*https://oreil.ly/WRGxE*). Geopolitical circumstances, given the souring relations between the US and China in recent years, have led to intense efforts to mitigate NVIDIA's dominance.

The right GPU for you should be sized for your purpose; the latest and greatest is not always the best. The criteria should include the compute requirements of the models you work with, your memory requirements (determined by your network and data), and the turnaround time you need, as well as your financial constraints. If you're interested in reading more on this topic, Tim Dettmers has written a couple of excellent articles about choosing the right GPU.[22]

Application-specific integrated circuits (ASICs)

In this section, you will learn about two specialized ASIC implementations: TPUs and IPUs.

---

20 Pierrard, Régis. 2022. "Faster Training and Inference: Habana Gaudi®-2 vs Nvidia A100 80GB." Hugging Face blog, December 14, 2022. *https://huggingface.co/blog/habana-gaudi-2-benchmark*.

21 Goldman, Sharon. 2023. "How Nvidia Dominated AI—And Plans to Keep It That Way as Generative AI Explodes." VentureBeat, February 23, 2023. *https://venturebeat.com/ai/how-nvidia-dominated-ai-and-plans-to-keep-it-that-way-as-generative-ai-explodes*.

22 Dettmers, Tim. 2023. "Which GPU(s) to Get for Deep Learning: My Experience and Advice for Using GPUs in Deep Learning." Tim Dettmers's blog, January 30, 2023. *https://timdettmers.com/2023/01/30/which-gpu-for-deep-learning/*; Dettmers, Tim. 2018. "A Full Hardware Guide to Deep Learning." Tim Dettmers's blog, December 16, 2018. *https://timdettmers.com/2018/12/16/deep-learning-hardware-guide*.

Tensor Processing Units (TPUs). Back in 2013, Google realized that the use of deep learning in its product portfolio had increased the company's compute requirements by 10x and that its data centers needed to scale to meet the growing demand. It went on to build its own ASIC chips with specialized microarchitectures for neural network computation, using a systolic array processing scheme: the Tensor Processing Unit.

The TPU is designed more as a co-processor to work alongside a CPU than as a standalone processor. The architecture of the TPU, shown in Figure 3-14, underscores the heavy utilization of memory buffers and specialized units for deep learning operations (activation, pooling) in addition to standard matrix multiply-accumulate operations.[23] TPUs' power consumption needs are much lower than GPUs', but they are mainly produced by Google and thus are exclusive to Google Cloud infrastructure.

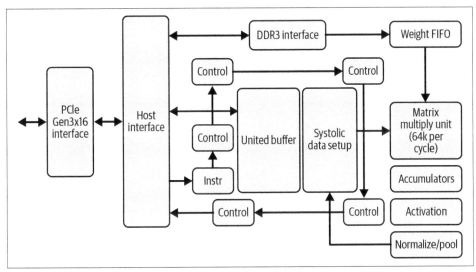

Figure 3-14. The high-level design of a TPU (adapted from Sato and Young, 2017)

As shown in Figure 3-14, TPUs cannot be truly classified as SIMD because as a unit they apply multiple operations on a synchronized systolic array. Instead, they fall into the synchronous class in Duncan's revised classification for parallel computing.[24]

23 Sato, Kaz, and Cliff Young. 2017. "An In-Depth Look at Google's First Tensor Processing Unit (TPU)." May 12, 2017. *https://cloud.google.com/blog/products/ai-machine-learning/an-in-depth-look-at-googles-first-tensor-processing-unit-tpu.*

24 Duncan, "A Survey of Parallel Computer Architectures," 5–16.

A big consideration in designing the TPU was "right-sizing" the data type. As shown in Figure 3-15, it takes four times more bits to represent a numeric value using single-precision floating point (fp32) than int8. Even with the reduced precision, int8 leads to results close to those of its fp32 counterpart, albeit slightly noisier. This quantization allows massive simplification and memory efficiencies in the design of the TPU. The bfloat16 format mentioned in Table 3-1 is also a key data format used in TPUs for higher precision than int8.

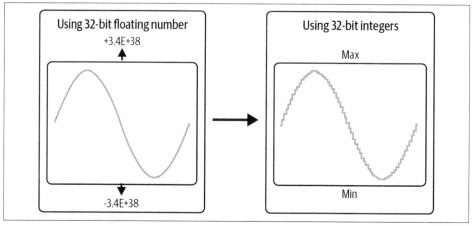

Figure 3-15. The impact of using int8 on accuracy of computation as compared to single-precision fp32 (adapted from Sato and Young, 2017)

Similar to a GPU's, the TPU's software stack includes a driver and a runtime, packaged in libtpu. All high-level libraries (PyTorch, JAX, TensorFlow, etc.) integrate with libtpu to accelerate the library functions when running on TPUs. Given the specialized nature of TPUs, the interface between hardware and software is a lot simpler, consisting of a single library as compared to the assorted set of purpose-built libraries and software packages provided by NVIDIA.

Currently in the fourth generation, Google has been adding more cores to the TPU to scale the computational capacity. TPU v4 comes with 8,192 co-processors combining to a peak of 1.1 exaFLOPs computational capacity over the pod.

Intelligence Processing Units (IPUs). IPUs, by Graphcore, are designed for the MIMD style of parallelism, making them a good candidate for scaling computation with mixed instruction sets. IPUs come with a core and local memory, but several IPUs on the chip share the memory. As shown in Figure 3-16, the components are analogous to those in other accelerators you have read about so far. The main difference here is that IPUs can run individual processing threads on smaller data blocks, in a highly

parallel fashion.[25] Each IPU core has hardware multithreading support for up to 6 threads, making the 1,472-core chip capable of running 8,832 threads. The memory bandwidth and interconnect capabilities of IPUs are comparable to other contemporary accelerators in the market today. The IPU offers a throughput of up to 31 TFLOPs for single precision, which is half the capacity of H100 single-precision benchmarks. Still in the early stages of development with only second-generation devices in the market, this is emerging technology.

Field programmable gate arrays (FPGAs)

FPGAs are integrated circuits that can be programmed and reprogrammed using a hardware description language (HDL). These circuits are useful in low-powered, small-footprint settings where lower latency than what the CPU can offer is required. FPGAs do not match the computational capabilities of GPUs or TPUs, but they're ideal for use in embedded devices and IoT solutions. They allow for a network setup that can be reconfigured down to the hardware level, meaning a software update can reconfigure the entire hardware network, greatly simplifying maintenance. The biggest challenge with FPGAs is the adaptation overhead, as reconfigurability comes with complexity in programming the hardware layer.

Around the time Google was exploring TPUs, Microsoft was looking into leveraging FPGAs for a configurable CNN accelerator with its Project Catapult (*https://oreil.ly/cyUR8*) and Project Brainwave (*https://oreil.ly/e3U0Q*). Figure 3-17 shows Microsoft's FPGA used in realizing the cloud-scale Brainwave deployment.

---

25 Jia, Zhe, Blake Tillman, Marco Maggioni, and Daniele Paolo Scarpazza. 2017. "Dissecting the Graphcore IPU Architecture via Microbenchmarking." arXiv, December 7, 2019. *https://arxiv.org/abs/1912.03413*.

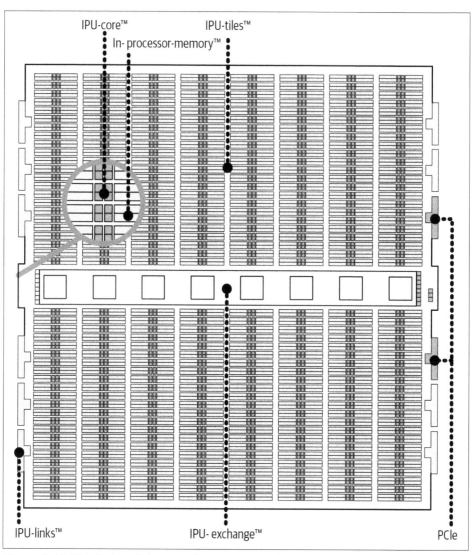

Figure 3-16. The design of the second-generation Colossus MK2 IPU processor (adapted from Graphcore (https://oreil.ly/VsORW))

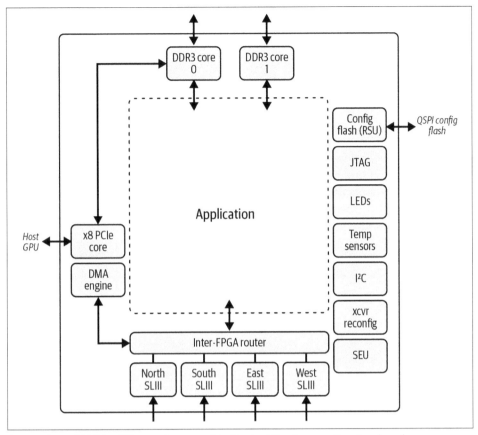

Figure 3-17. FPGA of Catapult as used in Project Brainwave for cloud-scale deployments[26]

Wafer Scale Engines (WSEs)

Cerebras has been developing wafer-scale computation engines known as WSEs since 2016. Currently in generation 2, these are large processors hosting hundreds of thousands of cores across the silicon surface area (the wafer). WSEs are MIMD-compatible processors. Each processor is a collection of grid-arranged dies, each of which can in turn host thousands of tiles. Tiles are units that contain the computational cores, memory, and routers. WSEs minimize the overhead of interconnects

26 Putnam, Andrew, Adrian M. Caulfield, Eric S. Chung, Derek Chiou, Kypros Constantinides, John Demme, Hadi Esmaeilzadeh, et al. 2014. "A Reconfigurable Fabric for Accelerating Large-Scale Datacenter Services." In Proceeding of the 41st Annual International Symposium on Computer Architecture (ISCA), 13-24. *https://www.microsoft.com/en-us/research/publication/a-reconfigurable-fabric-for-accelerating-large-scale-datacenter-services.*

because everything is integrated on the same wafer. They are more analogous to powerful AI-compute-ready CPUs than the heterogeneous accelerator-based computational devices we discussed earlier. The WSE-2 has about 2.6 trillion transistors for 850,000 cores, laid out over ~46K mm^2 (71.5 in^2); in contrast, one of the largest AI-ready CPUs has a silicon area of ~826 mm^2 (1.3 in^2) hosting 0.054 trillion transistors.[27]

Accelerator Benchmarking

MLCommons (*https://oreil.ly/D4kW5*) provides a suite of benchmarks to compare the performance of storage, clusters, training, etc. MLPerf is the performance benchmark by MLCommons that's used by all leading accelerator providers to benchmark the compute performance for distinct categories of training methodologies and techniques. This helps promote growth and fair competition at the intersection of hardware and deep learning training. Per the latest benchmarks (*https://oreil.ly/bSAeD*), NVIDIA continues to be leading the way; however, Intel's Habana accelerators and IPUs are catching up. You will read more about benchmarking and measuring to scale in Chapter 6.

Summary

Congratulations on making your way through this chapter. To many deep learning practitioners, the systems side can be less attractive than the algorithmic side. Nonetheless, having a fundamental understanding of the entire stack will go a long way in helping you scale your deep learning applications. Even if you work in a cross-functional team with experts to support you, standardized knowledge helps improve interaction and promotes healthy debate, all of which helps in developing efficient systems.

This chapter covered hardware and its implications for developing deep learning applications. You gained an understanding of data types and how they map to silicon and circuits. You also learned about computer architecture and explored various paradigms existing today to massively scale computation over data. Next, you delved into the various types of specialized accelerated devices used today in deep learning to accelerate development through heterogeneous computing paradigms. Several hardware-related considerations and nuances that may get in the way of scaling were brought forth. In the next chapter, you'll work through a few case studies to combine all you have learned thus far.

---

27 Cutress, Ian. "Cerebras Unveils Wafer Scale Engine Two (WSE2): 2.6 Trillion Transistors, 100% Yield." AnandTech, April 20, 2021. *https://www.anandtech.com/show/16626/cerebras-unveils-wafer-scale-engine-two-wse2-26-trillion-transistors-100-yield.*

## CHAPTER 4

Putting It All Together: Efficient Deep Learning

In Chapter 2, you read about the fundamentals and data flows of deep learning applications. In Chapter 3, you learned about the various computational units that are available today and how they enable number crunching at scale. This chapter builds on the content from the previous two chapters, demonstrating the acceleration provided by specialized computing hardware and providing some examples of how-tos. It also presents some tips and tricks for efficiently training a deep learning model on a single machine with at most one accelerated device.

There are two hands-on exercises in this chapter, one using a language model (OpenAI's GPT-2) and the second an image classification model (EfficientNet).[1] The GPT-2 exercise allows you to explore the level of acceleration a GPU provides and dig into the details of profiling tools to understand the underlying implications. In the second hands-on example, you'll explore building a multiclass image segmentation solution using the MIT Scene Parsing Benchmark (SceneParse150) dataset. After you go through these exercises, you'll look at several techniques you can apply to introduce efficiency in your code. More specifically, you will learn about graph compilation, mixed-precision training, efficiencies obtained via gradient tricks, memory layout tricks, and some `DataLoader` tricks to manage model input pipeline overheads. This chapter culminates with a small example of a custom kernel to demonstrate leveraging accelerated computing for custom operations.

---

1 Radford, Alec, Jeffrey Wu, Rewon Child, David Luan, Dario Amodei, and Ilya Sutskever. 2019. "Language Models Are Unsupervised Multitask Learners." *https://paperswithcode.com/paper/language-models-are-unsupervised-multitask*; Tan, Mingxing, and Quoc V. Le. 2019. "EfficientNet: Rethinking Model Scaling for Convolutional Neural Networks." arXiv, May 28, 2019. *https://arxiv.org/abs/1905.11946*.

Hands-On Exercise #1: GPT-2

ChaptGPT is an influential generative language model able to "converse" via free text prompts. The technology behind ChatGPT is OpenAI's Generative Pre-trained Transformer (GPT), a large Transformer-based language model. Scale has been a crucial factor behind the success of GPT; it is a large model, trained with vast volumes of data, and it employs many tricks, some of which are known and will be discussed in Chapter 10. It was the second version of GPT, GPT-2, that achieved impressive success. In this exercise, you will explore that model.

The task for GPT-2 is to predict the next word given the previous words within some text. GPT-2 has more than 10x as many parameters and is trained with 10x more data than the original GPT. More concretely, GPT-2 has 1.5 billion parameters and is trained from the text extracted from 8 million web pages.

 GPT-2 was released in early 2019. Since then (as of early 2024) GPT-3, -3.5, and -4 have also been released, albeit kept closed source (with very limited sharing of implementation details). A comparison of the versions across different criteria is provided in Table 4-1, in "Key contributors to scale" on page 115.

Exercise Objectives

The objectives of this exercise are as follows:

- Review examples of how to write infrastructure-agnostic code. This allows you to easily scale out to other infrastructure in the event of a computing bottleneck.
- Profile and monitor to measure the behavior of your model and training loop. These skills are useful in understanding the limitations and provide clues to optimize appropriately.
- Learn about techniques to leverage hardware capabilities to develop efficiently.
- Optionally, learn about Docker and other build toolchains to build runtimes suited to your development needs, rather than using Swiss army knife environments like NVIDIA GPU Cloud (NGC) containers.

The following section explores the architecture of the model and the implementation details. (For a more thorough walkthrough, see Jay Alammar's detailed explanation of GPT-2, which explains intricate concepts such as the Transformer, attention block, masked self- and cross-attention, and the role the query, key, and value play in predicting the possible next word/token).[2] The code for this exercise is available in the *chapter_4* (*https://oreil.ly/JjfeK*) folder of the book's GitHub repository.

Model Architecture

The key technique GPT employs is masking some words in the text corpus and training the model to predict the masked words by exploiting the remaining corpus of text. For example, the model might be shown the text "I brought a book to ___" and asked to predict the missing word, "read." As you can see, there may be more than one word that could fit here (e.g., "learn"). These possible words need to be scored to identify the recommended word. With attention blocks, Transformer architectures can attend to longer sequences of tokens in a parallelized fashion. This, combined with this masking ability, allows the model to develop a better language understanding and exploit the semantic meaning of text via word embedding.

GPT-2 is a decoder-only autoregressive model. The full architecture is shown in Figure 4-1, including a breakdown of the GPT block (the decoder component). This figure demonstrates how the text embedding and positional encoding flow through the network, which consists of a series of multiheaded masked attention blocks, composed together with LayerNorm (layer normalization) and Conv1d (1D convolution) layers. You may note that this network has several residual connections throughout. The attention block has both self- and cross-attention, so (as shown in the bottom-right corner of the figure) either the query, key, and value can all come from the same text sequence, or the query can come from one sequence and the key and value from another.

Key contributors to scale

Let's review some of the key features of GPT-2 that contributed to the scaling of this technique.

Transformer attention block.   Ashish Vaswani et al. initially proposed the multiheaded attention block that is used in GPT in their seminal paper "Attention Is All You Need."[3] The key feature of this architecture is that the words of the text are processed as a whole. Other contemporary architectures, like recurrent neural networks (RNNs) and long short-term memory networks (LSTMs), process words one by one in a temporal sequence and remember the representation of these words through

---

2 Alammar, Jay. 2019. "The Illustrated GPT-2 (Visualizing Transformer Language Models)." Jay Alammar's blog, August 12, 2019. *https://jalammar.github.io/illustrated-gpt2*.

3 Vaswani, Ashish, Noam Shazeer, Niki Parmar, Jakob Uszkoreit, Llion Jones, Aidan N. Gomez, Lukasz Kaiser, and Illia Polosukhin. 2017. "Attention Is All You Need." arXiv, December 6, 2017. *https://arxiv.org/abs/1706.03762*.

hidden states. The inability to process words in parallel was a key reason the capabilities of language models before Transformers were not rapidly improving. With the introduction of the Transformer, a larger context through a sequence of tokens/words could be provided. For GPT-2 this context size was 1,024 tokens, twice that of GPT (see Table 4-1). The context size has since been scaled up to a starting size of 8,192 tokens (*https://oreil.ly/zqlNt*) in GPT-4,[4] and the reasoning abilities of this network have scaled proportionately.

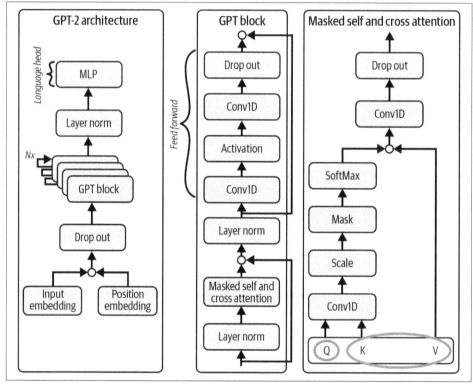

Figure 4-1. The architecture of GPT-2 and detailed breakdown of its subnetwork

Table 4-1. The evolution of various GPT models across versions

Name	Context size	Number of parameters	Layers	Depth of model	Comparable model (capacity-wise)
GPT-2 small	1,024	117M	12	768	GPT (original)
GPT-2 medium	1,024	345M	24	1,024	BERT

---

4 Bubeck, Sébastien, Varun Chandrasekaran, Ronen Eldan, Johannes Gehrke, Eric Horvitz, Ece Kamar, Peter Lee, et al. 2023. "Sparks of Artificial General Intelligence: Early Experiments with GPT-4." arXiv, April 13, 2023. *https://arxiv.org/abs/2303.12712*.

Name	Context size	Number of parameters	Layers	Depth of model	Comparable model (capacity-wise)
GPT-2 large	1,024	762M	36	1,280	
GPT-2 XL	1,024	1,542M	48	1,600	
GPT-3 small	2,048	125M	12	768	GPT-2 small
GPT-3 medium	2,048	350M	24	1,024	GPT-2 medium
GPT-3 large	2,048	760M	24	1,536	GPT-2 large
GPT-3 XL	2,048	1.3B	24	2,048	GPT-2 XL
GPT-3 2.7B	2,048	2.7B	32	2,560	
GPT-3 6.7B	2,048	6.7B	32	4,096	
GPT-3 13B	2,048	13B	40	5,140	
GPT-3 175B	2,048	175B	96	12,288	
GPT-4	8,192	Undisclosed (rumored to be 1.76T)	Undisclosed	Undisclosed	
GPT-4-32k	32,768	Undisclosed	Undisclosed	Undisclosed	

Unsupervised training. As discussed earlier, the training of GPT is achieved by masking certain tokens in the training dataset. Because of this technique, there is no labeling or supervision required for training these large language models. The training data thus remains easy to procure through a web crawler. Given the enormous amount of textual data available on the internet, it is only the quality of the inputs that remains a concern. OpenAI employs a filtering technique to choose pages of text that have received at least three user upvotes ("likes" of the page) more to ensure the quality of the content used to train the model. These scraped texts formed the vocabulary of GPT-2, which was also expanded to 50,257 from the 40,478 unique tokens used for training GPT.

Zero-shot learning. In the initial version of GPT, OpenAI focused on training a large language model through pretraining and fine tuning different versions of the model for various language purposes like question answering, text summarization, language translation, and reading comprehension. However, because the semantic relations between words remain consistent across applications of spoken language, with GPT-2 it was noted that the model could be repurposed for such tasks via zero- or few-shot techniques (discussed in Chapters 11, 12, and 13). In other words, it's possible to train a very good language model and repurpose it for various tasks at inference time. This is achievable because zero-shot techniques do not require backpropagation; thus, repurposing is highly cost-, compute-, and time-efficient.

This is a very important aspect of GPT that should be considered seriously for model development across related tasks. Repurposing an existing model for a related task via fine tuning or inference-time alignment, as in meta-learning and zero-shot learning, is a great optimization trick. This will be covered in detail in Chapter 11.

Parameter scale. As discussed already, GPT-2 is simply a scaled-up version of GPT (with a slight rearrangement of the `LayerNorm` layers). The scale in GPT-2 comes from the use of a larger context size and more GPT blocks (Figure 4-1 and Table 4-1). The subsequent versions of the model continued to scale; the largest GPT-3 model, for example, has 175 billion parameters.[5] For reference, humans are estimated to have 100 trillion synapses.

Implementation

Although the code for GPT-2 has been open sourced (*https://oreil.ly/23avQ*) by OpenAI, in this exercise, you will be using Hugging Face's Transformers library, which provides a PyTorch implementation of the GPT-2 architecture shown in Figure 4-1. Specifically, you will be using the library's `GPT2LMHeadModel`, a GPT2 model transformer with a language modeling head on top.

For wiring up GPT-2 you will use PyTorch Lightning, as in Chapter 2. You'll use the Hugging Face wikitext dataset (*https://oreil.ly/vR3_T*) for training.

As mentioned earlier, the code for this hands-on exercise is available in the book's GitHub repository (*https://oreil.ly/JjfeK*). The implementation is explained in the following sections.

model.py

The model implementation in this script is straightforward, as most of the complexity of the model is abstracted away in `GPT2LMHeadModel`. The model input pipeline tokenizes the text, and the `forward` call is dispatched to the `GPT2LMHeadModel`, which returns the cross-entropy loss between the predicted token and the true token. This script wraps the model from the Transformers library in the Lightning abstraction of `LightningModule`.

dataset.py

The dataset implementation is in `WikiDataModule`, which wraps v2 of the wikitext dataset. In this module, the raw text is downloaded, preprocessed, tokenized, and then grouped according to the block capacity of the model. The data is split into

---

5 Brown, Tom B., Benjamin Mann, Nick Ryder, Melanie Subbiah, Jared Kaplan, Prafulla Dhariwal, Arvind Neelakantan, et al. 2020. "Language Models Are Few-Shot Learners." arXiv, May 28, 2020. *https://arxiv.org/abs/2005.14165*.

training, validation, and test sets and a respective `DataLoader` is created for each of the modules.

app.py

The trainer code is included in *app.py*. Note specifically the entry point method `train_gpt2`, which defines various components integrated into the training regime, including callbacks and profilers (much like the hands-on PyTorch exercise in Chapter 2). The profilers should only be used during development and formal runs as they incur costs in terms of memory and compute resources. The trainer code is as follows:

```
datamodule = WikiDataModule(name=model_name, batch_size=batch_size,
                            num_workers=num_workers)
model = GPT2Module(name=model_name)

trainer = PLTrainer(
    accelerator="auto",
    devices=="auto",
    max_epochs=max_epochs,
    callbacks=[
        TQDMProgressBar(refresh_rate=refresh_rate),
        ckpt_cb,
        DeviceStatsMonitor(cpu_stats=True),
        EarlyStopping(monitor="val/loss", mode="min"),
    ],
    logger=[
        exp_logger,
        TensorBoardLogger(save_dir=result_dir / "logs"),
    ],
    profiler=torch_profiler,
)
trainer.fit(model, datamodule)
```

Notice the `accelerator` and `devices` arguments in this code. These parameters provide the ability to write platform-agnostic code so the same code can be run on CPUs, GPUs, TPUs, or other assorted accelerators. It also supports computation on Metal shaders, available in Apple's M-series GPUs. In other words, this snippet allows you to tick off the first objective of writing platform-agnostic code that you can run anywhere and scale out per your needs.

 There are a few other ways to do this, including using Hugging Face's `Trainer`, which provides a similar capability. However, for the sake of consistency and reusability, in these exercises PyTorch Lightning will be used as an orchestrator.

Running the Example

To run the code, execute the following command from your environment:

```
deep-learning-at-scale chapter_4 train_gpt2
```

Following are some examples of the results obtained after training this model on the wikitext dataset for 50 epochs. The prompt used was "I've been waiting for a deep learning at scale book my whole life. Now that I have one, I shall read it. And I." Here's some of the generated text:

- I have a feeling that it's going to be a long time before I retire from this.
- ive learned so much from it.
- ive no doubt that it's going to change my life.
- I'll be ready to do anything I can to help it. I'll be on the…
- ' ll be able to do anything I would normally do in life.
- ive to see how it all plays out.
- ive been waiting for a deep learning book for a long time.
- will be able to see what I can do to make it happen.

Experiment Tracking

This practice exercise (and others throughout this book) uses Aim (*https://oreil.ly/s-t5g*), an open source experiment tracking solution, to monitor and visualize the progress and metrics of training runs. I chose Aim as it's free to use with no commitment from you. There are, however, several alternatives that you can use instead, as you see fit. Some of these alternatives will be briefly discussed in Chapter 11 (see "Setting Up for Iterative Execution" on page 354). The following snippet is used to enable the experiment tracking logger:

```
exp_logger = AimLogger(
    experiment=exp_name,
    train_metric_prefix="train/",
    val_metric_prefix="val/",
    test_metric_prefix="test/",
)
```

This logger is then configured with the trainer API as `logger`: i.e., `trainer = Trainer(... , logger=[exp_logger])`, as shown in the earlier `Trainer` snippet.

You will have to start aim server locally by running command aim up to visualize the run logs in aumhub. Your runs will log both profiler logs and run logs that you can visualize using tensorboard and aimhub respectively (as done in Chapter 2). Results shown in Figures 4-2 and 4-3 can be visualized using these two tools.

Measuring to Understand the Limitations and Scale Out

This section presents the performance measures obtained by running the code on a high-end CPU and a GPU and compares the two to explore the limitations.

Running on a CPU

Figure 4-2 shows the results obtained when this code was run on a nonaccelerated computer with a 10-core CPU and 32 GB of memory (RAM). The batch size used in this run was set at 12.

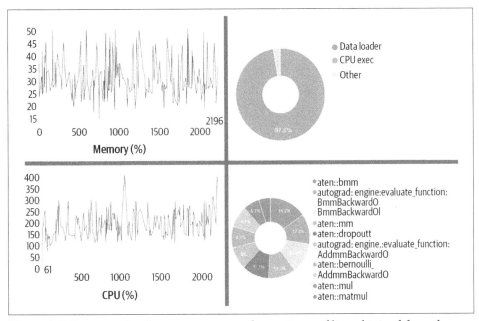

Figure 4-2. Screen grabs of resource usage and operator profiling obtained from the run of this example when trained on CPU-only compute

The average time to take one step (i.e., process one batch of data and do forward and backward passes) was about 304 seconds, with 97.46% of this time spent executing operations on the CPU and 2.54% spent on non-CPU operations. Noticeably, negligible time was spent to support the data loading operations (e.g., loading the wikitext dataset in memory for execution).

The profiler's memory consumption graph indicates a peak at 42.64 GB; however, if you look at the continuous monitoring of memory usage, in Aim's system metrics in this case, you may note the peak sits at 50 GB.

 Profilers are configured to sample steps during which the profiling should be run. You can see this in the schedule configured for the profiler in this example, `torch.profiler.schedule(wait = 1, warmup = 1, active =5, repeat = 10, skip_first = True)`. This is useful to minimize the overhead of profiling on the run, but it poses the risk of not capturing the usage appropriately. This is why high-level continuous monitoring is useful and schedule settings should be tweaked to ensure you get good coverage.

The system metrics also indicate that CPU utilization peaked at 410% in this run. Observing the main process via a tool like `htop` shows that it has a virtual size of a whopping 453 GB, which includes the physical memory, swap memory, files on disk that have been mapped into the process (e.g., shared libraries), and shared memory space (shared with other processes, for example).

Figure 4-2 shows the top 10 operations that took the longest time to compute, with the batch matrix-to-matrix operation `aten::bmm` accounting for the largest percentage of the time, at 15.2%. Increasing the batch size would allow you to reduce the total number of steps (that is, the total number of times this operation needs to be called per epoch).

At a batch size of 12, the total number of steps sums to 184. Hypothetically speaking, if the batch size were to be doubled to 24, the number of steps would be reduced to 92. Given the vectorized nature of the `aten::bmm` operation, if you had more compute cycles available, doubling the batch size would effectively halve the cost of this computation. However, as you increase the batch size the memory requirements to hold the input tensor (the token embedding) will increase, and so will the amount of memory required to hold the gradients. The gradients' memory requirement scales linearly with batch size; that is, the space complexity is given by $O(batch\_size)$. The implication for sample-wise losses and metrics would also increase in the same order.

For this reason, it's important to find the optimum balance between CPU and memory (both physical and virtual). In this instance, on the available CPU hardware, using a batch size of 24 was simply not possible as the system was running into out-of-memory (OOM) issues. In fact, even with a batch size of 12 the host system was sporadically unresponsive. There are autotuning techniques like Torch Memory-adaptive Algorithms (TOMA) (*https://oreil.ly/C2bvp*) that can find the most suitable batch size by retrying with a lower size if OOM errors occur; using these tricks can remove the manual overhead of right-sizing the batch size, and they can be easily enabled by using the `lightning.pytorch.tuner.Tuner.scale_batch_size()` API (*https://oreil.ly/RtPIi*).

As discussed in Chapter 3, managing the memory requirements by reducing the precision of the tensors is also an option; however, standard CPUs do not have specialized hardware for the various floating-point formats mentioned there. Accelerator units are more specialized in data crunching and have additional hardware to support lower-precision compute; CPUs are general-purpose hardware where this support is largely absent or emulated.

Given that at a batch size of 12 the system was sporadically unresponsive and took an average of 304 seconds to complete one step, it would take about 15.5 hours to finish one epoch (184 steps). Function tracing, as provided by a profiling tool such as the PyTorch profiler used in this example, is very helpful in understanding the duration and nature of operations that are occupying the process space (see Figure 4-3). This is useful in identifying suboptimal calls for further optimizations.

Figure 4-3. Function tracing provided by the PyTorch profiler when this example is run on a CPU

The main takeaway from this exercise is that right-sizing the memory and number of CPU cores and tuning the batch size will help you to get the best out of CPU-based training. However, the turnaround time for deep learning on a CPU may be insufficient—15+ hours for one epoch, as in this case, is a very impractical feedback cycle for rapid development and a good user experience.

In this following section, we'll look at how this example can be scaled out on a heterogeneous computer using a CPU similar to the one used in this section in conjunction with an NVIDIA A100 80 GB GPU.

Running on a GPU

In Chapter 3, you read about the execution model for accelerated computing and learned how the host/CPU facilitates operator (i.e., kernel) execution on a GPU in a parallelized fashion. You also learned about the steps involved to transfer data from the host into GPU memory and the overhead this may cause because of limited bandwidth.

In this exercise, the model input (data) pipeline loads the text data in memory, performs preprocessing and tokenization, and generates the embedding, as shown in Figure 4-1. These embeddings—the matrix tensors—are loaded into the GPU's VRAM. Then, as the computation proceeds, various kernel functions are called on the GPU to perform the required operations in a vectorized fashion over its thousands of cores.

Figure 4-4 is a screen grab obtained from a function trace of a training run of this example on an NVIDIA A100 SXM 80 GB GPU. The top trace pertains to a thread, spun up by the main process, that handles communication between the device and the host. This trace also shows another thread on the same host that manages the CPU-bound computations (e.g., the model input pipeline). The bottom part of the figure shows the stack for the thread corresponding to GPU computation. Note the corresponding dip in the streaming multiprocessor when the memory copy operations are in flight. The lowest row indicates the elapsed time for each of the kernel functions invoked during the stages of profiling. Notice how different the tracing obtained from a CPU and a GPU is (Figures 4-3 and 4-4, respectively).

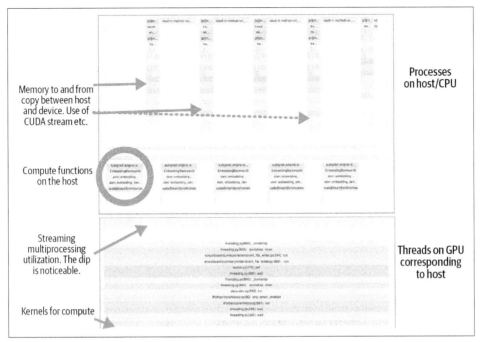

Memory to and from copy between host and device. Use of CUDA stream etc.

Compute functions on the host

Processes on host/CPU

Streaming multiprocessing utilization. The dip is noticeable.

Threads on GPU corresponding to host

Kernels for compute

Figure 4-4. Function tracing provided by PyTorch profiler when run on a GPU

To run this example on a GPU, you can use the same command you used to run it on a CPU (see "Running the Example" on page 120). Because the code is written to be platform-agnostic, no changes are needed. However, you will need to ensure that your hardware has an NVIDIA driver and runtime installed. Since one of the goals of this exercise is to be able to monitor the usage, you'll also need to have the CUDA Profiling Tools Interface (CUPTI) (*https://oreil.ly/aA7ZN*) installed. For pointers to the complete setup instructions, refer to "Setting Up Your Environment for Hands-on Exercises" on page xv.

 CUDA kernel profiling tools like CUPTI and NVProf are extremely helpful, but they only provide operator/kernel-level profiles. Unfortunately, they do not provide a higher-level perspective such as of the neural layer. This contextualization needs to be done by the user.

The first observation to make when running this exercise on an A100 80 GB GPU is that the memory utilization of the host has dropped significantly to marginal. In addition, at a batch size of 12 only about 40 GB of VRAM on the GPU is used. Also noteworthy is that the average step time has dropped to 4 s from 304 s on a pure CPU run. As you can see in Figure 4-5, GPU utilization is at 94.5%, with 0.4% used for memory copy, 1.5% for CPU-bound operations, and 3.7% for other operations. Notably, `DataLoaders` continue to account for a marginal fraction of this.

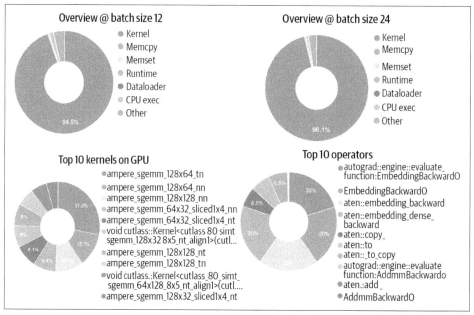

Figure 4-5. Screenshots of function/operator tracing and GPU kernel profiling obtained from the run of this example when trained on heterogeneous compute with an NVIDIA GPU

We have 80 GB and only 50% is used. Let's now increase the batch size to 24. The ideal utilization should be 100%, in theory, indicating all cores are being utilized at max capacity. At a batch size of 24, there is an increase of less than 2% in GPU utilization (to 96.1%), as shown on the right in Figure 4-5. There is a corresponding drop in CPU execution and "other" operation.

Looking at the bottom of Figure 4-5, we can see that when a GPU is brought into the mix the longest-running operator is no longer `aten::bmm` (as in the case of the CPU-only run, shown in Figure 4-2). Now, the most expensive operation is `auto grad::engine::evaluate_function:EmbeddingBackward0`, which pertains to gradient computation during automatic differentiation (i.e., backward propagation). The reason for this difference is that the batch matrix-to-matrix operation `aten::bmm` is much more easily scaled out on a GPU, and the turnaround drops massively because of parallelization. This is essentially a good application of Amdahl's law, since the scalable part of the computation—the matrix operation—is parallelized. Other expensive operations are related to copying, which is indicative of the challenges with memory loads.

As expected, as batch size increases, an increase in GPU utilization and a decrease in step time are observed. However, there is no impact on the order of top operations. The trace, as shown in Figure 4-5, continues to be similar, albeit with an increase in the utilization stats.

As discussed in Chapter 3, most modern accelerators, including NVIDIA GPUs, come with computation units for various precision formats. The A100 specifically comes with Tensor Core units capable of estimating the appropriate level of precision and executing at that level. The three available modes, `highest`, `high`, and `medium`, pertain to decreasing orders of internal precision, with the highest level ensuring the use of single-precision floating-point numbers (32-bit). Using the following configuration to activate this capability, you will notice a time savings of about 0.7 s per step at the medium precision level, for a new average step time of 3.3 s:

```
torch.backends.cuda.matmul.allow_tf32 = True
torch.set_float32_matmul_precision("medium")
```

As the profiler indicates, only about 37.6% of the GPU computation used the Tensor Core, indicating other operators were perhaps not compatible with the `tf32` format. This level of understanding is really helpful in optimizing the training run because it clarifies where most of the compute and memory expense is and, if critical, allows alternatives to these to be explored.

If you compare the model's accuracy with and without `tf32` enablement, you'll find that the impact of the loss of precision is negligible in this case. However, depending on your circumstances, it can be worth making this trade-off. This trick uses the Tensor Core architecture, which is specific to NVIDIA's Ampere and later GPU series. If your hardware is not equipped with Tensor Core capability, simplifying using standard-precision formats like `fp16` or mixed `fp16` may provide a significant gain too. We'll talk more about this in "Mixed precision" on page 139.

The activation of `tf32` compute overlaps with mixed-precision training. Depending on the `tf32` support of the operators used in your model, the use of mixed precision in addition to enabling `tf32` may provide advantages, but how much is dependent on your model and its functions.

Transitioning from Language to Vision

The exercise discussed here covers many aspects of language models. Before the Transformer architectures, the nuances of input modality (e.g., text, vision) drove the core modeling techniques and required specialized knowledge in dealing with domains specific to different input types. Just as sequence models dominated the language domain, convolution techniques were heavily used in computer vision models. The use of different modeling techniques per input modality is now reducing, as

Transformers are emerging as a ubiquitous technique with applicability across input modalities. Transformer-based architectures like Vision Transformer (ViT)[6] and Masked-attention Mask Transformer (Mask2Former)[7] are proving performant. Transformer networks have quadratic computation complexity with regard to the input dimension, however, which when applied to multimedia contents such as pixelated images explodes the resource requirements. Depending on the complexity of the task at hand, convolutional architectures may provide computationally less demanding yet efficient implementations.

The following section focuses on a computer vision exercise, using the convolution technique.

Hands-On Exercise #2: Vision Model with Convolution

The task for this exercise is to generate segmentation results for the images in the MIT Scene Parsing Benchmark (SceneParse150) dataset (*https://oreil.ly/ItHQf*), which are annotated with 150 categories of objects. Accounting for background or unknown, in total, you will be segmenting for 151 classes (*https://oreil.ly/XMBIA*). This exercise demonstrates the scale channel where the number of classes for which you are segmenting is fairly large.

Model Architecture

This exercise leverages convolutional neural networks (CNNs), a computer vision–based deep learning technique. More specifically, you will be using EfficientNet as a feature encoder and Convolve as a decoder blocker, assembled into a U-Net-based architecture.[8]

Key contributors to scale in the scene parsing exercise

Let's take a closer look at some of the key techniques used in this exercise. These techniques help with scaling to process large images for large numbers of classes in an efficient and scalable manner.

---

6 Dosovitskiy, Alexey, Lucas Beyer, Alexander Kolesnikov, Dirk Weissenborn, Xiaohua Zhai, Thomas Unterthiner, Mostafa Dehghani, et al. 2021. "An Image Is Worth 16x16 Words: Transformers for Image Recognition at Scale." arXiv, June 3, 2021. *https://arxiv.org/abs/2010.11929*.

7 Cheng, Bowen, Ishan Misra, Alexander G. Schwing, Alexander Kirillov, Rohit Girdhar. 2022. "Masked-Attention Mask Transformer for Universal Image Segmentation." arXiv, June 15, 2022. *https://arxiv.org/abs/2112.01527*.

8 Tan and Le, "EfficientNet: Rethinking Model Scaling for Convolutional Neural Networks," *https://arxiv.org/abs/1905.11946*; Ronneberger, Olaf, Philipp Fischer, and Thomas Brox. 2015. "U-Net: Convolutional Networks for Biomedical Image Segmentation." arXiv, May 18, 2015. *https://arxiv.org/abs/1505.04597*.

Scaling with convolutions. One of the main challenges when working with images is the scale of input. A 512x512 three-channel (color) image will have an input vector of size 786,432. The size of the input vector increases linearly with the increase in height or width of the images. However, these inputs are not independent; there is also a structural (spatial) and textural correlation that exists in the images. With a motivation to develop more efficient techniques to learn from images, convolutional networks were envisaged to exploit this correlation of image feature properties, leveraging sparsity and parameter sharing.

CNNs, first proposed by Yann LeCun in the 1980s,[9] were inspired by the computer vision technique "convolving," heavily used in image processing techniques like edge detection, blurring, etc. These techniques apply predetermined filters F of size fxf over the image in a sliding window operation shifting by stride s, effectively reducing the number of operations by a factor of s. This filtering operation is translation invariant because the same filter—say, the edge detection filter F—can be used to extract an edge from anywhere in the image (in the center, along an edge, or otherwise). The filters of the convolution layers (as in deep learning) are learned during backpropagation. The reusability of these learned filters F (see Equation 4-1) makes CNNs quite interesting and highly optimized, as not only is the number of parameters required in a CNN massively reduced, but they're also shared across each stride. This phenomenon is commonly known as *weight sharing*. Andrew Ng's Stanford CS230 lecture notes and Piotr Skalski's "Gentle Dive into Math Behind Convolutional Neural Networks" are good sources to explore the working of convolution layers further.[10]

Equation 4-1. Mathematical formula used by convolution layers for feature extraction from images

$$\sum_a^{f-1} \sum_b^{f-1} F_{ab} x_{(i+a)(j+b)}$$

The architecture of LeCun's CNN, LeNet-5, is shown in Figure 4-6.

9 LeCun, Y., B. Boser, J.S. Denker, D. Henderson, R.E. Howard, W. Hubbard, and L.D. Jackel. 1989. "Backpropagation Applied to Handwritten Zip Code Recognition." *Neural Computation* 1, no. 4: 541–51. *https://doi.org/10.1162/neco.1989.1.4.541.*

10 Ng, Andrew. *n.d.* Stanford CS230 lecture notes. *https://cs230.stanford.edu/files/C4M1.pdf.*; Skalski, Piotr. "Gentle Dive into Math Behind Convolutional Neural Networks." Towards Data Science, April 12, 2019. *https://oreil.ly/odnbI.*

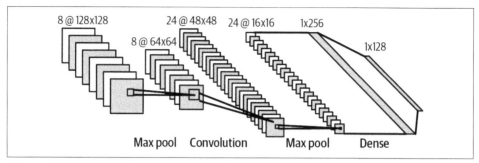

8 @ 128x128   24 @ 48x48   24 @ 16x16   1x256
8 @ 64x64   1x128

Max pool   Convolution   Max pool   Dense

Figure 4-6. LeNet-5 architecture (Source: https://alexlenail.me/NN-SVG/LeNet.html)

Scaling with EfficientNet.   EfficientNet, as the name indicates, is a neural network architecture that uses compound scaling, as shown in Figure 4-7, to scale out convolutional models in an efficient manner. It combines scaling across depth, width, and resolution in a more effective way to obtain a more performant model that maximizes resource use. EfficientNet was developed using a technique called neural architecture search (a subfield of AutoML) that you will read about in Chapter 11.

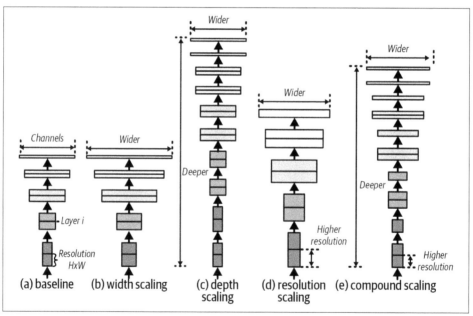

Figure 4-7. EfficientNet architecture (adapted from Tan and Le, 2019)

Implementation

As mentioned earlier, the final architecture used in the exercise is U-Net,[11] which uses EfficientNet as a backbone (see Figure 4-8).

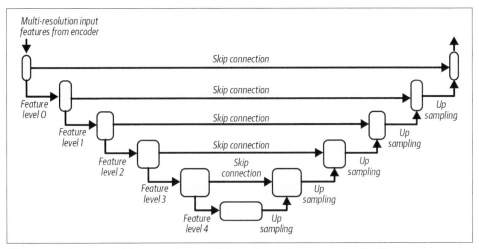

Figure 4-8. U-Net architecture (adapted from Ronneberger et al., 2015)

The code for this exercise is located in the *chapter_4* folder (*https://oreil.ly/Iaqxu*) of the book's code repository. Let's take a look at the implementation:

vision_model.py

> The model implementation is in UNetSegmentationModel. It wires up the EfficientNet encoder from the Hugging Face library timm and connects it with another head designed for the segmentation task. This head, the Decoder, acts as a feature decoder tasked with generating segmentation output. The EfficientNet encoder provides multilevel features that are combined with the decoder outputs in a hierarchical fashion, as shown in the U-Net skip connection architecture (see Figure 4-8).

> As in the previous exercise, this example uses PyTorch Lightning to leverage its ability to write infrastructure-agnostic code. The VisionSegmentationModule provides the LightningModule implementation.

---

11 Ronneberger et al., "U-Net: Convolutional Networks for Biomedical Image Segmentation," *https://arxiv.org/abs/1505.04597*.

dataset.py

The dataset implementation is in the `SceneParsingModule`, which wraps the SceneParse150 dataset. Note the specialized transformation used in this case to handle converting the images to tensors.

app.py

The entry point to this exercise is defined in *app.py*, in the method `train_vision_model`. Notice the use of `VisionSegmentationModule` and `SceneParsingModule` here. Otherwise, the implementation for this entry point is very similar to the previous exercise's entry point, `train_gpt2`.

Running the Example

To run the code for this example, execute the following command from your environment:

```
deep-learning-at-scale chapter_4 train_efficient_unet
```

Observations

The maximum number of samples that can fit in the memory of an A100 80 GB GPU is 85. On the baseline run of this sample, an average step time of 3.3 s per iteration can be achieved. This is higher than the step time observed in the GPT-2 example. One reason for the high latency is that a very large volume of data (85 images) is read, decoded, and further processed, creating an I/O-intensive process. This is a common challenge for vision-based modeling tasks.

We've now gone through two hands-on examples and explored various techniques they employ to develop efficient and effective models. In the following sections, you will learn about some orthogonal techniques to speed up your training code and explore the trade-offs of these techniques.

Graph Compilation Using PyTorch 2.0

As discussed in Chapter 2, PyTorch is a dynamic graph computation engine that incurs an additional cost of graph compilation. As you saw in Chapter 3, this cost is usually relatively small compared to the cost of the matrix computation required by the network—but as accelerators are getting faster, this gap is narrowing. Also, as deep learning practices are evolving, more practitioners are writing custom accelerated/GPU kernels to speed up their code. Ease of use is the first principle in the design of the PyTorch framework and APIs. However, the C++ development required for CUDA kernels reduced their usability for the deep learning practitioners who needed custom CUDA operators.

PyTorch 2.0 addresses both of the aforementioned challenges through its innovative approach to providing better performance and supporting dynamic tensor shapes while being backward compatible. These capabilities are realized by making compiler-level changes for graph execution. The frame evaluation API added to CPython in Python 3.6 via PEP 532 (also discussed in Chapter 2) has been critical in this design.

New Components of PyTorch 2.0

To provide this graph-compilation capability, four new components were added in PyTorch 2.0: PrimTorch, TorchDynamo, AOTAutograd, and TorchInductor. PrimTorch is a simplified minimal set of primitive operators that facilitates writing complex operators in Python. The main emphasis of this component is to support easier development of custom hardware-specific kernel functions that would otherwise have required complex C++ development with a corresponding CPython interface for Python.

TorchDynamo is an effort to provide graph compilation capability without losing usability by tracing dynamically using Python bytecode transformation. TorchScript, as mentioned in Chapter 2, followed a similar philosophy of tracing the graph to obtain a more efficient variant. However, TorchScript is limited in its ability to handle control flows. PyTorch offers a few other tracing utilities, like torch.fx and PyTorch/XLA (*https://oreil.ly/tKksZ*), but the key difference with TorchDynamo is the use of the frame evaluation API. In fact, torch.fx has now been migrated into TorchDynamo (see Figure 4-9).

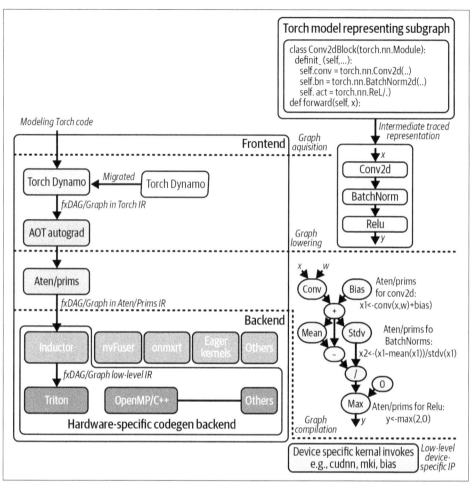

Figure 4-9. Key components of PyTorch 2.0 facilitating the ability to produce compiled graphs

Graph Execution in PyTorch 2.0

Graph execution in PyTorch 2.0 consists of three steps: graph acquisition, lowering, and compilation. Let's take a look at each of these in turn.

Graph acquisition

Your model computation graph is composed using a set of subgraph (i.e., `torch.nn.Module`) implementations. These subgraphs are compiled and consolidated (flattened) by one of the many backends of TorchDynamo (`aot_ts_nvfuser`, `cuda graphs`, `inductor`, `ipex`, `nvprims_nvfuser`, `onnxrt`, `tvm`), where possible. This compilation saves the overhead of generating graphs dynamically on every iteration (as is done in PyTorch 1.x, as discussed in Chapter 2). The caveat here is that, because of the Pythonic nature of PyTorch, not all of your control flow operations can be compiled into graphs or subgraphs. These unsupported parts of your control flow are integrated into the execution phase by falling back to eager mode. This seamless switching, made possible by the frame evaluation API, offers an effective technique to leverage the graph compilation capability of PyTorch 2.0. The efficiency it provides without losing ease of use while still being Pythonic is great. The PyTorch Dev Discussion thread "TorchDynamo: An Experiment in Dynamic Python Bytecode Transformation" (*https://oreil.ly/NzyrG*) discusses the internals in greater detail.

The following snippet demonstrates how the trace is realized using conv_block (*https://oreil.ly/Q63Ie*), which we used in the earlier vision exercises:

```
from torch.fx import symbolic_trace
symbolic_traced : torch.fx.GraphModule = symbolic_trace(conv_block)
```

The internal representation obtained via PyTorch's trace is shown here. This is another representation of the graph computation shown in Figure 4-9:

```
print(symbolic_traced.graph)
graph():
    %x : [#users=1] = placeholder[target=x]
    %conv : [#users=1] = call_module[target=conv](args = (%x,), kwargs = {})
    %bn : [#users=1] = call_module[target=bn](args = (%conv,), kwargs = {})
    %act : [#users=1] = call_module[target=act](args = (%bn,), kwargs = {})
    return act
```

The same graph, visualized in tabular format, is shown here, indicating the connectivity between the operations and input and outputs:

```
symbolic_traced.graph.print_tabular()
opcode          name     target    args       kwargs
-----------     ------   --------  -------    --------
placeholder     x        x         ()         {}
call_module     conv     conv      (x,)       {}
call_module     bn       bn        (conv,)    {}
call_module     act      act       (bn,)      {}
output          output   output    (act,)     {}
```

Graph lowering

In the graph lowering stage, all the graph operations are decomposed into their constituent kernels, specific to the chosen backend. In this step, the internal representation (IR) of the graph is obtained. PyTorch's ATen and primitive components (*https://oreil.ly/HJHqh*), a.k.a. *prims*, handle this stage. At this stage, the graph is more aligned/prepared for hardware-specific invocation.

Graph compilation

The graph compilation phase is when the kernels from the IR obtained in the preceding phase get translated to their corresponding low-level device-specific operations. This phase requires the backend to perform the compilation and also execute device-specific kernels. TorchInductor (a.k.a. `inductor`), the default engine for compilation, uses OpenAI Triton under the hood. However, other backends (such as `aot_ts_nvfuser`, `cudagraphs`, `ipex`, `nvprims_nvfuser`, `onnxrt`, and `tvm`) are also being actively developed.

In Chapter 2, you learned about the data flow of deep learning and compute requirements for arithmetic operations. In this section, you looked at clever improvements in PyTorch to mitigate dynamic graph inefficiencies. In the following section, we'll explore tricks and techniques, including graph compilation, that can be employed to train models efficiently on a single device.

Modeling Techniques to Scale Training on a Single Device

Most of the techniques described in this section are orthogonal and can be applied in combination or independently. These techniques can help you achieve efficiency by increasing computational speed or reducing memory requirements.

Graph Compilation

To leverage the advantages of using a compiled graph, use the orthogonal API `torch.compile`. Applying `torch.compile` on `torch.nn.Module` converts it to the `OptimizedModule` type, an internal representation for optimized graph modules. As per the benchmarks documented in PyTorch issue #93794 (*https://oreil.ly/cCV22*), this provides a 30% to 200% gain in performance depending on the type of architecture and underlying implementation.

The argument `fullgraph` is used to generate a static graph without eager mode fallback between the subgraphs. If your module does not have control flow (`if`/`else` and other conditional flows), then your chances of obtaining this type of graph will be higher. In general, using `fullgraph` will be a more efficient approach wherever possible. You can also choose your backend, as discussed previously; this defaults to `inductor` (see Figure 4-9).

There are three modes of compilation:

`default`

The default mode compiles the graph using the chosen backend, but does so efficiently without taking too much time or memory. In general, this mode will be more advantageous for large models.

`reduce-overhead`

This mode aims to remove overhead from the underlying framework and thus takes longer to compile and uses a small amount of extra memory. The `reduce-overhead` mode is more effective if your model and step inputs are smaller.

`max-autotune`

As the name indicates, this mode aims to provide a compiled graph with maximal tuning, which is thus faster. However, the compilation phase will be the longest of the three.

To see the difference before and after compilation, set the `mode` parameter, as shown here:

```
torch.compile(self.model, mode = "max-autotune")
```

and execute the following command from your environment:

```
deep-learning-at-scale chapter_4 train_gpt2 --use-compile
```

To observe the standard eager mode behavior, which is also the default behavior of the example script, run the same command with `--no-use-compile` instead.

 If you run into issues with compilation or notice suboptimal performance, using the environment variable `TORCH_LOGS=` `"graph_breaks,recompiles"` may help with debugging.

When running this example on an A100 SXM 80 GB GPU, you may note that at single precision (`fp32`), 24 is the optimal batch size for training. A batch size bigger than 24 will lead to OOM errors. You'll also find that by compiling the graph with the `default` option, you can get a 5% gain in the efficiency of your training compared to the baseline non-compile eager mode computation. Changing the mode to `max-autotune` will bump the gain to 12%. As the TorchDynamo error logs may indicate, the network is not fully Dynamo-compliant (due, for example, to the use of list objects). Fixing these errors will provide a higher gain in efficiency. Generally, the use of lists in training should be discouraged, especially in `DataLoaders`, as they can cause memory blowout due to how Python multiprocessing pickles list objects (see PyTorch issue #13246 (*https://oreil.ly/P5X5I*) for a discussion of this issue).

One of the techniques you can use to move from lists to tensors is to stack them (i.e., using `torch.stack([...]))`, if they are of the same dimensions. Otherwise, you can add padding to obtain a max-size stacked tensor. If your use case is specialized and neither of those tricks helps, you can try writing custom objects with suitable handling to implement the `.to()` method to handle device transfer.

In this section, you learned about a one-liner trick to gain about a 15% increase in efficiency. In the following section, you will explore how to gain more speed at the expense of precision.

Reduced- and Mixed-Precision Training

The memory consumed during training can be classified into two categories: memory consumed by model states and by residual states. We'll talk more about this in Chapter 9, but for now let's focus on the memory requirements during training in absolute form. These are determined by the following categories of numeric data, which are loaded in memory:

- Model parameters (weights and biases)
- Input data (generally loaded in chunks in memory)
- Activations/feature map (the results of the computations; i.e., the features extracted from the input data)
- Gradients (the error gradients required for backpropagation and error correction)
- Optimizer states (estimated to occupy 33–75% of memory)[12]
- Metrics and losses (numeric values to observe and monitor the progress of the training regime)

While the activation memory requirements are transitional, they scale linearly with the number of model parameters and size of the input data. Likewise, the memory requirements for backpropagation (i.e., gradients) increase linearly with batch size and number of parameters. Metrics and losses, in general, have negligible memory requirements. However, depending on the nature of the metrics (e.g., micro or macro), the requirements can scale on the order of the model's task objective. For example, storing metrics for a simple binary classifier will require much less space than storing micro-metrics for the 151-class multiclass/multilabel classifier we looked at earlier in this chapter. Likewise, for object detection/localization tasks such as semantic or instance segmentation, the metrics requirements might be extensive (e.g., MaskIoU and mean/average/precision calculation for various object sizes, as is done in Mask R-CNN models).

Training is typically done using the standard single-precision floating-point format (fp32). Various less precise formats, as listed in Table 3-1 in "Floating-point standards" on page 73, can be used to speed up training, both by increasing the batch size

---

12 Dettmers, Tim, Mike Lewis, Sam Shleifer, and Luke Zettlemoyer. 2022. "8-Bit Optimizers via Block-wise Quantization." arXiv, June 20, 2022. *https://arxiv.org/abs/2110.02861.*

(by reducing memory requirements as a result of the required data containers) and by leveraging the capabilities of hardware-optimized computation devices. Using a lower-precision format (e.g., fp16) may lead to suboptimal models. However, in scenarios where a highly precise outcome is not critical, the gain in efficiency achieved by reducing precision can be huge.

Mixed precision

Mixed precision, a technique that combines single- and half-precision floating-point formats, can also be used to manage the trade-off between computational efficiency and numerical accuracy. The Torch package `torch.cuda.amp` provides an implementation that enables the use of mixed precision for CUDA-compatible devices. Automatic mixed precision is realized by the `torch.cuda.amp.autocast` feature, which can manage data type conversions automatically. The Tensor Core architecture used in NVIDIA's Ampere and later GPU series can also multiply half-precision matrices, accumulating the result in either a single- or a half-precision output. All of these techniques facilitate mixed-precision training.

 When using automatic mixed precision, you should refrain from explicitly casting your tensors to any specific data type. Explicit casting hinders the automatic precision conversion, leading to suboptimal results.

There is a small memory penalty associated with mixed-precision training, because two copies of the model weights are loaded: one at single precision and the other at half precision. In effect, the memory requirements amount to 1.5x the requirements at single precision. Mixed precision is already implemented in the `torch.cuda.amp` and Lightning libraries, so you can enable it merely by calling `Trainer(precision = "16-mixed")`.

 Mixed precision is primarily an accelerated device feature. The standard CPU computers do not offer lower-precision compute capabilities. As a result, you will note that automatic mixed precision is generally supported only for training on heterogeneous systems. Mixed precision is also a relatively new implementation (introduced around 2017); as a result, older GPUs may not have support built in for such training.

The effect of precision on gradients

Because gradients are calculated based on the error factor (i.e., the contribution of the parameters to the error), the value can be either too small or too large. Too large a gradient results in overflowing values, leading to numerical instability in computation. This phenomenon is termed the *exploding gradients* problem.[13] As the numerical precision decreases, the capacity to hold a larger mantissa reduces, resulting in a higher risk of numerical overflow. Likewise, the capacity to hold very precise floating-point differences decreases, leading to an increased risk of underflow. Neither of the two scenarios is nice to have. Gradient scaling and clipping are two techniques that help avoid overflow and underflow issues during backward propagation.

Gradient scaling. PyTorch's gradient scaler, as the name indicates, scales out gradients to manage the precision loss. Generally, the scaler is initialized:

```
scaler = torch.cuda.amp.GradScaler()
```

and used during the training loop to scale the loss before backpropagation:

```
scaler.scale(loss).backward()
```

Frameworks like Lightning automatically take care of gradient scaling when mixed precision is used. This is why you may note that this chapter's hands-on examples do not feature an explicit use of `GradScaler`.

Gradient clipping. Gradient clipping is used to mitigate exploding gradients. Typically, the clipping is performed either on the value of the gradient or the norm of the gradient. In effect, it caps the maximum value (or norm) of the gradient during the training loop.

Lightning comes with a `clip_gradients` capability that can be activated via the infrastructure wiring code (e.g., by using `Trainer(gradient_clip_val = 0.5)`) and can be further customized using the `configure_gradient_clipping` function override of your `LightningModule`. You can find more detailed information in the documentation (*https://oreil.ly/Ut1dn*).

8-bit optimizers and quantization. As discussed previously, the data containers for gradients, even in mixed-precision training, are kept at `fp32`. Efforts to change the gradient precision to `fp16` have proven to lead to less than desirable results, because the variance in gradients can be large (depending on how each of the parameters contributes to the error). The challenge with gradient scaling and clipping is that both of these tricks are applied consistently across the entire gradient tensor.

Dynamic tree quantization is another interesting technique that can trade off between bits required to represent the mantissa and exponent (discussed in Chapter 3), by using an indicator bit to signal the beginning of the fractional partition of the number (see Figure 4-10). This dynamic quantization allows for right-sizing the

---

13 Bengio, Y., P. Simard, and P. Frasconi. 1994. "Learning Long-Term Dependencies with Gradient Descent Is Difficult." *IEEE Transactions on Neural Networks* 5, no. 2: 157–66. *https://doi.org/10.1109/72.279181*.

data type, resulting in more accurate outcomes. The gradient statistics (i.e., the optimizer states), however, are kept in lower-precision formats. Block quantization is another quantization technique that quantizes the optimizer states in chunks, providing better precision than half-precision and only slightly inferior precision to single-precision counterparts.

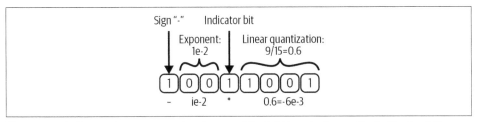

Figure 4-10. Dynamic tree quantization used in 8-bit optimizers: the indicator bit moves dynamically and allows for trade-offs between the fractional and decimal parts of the number (adapted from Dettmers et al., 2022)

The `bitsandbytes` library (*https://oreil.ly/SUEWg*) provides custom CUDA kernels that leverage dynamic tree quantization in addition to block quantization to provide a more accurate yet performant implementation of a suite of optimizers, including Adam. These implementations (e.g., `bnb.optim.Adam8bit`) can be swapped for `torch.optim.Adam` as a one-line change. (You may need a custom compilation of the library, however, based on your version of the NVIDIA runtime.) You will be using this library in the hands-on exercises in Chapters 7 and 9.

A mixed-precision algorithm

Considering the challenges mentioned previously, the summarized algorithm for mixed-precision training is given as follows:

1. Start with a master copy of weights at single precision (`fp32`).
2. Obtain another half-precision (`fp16`) copy of the weights.
3. Perform a forward pass using `fp16` weights and activations.
4. Scale the resulting loss by the scale factor *S*.
5. Perform a backward pass using the weights (`fp16`), activations (`fp16`), and their gradients (`fp32`).
6. Scale down the gradients by a factor of *S* (i.e., multiply by 1/*S*).
7. Execute additional optional gradient tricks such as gradient clipping, weight decay, etc.
8. Update the gradient statistics (`fp16`) in the optimizer states.
9. Update the master copy of weights (at `fp32`).

10. Repeat the iteration loop given by steps 3–9 until convergence.

Memory Tricks for Efficiency

As outlined in Chapter 1, efficiency is a crucial consideration in scaling. In this section we'll look at a few memory tricks that may be helpful in model development in memory-constrained environments.

Memory layout

The n-dimensional tensors need to be presented in 1D address space in memory. The memory layout defines the storage of n-dimensional tensors, describing how the tensors will be collapsed into the address space. Row-major and column-major are two commonly used formats to lay out the n-dimensional tensors contiguously in memory. As shown in Figure 4-11, row-major is analogous to the batch (N), channel (C), height (H), and width (W)–based scheme (i.e., NCHW, a.k.a. channels first), while column-major is analogous to the NHWC (channels last) scheme.

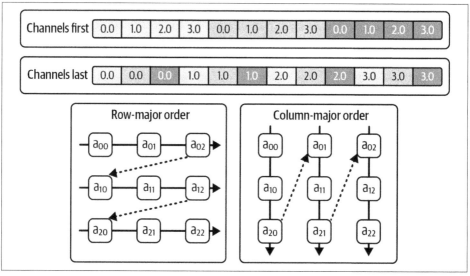

Figure 4-11. Memory layout of channels-first and channels-last tensors

If your operation parallelizes on the channel first, then storing and accessing tensors using the channels-first layout will be more efficient. Other image-based modeling techniques—specifically, convolutions that operate on and exploit spatial correlation of signals in images—access tensors in a more pixel-wise fashion. Thus, for convolution-based techniques, channels last may be a more efficient layout choice. PyTorch supports optionally switching to the channels-last memory layout and supports computation on the same native formats by implementing kernels for a series of operators (*https://oreil.ly/yIs-P*) in channels-last format in addition to the default channels-first format.

 Both PyTorch and NVIDIA cuDNN default to the channel-first (NCHW) layout. However, oneDNN and XNNPACK, the libraries PyTorch uses for pure CPU computation, default to channels last (NHWC). Aligning the layout across the entire stack provides more efficient execution of the training loop; otherwise, the access pattern of data becomes suboptimal, incurring a penalty during access of subtensors for relevant operations.

On a CPU, using the channels-last format for convolution-based networks can provide up to a 1.8x time performance gain through appropriate memory access patterns implemented by convolution, pooling, and upsampling layers.[14]

To switch the memory layout, you invoke .to(memory_format = torch.chan nels_last) on either the tensor or the module (to indicate operator preference).

In the second hands-on example in this chapter, you may note images = images.to(memory_format = torch.channels_last) and self.model = self.model.to(memory_format = torch.channels_last) applied when channels last execution is requested. Try this using the following command:

```
deep-learning-at-scale chapter_4 train-efficient-unet --use-channel-last
```

On a single A100 SXM 80 GB GPU, using the channels-last format provides about a 10% gain in performance compared to the channels-first configuration.

Likewise, when running the same example on the CPU with the mps backend, using channels last provides a 17% increase in performance over channels first with the same resource settings (a step time of 51.84 s per iteration, down from 62.48 s).

Feature compression

The pervasiveness of memory challenges in deep learning practice is indicated by how commonly GPU OOM errors are faced.[15] The use of data compression (both lossy and lossless) has been explored to reduce the memory footprint of feature maps

---

14 Ma, Mingfei, Vitaly Fedyunin, and Wei Wei. "Accelerating PyTorch Vision Models with Channels Last on CPU." PyTorch blog, August 24, 2022. *https://oreil.ly/Dr3Tt.*

15 Zhang, Ru, Wencong Xiao, Hongyu Zhang, Yu Liu, Haoxiang Lin, and Mao Yang. 2020. "An Empirical Study on Program Failures of Deep Learning Jobs." In *Proceedings of the ACM/IEEE 42nd International Conference on Software Engineering (ICSE '20)*, 1159–70. *https://doi.org/10.1145/3377811.3380362.*

from the forward pass until they are required again during backward propagation.[16] This technique can reduce the memory requirement by an average of 1.8x; however, it incurs performance overhead from compression/decompression and increased CPU-to-GPU communication. In general, this approach can be useful if there is sparsity or redundancy in the feature maps, but the observed gains will vary highly depending on the nature of the model and data.

Meta and fake tensors

Meta tensors are PyTorch's underlying mechanism to represent shape and data type without actually allocating memory for storage. PyTorch's *fake tensors* are very similar to meta tensors, except that a meta tensor is allocated to an abstract "meta" device whereas fake tensors are allocated to concrete devices (CPUs, GPUs, TPUs, etc.).

A meta tensor is initialized as follows:

```
meta_layer = torch.nn.Linear(100000, 100000, device = "meta")
```

We'll talk more about meta and fake tensors in Chapter 8, where we'll consider their importance in managing memory in a scaled-up setting.

Optimizer Efficiencies

So far you have looked at several techniques to improve the efficiency of your training runs, including using graph compilation and changing the memory layout and data formats. In this section, you will learn about some gradient tricks to scale out your training on a single host with at most one GPU.

Stochastic gradient descent (SGD)

Early versions of optimizers, such as gradient descent, used the entire training dataset in one step to derive the gradient. But as the dataset size begins to increase, because of memory limitations of computing devices, gradient descent becomes a bottleneck during training. To address this, an approximation technique called *stochastic gradient descent* (SGD) was devised. With this technique, instead of deriving gradients over the entire sample, the gradients are propagated in batches to arrive at an approximately comparable model.

SGD and other iterative gradient descent techniques are so commonly used these days that one tends to ignore their importance in scaling out large datasets. These techniques are only effective if the batch size is suitable for universal approximation. To develop a model to perform a complex task requiring learning over a highly var-

---

16 Jain, Animesh, Amar Phanishayee, Jason Mars, Lingjia Tang, and Gennady Pekhimenko. 2018. "Gist: Efficient Data Encoding for Deep Neural Network Training." In *ACM/IEEE 45th Annual International Symposium on Computer Architecture (ISCA)*, 776–89. *https://doi.org/10.1109/ISCA.2018.00070*.

iant dataset, larger batch sizes are needed to help with universal approximation. The memory budgets on the hardware, however, are limited.

Gradient accumulation

As discussed in the previous section, larger batch sizes are always preferable, as they enable universal approximation (leading to well-generalized models). In scenarios where the compute capacity is restricted but scaling the batch size is desired, *gradient accumulation* can be used to simulate larger batches.

With gradient accumulation, the standard model training loop, shown here, is transformed to include additional steps of normalizing the loss, accumulating the gradients, and taking the optimization steps every x interval of steps (instead of every step):

```
# Standard training loop
for epoch in range(...):
    for idx, (inputs, labels) in enumerate(dataloader):
        optimizer.zero_grad()
        # Perform the forward pass
        outputs = model(inputs)
        # Compute loss
        loss = loss_fn(outputs, labels)
        # Perform backpropagation
        loss.backward()
        # Update the optimizer
        optimizer.step()
```

The snippet for gradient accumulation follows, where `accumulation_step_count` indicates the frequency with which the optimization step is taken:

```
accumulation_step_count = ...

# Training loop with gradient accumulation enabled
for epoch in range(...):
    for idx, (inputs, labels) in enumerate(dataloader):
        optimizer.zero_grad()
        # Perform the forward pass
        outputs = model(inputs)
        # Compute loss
        loss = loss_fn(outputs, labels)
        # Perform gradient normalization
        loss = loss / accumulation_step_count
        # Perform backpropagation
        loss.backward()
        # Update the optimizer
        if ((idx + 1) % accumulation_step_count == 0) \
                or (idx + 1 == len(dataloader)):
            optimizer.step()
```

This technique is primarily designed to obtain more accurate models in settings where GPU resources are limited, rather than to provide computation efficiencies.

Gradient checkpointing

More popular optimization techniques used today, such as SGD and Adam, are stateful: they save the statistics of the past gradient values over time (e.g., the exponentially smoothed sum in SGD with momentum and the squared sum in Adam). Some optimizers have higher memory requirements than others. For instance, AdamW saves two states and hence has twice the memory requirements of SGD.

You can check this out by swapping `AdamW` for `SGD` in the `configure_optimizers` call in *vision_model.py* (*https://oreil.ly/v2YVL*) and observe the memory requirement dropout.

Gradient checkpointing is a technique that aims to be more memory efficient at the expense of computational overhead. If you look at the DAG (discussed in Chapter 2) generated for a `Conv2dReLUWithBN`, as used in hands-on exercise #2, you may notice that some nodes share the gradient propagation path. Traditionally, gradients for these nodes are saved in memory until all downstream children in the backward direction have been traversed and their respective gradients have been computed. The other extreme of this implementation is to not save the gradients and instead recompute them on demand. If computation latency is not extensive, then this trade-off might provide larger memory capacity to train the model or increase the batch size, for instance. These approaches are the two extreme ends of the spectrum. Gradient checkpointing, a.k.a. activation checkpointing, provides a middle ground: it allows saving gradients at known checkpoints, to find an optimal balance between freeing up memory and reducing redundant compute overhead.

This capability is packaged in PyTorch's `torch.utils.checkpoint.checkpoint` module. In Chapter 5, there are hands-on exercises that involve exploring gradient checkpointing.

Patch Gradient Descent

Patch Gradient Descent (PatchGD) is another very interesting technique that can be used to scale the training of gigapixel images that cannot fit into a single GPU (see Figure 4-12).[17] It's similar to the gradient accumulation technique, except in PatchGD the gradients are accumulated across the various spatial locations of the same image, rather than over independent samples. With this technique, each image is chunked in patches and bundles of patches are passed through the training loop in multiple steps.

---

17 Gupta, Deepak K., Gowreesh Mago, Arnav Chavan, and Dilip K. Prasad. 2023. "Patch Gradient Descent: Training Neural Networks on Very Large Images." arXiv, January 31, 2023. *https://arxiv.org/abs/2301.13817*.

During these steps, the gradients are accumulated in the corresponding gradient vector until all patches have been passed through.

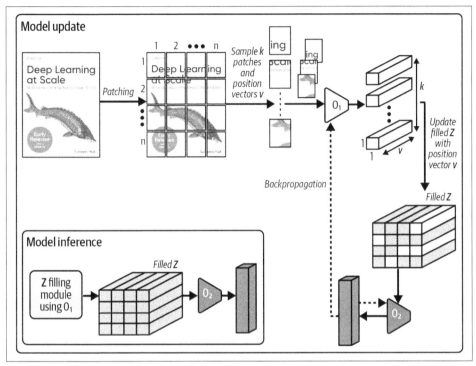

Figure 4-12. The workflow of PatchGD shown over a very large image sample

This technique is only effective for classification-like models where the gradient's size is much smaller than for models used for more dense tasks, like detections. With PatchGD, the input is chunked, but the gradient is maintained in memory at its full size. Thus, for this trick to work, the estimated gradient vector must fit in memory.

Learning rate and weight decay

The learning rate is another crucial parameter with deep ties to convergence time. As discussed in Chapter 2, with a slower learning rate, it will typically take a lot longer and many more steps to arrive at convergence or global minima. Conversely, a very high learning rate may lead to navigating the loss curvature too fast, resulting in missing out on the global minima and arriving at a suboptimal model. Weight decay can be applied through optimizers as well to enforce regularization (via L2 normalization) to mitigate overfitting. Both learning rate and weight decay influence convergence time.

For this reason, right-sizing the learning rate is a fruitful exercise. Unfortunately, due to its stochastic nature, conducting hyperparameter tuning might be the only solution to optimize the learning rate. In Part II of this book, we will take a deep dive into experimental design and parameter search, and you'll work through some exercises to tune the model's parameters.

Model Input Pipeline Tricks

In both of this chapter's hands-on examples, a very small portion of the compute cycles were used by the model input pipeline (i.e., the `DataLoaders`). As the volume and data size per sample increases, the increase in computation required to load, uncompress, and read and further transform the dataset could become quite challenging. In Chapter 6, you will learn about training with massive-scale datasets, including techniques to develop efficient `DataLoaders` to keep GPUs busy and maximize SM utilization. Some of these techniques involve choosing the right compression for your data, scaling out CPU-bound operations with thread and process parallelism (covered in detail in Chapter 3), and moving scalable transformations to the GPU, either via libraries providing GPU-compliant transformations, such as Kornia, or understanding the CPU–GPU memory bandwidth bottlenecks to right-size your inputs. Chapter 7 will feature a hands-on exercise that dives into the details of writing efficient input pipelines.

In the following section, we'll look at a small example of writing custom CUDA kernels in PyTorch 2.0 using OpenAI Triton (*https://oreil.ly/tVhs4*).

Writing Custom Kernels in PyTorch 2.0 with Triton

Triton's programming model is analogous to CUDA programming in that both support SIMD(/T) parallelism. Triton can facilitate the construction of high-performance compute kernels for neural networks using SIMD-style programming paradigms. Its programming model is different than CUDA's, however, in that the programs—rather than threads—are blocked.

A hands-on example to write a custom kernel for NVIDIA, *custom_kernel_example.py* (*https://oreil.ly/0oR8a*), is available in the book's GitHub repository.

In this code, the kernel `multiply_kernel` is called on a block of 1,024 elements of the tensors to perform multiplication and store the output in relevant positions. In this example, `MultiplyWithAutoGrad` implements a function with an automatic differentiation feature. This function can be invoked as follows:

```
MultiplyWithAutoGrad.apply(
    torch.ones((1999, 1999, 10)).to(device),
    torch.ones((10, 1999, 1999)).to(device)
)
```

Another emerging PyTorch compiler backend, Hidet (*https://oreil.ly/gGKXu*), allows more fine-grained compiler optimization than Triton because of its ability to operate at the thread level (unlike Triton, which operates at the block level) and support for additional paradigms like task mapping and fusion to further optimize at the operator and tensor level.[18] This compiler can shave off about 50% of compute time as compared to Triton/max-autotune. It is, however, currently limited to inference only, with training on the roadmap.

Summary

In this chapter, you learned about GPT-2 and EfficientNet as two architectures for two different input formats: text and images. In addition to these hands-on examples, you learned about a variety of techniques to develop models more efficiently. This chapter concludes the first part of the book, focusing on introducing various fundamental techniques required for accelerating and scaling your deep learning model training.

In the next part of this book, you will learn techniques to scale out model training from one to many accelerated devices, using many more hosts connected over the network.

---

18 Ding, Yaoyao, Cody Hao Yu, Bojian Zheng, Yizhi Liu, Yida Wang, and Gennady Pekhimenko. 2023. "Hidet: Task-Mapping Programming Paradigm for Deep Learning Tensor Programs." arXiv, February 15, 2023. *https://arxiv.org/abs/2210.09603*.

## PART II

Distributed Training

This section delves into the details of distributed training, offering a comprehensive understanding of its foundational concepts and practical applications. It begins by introducing distributed systems and communication challenges, which are essential to understand for scaling hardware resources effectively. Building upon this foundation, the section extends into theoretical frameworks for distributed deep learning training techniques and explores data parallelism in depth, complemented by practical exercises. Furthermore, it provides insights into scaling model training through various parallelism techniques like model, pipeline, tensor, and hybrid parallelism, highlighting their challenges and limitations through hands-on experiences. Finally, the section consolidates this knowledge, offering expertise in realizing multidimensional parallelism for efficient deep learning at scale.

## CHAPTER 5

Distributed Systems and Communications

Part I of this book presented the fundamental concepts of full-stack deep learning, describing the theoretical and technical priors of developing deep learning models efficiently. The first four chapters brought forth the interaction involved between hardware, software, data, and algorithms to materialize deep learning applications. Part II will extend the knowledge you have acquired so far to apply to distributed systems and explore how a fleet of computational devices can be used to scale out model development.

In this chapter, you will learn about the types of distributed systems and their corresponding challenges. You will also learn about the various communication topologies and techniques that exist today to enable deep learning in a distributed setting. To ease the infrastructure entry barrier, this chapter briefly discusses some of the software and frameworks for managing your processes and infrastructure at scale.

This chapter also highlights some of the attractive massive-scale deep learning infrastructure that exists today. Managing infrastructure is quite an involved process and should be owned by experts like DevOps and MLOps. You may choose to skip "Scaling Compute Capacity" on page 173 if this content isn't relevant to your particular role. Finally, this chapter introduces the different types of distributed deep learning techniques that are available, to provide context and an overview of the existing patterns for scaling out model training. The remaining chapters in Part II (Chapters 6–9) discuss these in more detail and include hands-on exercises.

Let's start by answering the question, what is a distributed system?

Distributed Systems

A distributed system can be defined as "a collection of independent computers that appear to their users as a single coherent system."[1] In a distributed system, physically separated independent computational units (nodes) coordinate to achieve a common goal. Scaling is achieved through divide-and-conquer semantics, wherein each node takes responsibility for executing different parts/chunks of the shared task in order to meet this common goal. This partitioning and distribution of tasks across the system underscores the criticality of coordination between the nodes.

The total physical independence of the computational units enables loose coupling and is in line with the "share nothing" architectural principle, where sharing of resources is discouraged.[2] Sharing nothing facilitates horizontal scale-out, but in practice, it is incredibly hard to achieve. In fact, distributed systems do share the same network—the means through which these nodes interconnect, communicate, and coordinate (see Figure 5-1). All the considerations discussed in Chapter 1 apply to distributed systems as well, though the extent of these challenges amplifies as the number of nodes increases.

In addition, a class of faults known as *partitioning faults* may surface, and these require careful consideration and management. A partitioning fault is defined as a communication breakdown between parts/partitions of the distributed system, leading to loss or delay in communication. The challenges arising from partitioning are so often underappreciated and misunderstood that they have been codified as "the fallacies of distributed computing" (*https://oreil.ly/czOYx*).

---

1 Van Steen, M., and A.S. Tanenbaum. 2016. "A Brief Introduction to Distributed Systems." *Computing* 98: 967–1009. *https://doi.org/10.1007/s00607-016-0508-7.*

2 Stonebraker, Michael. 1986. "The Case for Shared Nothing Architecture." *Database Engineering* 9, no. 1: 4–9. *http://db.cs.berkeley.edu/papers/hpts85-nothing.pdf.*

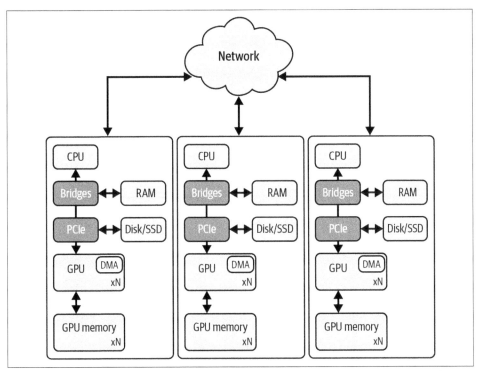

Figure 5-1. Multiple nodes with their resources are connected to each other over the network forming a distributed system (a.k.a. cluster of nodes)

The Eight Fallacies of Distributed Computing

The fallacies of distributed computing were formulated by Laurence Peter Deutsch and colleagues at Sun Microsystems to highlight the underappreciation of the challenges of managing effective interconnection between the nodes of a cluster. These fallacies are:

- You have a reliable network.
- Your network latency is zero.
- You have infinite bandwidth.
- Your transport cost is zero.
- You have a secure network.
- Your (network) topology does not change.
- A single administrator would suffice.
- You have a homogeneous network.

These eight fallacies are directly applicable to distributed deep learning as well. In addition, distributed deep learning introduces a few other fallacies:

Embarrassing parallelism exists
> As discussed in previous chapters, while there are several opportunities for parallelism to enable scale-out, you are often limited by either capacity (e.g., the bandwidth limitation discussed in Chapter 3) or coordination challenges (e.g., throttling at gradient or parameter synchronization or loading and transferring of data).

Heterogeneity is fine
> Heterogeneity offers different combinations of compute capabilities, allowing you to choose the best (most efficient) option for the task. However, the collective performance of a task at scale run on a heterogeneous system is mostly defined by the weakest (slowest) participating member (worker/node/computer). Deep learning workloads may feature different sources of heterogeneity, such as:

> *Computation devices*
>> As discussed in Chapter 3, most accelerated computing devices are heterogeneous (combining one or more CPUs and GPUs). However, there's also heterogeneity among accelerated devices, because of their potentially varying abilities.

> *Networking*
>> Different communication channels may be used in distributed deep learning systems; for example, GPU–GPU direct interconnects, GPU–GPU via PCIe, and GPU–CPU. The latency and bandwidth of these communication channels may vary.

These fallacies capture various sources of partitioning faults. In the following section, we'll look at a theorem for designing reliable distributed systems.

The Consistency, Availability, and Partition Tolerance (CAP) Theorem

The CAP theorem, proposed by UC Berkeley professor of computer science Eric Brewer in 2000, is one of the fundamental theorems of distributed system design. It states that of the three main desirable characteristics of a distributed system, only two can be guaranteed at any given point in time. Those properties are:

Consistency
> Every read receives the latest value or an error.

Availability
> All requests return valid responses, without any guarantee that the response contains the latest value.

Partition (fault) tolerance
   The system remains functional when network partitions (communication faults) occur.

Ideally, your system will be highly fault-tolerant, but that is so hard to achieve that you will need to compromise on either consistency (i.e., having all nodes see the same data simultaneously) or availability (having all the nodes of your system simultaneously humming along, crunching numbers and learning from the data). Figure 5-2 illustrates the intersection of these three network characteristics.

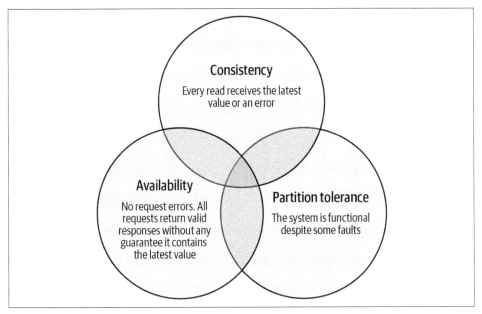

Figure 5-2. The CAP theorem

Later in this chapter, we'll revisit this theorem to explore which dimensions of CAP are traded off in deep learning, and under what circumstances. For now, let's look at the implications of these challenges on scaling law and how they apply to distributed systems.

The Scaling Law of Distributed Systems

Amdahl's law, discussed in Chapter 3, only considered concurrency—i.e., the ability to parallelize parts of the process for scale-out. Distributed systems require a revision of the scaling law to account for challenges and bottlenecks that arise not only from concurrency but also from consistency, coherency (a close cousin of consistency), and contention (i.e., delay caused by waiting for required resources).

Neil Gunther used these three Cs—concurrency, coherency (consistency-related), and contention—to extend Amdahl's law for distributed systems and define the universal scalability law (USL).[3] According to USL, the scale-up achievable by increasing the number of nodes (or GPUs/processes) N is given by:

$$S(N) = \gamma N / (1 + \alpha(N - 1) + \beta N (N - 1))$$

where α, β, and γ are the coefficients of contention, coherency, and concurrency, respectively (see Figure 5-3).

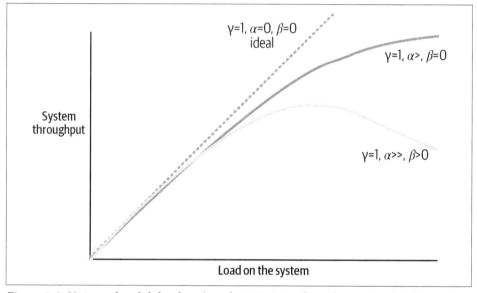

Figure 5-3. Universal scalability law (per the USL Manifesto (https://oreil.ly/bEm1t))

3 Gunther, Neil. 2018. "USL Scalability Modeling with Three Parameters." *The Pith of Performance* (blog), May 20, 2018. *http://www.perfdynamics.com/Manifesto/USLscalability.html*.

More practically, USL implies that to scale effectively as concurrency (γ) is increased, contention (α) and coherency (β) should be minimized. This will help maximize scalability (S). In scenarios where contention (α) coherency (β) or both increase, the scalability will be limited even if concurrency (γ) is increased. As shown in Figure 5-3, the increasing contention (α) or coherency (β) will increase the risk of regressive performance as scaling leads to diminishing returns, pushing you into the retrograde scalability region where system throughput ceases to increase.[4]

 The universal scalability law is a specialization of the general scaling law discussed in Chapter 1. USL acknowledges additional variables that influence the scalability of your solution.

Fundamentally, to scale efficiently you *overlap communication and computation* (i.e., continue computation while communication is ongoing). Additionally, you reduce latency where possible and, where not possible, hide it.

In the following section, we'll look at different types of distributed systems and explore the practical aspects of their composition, configuration, and limitations.

Types of Distributed Systems

Based on the coordination styles, distributed systems are divided into two categories: centralized and decentralized (see Figure 5-4). Both of these types of distributed systems are used for scaling out model training and development.

---

4 Gunther, "USL Scalability Modeling with Three Parameters," *http://www.perfdynamics.com/Manifesto/USLs calability.html*

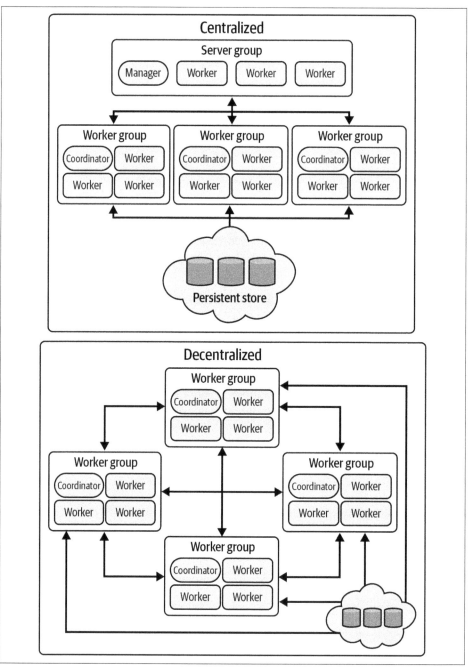

Figure 5-4. Types of distributed systems used in deep learning

Centralized

Centralized distributed systems are orchestrated such that of all N members of the system, one or more members $s \ll N$ assume the responsibility of "server" and coordinate and communicate with other "worker" members w responsible for executing independent parts of the given task. As shown on the left side of Figure 5-4, the workers in a centralized system do not talk to each other, but only to the server(s). This style of communication and coordination places a heavy burden on the server(s) and requires collation of output generated during the computing phase across all w workers.

The advantages of a centralized system are:

Asynchronous communication
Independent communication between workers and server(s) enables a more scalable asynchronous style of communication. This is a more effective communication style when the interconnection fabric saturates.

Simplicity
The centralization given by servers simplifies the collation algorithm, as all output needing collation is available on a single machine at the same time.

These advantages come at the expense of three main disadvantages:

- During the computing phase of the program, the *compute capacity of the server(s) is not effectively utilized*. While the workers perform their respective parts of the task, the server is predominantly only managing the workers and not computing.

- During the collation phase, on the other hand, the server(s) are overloaded with information from all workers, leading to *communication throttle* and *compute waste* as the workers wait for the next part of their work.

- The *scalability is limited* by the capacity of the server group. While having only one server in the group creates a single point of failure in the system, adding more increases the complexity of coordination due to necessary partitioning of the responsibilities. In some distributed system configurations, servers are added for redundancy (i.e., to manage failover). This type of orchestration is better than having only a single server, as it mitigates the single point of failure; however, it is very inefficient as the secondary server(s) in the group predominantly sit idle and do not actively participate in computing.

Centralized distributed systems are analogous to generic client/server computer systems; however, in the context of deep learning model development, the clients are simply the worker units. In practice, centralized distributed deep learning systems are usually implemented using the parameter server framework, where the server group keeps the main copy of the parameters and the workers provide the gradients or updates to the parameters.

In centralized distributed systems, the onus of CAP—i.e., ensuring consistency and availability—lies on the server group, which is also largely responsible for the allocation of work.

Decentralized

Decentralized systems remove the dedicated server roles and distribute them amongst the workers. As a result, as shown on the right side of Figure 5-4, all worker nodes get to talk to other worker nodes about their parts of the work. With a decentralized system, the biggest advantage is *effective utilization of resources*. Compared to a centralized system, in a decentralized system resource use tends to be much more efficient, due to interleaving and independent execution. Having said that, the system becomes increasingly complex, and the communication burden increases. Unlike in a centralized system, the burden of consistency is shared amongst all the workers, requiring workers to communicate more. As a consequence, the complexity of the consensus (for consistency) algorithm increases.

Communication in Distributed Systems

Communication is a critical aspect of any distributed system. In this section, we'll first look at the communication paradigm pervasively used in distributed systems and follow that up with an exploration of communication technologies used in enabling distributed deep learning.

Communication Paradigm

As you've seen there are two broad categories of communication: synchronous and asynchronous. In synchronous (sync) communication, the sender sends a message and waits for a response from the receiver in a blocking call, whereas asynchronous (async) communication eliminates the blocking call and gravitates toward a more push/pull style of communication. In async communication, the sender sends a message and continues with its work, and the receiver processes the message upon reception and handles it accordingly.

As per a USL simulation conducted by Jim Holtman and Neil Gunther to analyze successfully scalable systems,[5] each system has three scalability zones (see Figure 5-5): concurrency-limited (α, β, ~0), contention-limited ($\alpha > 0$, β, ~0), and coherency-limited (α, $\beta > 0$). The concurrency-limited zone is the ideal target zone you want your system to be in, and asynchronicity is the key to being in this zone. This is

---

5 Holtman, Jim, and Neil. J. Gunther. 2008. "Getting in the Zone for Successful Scalability." arXiv, September 15, 2008. *https://arxiv.org/abs/0809.2541*.

because asynchronous systems can hide latency quite effectively. (This is also why async communication is used more often in scaling model development.)

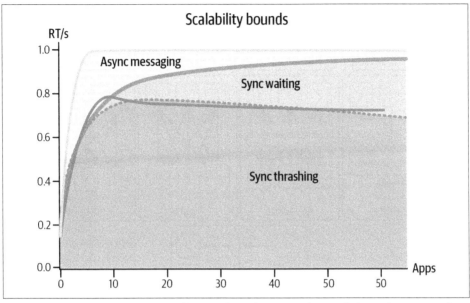

Figure 5-5. The scalability zone of a distributed system, obtained through a series of performance-based simulations (adapted from Holtman and Gunther, 2008)

Communication Patterns

Communication patterns describe how the processes running on each of the nodes in a given distributed system may communicate. Depending on the nature of the communication algorithm (e.g., consensus), one or more of these communication patterns may be used in your application. In practice, you will not be implementing these communications patterns explicitly; your underlying deep learning framework (e.g., PyTorch, JAX, TensorFlow) already transparently implements them and exposes them to you through APIs. You'll read about the technologies used in implementing these patterns in "Communication Technologies" on page 167. First, let's review the communication patterns and see how they relate to distributed systems and deep learning.

The communication patterns are divided into two categories: *basic* and *collective*. Most of these patterns are implemented to allow for sync and async communication. Figure 5-6 outlines the communication patterns used in distributed deep learning.

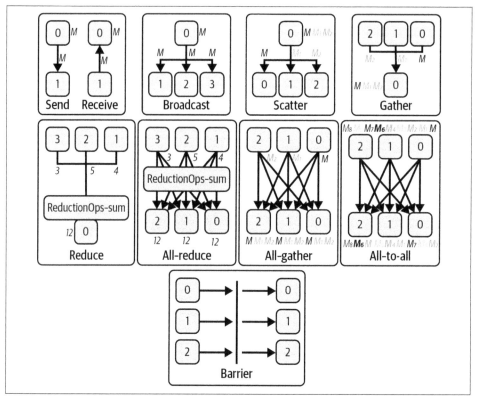

Figure 5-6. Communication patterns

Let's start by looking at the two basic patterns, then move on to the collective patterns. In these sections, *m* represents data, α represents the latency, β the communication cost per word, *p* the number of processes, and *n* the message size.

Basic communication patterns

The basic communication patterns are point-to-point, describing how a sender and a receiver may communicate to transmit data. They are:

Send

As shown in Figure 5-6, in the send pattern, the sender sends the message to the receiving endpoint. The cost function for send is given by α + *n*β.

Receive

As shown in Figure 5-6, in the receive pattern, the receiver receives the message from the sender. The cost function for this communication is given by α + *n*β.

Collective communication patterns

As the name indicates, the second category of communication patterns describe how a collective group of processes p consisting of one or more senders and receivers may communicate. Typically, collective communications are the one of the biggest sources of bottlenecks when scaling deep learning workloads. You will read more about these in Chapterse 7, 8, and 9.

The collective communication patterns can be grouped into the following three subcategories:

One-to-all

> The patterns in this subcategory follow a fan-out approach, where one sender sends the message out to the remaining $p - 1$ receiver. They are:

> *Broadcast*

>> In the broadcast pattern, a sender sends a message m to the remaining $p - 1$ members, enabling an announcement-like communication. Successful broadcast results in all processes in the collective group having the same data (i.e., m). While a naive implementation of the broadcast pattern can be a loop, more mature implementations exploit minimal spanning tree, ring, or hypercube-based algorithms. The cost function for this communication style varies per implementation; for the tree-based algorithm, it can be given by $\alpha \log p + n\beta$.

> *Scatter*

>> In the scatter pattern, the sender chunks up the message m into $p - 1$ parts and distributes each part amongst the remaining $p - 1$ members. The difference between scatter and broadcast is that broadcast sends the same message to all members, whereas scatter sends each member a chunk. It's quite useful for implementing a divide-and-conquer approach where the workload is split amongst the collective group. For example, a tensor of dimension 10x10 can be divided amongst 10 processes, where each process sums 1/10 chunks of the tensor before these results are aggregated together to obtain the final sum of the tensor. Scatter, like broadcast, can be implemented using spanning tree, ring, or hypercube-based algorithms. This is a fan-out operation and can cost $\alpha \log p + n\beta$.

All-to-one

> The patterns in this subcategory follow a fan-in approach, where $p - 1$ senders send the message out to the receiving members. They are:

> *Gather*

>> Gather is the reverse of scatter. In the gather pattern, the receiver receives the message m in chunks from the remaining $p - 1$ members, which act as

senders. This is a fan-in operation and can cost the same as scatter; i.e., $\alpha \log p + n\beta$.

Reduce

Reduce is an interesting collective operation that in principle is similar to gather, except it applies an additional function f_n on the messages gathered from senders. In doing so, it reduces the messages to a final global result to be received at the receiving end. This is a fan-in operation and costs the same as scatter; i.e., $\alpha \log p + n\beta$.

All-to-all

The patterns in this subcategory follow the approach where all members send the message m out to the remaining $p - 1$ members. They are:

Barrier

The barrier pattern is used to ensure that all processes are synchronized and ready before they begin to interact with each other using any of the other collective communication patterns. As you may have noted, this is a blocking pattern enforcing synchronization and should be used sparingly. The cost of this operation is $\alpha \log p$.

All-gather

All-gather is an extension of gather where all the chunks from processes p are combined to generate the final (gathered) message, such that at the end of the operation all the processes have the same final result. This pattern is used to collect data from all processes and store the collected data on all processing units. It can be implemented in multiple ways; e.g., using a combination of gather and broadcast. The cost of this operation is $\alpha \log p + np\beta$.

All-reduce

All-reduce is an extension of reduce where all the chunks from processes p are reduced to produce a final message, and this message is distributed back to all the processes at the end of the operation. The all-reduce pattern plays a key role in distributed model training because of its ability to collate data from all workers, reduce it, and redistribute the final result back to all the processes. For example, all-reduce is used to perform gradient synchronization across all workers. Several implementations of all-reduce exist, spanning from using a combination of reduce and broadcast operations to tree-based algorithms to more optimized butterfly networks.[6] Generally, the cost of this operation is $\alpha \log p + n\beta$.

---

6 Patarasuk, Pitch, and Xin Yuan. 2009. "Bandwidth Optimal All-Reduce Algorithms for Clusters of Workstations." *Journal of Parallel and Distributed Computing* 69, no. 2: 117–24. *https://doi.org/10.1016/j.jpdc.2008.09.002*.

All-to-all

The all-to-all pattern redistributes n length of message n from each process p such that each process ends up with another unique set of n length of message m wherein each chunk of this message belongs to a chunk from another process p before the communication commenced. For instance, if a tensor of dimension 10x10 is split across 10 processes such that each ith row is at the p_i^{th} process, then after all-to-all communication each p_i^{th} process will end up with the ith column of the original 10x10 tensor. In essence, all-to-all transposes the data split across the processes. The cost of this operation is $log\ p(\alpha + np\beta)$.

 To optimize by eliminating the need to send the same data multiple times between various remotely connected endpoints, some networking technologies, like Mellanox's Scalable Hierarchical Aggregation and Reduction Protocol (SHARP), offload parts of the collective communication from the CPU and perform the work at the (network) switch level. This technique decreases the amount of redundant data traversing the network during collective operations, increasing the efficiency of the communication. Such techniques can also free up memory space on the CPU for other computational purposes.

Communication Technologies

Several communication technologies have evolved over the years to facilitate distributed systems. These include, but are not limited to, Remote Procedure Call (RPC), Remote Method Invocation (RMI), Distributed Common Object Model (DCOM), Common Object Request Broker Architecture (CORBA), and Message Passing Interface (MPI). Two of these techniques, RPC and MPI, have been actively utilized in developing distributed deep learning systems. We'll look at those next, along with a useful library for multi-GPU communications.

RPC

RPC is a high-level communications technique that uses a low-level transport protocol, such as Transmission Control Protocol/Internet Protocol (TCP/IP) or User Datagram Protocol (UDP). RPC allows the invocation of a method on a remote system as if it were a local method. It can take care of serialization and deserialization and uses optimized methods to send large blobs of data in chunks transparently.

RPC can be used to implement the communication paradigms discussed in "Communication Patterns" on page 163. However, all known implementations of RPC today are CPU-only. This is the biggest limitation of RPC-supported distributed training, because in such a scenario, for the communication to transpire the tensors and data need to be loaded back onto the CPU from the accelerator. So, even though the computation can be performed on the accelerator, RPC causes a CPU-offloading bottleneck. The challenges from such bottlenecks increase as the data volume—either directly from input data or from gradients, optimizers, parameters, etc.—increases. Because of this limitation, the use of RPC for distributed training is more successful in CPU-bound training.

 In a centralized distributed training setting, the parameter server(s) act as the RPC servers and the workers are the clients, whereas (in theory) in decentralized settings, each process acts as both server and client. However, decentralized RPC distributed training has not been widely explored. Overall, RPC is not a natural fit for scaling out accelerator-bound deep learning, as a much more significant (25x) gain in speed can be obtained by using DirectGPU RDMA (discussed in the following section).[7]

---

gRPC

Google's RPC framework, more commonly known as gRPC, is a high-performance modern implementation that uses protocol buffers (a.k.a. protobuf) (*https://proto buf.dev*). gRPC is more performant than its classical RPC counterpart, for two reasons:

- Reduced latency due to the use of HTTP/2 protocol
- Use of a more optimized binary data format than the verbose JSON counterpart used in RPC

While gRPC is actively used in deep learning frameworks like TensorFlow, in the PyTorch ecosystem its use is limited to inference and serving and it has not been explored for use in RPC-style distributed training. PyTorch uses `tensorpipe` (*https://oreil.ly/ZzNFi*) as the default backend for RPC-style distributed training.

The toy example shown here demonstrates the internal workings of RPC, where the `server` process started through `ThreadedServer` is invoked by the client process as if the `say_hello` API were local:

```
import rpyc
from rpyc.utils.server import ThreadedServer
```

---

7 Xue, Jilong, Youshan Miao, Cheng Chen, Ming Wu, Lintao Zhang, and Lidong Zhou. 2018. "RPC Considered Harmful: Fast Distributed Deep Learning on RDMA." arXiv, May 22, 2018. *https://arxiv.org/abs/1805.08430*.

```
# Class GreetingService defines say_hello capability.
# Any process hosting this service will expose the say_hello
# API over RPC on host localhost over port 8082.
@rpyc.service
class GreetingService(rpyc.Service):
    @rpyc.exposed
    def say_hello(self, user: str):
        print("say_hello is called")
        return f"Hello {user}!"

# Start a server
server = ThreadedServer(GreetingService, port=8082)
server.start()
```

On the client, the following snippet is run:

```
# On client side
import rpyc

# Connect to the server and invoke remote API as if it was local
connection = rpyc.connect("localhost", 18811)
print(connection.root.say_hello("Jo"))
```

MPI

MPI defines a standard for sending and receiving messages and performing collective operations, discussed in "Communication Patterns" on page 163. It was introduced in 1992 by Jack Dongarra, founding director of the Innovative Computing Laboratory at the University of Tennessee, and colleagues. MPI has been implemented for many distributed memory architectures and has been adopted so widely that there are various hardware-optimized implementations for it. This makes MPI both fast and easily adaptable. Unlike RPC, MPI does not dictate a centralized system and supports SIMD at the process level, not the node level. When applied in a distributed setting, it uses the concept of *slots*: allocatable units where you can launch a process that maps to the number of cores. MPI supports under- and overallocation to allow managing workload orchestration.

A toy example of MPI is included in the book's code repository, in the file *mpi_probe.cpp* (*https://oreil.ly/3TrhZ*). In this example, the main process broadcasts a number entered by the user to other member processes. By the end of the program, every process in the group has received this number. To run this example, you will have to install Open MPI (*https://oreil.ly/MLAOi*) and compile the sample to an executable probe, using:

```
mpicc -o probe ./deep_learning_at_scale/chapter_5/mpi_probe.cpp
```

After this, you can run probe over as many processes as you like by controlling the number of processes argument, nb:

```
mpirun -np 2 ./probe
```

This command will present you with a prompt asking you to enter a number to send to the other processes: "I am the root Process! Enter your number to broadcast?" All processes in the group with ranks >0 will receive the number you enter. Notice the terminology of world_rank and world_size. world_rank is used to identify the ID of the process, and world_size is used to describe the total number of processes "doing" the probe task. This is MPI terminology that's been widely adopted in all implementations of distributed training.

You can explore this example in a distributed setting or simulate one locally using host slots (e.g., localhost:1), using a command like the following:

```
mpirun -np 3 -H localhost:1,localhost:2,localhost:3 ./probe
```

Similar to this example, you can perform computations (e.g., computing the sum of a large array) by distributing them over various processes: each process gets a different chunk of the array and returns the sum of that chunk back to the root, which computes the final sum. You can find one such hands-on exercise on the GeeksforGeeks platform (*https://oreil.ly/5ce0P*).

There are several implementations of MPI, including but not limited to Open MPI, MPICH, MVAPICH(2), CRAY MPI, and Intel MPI. From version 2 on, MPI implementations can be made CUDA-aware, which can eliminate overhead from CPU offloading and CUDA memory copy. The Unified Virtual Addressing (UVA) feature of CUDA 4.0 allows memory pinning between host and GPU, meaning memory address space is shared across the CPU and all GPUs of the node.

Additionally, CUDA-aware MPI can exploit GPUDirect technologies, allowing more efficient peer-to-peer (P2P) or RDMA communication between local and remote GPUs (as shown in Figure 5-7). GPUDirect decouples the GPU memory transfer from the CPU, thus bypassing any kernel overhead, such as memory paging.[8] Version 3 of MPI also enables a new interprocess shared memory extension (MPI SHM) to create regions of shared memory that are accessible by the MPI processes to facilitate more performant interprocess communication.

---

8 Kraus, Jiri. 2013. "An Introduction to CUDA-Aware MPI." NVIDIA Technical Blog, March 13, 2013. *https://developer.nvidia.com/blog/introduction-cuda-aware-mpi/* (*https://oreil.ly/lK-wN*).

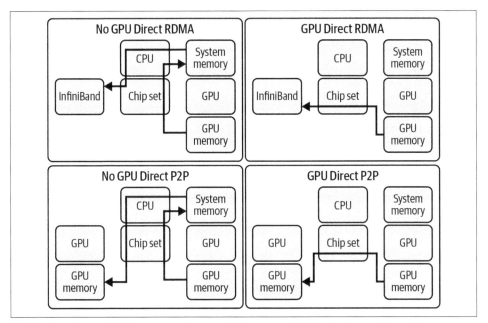

Figure 5-7. Cross-GPU communication P2P or over RMDA (adapted from Kraus, 2013)

The CUDA-aware API has been implemented in libraries such as MVAPICH2, CRAY MPI, and Open MPI. You can use any of these implementations as a backend for distributed training.

MPI-based backends may require a custom build from source to include MPI in the runtime. For more details, see the PyTorch tutorial "Writing Distributed Applications with PyTorch" (*https://oreil.ly/-Y5bL*).

NCCL

The NVIDIA Collective Communication Library (NCCL) implements multi-GPU and multinode communication primitives optimized for NVIDIA GPUs and networks (NVLinks, NVSockets, etc.). NCCL provides routines for several of the communication patterns discussed in "Communication Patterns" on page 163—including all-gather, all-reduce, broadcast, reduce, and reduce-scatter as well as the basic point-to-point patterns—that are optimized to achieve high bandwidth and low latency over PCIe and NVLink high-speed interconnects within a node and over NVIDIA Mellanox networks across nodes.

NCCL's implementation closely aligns with MPI's; it uses similar constructs but does not strictly follow MPI standards. A comparison between NCCL and MPI is provided in the NVIDIA documentation (*https://oreil.ly/udsyF*). One notable difference is `ncclReduceScatter`, which differs from `MPI_Reduce_scatter` to align more with the thread block schematics of the CUDA paradigm. NCCL also omits several implementations of MPI specifications that are not relevant for CUDA-related operations, such as `scatterv` and `gatherv`.

In principle, NCCL can be used in conjunction with MPI to leverage CPU-to-CPU and GPU-to-GPU coordination and parallelization. However, such mixing can lead to deadlocks for a variety of reasons and should be avoided.

Communication technology summary

In the PyTorch ecosystem, RPC, MPI, NCCL, and Gloo are four distribution backends that are widely available. Gloo is an open source library developed by Facebook that implements collective communications over standard TCP/IP. It is compatible with both CPUs and GPUs, implementing all the communication patterns discussed so far; however, its GPU implementation is not as optimized as NCCL's (*https://oreil.ly/4WIF1*). MLBench documents the performance benchmarks (*https://oreil.ly/KJSGd*) of these backends: NCCL leads for the most part, except when tensors are very small (in which case MPI excels). All of these technologies leverage networking communications standards for high-performance computing, such as InfiniBand to provide very high throughput and very low latency communication. InfiniBand is suitable for direct or switched interconnect and is widely used in NVIDIA GPUs.

Communication Initialization: Rendezvous

In the previous sections, you learned about communication patterns used in distributed learning and technologies that are used to enable these patterns, and you explored some of the backends available in the PyTorch ecosystem. The first step in establishing the communication network is commonly known as *rendezvous*. Rendezvous is essentially communication initialization, after which every worker has established a connection to any other worker/server it may need to communicate with. The full bisection bandwidth topology is a popular choice for ensuring two-way communications are established between all workers. This pattern is commonly used in distributed learning.

During rendezvous, each process of the collective communication group, with the `world_rank` ranging from 0 to `world_size` – 1, registers itself to a central point (see "MPI" on page 169 for more information on `world_rank` and `world_size`). This central point is either a server (identified by hostname/IP address and port) or a shared filesystem that every process can see or has access to. You'll see examples of this initialization in the hands-on exercises in the following three chapters, and additional information is available in the PyTorch docs (*https://oreil.ly/sJueH*).

Hands-On Exercise

I've included a toy example to demonstrate how PyTorch handles distributed processes in the example repository, in the script *torch_dist.py* (*https://oreil.ly/eYosx*). In this example, a group of processes are initialized, and communications are established between them. All the processes in this group perform an all-reduce collective communication operation to obtain the cumulative sum of each process's tensor.

You can use the `--no-use-async` argument to opt for the communication pattern to be synchronous, or use `-use-async` to choose async communication. To control the number of processes in the group, use the `--world-size` argument.

For example, to specify synchronous communication among three processes, you would execute this command:

```
python deep_learning_at_scale/chapter_5/torch_dist.py --no-use-async
--world-size 3
```

You've learned about how distributed systems enable horizontal scaling and how processes and nodes communicate to coordinate and complete the task at hand. Next, we'll briefly review the options for scaling and managing your compute capacity.

Scaling Compute Capacity

In Chapter 1, you read about several considerations for scaling efficiently. Scaling out compute capacity is largely a hardware affair, requiring consideration of CapEx and OpEx budgets, maintainability and management, and failover strategies. DevOps and MLOps engineers dedicate a significant amount of their time to ensuring systems are reliable and robust. This is a broad topic that is, unfortunately, outside the scope of this book; instead, in this section we will look at a few setups that are commonly used today to scale out compute capacity, followed by a brief review of some of the tools used in workload management to distribute a workload over a fleet of nodes in a distributed system.

Infrastructure Setup Options

Various infrastructure setups are available for distributed systems, depending on how the hardware is procured, assembled, and architected. This section provides an overview of the different options.

Private cloud (on-premise/DIY data centers)

On-premises data centers are built and managed internally. An in-house team handles everything from hardware and networking to maintenance and continual operation. This type of setup provides complete configurability and customizability, but it requires significant capital and operational investments.

Companies using customized hardware for their AI programs (say, Tesla's Dojo chip and supercomputer) often have good reasons to manage their own computing systems. Research institutes and other companies may also adopt this approach for security, privacy, and compliance purposes, such as to meet General Data Protection Regulation (GDPR) requirements. There are also organizations that prefer to manage their own data centers because their total capacity requirements are low, so procuring and managing hardware ends up being more cost effective than renting it in the long run, and they have the required expertise in-house. In the absence of such expertise, private cloud setups limit your upper bound of scale, as increasing the cluster capacity is a nontrivial effort.

Public cloud

Various platform as a service (PaaS) companies offer compute capacity for deep learning workloads, including Amazon Web Services (AWS), Google Cloud Platform (GCP), Microsoft Azure, and Lambda Labs. These PaaS providers offer virtualized nodes, and depending on the configuration and services the accelerated devices may be either bare metal or virtualized. Most offer assorted sets of services with varying levels of ease of use, abstraction, customizability, and cost.

Google's Vertex AI, Amazon SageMaker, and the Azure AI platform are some of the packaged services that are useful for quickly getting set up for deep learning development. At the other end of the spectrum are more highly customizable offerings such as Google Compute Engine, Amazon Elastic Compute Cloud (EC2), and Azure high-performance computing (HPC). Often PaaS providers have a custom high-speed interconnect—for example, AWS's Elastic Fabric Adapter (EFA), which requires a custom plug-in (*hhttps://oreil.ly/y9rGi*) for collective communication libraries—to enable more efficient use of custom networking.

Public cloud setups are flexible and highly scalable, but they present two challenges:

- The cloud provider's pool is limited, and you are sharing these resources with everyone. You may find yourself in situations where you've requested certain resources, but due to high demand those resources are not available. These scenarios often present themselves around big conference deadlines, like the Conference on Neural Information Processing Systems (NeurIPS) and the International and European Conferences on Computer Vision (ICCV and ECCV). The availability of compute resources is subjected to demand at your provider's end. This is also why many organizations using purely public cloud platforms reserve instances to ensure they have dedicated capacity available for their use at any time. Reserve instance schemes exist to reserve a block of compute for a fixed duration of time to guarantee availability. They are, however, generally for multiyear commitment and thus require significant planning and consideration.

- Renting accelerated devices can be an expensive affair. These costs can be somewhat reduced by opting in to preemptible instances that are offered at a lower price under the agreement that they can be taken away at any time. Making your application robust to these faults allows one to exploit these capabilities. When you're renting hundreds or thousands of these devices, even a small discount can amount to a decent savings.

> To make your application robust to faults, you must be able to restart your work from the last known working state. Checkpointing, as used in most of this book's hands-on exercises, is a useful way to maintain state so it can be used to resume the workload.
>
> You should also ensure that in case of a partitioning failure event (e.g., loss of nodes in a worker group), your deep learning application adapts and continues to function. Chapter 6 will explore this topic further.

Hybrid cloud

Hybrid cloud solutions offer the ability to combine one or more cloud providers and private data centers into a seamless interface and run your workloads over the combined capacity of these infrastructures. Organizations sometimes use this approach to enable them to migrate from private to public cloud infrastructure or vice versa at their own pace, or to provide elasticity to private cloud solutions. Google Cloud Anthos, Azure hybrid cloud environments, AWS Elastic Container Service (ECS) and Elastic Kubernetes Service (EKS) Anywhere, and other suites of services under the hybrid umbrella can be used to establish a hybrid system.

Multicloud

Multicloud is a variant that's similar to a hybrid cloud setup, except in a multicloud setting each cloud has nonoverlapping responsibility for certain operations. One example might be a setup where data is coming from a private cloud/data center but compute resources are provided by a public cloud, or vice versa (e.g., using data from Google's BigQuery but a private cloud for compute). High-speed interconnects like AWS Direct Connect are crucial for such a setup, especially if your data volume is large. This type of setup also allows to diversify your cloud infrastructure by bringing in specialists for accelerated computing to both maximize the availability and provide competitive pricing. Providers like LambdaLabs (*https://lambdalabs.com*) can be considered for such specialized extension.

Federation

Federated systems combine assorted compute capacities to create a highly dynamic and pseudopublic cluster where nodes can register and deregister depending on their own availability. Most federated systems are created in the public domain and are inspired by the idea of crowdsourced learning. There is a special class of deep learning known as federated learning that we'll revisit in Chapter 8, where we'll discuss the implications and algorithmic considerations of such systems.

Federated systems are very hard to manage and coordinate, and they require extreme robustness and tolerance of failure. This is an emerging computing pattern that faces several challenges, including the use of heterogeneous computing discussed in Chapter 1.

Given the variety of compute and infrastructure categories that exist today, it is always a good strategy to separate and decouple applications from infrastructure and orchestration code. This allows for seamless switching from one platform/environment to another. If you are intending to scale your deep learning application, this should be your guiding principle when defining the interaction layer between the application and the infrastructure.

Provisioning of Accelerated Devices

Infrastructure setup provides access to hardware and bare metal. While in a private cloud the setup may allow for full bare metal access, all cloud-based nodes are provisioned through virtualization technologies like hypervisors that surface one or more systems on the same hardware components. For instance, one node of 1 TB RAM and 16 CPUs can be virtually sliced into two nodes of 500 GB RAM and 8 CPU nodes each. Virtualization technologies enable superior management and more robust operations of large-scale compute infrastructure; however, the software layer introduces a performance penalty. These penalties vary but are mostly fractional if set up correctly.

GPUs in data centers can be virtualized as well, enabling two possible configurations through which GPUs are exposed for consumption (see Figure 5-8):

GPU passthrough/bare metal
> In a GPU passthrough setup, GPUs are exposed directly through the host as devices. This means the access and communication pathway to the GPU will be exactly the same as if you had access to this node physically.
>
> With this setup, it's possible to share a GPU across multiple virtual machines (VMs) hosted on the same node that the card is installed on. This approach can be useful in graphics processing, in cases where a single GPU card provides more than the required capacity. Technologies like NVIDIA's Multi-Instance GPU

(MIG) feature, available in Ampere and later GPUs, allow slicing a GPU into "chunks" for such scenarios; however, these MIG GPUs currently cannot be used for distributed deep learning training due to limited NCCL support.

Virtualized GPU (vGPU)

As mentioned previously, in virtualized GPU settings, the GPUs are surfaced as vGPUs. The communication pathway between GPU and CPU in this case goes through the virtualization layer (e.g., hypervisor). This extra interface may incur some overhead. (In a benchmark I performed using an A100 node, the pass-through GPU performed better than the vGPU, but the differences were marginal.)

A limitation of the vGPU approach is that if multiple GPUs need to be surfaced, they must all be of the same type. Additionally, not all virtualization tools currently support multiple vGPUs.

 Paravirtualization (PV) is a type of virtualization technique that is faster and more secure than traditional full virtualization. It has been widely adopted by the virtualized industry.

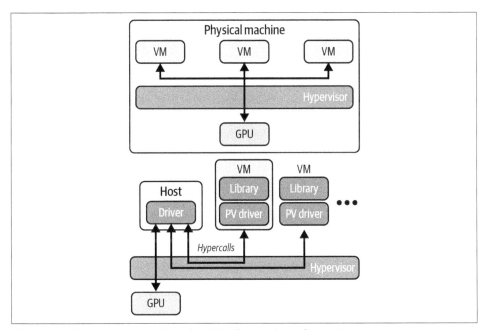

Figure 5-8. Passthrough (top) and vGPU (bottom) configurations

Workload Management

So far in this section, you've learned about different ways of provisioning a fleet of nodes and provisioning GPUs on those nodes. Let's assume the nodes are provisioned with operating systems and the required accelerated device drivers, and they're hooked up to a network where they can communicate with each other via their IP addresses on designated ports. Your next challenge is how to distribute and parallelize your application over these nodes. Considering how to manage your deep learning workload is also critical.

Hypothetically speaking, if your distributed setup were centralized (as discussed in "Types of Distributed Systems" on page 159), you might want to run a command such as the following to start your training:

```
train_my_amazing_model --data my.object.store.endpoint --server server.ip
--worker worker1.ip --worker worker2.ip --worker worker3.ip
```

This command indicates that you want to start training on three workers, `worker1`, `worker2`, and `worker3`, managed by the server identified by `server.ip`. The data is coming from a shared/common location, and your training logic is embedded in the `train_my_amazing_model` code. The command to run the same workload in a decentralized setting might look like this:

```
train_my_amazing_model --data my.object.store.endpoint --worker worker1.ip
--worker worker2.ip --worker worker3.ip --worker server.ip
```

This command indicates that you want to train your amazing model on four nodes: `worker1`, `worker2`, and `worker3`, as well as the node identified by `server.ip`.

In distributed training, if using acceleration, the rank is given per accelerator—that is, the `world_size` should reflect the total number of accelerators on which the training is to be conducted. This holds true even if one node hosts more than one accelerator. In essence, the scale-out is a function of the number of accelerators.

This section introduces various tools for launching, scheduling, and managing the lifecycle of distributed processes involved in conducting distributed training.

Slurm

The Simple Linux Utility for Resource Management, more commonly known as Slurm (*https://oreil.ly/B8zOx*), is a workload management application that itself can run in a distributed fashion. It has a main server node that manages the job queue and allocates jobs to the cluster, consisting of one or more worker nodes. Each worker node has a daemon process, `slurmd`, that coordinates with the server controller, `slurmctld`, to schedule, execute, and synchronize on the results of jobs. An overview of the Slurm architecture is shown in Figure 5-9.

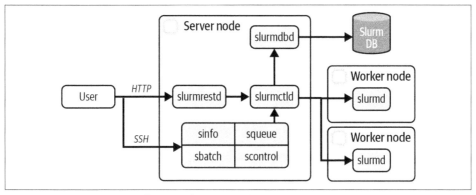

Figure 5-9. Architecture of Slurm (https://oreil.ly/B8zOx)

Slurm permits scheduling and execution of one or more jobs through the `srun` and `sbatch` client commands. Users can define dependencies between jobs by using the `--dependency` option, and the arguments of the main script can be amended for a particular group of jobs, known in Slurm terminology as a *job array* and specified using the `--array` argument, as shown here:

```
$ sbatch --gpus-per-node=v100:1 --array=1-4 -J train_my_amazing_model --data
my.object.store.endpoint --word_count 4
Submitted batch job 21845

$ squeue
 JOBID    PARTITION    NAME    USER  ST  TIME NODES NODELIST
 21845_1   canopo     amaze   small  R  0:13   1     mario
 21845_2   canopo     amaze   small  R  0:13   1     mario
 21845_3   canopo     amaze   small  R  0:13   1     mario
 21845_4   canopo     amaze   small  R  0:13   1     mario
```

GPUs in Slurm are surfaced as Generic Resources (GRES). As shown in the preceding command line, you can configure the number of GPUs per job using the `--gpus-per-node` option. In this example, the batch job (with an ID of `21845`) is running on a node named `mario`; the individual jobs in the array are identified with the suffixes `_1` through `_4`.

Slurm was designed for scale and can cope with about 100K jobs in flight or queued, synchronously executing jobs in parallel or as arrays (grouped jobs). With its centralized design, it can schedule multiple tasks in parallel, allowing you to scale ML frameworks to tens of thousands of cores.

Slurm supports containers (*https://oreil.ly/CDDTl*) (Docker, Podman, etc.), providing flexibility in how you can create and isolate your runtime without polluting the host operating system. This support is limited; for example, containers can't run as root (which may mean you can't run debuggers, which often require root permissions). Container support in Slurm is enabled by the `--container` argument.

A limitation of Slurm is that it is purely workload management software and does not provide predicates for deep learning–based operations such as hyperparameter optimization, etc. It provides crude commands to manage the state of your workload but can neither add fault tolerance nor automatically retry jobs in the event of failure.

Kubernetes

Kubernetes is a container orchestration platform that provides a full feature set to manage and run containerized workloads efficiently and at scale, in a fault-tolerant and resilient manner. Kubernetes follows a declarative deployment paradigm: you specify what you want to deploy, and it takes that as an instruction and works toward achieving that state by automatically provisioning, restarting, and autoscaling (if configured) resources until the final desired state is achieved. It uses a centralized architecture to provision and manage the workload (see Figure 5-10), where the controller directs the deployment of containers and the workload on the nodes. The servers in the server group share the management responsibility, using a very effective coordination technique (using a distributed data store, etcd, that implements the Raft consensus algorithm), making Kubernetes highly available and scalable.

Kubernetes in itself is a vanilla scalable distributed system platform that can run in public, private, and hybrid environments. Additional components can be installed in Kubernetes clusters to provide specialized predicates for specific workloads such as deep learning. Two such components that offer a rich deep learning feature set are Kubeflow and Ray; we'll look at Ray in the next section.

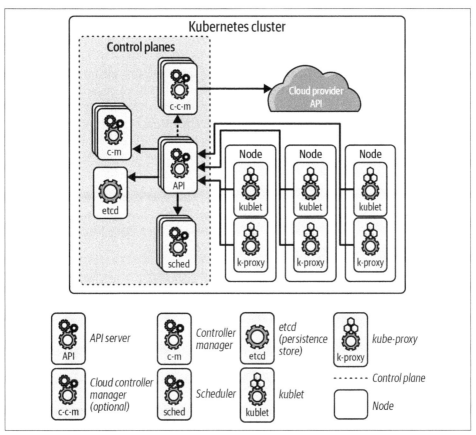

Figure 5-10. Kubernetes architecture (adapted from Kubernetes.io (https://oreil.ly/ Qx7fa))

The full feature set of Kubernetes can be very hard to manage. For this reason, a popular alternative is to use K3s (*https://k3s.io*), a lightweight version that provides all the key workload management features without requiring the huge undertaking of managing a full Kubernetes distribution. There are also cloud-managed versions, like Google Kubernetes Engine (GKE), Amazon Elastic Kubernetes Service (EKS), etc. that can handle the operational overhead for you.

GPUs in Kubernetes are exposed through the use of device plug-ins (*https://oreil.ly/ _KiNQ*). NVIDIA also provides a GPU Operator (*https://oreil.ly/KL-AG*) that can be used to expose GPUs to the containers and make them available as resources in the cluster.

Ray

Ray was created by researchers at the RISELab at UC Berkeley to provide simple abstractions for distributed programming and efficient ways to scale up workloads by distributing them across cores and nodes. Compared to kits like Open MPI, discussed in "MPI" on page 169, Ray is a high-level parallelization framework. It translates Python functions and classes into tasks and actors, allowing serial applications to be easily parallelized without any low-level changes to the application code or design. The core of Ray is written in C++; however, it is Python-first and provides a full set of predicates for deep learning workloads through the Ray AI runtime (AIR).

The architecture for Ray is shown in Figure 5-11. It's very similar to Slurm, except that it features a distributed memory layer and provides higher-order machine learning/deep learning predicates for specialized workloads like data loading, training, serving, inference, and hyperparameter tuning.

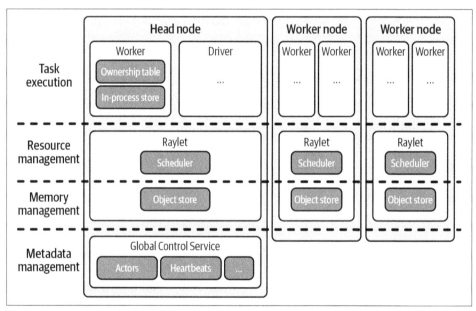

Figure 5-11. Ray architecture[9]

Distributed memory layer. Ray uses Plasma, a high-performance shared memory object store that has now moved to Apache Arrow, to create distributed object stores, providing a consistent store to keep and manage data objects in memory that workers

---

9 Pumperla, Max, Edward Oakes, and Richard Liaw. *Learning Ray*. Sebastopol, CA: O'Reilly Media. *https://oreil.ly/NCE2h*.

across the Ray cluster can share. This data store is not only used for application-level data storage, like in Ray Data (*https://oreil.ly/WMb2B*), but also used internally by Ray Core for interworker communications.

One of the key advantages this provides is zero-copy serialization, essentially eliminating all the overhead that Python multiprocessing faces. In Python, interprocess communication occurs by sending serialized Python objects (obtained via pickling) to other processes that then create their own copies of the deserialized Python objects. This not only results in significant memory overhead but also creates processing overhead and limits the abilities of what can be pickled (for example, lambda functions cannot be pickled). Because of this pickling challenge, packages like Dill (*https://oreil.ly/9bD5z*) (a module for serializing and deserializing Python objects) are increasingly used. To overcome similar challenges, PyTorch also provides a custom package for multiprocessing, a wrapper around the native `multiprocessing` module (*https://oreil.ly/J2a3p*). This PyTorch implementation not only has special serde (serialize/deserialize) handling but also uses shared memory for data exchange between the processes.

Asynchronous model.   Ray provides synchronous and asynchronous paradigms for parallelizing workloads. Its asynchronous model is inspired by Akka's actor framework, which leverages asynchronous messaging for efficient scale-up. Ray also uses gRPC (discussed in "gRPC" on page 168) for efficient communication.

Let's revisit the arXiv crawler exercise from "Scenario walkthrough: A web crawler to curate a links dataset" on page 88, so I can show you how easy it is to switch to using Ray. The first thing you need to do is import Ray, with `import ray`. Since the implementation is object-oriented, not functional, you will be using the decorator `@ray.remote` to annotate the class `TextMatcher`. After this, you will need to make the following changes to distribute your links to workers so they do the text matching in parallel:

```
matcher = TextMatcher.remote(phase_pattern=phase_pattern)
futures = [matcher.find_matched_sentences.remote(link) for link in links]
values = ray.get(futures)
```

Notice the use of the `remote` API (`matcher.find_matched_sentences.remote`) in the second statement. Besides that, the entire implementation is analogous to Python's multithreading/multiprocessing executor. The full example is located in the *ray_crawler.py* script (*https://oreil.ly/nWea9*) in the code repository.

Amazon SageMaker

Amazon SageMaker is a fully managed service for ML development, offering various APIs via the SDK to start workloads around building, training, and deploying ML models. The intention of this service is to abstract away the infrastructure and orchestration aspects so you just have to specify what you want to run and on what kinds of devices. The following code snippet shows the starting of a SageMaker training job:

```
import sagemaker as sage
from sagemaker.estimator import Estimator

session = sage.Session()

dataset_uri = session.upload_data("/your_data_dir", key_prefix="your_data")
ecr_image = "{}.dkr.ecr.{}.amazonaws.com/{}:latest".format(
        "your_aws_account_id", "your_aws_region", "your_container_name")

hyperparameters = {"epochs": 1}

estimator = Estimator(
    role="your_aws_role",
    train_instance_count=1,
    train_instance_type="ml.m4.xlarge",
    image_name=ecr_image,
    hyperparameters=hyperparameters,
)

estimator.fit(dataset_uri)
```

You can find more hands-on examples of using SageMaker in the AWS Amazon SageMaker Examples repository (*https://oreil.ly/r0TPZ*).

Google Vertex AI

Google offers packaged services for AI workloads, similar to SageMaker, with its Vertex AI. Essentially, Vertex AI provides an SDK that enables you to interact with high-level API abstractions to start ML/AI workloads. The following snippet shows how you can start a containerized training job by simply providing the details of your application (i.e., the Python package, container, and task) and specifying the machine type. Vertex AI handles the infrastructure and provisioning for you:

```
import google.cloud.aiplatform as aiplatform

job = aiplatform.CustomPythonPackageTrainingJob(
    display_name="you_experiment",
    python_package_gcs_uri=f"{YOUR_BUCKET_URI}/trainer.tar.gz",
    python_module_name="trainer.task",
    container_uri="your_container_image",
)

CMDARGS = [
    f"--model-dir={YOUR_BUCKET_URI}",
    f"--dataset-uri={YOUR_DATASET_URI}",
    "--epochs=5",
    "--experiment=your_experiment",
```

```
    "--run=run-1",
]

job.run(
    args=CMDARGS,
    replica_count=1,
    machine_type=YOUR_COMPUTE_TYPE,
)

job.delete()
```

You can find additional examples to get you started with Vertex AI in the Google Cloud Vertex AI Samples GitHub repository (*https://oreil.ly/9_ZC9*).

Deep Learning Infrastructure Review

TOP500 (*https://www.top500.org*) is an independent body that maintains statistical comparisons of high-performance computing systems around the world. The LINPACK Benchmarks, introduced by Jack Dongarra, founding director of the Innovative Computing Laboratory at the University of Tennessee and an HPC legend, are used in ranking the systems; they test a system's performance at solving a dense system of linear equations, providing a measure of its floating-point computing power. Currently, HPL (*https://oreil.ly/eL4Lz*), an implementation of LINPACK that transparently uses libraries such as MPI and BLAS, is used by TOP500.

Overview of Leading Deep Learning Clusters

In this section I'll discuss some of the leading HPC systems at the time of writing (based on benchmarks gathered in November 2023). These systems are heavily used in large-scale computing, including large-scale deep learning training. Reviewing their configuration provides insights into the kinds of hardware that are widely used in large-scale supercomputers for deep learning today, and their abilities. The top 10 supercomputers as late 2023 include:

Frontier
> Housed at the Oak Ridge National Laboratory (ORNL) in Tennessee, the HPE Cray EX system Frontier achieved 1.194 EFLOPs on the LINPACK benchmark using 8,699,904 cores. It combines third-generation AMD EPYC CPUs optimized for HPC and AI with AMD Instinct 250X accelerators and a Slingshot-11 interconnect.

Aurora
> Housed at the Argonne Leadership Computing Facility in Illinois and operated for the US Department of Energy, newcomer Aurora catapulted nearly to the top of the list by achieving 585.34 PFLOPs on the LINPACK Benchmark using 4,742,808 cores. Notably, this score was achieved with a measurement on half of

the planned final system. Based on the HPE Cray EX Intel Exascale Compute Blade, Aurora uses Intel Xeon CPU Max Series processors and Intel Data Center GPU Max Series accelerators with a Slingshot-11 network interconnect.

Eagle

Installed in the Microsoft Azure cloud, Eagle, another newcomer, achieved 561 PFLOPs on the LINPACK Benchmark using 1,123,200 cores. Eagle is a Microsoft NDv5 system based on Xeon Platinum 8480C processors and NVIDIA H100 accelerators.

Fugaku

Housed at the RIKEN Center for Computational Science (R-CCS) in Kobe, Japan, Fugaku features 7,630,848 cores and achieved 442 PFLOPs on the LIN-PACK Benchmark. Fugaku, however, does not have accelerated computing capability.

LUMI

Housed at the EuroHPC center at the IT Center for Science (CSC) in Finland, LUMI is another HPE Cray EX system that clocked 380 PFLOPs on the LIN-PACK Benchmark using 2,752,704 cores. It consists of third-generation AMD EPYC 64C 2 GHz CPUs optimized for HPC and AI, with AMD Instinct 250X accelerators and a Slingshot-11 interconnect.

Leonardo

Housed at Cineca, a EuroHPC site in Italy, Leonardo is an Atos BullSequana XH2000 system that clocked 238.7 PFLOPs on the LINPACK Benchmark using 1,824,768 cores. It consists of Xeon Platinum 8358 32C 2.6 GHz CPUs with NVI-DIA A100 SXM4 64 GB accelerators and a quad-rail NVIDIA HDR100 Infini-Band interconnect.

Summit

Housed at ORNL in Tennessee, Summit is an IBM-built system that achieved 148.8 PFLOPs on the LINPACK Benchmark using 2,414,592 cores. It consists of IBM POWER9 CPUs with NVIDIA Tesla V100 accelerators and a dual-rail Mel-lanox EDR InfiniBand interconnect.

Rounding out the global top 10 list as of November 2023 are two more newcomers, the MareNostrum 5 ACC system and NVIDIA's Eos, along with Sierra, another IBM-built system with a similar architecture to Summit. You can find details on these on the TOP500 website (*https://oreil.ly/hjmdr*). In addition to the world's top 10 super-computers, there are a few others that I'd like to highlight due to their scale:

Jean Zay

Jean Zay is a French supercomputer designed for AI, acquired by the French Ministry of Higher Education, Research, and Innovation. Built in collaboration with Hewlett Packard Enterprise (HPE) and installed at IDRIS, a national computing center for the Centre National de la Recherche Scientifique (CNRS), it clocked 36.85 PFLOPs at peak performance following updates made in June 2022. The system consists of assorted sets of CPU (AMD) and GPU (NVIDIA) nodes, with the GPUs NVLink-interconnected in a dedicated subnet to efficiently communicate over NCCL. A full description of the architecture is available on the IDRIS website (*https://oreil.ly/1x308*).

The servers are virtualized by hypervisor technologies and surfaced for use by Slurm. Jean Zay was used to train BLOOM (*https://oreil.ly/ztufH*), the world's largest open multilingual language model.

Microsoft Azure

AI capability at Google, AWS, and Microsoft is powered by in-house infrastructure they own as PaaS providers. Not a lot of details of their infrastructure capabilities are publicly known, possibly for commercial reasons. However, Microsoft Azure is known to power or supplement the compute capacity of heavy hitters such as:

OpenAI

OpenAI implements hybrid supercomputer environments combining public and private cloud infrastructure. OpenAI has been using Azure's supercomputers since 2020 to power its AI development,[10] with 40 GB ND and 80 GB NDm A100 v4 VMs reportedly used to handle large-scale production workloads.[11] It uses Kubernetes to orchestrate and deploy its AI workload, which is known to scale to at least 7.5K nodes; a post on the OpenAI blog describes in detail the configuration of the cluster, including how they test.[12]

Meta

Meta also implements hybrid supercomputer environments using Azure, AWS (in the past, certainly,[13] although more recent trends seem to favor Azure), and its own private AI cluster known as the "AI Research SuperCluster." Meta seems to be investing heavily in compute. In 2022, it announced

---

10 Langston, Jennifer. 2020. "Microsoft Announces New Supercomputer, Lays Out Vision for Future AI Work." Microsoft, May 19, 2020. *https://oreil.ly/7yPhM*.

11 Wang, Sherry. 2021. "Microsoft Expands Its AI-Supercomputer Lineup with General Availability of the Latest 80GB NVIDIA A100 GPUs in Azure, Claims 4 Spots on TOP500 Supercomputers List." Azure Compute Blog, November 15, 2021. *https://oreil.ly/rUWVb*.

12 Sigler, Eric, and Benjamin Chess. 2021. "Scaling Kubernetes to 7,500 Nodes." OpenAI blog, January 25, 2021. *https://openai.com/research/scaling-kubernetes-to-7500-nodes*.

13 Hellard, Bobby. 2021. Meta Picks AWS to Help Expand Its AI Services. ITPro, December 2, 2021. *https://www.itpro.com/cloud/cloud-computing/361723/meta-selects-aws-as-strategic-cloud-provider-ai*.

plans to scale to 16,000 NVIDIA A100 GPUs, interconnected over 16 TB/sec InfiniBand and supported by Pure Storage for secondary storage.[14] Later that year, the company also announced it would be building secondary clusters including 5,400 NVIDIA A100 GPUs and 1,350 AMD Milan Epyc 7V13 CPUs delivered using the NDm A100 v4-series instances on Azure.[15] More recently, Meta revealed its intention to build a cluster of 350K NVIDIA H100 nodes.[16]

Tesla Dojo

In 2021, Tesla announced its own specialized acceleration chip, the D1, and a supercomputer built using this chip, known as Dojo.[17] Dojo is specially designed for video processing and vision-based AI development for training and auto-labeling systems (a.k.a. a data engine, discussed in Chapter 1). Prior to Dojo, Tesla reportedly used 720 8x NVIDIA A100 Tensor Core GPUs to power its AI development.[18]

Similarities Between Today's Most Powerful Systems

As you reviewed some of the world's most powerful systems that are fueling deep learning training today, you may have noted that all these clusters are heterogeneous. The key features of these clusters are CPU units, GPU units, and a high-speed inter-connect, be it via Slingshot or InfiniBand. It's interesting to note that while NVIDIA is currently dominating the GPU industry, as discussed in "Graphics processing units (GPUs)" on page 94, only about half of the leading supercomputers use NVIDIA accelerators. Frontier, LUMI, and others, for example, are based on AMD GPUs. This is in line with the discussion of the competition landscape in Chapter 3.

---

14 Lee, Kevin, and Shubho Sengupta. 2022. "Introducing the AI Research SuperCluster — Meta's Cutting-Edge AI Supercomputer for AI Research." AI at Meta Blog, January 24, 2022. *https://ai.meta.com/blog/ai-rsc.*

15 Moss, Sebastian. 2022. "Meta/Facebook to Use Dedicated Microsoft Azure Cluster for AI Supercomputing." DCD, May 26, 2022. *https://www.datacenterdynamics.com/en/news/metafacebook-to-use-dedicated-microsoft-azure-cluster-for-ai-supercomputing.*

16 Quach, Katyanna. 2024. "Zuckerberg Wants to Build Artificial General Intelligence with 350K Nvidia H100 GPUs." The Register, January 20, 2024. *https://www.theregister.com/2024/01/20/metas_ai_plans.*

17 Lambert, Fred. 2021. "Tesla Unveils Dojo Supercomputer: World's New Most Powerful AI Training Machine." Electrek, August 20, 2021. *https://electrek.co/2021/08/20/tesla-dojo-supercomputer-worlds-new-most-powerful-ai-training-machine.*

18 Shahan, Zachary. 2021. "NVIDIA: Tesla's AI-Training Supercomputers Powered By Our GPUs." Clean-Technica, August 19, 2021. *https://cleantechnica.com/2021/08/19/nvidia-teslas-ai-training-supercomputers-powered-by-us.*

Summary

In this chapter, you learned about distributed systems and explored various communication strategies and patterns actively utilized in scaling out deep learning training. You learned about the advantages and limitations of some of these communication paradigms and technologies, and you looked at various options to expand your infrastructure and how to choose infrastructure and services for your scale-out. You also learned a little about the composition of the world's leading supercomputers that are powering many deep learning use cases.

Building on these concepts, in the following chapter, you will explore the theoretical concepts involved in distributing the deep learning training workflow and explore patterns leveraged in scaling out training. You will revisit the data flow you read about in Chapter 2 and explore the implications of the distribution of training workloads across a cluster of workers on that data flow. You'll also learn about various distribution strategies for parallelizing deep learning and explore how best to choose the right strategy for your use case.

## CHAPTER 6

Theoretical Foundations of Distributed Deep Learning

This chapter introduces the key concepts and theoretical formulations of distributed deep learning (DDL), building on your learning from Part I of this book. You will revisit centralized and decentralized systems (described in the previous chapter) through the lens of DDL and explore the impact on the data flow and computation graphs when using these techniques. In this chapter, you will also learn about the different types of distributed learning and how to decide what type of DDL might be most suitable to scale out your training.

Distributed Deep Learning

Chapter 2 described the data flow during training, explaining the *gradient computation flow*, which involves the forward pass and backward pass, and the *parameter update flow*, which is guided by optimization techniques such as gradient descent. A pictorial presentation of these flows is shown in Figure 6-1. As shown in this figure, the gradient computation flow (indicated by the solid arrows) is local to the computation graphs, while the parameter update flow (indicated by the dashed arrows) closes the loop to complete the learning for each optimization step.

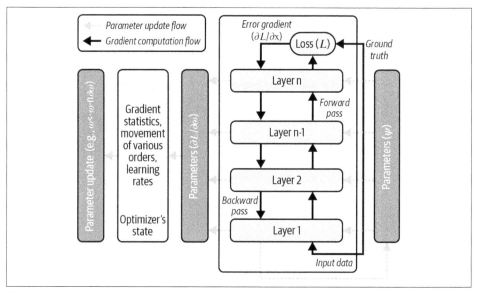

Figure 6-1. Revisiting the data flow in deep learning training

Within the framework of distributed systems, the data flow in training is distributed such that the independent processes execute the local gradient computation flow and communicate and collaborate to achieve a global parameter update flow (see Figure 6-2 in the next section). Optimizers play a crucial role in the parameter update flow, as they guide the rate at which gradient updates are applied. Due to this global role, scaling out training necessitates that the implementation of optimizers be distributed so that training can cope with gradients coming from several independent processes, each executing its own respective local gradient flow.

With this in mind, let's explore how training is distributed for the centralized and decentralized paradigms. The following sections will dive into the details of these DDL modes.

Centralized DDL

As you learned in Chapter 5, centralized systems have a server group (with one or more members) that coordinates the distributed workload. In DDL, the servers in this group are commonly known as parameter servers. In centralized DDL, the local flow (gradient computation) is scaled out on a set of worker processes, while the global flow (parameter updates) is centralized to the parameter server group.

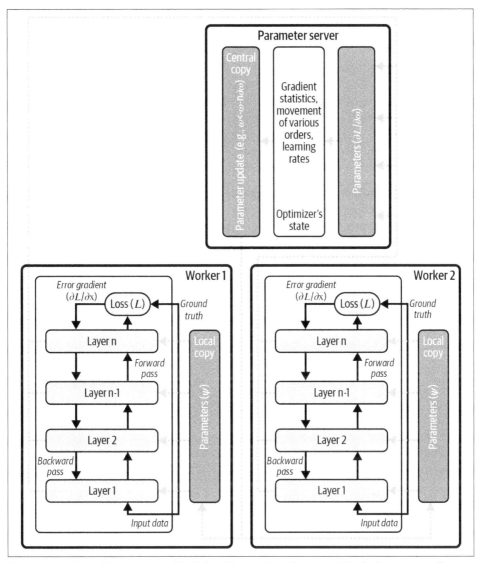

Figure 6-2. Data flow in centralized distributed deep learning (dashed arrows indicate the global parameter update flow and solid arrows indicate the local gradient flow)

Scaling in centralized DDL is achieved by increasing the number of workers computing the local flow. The reliability of this mode, on the other hand, comes from ensuring consistency and availability of the server group. Having only one member in the parameter server group creates a single point of failure. Having one or more redundant/inactive replicas improves reliability, but leads to inefficient use of resources.

One way to improve the reliability and efficiency of the parameter server group could be to parallelize the global parameter update flow by partitioning the task among the group's members and having them collaborate to collectively perform updates. Considering that the majority of optimization algorithms can execute independently for each parameter of the model, distributing the parameter server load in this way is possible. In practice, however, this is very hard to achieve, not only because of the increased complexity of the optimization algorithms (and implementation thereof) but also because of the increased communication overhead.[1] For these reasons, the most common paradigm with centralized DDL is using a single parameter server. However, this setup is not reliable and can quickly become a bottleneck as the number of workers is scaled out.

In the following section, you will learn about an alternative configuration where the responsibility of the parameter server(s) is migrated to the workers themselves.

Parameter server configurations

There are four possible parameter server configurations in centralized DDL:

Single parameter server
> In this configuration, a single parameter server instance is used for centralization purposes. As discussed earlier, this server is a single point of failure.

Parameter server with replica(s)
> This is an extension of the single parameter server configuration wherein one or more replicas are maintained for redundancy. In the event of the failure of the parameter server, a replica takes over and becomes the main server. This is not a commonly used setup, because not only does the switchover require additional management, but also maintaining replicas makes for ineffective utilization of resources.

Group of parameter servers
> In this configuration, multiple parameter servers are run and the server's responsibility is partitioned amongst them. This configuration increases reliability, but again at the expense of efficiency in resource utilization.

Joint worker/server
> This is a refinement of the group of parameter servers configuration wherein the parameter server's responsibility is partitioned between the workers. There are two possible subconfigurations in this category:

---

1 Zhang, Sixin. 2016. "Distributed Stochastic Optimization for Deep Learning." PhD diss., New York University. arXiv, May 7, 2016. *https://arxiv.org/abs/1605.02216.*

Weight-partitioned joint worker/server

In this configuration, each worker takes on the responsibility of updating a chunk of the parameter weights, thus parallelizing the parameter update workflow. This is shown on the left in Figure 6-3: each worker updates only their respective chunk, w_i, and communicates the updated chunk to the other workers. A major drawback here is that the failure of any worker will result in full system failure.

Gradient-partitioned joint worker/server

This configuration provides more reliability than the previous one. In this case, each worker updates all the parameters and communicates its results to the others using the all-reduce communication paradigm, meaning the failure of any worker merely results in loss of information (in line with the CAP theorem) and not total system failure. This configuration, shown on the right in Figure 6-3, is thus more popular and more widely used. The drawback in this case is that significant communication bandwidth is required to exchange all the gradients and model parameters.

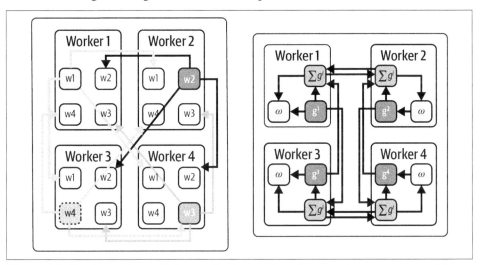

Figure 6-3. Configurations of joint worker/server-based parameter servers as used in centralized DDL[2]

---

2 Langer, Matthias, Zhen He, Wenny Rahayu, and Yanbo Xue. 2020. "Distributed Training of Deep Learning Models: A Taxonomic Perspective." arXiv, July 8, 2020. *https://arxiv.org/abs/2007.03970*.

Subtypes of centralized DDL

The workers in DDL can be configured to communicate synchronously or asynchronously. The optimization algorithm and the server group need to be configured accordingly to handle the (sync or async) communication from workers to ensure good collaboration and convergence. As discussed in Chapter 5, the CAP theorem is considered in ensuring the server/worker communication flows effectively.

Depending on the communication pattern, centralized DDL is subclassed into two types, as discussed in the following subsections.

Synchronous centralized DDL. Synchronous centralized DDL training has the simplest distributed algorithm implementation, as it employs the barrier communication pattern to wait until gradient communications from all workers have been received. This is shown in Figure 6-4, which highlights how the parameter server collects gradients from all the workers, conducts the parameter update, and broadcasts the updated weights to all the workers.

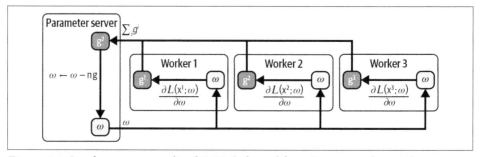

Figure 6-4. Synchronous centralized DDL (adapted from Langer et al., 2020)

The algorithmic approach in this implementation requires all workers to be initialized with the same initial weight values. This is followed by the local gradient computation flow and synchronous reduction of the gradients, leading to weight updates on each worker. The high-level algorithm for the parameter server and workers is given by the following pseudocode. On the parameter server:

1. Initialize the server with model weight w_0 and learning rate η
2. For each mini-batch (i.e., step $t \leftarrow 0, 1, 2, 3\ldots$):
   a. Broadcast w_t to all workers n.
   b. Wait until gradients g_i from all workers n are received.
   c. Apply $w_{t+i} \leftarrow w_t - \eta\sum_{i=0}^{n} g_i$.

On the worker processes:

1. For workers n, for each mini-batch (i.e., step $t \leftarrow 0, 1, 2, 3\ldots$):

    a. Wait to receive w_{t-1} from the server.

    b. Conduct forward and backward pass on the mini-batch data.

    c. Deduce gradients g_i on the worker, using $g_i \leftarrow \frac{\delta L\ (x_i,\ w_t)}{\delta w_t}$.

    d. Send g_i to the server.

Asynchronous centralized DDL. In asynchronous centralized DDL training, the server applies the gradients received from workers as they come in, without waiting to receive gradients from all workers. This decoupling allows all communications between the workers and the server to be asynchronous, resulting in increased efficiency through communication interleaving and latency hiding. A pictorial representation of asynchronous centralized DDL is shown in Figure 6-5, outlining the weight updating and weight sharing happening asynchronously.

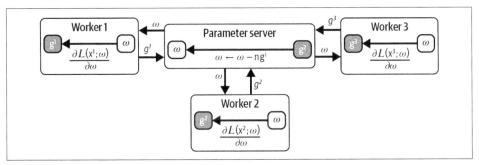

Figure 6-5. Asynchronous centralized DDL (adapted from Langer et al., 2020)

The high-level algorithm for asynchronous centralized DDL is similar to that for synchronous centralized DDL, except that gradients from each worker (computed during the local gradient flow) are received asynchronously, followed by a weight update if the gradients are received within the desired time range. Otherwise, the update is ignored.

The pseudoworkflow for the parameter server and workers for asynchronous centralized DDL is as follows. On the parameter server:

1. Initialize the server with model weight w_0 and learning rate η.

2. Broadcast w_0 to all workers n.

3. While step $t \leftarrow 0, 1, 2, 3\ldots$:

    a. Receive (asynchronously) gradients $g_{t-\delta}^i$ from worker i, where δ is the delay in steps.

    b. If δ is in the acceptable range:

c. Update weights: $w_{t'} \leftarrow w_t \, \eta \, g^i_{t\text{-}\delta}$.

d. Send $w_{t'}$ to worker i (asynchronously).

On the worker processes:

1. For workers n, for each mini-batch (i.e., step $t \leftarrow 0, 1, 2, 3\ldots$):

    a. Receive (asynchronously) w_{t-1} from the server.

    b. Conduct forward and backward pass on the mini-batch data.

    c. Deduce gradients g_i on the worker, using $g_i \leftarrow \dfrac{\delta L \;(x_i,\; w_t)}{\delta w_t}$.

    d. Send (asynchronously) g_i to the server.

Because of this async workflow, the last worker to update the parameters drives the direction of convergence. Figure 6-6 shows an example of two workers (and the parameter server) collaborating asynchronously to converge to an optimal minimum. As the server receives gradients from each worker, the model gets pulled in the direction of that worker's gradient. In the subsequent update, the next worker then pulls the model in the direction of its own gradients, but also gets pulled in the direction of the other worker itself through the server's weight download. Through such repeated updates, the workers navigate the loss curve both workers collectively to achieve convergence.

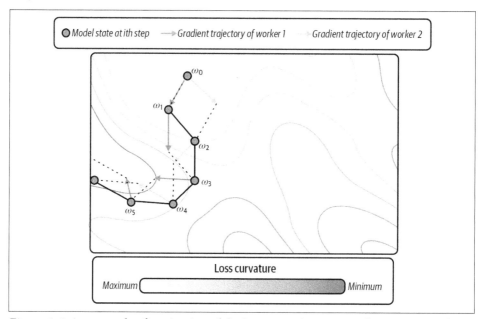

Figure 6-6. An example of navigation of the loss curve during asynchronous centralized DDL (adapted from Langer et al., 2020)

Consistency and alignment of all workers are crucial for the success of DDL. For example, in cases where one or more workers become biased, slow or even no convergence becomes possible. Noisy gradients and stale workers pose a significant risk of destabilizing the asynchronous centralized DDL training. Optimization techniques like Adam[3] that capture gradient statistics and account for gradient moments provide more stability in training, but this risk is always present in any scaled-out DDL scenario. Metrics to manage this will be discussed in "Time to convergence" on page 221.

Decentralized DDL

In decentralized DDL, there are only workers; there is no dedicated central server(s). In decentralized training, one of the workers is elected as a leader, which then coordinates any collaboration as needed. The leader is traditionally identified with rank 0.

The data flow observed in decentralized DDL is shown in Figure 6-7. In this configuration, each worker not only computes its own gradient computation flow but also performs the parameter update flow locally. These local updates are then synced globally on the leader of the decentralized group. The workers are highly decoupled, as they conduct the entire training cycle independently. This decoupling of parameter updates allows the workers to independently progress training with minimal communication and network bandwidth requirements, compared to their centralized counterparts. This independence is introduced with the assumption that workers will eventually converge, even though they may take different optimization trajectories to navigate loss curves. However, there is a risk of workers significantly diverging over a period of time, so decentralized DDL requires that measures be implemented to limit divergence amongst the workers. While this type of distribution is more scalable, the algorithm to update a model while maintaining consistency to achieve convergence is more complex, and limiting divergence remains a key challenge of decentralized DDL.

---

3 Kingma, Diederik P., and Jimmy Ba. 2014. "Adam: A Method for Stochastic Optimization." arXiv, December 22, 2014. *https://arxiv.org/abs/1412.6980*.

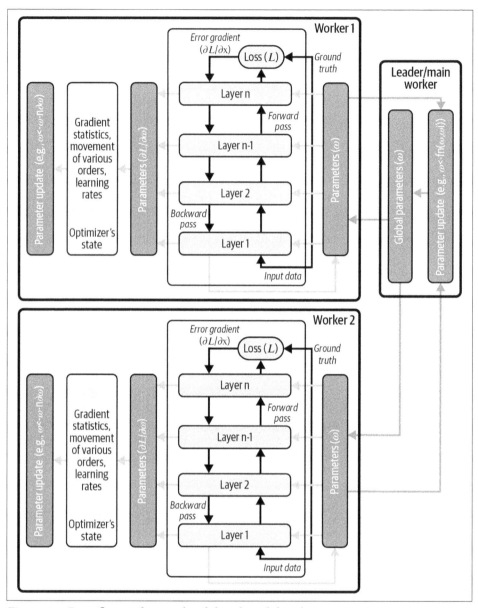

Figure 6-7. Data flow in decentralized distributed deep learning

Limiting divergence

To limit divergence between workers, two additional phases are introduced: exploration and exploitation.[4] During the *exploration* phase, the workers are independently following their training regime and navigating the loss curve, guided by the optimization algorithm. In the *exploitation* phase, local optimization is interrupted in order to sync the model parameters with the leader, which merges the updates from all the workers and sends them a revised global state to provide better averaging over the training conducted so far. The iteration of the decentralized worker training loop through exploration and exploitation allows optimizers to find the majority consensus (amongst the workers) minima (of loss).

Figure 6-8 demonstrates this process as the workers navigate the loss curve. This type of learning is somewhat collaborative, as the individual workers explore subregions and then corroborate their findings, collectively converging to a new state until final convergence is achieved. In this process, any workers that become biased also get an opportunity to correct their alignment.

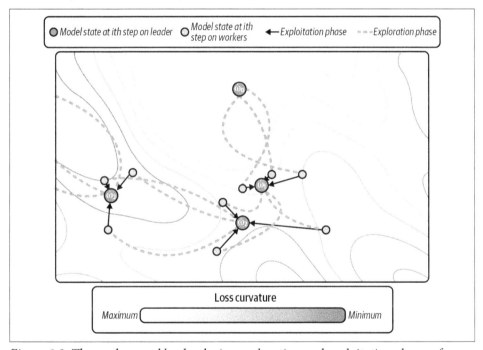

Figure 6-8. The workers and leader during exploration and exploitation phases of training (adapted from Langer et al., 2020)

---

4 Langer et al., "Distributed Training of Deep Learning Models," *https://arxiv.org/abs/2007.03970*.

Since decentralized DDL requires each worker to conduct training independently, this is not suitable for scaling out training in scenarios where workers have insufficient resources (GPU/memory/CPU) to conduct both the gradient computation and parameter update flows. This is the key limitation of decentralized DDL. For instance, if your minimum training time GPU VRAM requirement is 34 GB but your GPU has 32 GB VRAM capacity, then it will not help. In Chapters 8 and 9 you will read about training techniques to tackle such memory limitations. The workflows discussed in this chapter predominantly relate to data parallel techniques, discussed in detail in Chapter 7, but also form the basis for scaling beyond data parallelism.

Subtypes of decentralized DDL

Depending on the communication paradigm, decentralized DDL can be set up in two ways, as discussed in the following subsections.

Synchronous decentralized DDL. In synchronous decentralized DDL, each worker completes the exploration and exploitation phases independently for τ steps. After the τ steps, the leader synchronizes the weights across the workers before the loop begins again. An example of synchronous decentralized DDL is SparkNet, a framework for training deep networks on Apache Spark.[5] SparkNet implements synchronous decentralized training using the barrier communication pattern (discussed in Chapter 5), allowing synchronization of weights after every τ steps. Figure 6-9 demonstrates this workflow, showing how broadcast and all-reduce (synchronous) are used to realize this type of DDL. The exploration and exploitation phases of synchronous decentralization follow the pattern shown in Figure 6-8, where periodic synchronization facilitates consistency across the workers intermittently.

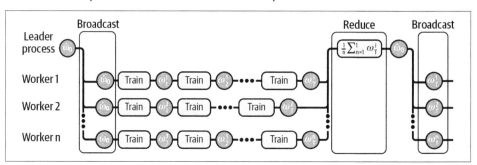

Figure 6-9. A pictorial representation of synchronous decentralized DDL (adapted from Langer et al., 2020)

5 Moritz, Phillip, Robert Nishihara, Ion Stoica, and Michael I. Jordan. 2016. "SparkNet: Training Deep Networks in Spark." arXiv, November 19, 2015. *https://arxiv.org/abs/1511.06051*.

The core of synchronous decentralization rests in periodic synchronization of all workers every τ steps, but independent execution within that τ-step range. The barrier communication pattern is used every τ steps to enforce this synchronization across all workers.

The pseudo-workflow of asynchronous centralized DDL for the leader and worker processes is as follows. On the leader process:

1. Initialize the model weight w_0, the number of workers n, and the step counter $t \leftarrow 0$.

2. Broadcast w_0 to all workers n.

3. At every step τ, repeat:

    a. Receive weights $w^i_{t+\tau}$ from worker i.

    b. Apply all-reduce weight averaging strategy (e.g., linear average):

    c. Update the weights: $w_{t+\tau} \leftarrow \dfrac{1}{n \Sigma w^i_{t+\tau}}$.

    d. Update $t \leftarrow t + \tau$

4. End while.

On all worker processes:

1. Configure each worker n with training data d^i, learning rate η, and step counter $t \leftarrow 0$.

2. While training, repeat:

    a. Receive w_t from the leader's broadcast.

    b. Replace local weights: $w^i_t \leftarrow w_t$.

    c. For each step $s \leftarrow range(0, \tau)$, repeat:

        i. Conduct forward and backward pass on the mini-batch data.

        ii. Deduce gradients g_i on the worker using $g_i \leftarrow \dfrac{\delta L\ (x_i,\ w_i)}{\delta w_i}$.

        iii. Update the worker's weights: $w^i_s \leftarrow w^i_{s-1} - \eta g_i$.

    d. End for.

    e. Send the weights w^i_s to the leader.

    f. Update $t \leftarrow t + \tau$.

3. End while.

Asynchronous decentralized DDL. In asynchronous decentralized DDL, the weight aggregation from the workers happens asynchronously on the leader without any synchronization barrier. Similar to with centralized async DDL, the leader's weights are pulled in the direction of the weights of the last worker to update. The lack of a periodic collective consensus (as present in this approach's synchronous counterpart) results in an increased degree of freedom in the pull applied on the leader by the individual workers, creating a significant risk of instability.

An example of the exploration and exploitation stages as observed in asynchronous decentralized DDL is shown in Figure 6-10, underscoring the independent trajectories taken by the workers. The navigation of the loss curve can get very noisy, as is evident in this figure, increasing the risk of workers getting stuck in poor minima or failing to converge.

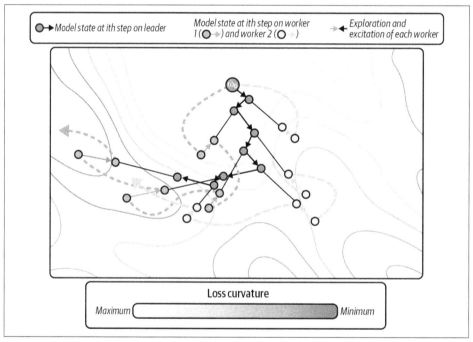

Figure 6-10. The workers, including the leader, during the exploration and exploitation phases of asynchronous decentralized DDL training (adapted from Langer et al., 2020)

The asynchronous decentralized training workflow is shown in Figure 6-11, to demonstrate how broadcast and async send and receive communication is used to realize this type of DDL.

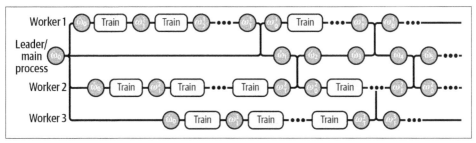

Figure 6-11. A pictorial demonstration of asynchronous decentralized training and coordination with workers

Several algorithms have been proposed to realize parallel asynchronous gradient descent to enable convergence.[6] *Elastic averaging stochastic gradient descent* (EASGD) is one such algorithm, recommending linear interpolation of weights by a known rate ranging between 0 and 0.5 to simulate a controlled push and pull between the workers and leader.[7] EASGD recommends updating the weights of the workers (w^i_w) and leader (w_l) in opposite directions at their own respective rates r_w and r_l, such that after τ steps, the worker updates its weights by $w^i_w \leftarrow w^i_w - r_w(w^i_w - w_l)$ while the leader updates its by $w_l \leftarrow w_l + r_l(w^i_w - w_l)$. This style of weight adjustment corresponds to the squared L2 norm of the leader and worker weights.[8]

Overall, the stability in asynchronous decentralized DDL is managed by elastic weight averaging factors r_l and r_w and the length of the exploration phase (i.e., step interval τ. Due to the high independence and decoupling of workers, computationally asynchronous decentralized DDL scales roughly linearly; however, overall convergence is harder to achieve, not only because of the higher degree of freedom to navigate the loss landscape, but also the lack of collective consensus.

The pseudo-workflow of asynchronous decentralized DDL for the leader and worker processes is as follows. On the leader process:

1. Initialize the model weight w_0, the number of workers n, and the elastic averaging factor r_l.

2. While in training, do:

    a. If i^{th} worker requests weights, then:

    b. Send leader's current t^{th} model weights w_{l_t} to the worker.

---

6 Langer et al., "Distributed Training of Deep Learning Models," *https://arxiv.org/abs/2007.03970*

7 Zhang, Sixin, Anna Choromanska, and Yann LeCun. 2014. "Deep Learning with Elastic Averaging SGD." arXiv, December 20, 2014. *https://arxiv.org/abs/1412.6651.*

8 Langer et al., "Distributed Training of Deep Learning Models," *https://arxiv.org/abs/2007.03970*

   c. End if.

   d. If receive the difference in weights (i.e., $\delta^i \leftarrow w_i^w - w_{l,t}$) from i^{th} worker, then:

   e. Apply the weight update strategy (e.g., as in EASGD): $w_{l,t+\tau} \leftarrow w_{l,t} + r_l \delta^i$.

   f. End if.

3. End while.

On all worker processes:

1. Configure each worker n with training data d^i, learning rate η, step counter $t \leftarrow 0$, and elastic weight averaging rate r_w.

2. Receive w_0 from the leader and initialize the worker's weights: $w_i \leftarrow w_0$.

3. While training, with step as t, do:

   a. For each step $s \leftarrow range(0, \tau)$, repeat:

      i. Conduct forward and backward pass on the mini-batch data.

      ii. Deduce gradients g_i on the worker, using $g_i \leftarrow \frac{\delta L\ (x_i,\ w_i)}{\delta w_i}$.

      iii. Update the worker's weights: $w_s^i \leftarrow w_{s-1}^i - \eta g_i$.

   b. End for.

   c. Download the weights w_{l_t} from the leader.

   d. Estimate the difference of weights: $\delta^i \leftarrow w_w^i - w_{l_t}$.

   e. Send δ^i to the leader.

   f. Update the local weights: $w_w^i \leftarrow w_w^i - r_w \delta^i$.

   g. Update $t \leftarrow t + \tau$.

4. End while.

Decentralized DDL has significant potential to provide compute efficiency, but as worker independence increases, the risk of an adverse impact on convergence also increases. The risk also rises as the number of workers grows, due to the increased risk of noisy gradients and incompatible models. Consequently, decentralized DDL techniques are less commonly used in practice than centralized techniques, despite their potential for huge efficiency gains.

You now have a theoretical understanding of distributed deep learning and how it relates to distributed systems in the context of deep learning and model training. With these concepts in mind, the following section will dive into details of how your training regime is parallelized to realized distributed deep learning.

Dimensions of Scaling Distributed Deep Learning

You have read about the implications of data flow in your training regime should you scale your training workload and distribute it across a fleet of machines. In this section, you will read about different options for distributing the training workload and what your dimensions of scalability are. We'll also briefly review how these dimensions are leveraged to implement various types of distributed deep learning training techniques.

Partitioning Dimensions of Distributed Deep Learning

In the previous section, you learned about data flow in distributed deep learning and explored how optimization techniques are adapted to coordinate across workers to achieve collaborative learning. The key to DDL is to allow each worker to work independently on different parts of the problem. So, what are the dimensions of deep learning that these workers could be partitioned on?

To partition model training, you can partition the input or the computational operations. From an input perspective, you can partition either the hyperparameters or the training data across workers. With regard to computational operations, you have the directed acyclic graph (DAG) representing the model hierarchy (i.e., the network architecture). The network is composed of blocks of layers, and each layer is composed of a set of operations and (learnable and non-learnable) parameters. The layers' operations (the kernels) are already vectorized for parallelization at the tensor level, such that partitioning occurs across the dimension of tensors. This leaves you with the two remaining partitioning opportunities:

Partitioning on blocks of layers
> This is an inter-layer partitioning where the network is partitioned into blocks of layers to be computed in parallel.

Partitioning the layer itself
> This is an intra-layer partitioning where, following SIMD, the layer's operations can be applied in parallel over chunks of (the layer's) parameter tensors.

These potential dimensions of partitioning and parallelism are shown in Figure 6-12.

All together, these four dimensions are utilized in various combinations to realize seven actively used distributed training strategies, discussed in the following section.

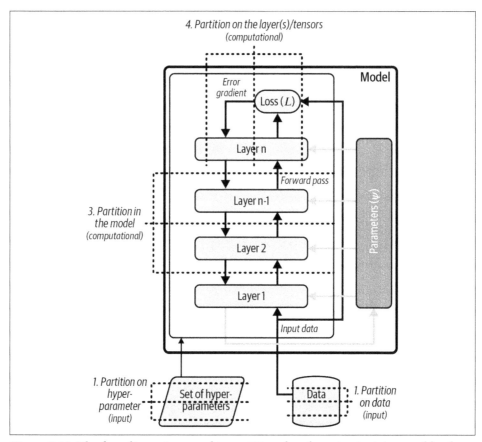

Figure 6-12. The four dimensions used to partition deep learning training workloads: data, hyperparameters, network (model), and layers (i.e., parameters)

Types of Distributed Deep Learning Techniques

Ensembling, federated learning, and data, model, pipeline, tensor, and hybrid parallelism are all actively used distributed deep learning techniques. In this section, we'll take a look at each of these techniques.

Ensembling

Ensembling is a sporadically used technique in classical ML that has proven its value in the deep learning landscape as well. With this approach, multiple models are developed for the same task, and their predictions are combined through a process known as *ensemble learning*. The models are bundled together as a unified system, and the resulting ensemble model is used upon inference to decide on the output for a given input. Ensembling can be seen as a distributed learning technique because multiple models are trained in parallel, either on different sets of hyperparameters or different data or tasks; see Figure 6-13(a).

The premise behind ensembles is to increase the statistical performance of the model by mixing together the contributions of various "expert" models to provide a more generalized and robust outcome. Bagging, boosting, bucketing, stacking, and random forests are some popular ensembling techniques. Alternatively, an ensemble can be created by training multiple highly specialized models for specific chunks of a task and assembling them via routing/gating logic, as in the mixture of experts (MoE) approach[9] shown in Figure 6-13(b).

Ensembling is also used in settings where training data is limited. In such scenarios, k-fold cross-validation techniques are used to develop k models, each trained on a different subset or "fold" of the dataset. These k models are then combined to create a more generalized expert model that will effectively have learned from the entire dataset. The challenge with this technique is that it requires k times more training effort and thus is k times as expensive to develop. Recently, techniques like model souping and population model weight averaging have emerged to provide greater compute efficiency during inference by reducing (via averaging techniques) these trained expert models into a single expert model.[10]

From an engineering viewpoint, ensembling is a highly parallelizable training regime due to the total independence and isolation of each of the models during training. As shown in Figure 6-13(a), both the gradient computation flow and the parameter update flow are kept completely isolated for each model in the ensemble. This makes ensembling embarrassingly parallel in itself. However, each model in an ensemble can still employ one or more of the following distributed learning approaches to scale out individual learning, as needed.

---

9 Shazeer, Noam, Azalia Mirhoseini, Krzysztof Maziarz, Andy Davis, Quoc Le, Geoffrey Hinton, and Jeff Dean. 2017. "Outrageously Large Neural Networks: The Sparsely-Gated Mixture-of-Experts Layer." arXiv, January 23, 2017. *https://arxiv.org/abs/1701.06538*.

10 Mitchell Wortsman, Gabriel Ilharco, Samir Yitzhak Gadre, Rebecca Roelofs, Raphael Gontijo-Lopes, Ari S. Morcos, Hongseok Namkoong, et al. 2022. "Model Soups: Averaging Weights of Multiple Fine-Tuned Models Improves Accuracy Without Increasing Inference Time." arXiv, July 1, 2022. *https://arxiv.org/abs/2203.05482*; Jolicoeur-Martineau, Alexia, Emy Gervais, Kilian Fatras, Yan Zhang, and Simon Lacoste-Julien. 2023. "PopulAtion Parameter Averaging (PAPA)." arXiv, May 24, 2023. *https://arxiv.org/abs/2304.03094*.

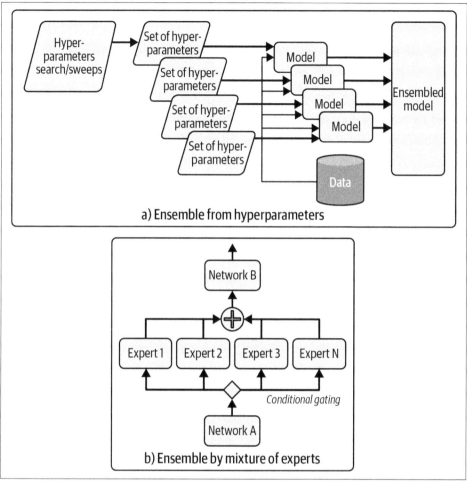

Figure 6-13. Examples of two distinct ensembling techniques: (a) an ensemble created from models trained on different partitions of hyperparameters and (b) an ensemble created by training multiple simultaneous experts for subsets of tasks

Chapter 11 dives into the details of MoE and related tricks and techniques, with some hands-on examples.

Data parallelism

Most deep learning algorithms operate under the assumption that each data sample is independent and identically distributed. If the entire training data corpus can be split into n chunks while guaranteeing an approximately similar distribution in each chunk, then perhaps *n* workers can independently perform the gradient computation flow and collaborate to conduct the parameter update flow to commence the model training. This is the premise of data parallelism. With this approach, the workers partition the training task across the data dimension such that each worker keeps a copy of the model and they conduct the training task jointly. Figures 6-2 and 6-7 provide overviews of the data flow in centralized and decentralized distributed deep learning that directly transfer to the data parallel technique. The key scalability criterion with this technique is to increase sample throughput (i.e., how many samples per optimizer step your distributed system processes to achieve convergence). This is accomplished by increasing the batch size.

Google's DistBelief, introduced in 2012, was one of the first frameworks to scale out training on tens of thousands of CPUs using data parallelism. More specifically, it used centralized asynchronous DDL, proposing a custom stochastic gradient optimization termed "downpour SGD."[11] In 2017, Krizhevsky et al. were the first to succeed at executing distributed learning on GPUs, training the 60M-parameter AlexNet to classify the 1.2 million images in the ImageNet dataset into 1,000 classes on two GTX 580 3 GB GPUs. Training completed in about six days, resulting in top-1 accuracy of 37.5% (a record at the time).[12] Both of these early works utilized data parallel techniques in combination with model parallel techniques, discussed in the following section, due to limited computing resources. However, with the advancements in hardware and acceleration—specifically, increases in GPU memory specifications—nowadays data parallelism is more commonly used independently.

This technique is popular and effective if the model size is not your bottleneck. It's relatively easy to implement and scales out easily. In Chapter 7, you'll learn more about data parallelism and try out some hands-on examples.

Model parallelism

In model parallelism, the model is partitioned across the workers such that each worker computes a portion of the computation graph. Because the split is applied on the computation graph, the input and output of each worker diverge as workers are serially interleaved to compute their respective graph partitions. Figure 6-14 shows an example where a three-layer model is partitioned across workers such that worker 1 (on device 0) consumes the trainable data but worker 2 (device 1) requires input

---

11 Dean, Jeffrey, Greg S. Corrado, Rajat Monga, Kai Chen, Matthieu Devin, Quoc V. Le, Mark Z. Mao, et al. 2012. "Large Scale Distributed Deep Networks." In *NIPS '12: Proceedings of the 25th International Conference on Neural Information Processing Systems*, 1223–31. *https://proceedings.neurips.cc/paper_files/paper/2012/file/6aca97005c68f1206823815f66102863-Paper.pdf*.

12 Krizhevsky, Alex, Ilya Sutskever, and Geoffrey E. Hinton. 2012. "ImageNet Classification with Deep Convolutional Neural Networks." In *Advances in Neural Information Processing Systems (NIPS 2012)* 25, no. 2. *https://papers.nips.cc/paper_files/paper/2012/file/c399862d3b9d6b76c8436e924a68c45b-Paper.pdf*.

from worker 1, and so on, indicating a need for chaining the flow together to distribute this graph across workers.

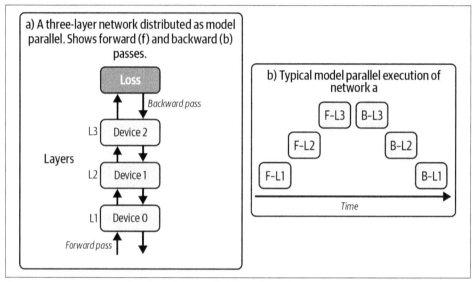

Figure 6-14. An example of model parallel distributed training

Partitioning a model such that the overhead is minimal and there are no bottlenecks is quite a specific task, and it varies from model to model. Interconnecting the model layers to map to the computing resources of your cluster is an intricate process, and the results are inflexible; any changes to, say, the batch size or the computation graph can quickly change your optimal memory layout, requiring reconfiguration of layer mapping across the cluster. Likewise, scaling out by adding more compute resources requires a rethinking of the workload distribution. For these reasons, implementing model parallelism can be quite tedious, and it's not easily dynamically scalable.

Another challenge with model parallelism is that it creates a period of idle time on devices as they wait to receive input from the preceding step, increasing the likelihood of ineffective compute utilization. Having said that, if your model is too big to fit on your hardware, or it's big enough to fit the model but not the model and the model states (gradients, optimizer states, etc.), then partitioning the model across workers is an effective technique.

Both DistBelief and AlexNet utilize model parallel (in conjunction with data parallel) training to scale out. More recently, libraries like GPipe[13] have emerged to facilitate model parallelism.

In Chapter 8, you will learn more about this technique and try out some hands-on examples.

Pipeline parallelism

In pipeline parallelism, the computations are interleaved to scale out model parallelism more efficiently. The inputs (i.e., feature signals) passing through the partitioned model are streamlined to better utilize the available resources and to increase the sample throughput. The key technique in pipeline parallelism is to introduce micro-batches for more fine-grained computation. These micro-batches are then interleaved across the devices to increase compute utilization and reduce the "idle bubble" that's generally present when standard model parallel techniques are used. Figure 6-15 illustrates this; compare the size of the idle bubble in pipeline parallel execution of the example network from Figure 6-14 to that observed in model parallel execution.

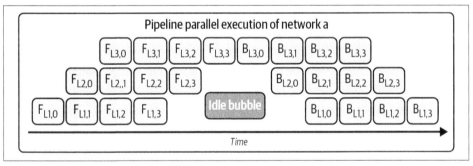

Figure 6-15. An example of pipeline parallel distributed training

Model parallelism is known to be compute-inefficient, whereas with pipeline parallel techniques compute utilization of up to 90% can be achieved. (As shown in Figure 6-15, achieving 100% compute utilization at training time is not possible even with these techniques.) Pipeline parallelism has higher network bandwidth requirements compared to model parallelism, however. For this reason, in cases where network capacity is limited, model parallelism may be a more feasible (albeit inefficient)

---

13 Huang, Yanping, Youlong Cheng, Ankur Bapna, Orhan Firat, Mia Xu Chen, Dehao Chen, HyoukJoong Lee, et al. 2019. "GPipe: Efficient Training of Giant Neural Networks Using Pipeline Parallelism." arXiv, July 25, 2019. *https://arxiv.org/abs/1811.06965*.

technique. GPipe, PipeDream, Chimera, and DAPPLE are some implementations of pipeline parallel techniques; these will be discussed in more detail in Chapter 8.

Tensor parallelism

While pipeline parallelism aims to achieve efficiency by interleaving layerwise computations, tensor parallelism seeks to further partition the model by slicing the layers themselves (i.e., intra-layer partitioning) to provide a more fine-grained workload distribution. In other words, the tensors in the individual layers of the model (representing the model parameters) are split across workers, and the workers collectively apply the operators over their respective chunks of tensors. Megatron-LM is an example of a library that uses tensor parallelism to scale out large models.[14] Figure 6-16 demonstrates this technique, showing how the GELU activation is split into two vertical chunks and executed in parallel by separate devices, A_1 and A_2. Another example of a system that uses tensor parallelism is Tofu.[15] This type of parallelism is discussed further in Chapter 8, supported by hands-on examples.

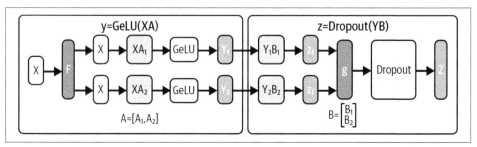

Figure 6-16. An example of tensor parallelism, borrowed from Megatron-LM(adapted from Narayanan et al., 2021)

Hybrid parallelism

Hybrid parallelism, as the name indicates, involves the application of more than one parallelism technique to scale out model training. PTD-P, for example, combines pipeline, tensor, and data parallelism into a hybrid strategy by chunking several layers and assigning separate chunks to each worker (associated with a unique device),

---

14 Shoeybi, Mohammad Mostofa Patwary, Raul Puri, Patrick LeGresley, Jared Casper, and Bryan Catanzaro. 2020. "Megatron-LM: Training Multi-Billion Parameter Language Models Using Model Parallelism." arXiv, March 13, 2020. *https://arxiv.org/abs/1909.08053*.

15 Wang, Minjie, Chien-chin Huang, and Jinyang Li. 2019. "Supporting Very Large Models Using Automatic Dataflow Graph Partitioning." arXiv, February 20, 2019. *https://arxiv.org/abs/1807.08887*.

such that each worker also only gets a unique chunk of data.[16] Another example of hybrid training is Alpa, which combines both tensor (intraoperation) and pipeline (interoperation) parallelism in one training task.[17]

Hybrid parallelism is discussed further in Chapter 8, with a practical example.

Federation/collaborative learning

High-profile data breaches such as Cambridge Analytica's (*https://oreil.ly/Or6sF*) underscore the importance of data privacy and data preservation. Large-scale training on data relating to people's behavior (shopping, social media use, advertising interactions, etc.) requires due consideration of the appropriate processes for procuring and managing such highly personalized information. The concerns are not just limited to obtaining the data but also to securing it, to avoid any misuse of personal data or sharing without consent. Several privacy laws have emerged over the last decade to provide legal guardrails in digital data privacy, including Europe's GDPR, the California Consumer Privacy Act (CCPA), and the Australian Privacy Principles (APPs).

Federated learning was first envisaged by Google to account for these data privacy and protection concerns. In the federated learning style of training, personal data never leaves the premises; what's exchanged is only the learnings (i.e., latent information) extracted from that data. Federated learning thus aims to create a highly collaborative learning environment where data privacy is respected.

In some ways, federated learning can be seen as an extension of the data parallel technique where collaborators use their own data to learn from and determine their own training schedules and regimes. For example, collaborators can choose to train for a varying number of steps, ranging from a few steps to a few epochs or even full model convergence, before sending their latent learnings back for updates. In federated learning, the sharing can be based on either model weights or just accumulated gradients. Federated averaging (FedAvg)[18] and federated learning with fair averaging

---

16 Narayanan, Deepak, Mohammad Shoeybi, Jared Casper, Patrick LeGresley, Mostofa Patwary, Vijay Korthikanti, Dmitri Vainbrand, et al. 2021. "Efficient Large-Scale Language Model Training on GPU Clusters Using Megatron-LM." arXiv, August 23, 2021. *https://arxiv.org/abs/2104.04473*.

17 Zheng, Lianmin, Zhuohan Li, Hao Zhang, Yonghao Zhuang, Zhifeng Chen, Yanping Huang, Yida Wang, et al. 2022. "Alpa: Automating Inter- and Intra-Operator Parallelism for Distributed Deep Learning." arXiv, June 28, 2022. *https://arxiv.org/abs/2201.12023*.

18 McMahan, H. Brendan, Eider Moore, Daniel Ramage, Seth Hampson, and Blaise Agüera y Arcas. 2016. "Communication-Efficient Learning of Deep Networks from Decentralized Data." arXiv, February 17, 2016. *https://arxiv.org/abs/1602.05629*.

(FedFV)[19] are examples of techniques used to realize federated learning that aggregate the weights on the main server.

Due to a variety of security and privacy considerations, the information exchange in federated learning happens via secure channels, and ideally encryption is applied during any data exchange. This is in stark contrast to any of the previously discussed parallelism techniques.

In principle, federated learning is an asynchronous decentralized learning technique. However, it is not fully decentralized, because the parameter update flow requires each worker to encrypt and send its version of the model to the central server to combine into the updated version. There is ongoing research into leveraging blockchain in federated learning (e.g., BlockFL[20]) to build zero-trust models, but these techniques are still evolving.

NVIDIA's Clara is one successful implementation of a federated learning system created for the healthcare domain, where collecting and sharing patient data is often very challenging. In its paper describing this work, NVIDIA shows that federated learning can achieve comparable results to on-premise (trained) models.[21] Running on NVIDIA EGX, as shown in Figure 6-17, Clara allows hospitals and other premises to send out only their learnings to the central server, which then updates the model if the contributions are accepted as per merging policies. The merging policies are designed to guide convergence and eliminate the risk of highly biased models adversely influencing the central model. Federated learning also has a lot of potential in pervasive systems such as mobile and IoT devices, where access to the data can be highly personal and sensitive. The data on such devices is generally quite rich and useful for developing behavior systems such as recommendation engines.

19 Wang, Zheng, Xiaoliang Fan, Jianzhong Qi, Chenglu Wen, Cheng Wang, and Rongshan Yu. 2021. "Federated Learning with Fair Averaging." arXiv, June 16, 2021. *https://arxiv.org/abs/2104.14937*.

20 Kim, Hyesung, Jihong Park, Mehdi Bennis, and Seong-Lyun Kim. 2019. "Blockchained On-Device Federated Learning." arXiv, July 1, 2019. *https://arxiv.org/abs/1808.03949*.

21 Li, Wenqi, Fausto Milletarì, Daguang Xu, Nicola Rieke, Jonny Hancox, Wentao Zhu, Maximilian Baust, et al. 2019. "Privacy-Preserving Federated Brain Tumour Segmentation." arXiv, October 2, 2019. *https://arxiv.org/abs/1910.00962*.

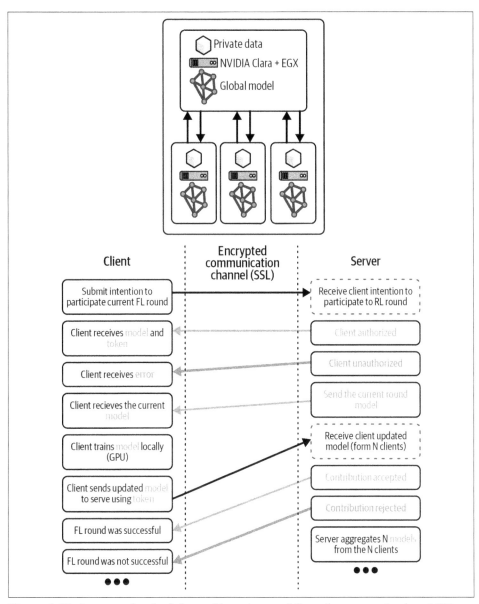

Figure 6-17. An example of a federated learning workflow, demonstrating how NVIDIA's Clara is trained in a federated setting[22]

22 Wen, Yuhong, Wenqi Li, Holger Roth, and Prerna Dogra. 2019. "Federated Learning Powered by NVIDIA Clara." NVIDIA Technical Blog, December 1, 2019. *https://developer.nvidia.com/blog/federated-learning-clara.*

Federated learning is still evolving and faces many challenges, including but not limited to the following:

Opaque heterogeneity of data and devices
> The distribution of data and nature of devices is opaque to the central system, but they can have a high degree of variance as a result of demography, ownership, etc.

Data privacy
> Just isolating data is, unfortunately, insufficient to guarantee privacy and security because of the possibility of reverse engineering and information leaks in latent learning. For this reason, techniques such as differential privacy, secure multiparty computation, and homomorphic encryption are being explored for use in federated learning.

Reproducibility, debugging, and development
> Highly distributed systems are hard to debug, and decentralization adds more complexity to them. In a federated system, not having access to data increases development and debugging challenges.

In terms of training frameworks, Flower (*https://oreil.ly/5_uRf*) is an emerging tool for federated deep learning. More generalist frameworks like PySyft (*https://oreil.ly/_Y-UT*) are highly popular and can be used to manage the decentralized setup.

Choosing a Scaling Technique

This chapter has introduced various distributed learning techniques and their scaling criteria. Along the way, I've also discussed concepts and criteria to help you decide on suitable techniques. Let's distill them down through a series of questions that you should consider if you're thinking about scaling your model training:

What dimensions should we scale on?
> A good first step is determining which of the four dimensions discussed in "Partitioning Dimensions of Distributed Deep Learning" on page 207 you should use to partition your training workload. Partitioning on hyperparameters is perhaps the simplest option; this can be realized by techniques such as parameter sweeps that can be scaled out using frameworks like Ray, Kubeflow, Slurm, etc. (We'll discuss hyperparameter optimization in Chapter 11.) If your data size is large, then augmenting parameter sweep runs with data parallelism allows scaling for both hyperparameters and data. Likewise, a combination of scaling strategies can be employed to realize aggregated distributed training.
>
> To scale out your training data, the synchronous centralized data parallel training is generally the most stable and should be explored first. This is because by scaling the workers, one effectively scales the batch size, but the synchronous

update simplifies the convergence by increasing the data variance while keeping the data distribution unique. Distributing the parameter server workload, as discussed in "Parameter server configurations" on page 194, mitigates the bottleneck of central servers. As you move toward more asynchronous techniques, the independence of the workers, as discussed earlier, creates a situation where each worker may be working on a different data distribution, leading to slower convergence.

What are the bounds of compute, clusters, and hardware resources?

Understanding the specification of your compute resources and the extent to which you can scale these resources helps understand your infrastructure limits to define the shape of suitable training parallelism. For instance, if you are limited by independent training of workers (e.g., memory bottlenecks), applying simple model parallelism is a good first step. Conversely, if network bandwidth is your limit but your dataset is huge, using decentralized asynchronous data parallel training may be a more suitable option.

Should we have a homogeneous or heterogeneous cluster?

The ability to compose and exploit heterogeneous clusters is advantageous, to the extent that you are not blocked by the availability of a particular type of resource. This is an important consideration that impacts your ability to conduct training. For instance, in data parallel training, the slowest worker defines the speed of your training. Mixing hardware with varying capabilities may mean your more performant devices are not efficiently utilized. However, with model parallelism, you can use your creativity to partition layers right-sized to the available devices.

How dynamic does scaling need to be?

Do you need your scale-out to be just enough to conduct training, or are you also optimizing for a faster development cycle? Is your compute budget fixed, or do you need to be able to scale out dynamically to fit on a range of resources depending on availability? These questions are important considerations, especially because some scaling techniques (like data parallelism, federation, and ensembling) are easily dynamically adjusted, while others (like model parallelism) require careful planning.

How resilient does training need to be?

Some techniques are more tolerant of partitioning failures than others. For example, a vanilla model parallel technique that maps layers across workers has no fault tolerance built in. Failure of any of the workers may result in a full system halt. While in general pipeline parallelism is also susceptible to faults, techniques like FTPipeHD[23] utilize replication across workers to maintain tolerance to partitioning failure.

Decentralized data parallel techniques are designed to be fault tolerant and are most robust to failure. Some configurations of centralized data parallel techniques (as discussed in "Synchronous centralized DDL" on page 196) that migrate full model weights to workers are also robust to failure.

In general, the training configuration should be such that in case of partitioning events, the run continues. This can be hard to achieve and may not suit your other more pressing requirements. At a minimum, you should implement checkpointing, as discussed in previous chapters, and ensure that you are able to resume from the last successful point. The advantages of such measures are easy to underappreciate, but they are hugely beneficial and can save the day (and your compute budget!) when disasters do strike.

In this chapter, you've read about DDL architectures and techniques to parallelize model training. In the following two chapters, you will explore some practical examples to realize distributed training using the techniques discussed so far. Before diving into the practical exercises, though, let's discuss some additional considerations in scaling out training and how to measure to arrive at optimal scaling configurations.

Measuring Scale

Chapter 1 introduced the concept of "measure twice, cut once" when discussing considerations for effective scaling. But due to the stochastic nature of deep learning, the measurements are often not reproducible. There are several reasons why reproducibility in deep learning is hard to come by (*https://oreil.ly/fhnoe*), including but not limited to the use of SGD, adaptive techniques such as AdaptiveAvgPool2d layers, or efficiency tricks that leverage runtime dynamism to optimize for compute efficiency. The CUDA Basic Linear Algebra Subroutine (cuBLAS) library (*https://oreil.ly/vtYx5*), for example, has optimizations for selecting internal workspace for the routines running in parallel streams that lead to nondeterminism.

Similarly, convolution algorithms in CUDA (discussed in Chapters 3 and 4) have several implementations, but the fastest one is chosen at runtime using its autotuning feature (*https://oreil.ly/VLY7Q*).[24] Because of this dynamism, the benchmark results should not only be repeated but also processed with an allowed variance

---

23 Chen, Yuhao, Qianqian Yang, Shibo He, Zhiguo Shi, and Jiming Chen. 2021. "FTPipeHD: A Fault-Tolerant Pipeline-Parallel Distributed Training Framework for Heterogeneous Edge Devices." arXiv, October 6, 2021. *https://arxiv.org/abs/2110.02781*.

24 Riach, Duncan. 2019. "Determinism in Deep Learning (S9911)." *https://developer.download.nvidia.com/video/gputechconf/gtc/2019/presentation/s9911-determinism-in-deep-learning.pdf*.

margin. For context, MLPerf requires 5–10 runs of deep learning benchmarks to ensure 90% of entries have 5–10% variance at most.[25]

End-to-End Metrics and Benchmarks

As discussed in "Questions to ask before scaling" on page 26, it is critical to acknowledge that while you're scaling out your model training, your key objective is to obtain a statistically performant model. Achieving computational performance excellence is a significant win for cost and operational efficiency, as long as it's not at the expense of statistical performance. Interestingly, these two performance dimensions—statistical and operational (a.k.a. computational)—are not completely orthogonal. This is also why, since the introduction of DAWNBench,[26] performance measures tend to be considered holistically, end to end, accounting for both these dimensions. Let's discuss some of these measures.

Time to convergence

Given the interdependency of statistical and operational efficiency, DAWNBench proposed measuring time to convergence—a.k.a. time to accuracy or time to (statistical) performance—to provide a measure of overall efficiency gains across the system.

In the practical exercises in Chapter 4, if you recall, you were optimizing for step rate and compute efficiency. In those exercises, the focus on the statistical performance of the model was largely absent. Luckily, the techniques you applied there didn't affect this; however, to assume statistical performance will always hold is to deceive yourself. For example, as shown in Figure 6-18, DAWNBench benchmark results for a ResNet56 model trained on the CIFAR10 dataset using an NVIDIA Tesla P100 GPU indicated that both too small and too large batch sizes led to poor convergence, while optimal convergence was achieved with an intermediate batch size.

25 Mattson, Peter, Christine Cheng, Cody Coleman, Greg Diamos, Paulius Micikevicius, David Patterson, Hanlin Tang, et al. 2020. "MLPerf Training Benchmark." arXiv, March 2, 2020. *https://arxiv.org/abs/1910.01500*.

26 Coleman, Cody, Deepak Narayanan, Daniel Kang, Tian Zhao, Jian Zhang, Luigi Nardi, Peter Bailis, et al. 2019. "DAWNBench: An End-to-End Deep Learning Benchmark and Competition." NIPS ML Systems Workshop. *https://dawn.cs.stanford.edu/benchmark/papers/nips17-dawnbench.pdf*.

For optimal time to convergence, the interdependency of hyper-parameters should also be considered.[27] For example, the scaling law of learning rate when batch size is increased. There are two laws:

- Linear scaling: When learning rate is scaled at the same rate batch size is. This scaling is found to be more useful when stochastic gradient descent is used.

- Power law scaling: When learning rate should be scaled by the square root of the rate of scale of batch size (i.e., learning rate is scale by r when batch size is scaled by r^2).

For more information on this, please see Sadhika Malladi's detailed explanation (*https://oreil.ly/3PqcR*).

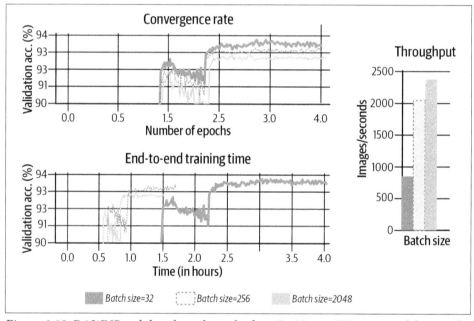

Figure 6-18. DAWNBench benchmark results for a ResNet56 CIFAR10 model trained on a P100, indicating building for highest throughput may not be the optimal choice[28]

---

27 Nitish Shirish Keskar, Dheevatsa Mudigere, Jorge Nocedal, Mikhail Smelyanskiy, and Ping Tak Peter Tang, "On Large-Batch Training for Deep Learning: Generalization Gap and Sharp Minima," ICLR 2017, Feburary 9, 2017, *https://arxiv.org/abs/1609.04836*

28 Coleman et al., "DAWNBench: An End-to-End Deep Learning Benchmark and Competition."

There are several other scenarios where the trade-off between statistical and operation efficiency needs to be managed to obtain the shortest time to convergence (which can be defined as the time taken by a training regime to reach the most optimal or a predetermined value for a preset metric; e.g., time taken to achieve a validation accuracy of 0.98 or time taken to train until loss ceases to improve). In a hypothetical scenario, if reducing precision (for example, using mixed-precision training) reduces the step rate by half but it takes twice the number of steps to converge due to the lack of precision, then the benefit of the precision trick dissipates pretty quickly. Additionally, the challenges of asynchronous parameter update flow, as discussed earlier in this chapter, may introduce similar convergence issues, requiring a longer lead time during distributed training.

For these reasons, time to convergence is a good end-to-end metric to measure while keeping the variance in the system configuration to a minimum (see also "Measuring Incrementally in a Reproducible Environment" on page 226).

For optimal time to convergence, the interdependency of hyperparameters should also be considered.[29] For example, the scaling law of learning rate when batch size is increased. There are two laws:

- Linear scaling: When learning rate is scale at the same rate batch size is. This scaling is found to be more useful when stochastic gradient descent is used.

- Power law scaling: When learning rate should be scaled by square root of the rate of scale of batch size (i.e., learning rate is scale by r when batch size is scaled by r^2).

For more information on this, please see Sadhika Malladi's detailed explanation (*https://oreil.ly/ORPQF*).

Cost to train

Cost to train is a useful metric to contextualize the scalability versus cost trade-off to find the optimal scalability range from a budgetary viewpoint. This might simply be an equation of hardware (renting or owning), storage requirements, and bandwidth/network requirements, but it can be very helpful in understanding the ROI of the scale-out spend. This metric can be beneficial if your compute infrastructure is hybrid or elastic (see "Infrastructure Setup Options" on page 173), helping you

---

29 Nitish Shirish Keskar, Dheevatsa Mudigere, Jorge Nocedal, Mikhail Smelyanskiy, and Ping Tak Peter Tang, "On Large-Batch Training for Deep Learning: Generalization Gap and Sharp Minima," *https://doi.org/10.48550/arXiv.1609.04836*.

choose the most optimal setup, type of resources, and configuration of clusters for your scale-out efforts.

Ben Cottier's article "Trends in the Dollar Training Cost of Machine Learning Systems"[30] provides detailed insights on growing trends in training cost and outlines a few methods to estimate your cost.

Multilevel benchmarks

End-to-end metrics measure the integral impact of every component of the system. They need to be supported by benchmarks of varying granularity to provide clear insights on how each component is performing, how they're interacting with each other, and where the bottlenecks are coming from. This premise has been discussed in several of the preceding chapters. Various benchmarking frameworks, such as DAWNBench (*https://oreil.ly/hVPrQ*), MLPerf (*https://oreil.ly/b0YnV*), Deep500 (*https://oreil.ly/1jbbx*), and Alibaba's AI Matrix (*https://oreil.ly/cBfXl*), have collectively developed the principles of benchmarking DL performances. Some of these frameworks, including Deep500[31] and AI Matrix,[32] explicitly outline and define multilevel benchmarks. While these definitions may vary, conceptually, the levels are as follows:

Operator

The operator level pertains to tensor-level algebraic computations, like matrix multiplications. Benchmarking at this level provides detailed information about lower-level (kernel, operator, etc.) compute expenditure. You may recall looking into operator-level benchmarks in practical exercises in Chapter 4.

As discussed in Chapter 3, under the hood operators utilize highly tuned libraries for algebraic calculations, such as NVIDIA cuBLAS. The auto-tuning feature of these libraries is such that even varying the dimension of metrics may result in the selection of different algorithms, leading to different performance characteristics.[33] The finer-grained benchmarking at this level also provides details on the

30 Cottier, Ben. 2023. "Trends in the Dollar Training Cost of Machine Learning Systems." Epoch, January 31, 2023. *https://epochai.org/blog/trends-in-the-dollar-training-cost-of-machine-learning-systems*.

31 Ben-Nun, Tal, Maciej Besta, Simon Huber, Alexandros Nikolaos Ziogas, Daniel Peter, and Torsten Hoefler. 2019. "A Modular Benchmarking Infrastructure for High-Performance and Reproducible Deep Learning." arXiv, June 13, 2019. *https://arxiv.org/abs/1901.10183*.

32 Zhang, Wei, Wei Wei, Lingjie Xu, Lingling Jin, and Cheng Li. 2019. "AI Matrix: A Deep Learning Benchmark for Alibaba Data Centers." September 23, 2019. *https://arxiv.org/abs/1909.10562*.

33 Oyama, Yosuke, Akihiro Nomura, Ikuro Sato, Hiroki Nishimura, Yukimasa Tamatsu, and Satoshi Matsuokal. 2016. "Predicting Statistics of Asynchronous SGD Parameters for a Large-Scale Distributed Deep Learning System on GPU Supercomputers." In *Proceedings of the 2016 IEEE International Conference on Big Data (Big Data)*, 66–75. *https://doi.ieeecomputersociety.org/10.1109/BigData.2016.7840590*. See also *https://oyamay.github.io/slides/20161207_bigdata2016.pdf*.

dependencies of operators and insights on throttling due to other factors, such as memory bandwidth loading, compute resources waiting for data, etc.

Any challenges or bottlenecks arising from the Python–C interface or CPU–GPU handoff are much easier to identify at this level of benchmarking. Estimated time to complete, computing rate in FLOPs, memory consumed, and statistical accuracy are examples of some of the metrics to use at an operator level.

Computation graph

Computation graph benchmarks relate to the neural network, the layers, the interaction between the layers, and the software and hardware stack. Estimated time to do forward pass, number of parameters, memory and compute required for the full pass, overhead from software and hardware (if any), and accuracy of calculating error, loss, etc. are examples of metrics to explore.

Standalone training

Standalone training benchmarks capture the performance of not only computation graphs but also the parameter update flow, including backpropagation, optimizer steps, and the model input pipeline. Key metrics include step rate, time per epoch, time to convergence, memory and compute utilization, and model input pipeline latency. In addition, statistical metrics to benchmark training and validation-time performance (accuracy, loss, etc.) and dataset metrics to understand the characteristics of the datasets and identify potential sources of bias are typically measured in standalone training.

Distributed training

Distributed training benchmarks measure the impact of scale-out of the training and interactions between the workers, concentrating on the communication volume, I/O latency, performance of distributed optimizers, and performance of individual workers (and servers, in a centralized setting). The metrics used are the same as in standalone training (except these are now required per worker), in addition to metrics to capture communication and coordination. *Goodput* is a metric that combines system throughput with statistical efficiency;[34] it provides a useful overview of how effective your scaling efforts are and is increasingly being used in distributed deep learning training settings (although the concept is generic enough to be customized to other metrics you might care about in your scalability exercises).

---

34 Qiao, Aurick, Sang Keun Choe, Suhas Jayaram Subramanya, Willie Neiswanger, Qirong Ho, Hao Zhang, Gregory R. Ganger, and Eric P. Xing. 2020. "Pollux: Co-Adaptive Cluster Scheduling for Goodput-Optimized Deep Learning." arXiv, August 27, 2020. *https://arxiv.org/abs/2008.12260*.

The advantage of using profiling tools such as one used in the exercises in Chapter 2 is that they already capture detailed metrics at the different levels involved in training. The majority of the time, these tools will provide a good overview of full system performance, which can be used to direct further investigation into specific levels in cases where further tuning or profiling may be needed.

Measuring Incrementally in a Reproducible Environment

Previous chapters have discussed the importance of having a fixed, reproducible environment. Having a fixed version of the software stack, hardware, and drivers enables repeatability. This not only allows easier debugging and development, but also reliable benchmarks. The same concept extends to the code and the data flow. MLPerf experiments have demonstrated how just varying the randomization seeds while keeping everything else fixed, including the runtime and hyperparameters, significantly altered the benchmark results for MiniGo.[35] While 100% reproducibility in deep learning comes at the cost of a severe compute penalty, it's important to do your best to minimize the variance and maximize the reproducibility of your system, especially when benchmarking.

Reproducibility is also a consideration with regard to feature or capability introduction. In deep learning, the interplay of hyperparameters is extremely complex. The interaction between hyperparameters that have independently provided a significant gain in time to convergence may be counterproductive, leading to inferior results. This was demonstrated by DAWNBench experiments[36] with training a ResNet110 model on the CIFAR10 dataset using the Adam optimizer, stochastic depth (a form of regularization similar to dropout), and single-node multi-GPU training on four NVIDIA K80 GPUs with different batch sizes, individually and all combined. The researchers observed a reduction in the time to convergence (as measured by top-1 accuracy) with each of these hyperparameters independently, and with certain combinations of two; however, when they were all combined, the model's performance was worse than the baseline without any optimizations. Benchmarking features and capability incrementally allows one to manage the interplay more effectively.

35 Mattson et al., "MLPerf Training Benchmark," *https://arxiv.org/abs/1910.01500*.

36 McMahan et al., "Communication-Efficient Learning of Deep Networks from Decentralized Data," *https://arxiv.org/abs/1602.05629*

Summary

In this chapter, you learned about the theoretical foundations of distributed deep learning and explored several techniques to scale out deep learning training. You saw how training can be partitioned along various dimensions (data, hyperparameters, model, and tensors) and learned about several distributed deep learning techniques, including ensembling, federation, and data, model, tensor, pipeline, and hybrid parallelism. In Chapters 7, 8, and 10, you will be completing practical exercises to scale out training using some of these techniques. In preparation for those exercises, this chapter also introduced the standard benchmarking frameworks and metrics for measuring the impact of scale. In the following chapters, you'll make use of these concepts as you look into scaling out your training workload.

Data Parallelism

In Chapter 6, you read about the fundamentals of distributed training and explored various parallelization techniques to scale out your model training workload. Building on the concepts from the preceding chapters, this chapter will take a deep dive into the data parallel technique. The objective of this chapter is to provide a full-stack understanding of how data parallel training comes to fruition. To meet this objective, it will introduce data partitioning techniques, explore how the workers get involved in distributing the load, and discuss related concepts along the way. The material in this chapter is hands-on, so most scenarios will include dedicated examples that walk through the concepts.

Data Partitioning

As discussed in the previous chapter, data parallelism scales out training by partitioning the training corpus amongst the workers in the system. Creating equal-sized subsets of your training corpus is one example of a very simplistic partitioning strategy. With this approach, if you have 10 workers and your main training corpus has 100 records with IDs [0, 1, 2, … 99], it will be divided (a.k.a. sharded or subsetted) into 10 parts, with each worker receiving 10 unique records offset by, say, its own rank. In this case, the first worker (w_0) will receive records [0, 1, 2, … 9] while the tenth worker (w_0) will receive records [90, 91, 92, … 99]. An example of this implementation that uses `torch.utils.data.Subset` to create such data partitioning is included in the *rpc_ddp.py* script (*https://oreil.ly/qEOeC*) in the book's code repository.

Another way to implement data partitioning is via sampling, where you select a representative subset of the dataset to send to each worker. This approach more naturally fits with the roles and responsibilities of datasets and `DataLoaders`. There are two higher-order implementations in PyTorch for sample-based partitioning:

- `torch.utils.data.distributed.DistributedSampler`
- `torch.distributed.elastic.utils.data.elastic_distributed_sam` `pler.ElasticDistributedSampler` (extends `DistributedSampler`)

PyTorch defined two types of dataset: *map-style* and *iterable-style*. Map-style datasets are fixed-size datasets that allow for random access, whereas iterable-style datasets are of unknown size and are accessed sequentially.

Partitioning has been well explored for fixed-size datasets, so map-style datasets have very good support for partitioning and scale-out. Support is limited, however, for automatic partitioning of iterable-style datasets, where not only is the total size unknown but sequential access is enforced. As a result, the partitioning logic needs to be handled in the `IterableDataset` implementation. A simple example of partitioning an iterable dataset is where each worker reads from the sequence in round-robin order. This technique is analogous to sharding the dataset by workers.

Let's look at an example of partitioning an iterable dataset across N workers. We'll create a dataset containing the first x numbers of the Fibonacci sequence and partition it such that each worker only sees every ith number in the sequence. The full code for this example is located in the *distributed_dataset.py* script (*https://oreil.ly/ kO8Dp*) in the GitHub repository and can be executed using the following command:

```
deep-learning-at-scale chapter_7 distribute-iterable start-worker
```

In this example, the `DistributedFibonacciDataset` (shown here) yields the next number in the sequence only if the worker's rank is the same as the assumed shard index:

```
class DistributedFibonacciDataset(torch.utils.data.IterableDataset):
    def __init__(self, rank: int, world_size: int, max: Optional[int] = 100):
        super().__init__()
        self.f = fibonacci(max=max)
        self.sequence = itertools.cycle(range(0, world_size))
        self.rank = rank

    def __iter__(self):
        for shard, value in zip(self.sequence, self.f):
            if shard == self.rank:
                yield value
```

Sharding is a useful technique that is widely adopted for partitioning datasets. For example, Hugging Face's `datasets` library uses sharding to split the dataset via the `distributed.split_dataset_by_node` API, which can partition both map- and iterable-style datasets. Dynamic sharding has its limitations, however; because of its sequential nature, a data slowdown or complexity in loading a specific record can throttle the other workers.

Implications of Data Sampling Strategies

It's important to choose your sampling strategy carefully, in order to ensure the data is distributed appropriately. This is especially true in nonstandard scenarios where, for example, class imbalances exist in the data. In such cases, you need to carefully consider additional strategies to manage the data distribution.

You'll need to take special care when data sampling strategies are combined with partitioning techniques (distributed samplers). For instance, PyTorch's `WeightedRandomSampler` is not compatible with distributed training (*https://oreil.ly/PVdeo*), requiring a custom implementation to combine the effects of `DistributedSampler` and `WeightedRandomSampler`. PyTorch Lightning simplifies this by offering a wrapper class, `DistributedSamplerWrapper`, that automatically wraps your custom samplers (*https://oreil.ly/OuffD*) by default.

Batch sampler `torch.utils.data.BatchSampler` is another technique to sample data for mini-batches. This technique is especially useful in scenarios where loss computation are interdependent on samples in batches (e.g., contrastive training) or special sampling use-cases where batches are cherry-picked to amplify signals for specific class or type (e.g., maximize signal for sod roofs so sample sod roofs every ith iteration).

Working with Remote Datasets

If you're working with remote data (e.g., object stores such as S3), your dataset implementation will require a connection to the server to access (load and read) the data. The implementation for this access interface can cause friction, as each cloud provider has its own APIs for accessing files. Additionally, when you cache the datasets locally, not having a common translation between these interfaces can pose maintenance challenges. The Filesystem Spec (`fsspec`) project (*https://oreil.ly/6d13a*) provides a Pythonic interface to local, remote, and embedded filesystems and bytes storage and is interoperable.

In recognition of some of the friction that can surface as a result of increased demand for integration with various storage systems and their APIs, more modular and reusable abstractions for data have also been implemented via the `torchdata` library (*https://oreil.ly/a4jIu*). These interfaces provide more seamless integration with the cloud stores underpinning `fsspec` (you can find more on this in the PyTorch `DataPipe` tutorial (*https://oreil.ly/eqdmr*)). This library was still in the beta stage at the time of writing, so the Hands-On Exercises in this book use the `DataLoader` API. The `DataLoader2` API introduced in `torchdata`, which is designed to decouple the loading and manipulation of data and to support features like snapshotting and multiple backends for loads, is worth a look; however, further development of this library has paused as of July 2023, pending a reevaluation of the technical design and user needs.

There are several other considerations to keep in mind when working with a high volume of training data. Chapter 9 dives more specifically into the details of many of these tricks and techniques. This chapter treats data as more of an opaque element and discusses the scale-out from an engineering viewpoint.

Now that you have partitioned your dataset, let's explore how workers will interact to learn and converge to the local minima.

Introduction to Data Parallel Techniques

Data parallel distributed training is a SIMD paradigm, but it's applied at a macro program/process level. With this technique, every worker process loads the model in memory, creating a unique model instance. Each of these model instances reads its own process's partition of the data and begins learning independently.

As discussed in Chapter 6, if the system configuration is centralized, each worker sends its gradients to the central server after completing the gradient computation flow (as per the chosen communication style, synchronous or asynchronous). The central server then applies reduction (i.e., averaging) and performs a parameter update before sending the parameters back to the workers for subsequent training steps. If the configuration is decentralized, the workers use collective communication techniques (mainly all-reduce) to arrive at the final gradients before applying the parameter update and continuing training. See Figures 6-2 and 6-3 in "Centralized DDL" on page 192 for the workflow for these two approaches.

Let's look at an example to see how a centralized parameter server system can be configured and explore the interactions involved in that process.

Hands-On Exercise #1: Centralized Parameter Server Using RCP

PyTorch treats synchronous centralized training approaches (specifically the gradient-partitioned joint worker/server approach discussed in "Parameter server configurations" on page 194) as first-class citizens but also exposes RPC-based APIs (*https://oreil.ly/P2wA_*) for other modes of centralized training. Because of limited support for accelerated computing in the RPC APIs, use of RPC-based centralized distributed training is more common in CPU-only workloads. The RPC module uses the `tensorpipe` (*https://oreil.ly/yyfK9*) package under the hood for point-to-point communication, and this package will be transparently used in this example.

The code for this example is located in the *rpc_centralized.py* script (*https://oreil.ly/ f3Uxg*) in the GitHub repository.

Setup

This exercise is an extension of the MNIST digit classification exercise from Chapter 2 (see "Hands-On Exercise #2: Getting Complex with PyTorch" on page 57). In this extension, you will use the same example to create a parameter server and a worker, where the model resides on the parameter server and the worker references it using RPC to conduct the computations on the dataset.

This setup is an example of a centralized parameter server configured using RPC. For simplicity, in this example, subsetting is used to partition the dataset (see *rpc_centralized.py* (*https://oreil.ly/7HvMg*)). This ensures that all workers are doing unique and not duplicate work.

In this example, you have a `SimpleNetwork` imported from the `MNISTModel` of Chapter 2. There is also a `ParameterServer` module that wraps all the parameters of the network into `rpc.RRef`. This wrapping allows for all the parameters to be referenced remotely over RPC. The processes (i.e., the parameter server and the worker) are spun up using `torch.multiprocessing.spawn`, which triggers the invocation of the `run_worker` method. If you look at the `run_worker` method, you may note that the parameter server is designated the highest rank, implying all lower ranks are assigned to the worker(s).

As a first step, each process is initialized through the `rpc.init_rpc` call, which uses `TensorPipeRpcBackendOptions` to provide connection details like the master host, port, timeout, and related configurations required for communication. This sets up a dedicated RPC communication channel between the processes.

Although each process in this exercise is local, the same setup can be executed by decoupling each process to be distributed. In that case, you'll just need to swap the process spawning logic (i.e., `torch.multiprocessing.spawn`) to be run on different remote nodes. Tools like Slurm and Kubernetes, as discussed in "Workload Management" on page 178, can be used to distribute these processes on remote nodes.

You may also note that in this example, the process group is not initialized—that is, there's no call to `dist.init_process_group`. Likewise, there is no backend used for collective communications (discussed in Chapter 5). Since this example demonstrates centralized distributed training, the workers do not communicate directly with each other, so collective communication is not necessary (this will be the case even with multiple workers). The communication pathway is directly between the worker(s) and the parameter server (the central server). In a decentralized version of this example, configuring the backend and initializing the process group would be necessary.

The crux of the training happens in run_training_loop, which is executed only by workers and not parameter servers. This is in line with the concepts discussed in "Centralized DDL" on page 192. In this method, you will note that each worker obtains a reference to the network parameters via remote reference and begins the training loop. The snippet in question is located in lines 125–135 of the *rpc_centralized.py* script (*https://oreil.ly/ANe0E*) in the GitHub repository and reproduced here:

```
worker = Worker()
param_rrefs = worker.get_global_param_remote_references()
opt = DistributedOptimizer(optim.SGD, param_rrefs, lr=0.01)
for i, (data, target) in enumerate(train_loader):
    with dist_autograd.context() as context_id:
        model_output = worker(data)
        loss = F.nll_loss(model_output, target)
        if i % 5 == 0:
            print(f"Rank {rank} training batch {i} loss {loss.item()}")
        dist_autograd.backward(context_id, [loss], retain_graph=True)
        opt.step(context_id)
```

The forward and backward loops are standard; however, note the change in use of optimizer. Here, the SGD optimizer is wrapped in torch.distributed.optim.Dis tributedOptimizer. This distributed optimizer, along with dist_autograd, handles the aggregation of gradients from workers, which are then used on the parameter server for parameter updates. For subsequent epochs, this process of obtaining parameters and looping over the dataset will be repeated.

Observations

To run this example, use the following command:

```
deep-learning-at-scale chapter_7 rpc train --world-size 2
```

Inspecting involved processes.   When you run the example, you may note that three additional processes are created alongside your main process: one for the parameter server, one for the worker, and one for the resource tracker. The resource tracker is an implementation detail of the multiprocessing package that gets used in spawn or forkserver-based process provisioning to keep track of shared resources, etc. You can read more about this in the Python documentation (*https://oreil.ly/O9FDy*).

You can inspect the additional processes using the following command, where *<your_main_process_id>* will be logged at the beginning of the run you just started:

```
ps axo pid,ppid,user,command | egrep <your_main_process_id>
```

Here's a sample log, for reference:

```
$ deep-learning-at-scale chapter_7 rcp train --world-size 2
==== Main process id is 95021 =====
Worker 0 initialized with RPC @ tcp://localhost:29501
Worker 1 initialized with RPC @ tcp://localhost:29501
RPC initialized!
Rank 0 training batch 0 loss 2.285827159881592
Rank 0 training batch 5 loss 2.2682082653045654
Rank 0 training batch 10 loss 2.3351123332977295
Rank 0 training batch 15 loss 2.2401435375213623
Rank 0 training batch 20 loss 2.215524435043335
..
```

Inspecting connections.   You can also track the ports on your machine, and you may note that while your processes were running ports 29501 (for RPC) and 29504 (for the gloo backend/collective communications) were both open and actively listened on. You can use the lsof command for such inspection, as follows:

```
sudo lsof -iTCP -sTCP:LISTEN -n -P | grep 29504
sudo lsof -iTCP -sTCP:LISTEN -n -P | grep 29501
```

Communication patterns.   This exercise includes implementations for both synchronous and asynchronous communication patterns. This is achieved by making use of the appropriate RPC API calls; i.e., rpc_sync or rpc.rpc_async from PyTorch's distributed package. For reference, see the following snippet from *rpc_centralized.py* (*https://oreil.ly/sroSQ*):

```
sync_fn = rpc.rpc_sync if self.sync else rpc.rpc_async
result = sync_fn(rref.owner(), Worker.call_method, args=args, kwargs=kwargs)
```

Both APIs function similarly, except rpc_sync is blocking and returns an absolute value whereas rpc_async returns a Future that can be waited on.

Discussion

When you run this example, you will note that your loss starts at about 2.286 before converging to about 0.609 by the end of the epoch, at the 936th step. This indicates that your worker is able to fetch parameters from the central server, compute the graph given batches of the data, and suitably take optimization steps. If you scale out this training using the following command to have two workers and one parameter server, you will have four processes (two for each worker, and one each for the parameter server and the resource tracker):

```
deep-learning-at-scale chapter_7 rcp train --world-size 3
```

Note that in this case each worker runs only 465 iterations, essentially halving their respective runtime.

In this exercise you looked at how to set up centralized data parallel training using RPC as a communication technique, in the context of both synchronous and asynchronous communication patterns. As discussed in the previous chapter, the use of a single parameter server is not very reliable. In the following Hands-On Exercise, you'll attempt the same problem but apply a more reliable technique for distributed training.

Hands-On Exercise #2: Centralized Gradient-Partitioned Joint Worker/Server Distributed Training

In "Parameter server configurations" on page 194, you read about five different parameter server configurations for centralized distributed training. As you saw, the gradient-partitioned joint worker/server configuration is the most reliable, as in this case each worker acts as server and also holds all the information (at the expense of communication overhead), making the system more capable of handling failures in any of the workers. In this example, you will see a toy implementation of centralized gradient-partitioned joint worker/server distributed training.

This setup requires each worker to communicate with the others, thereby requiring configuration for collective communication, as discussed in Chapter 5. The backend can be gloo, mpi, or nccl, depending on the resources at your disposal. In this exercise, you will be using the gloo backend and repurposing the previous problem for this distributed setting.

The code for this exercise is available in the GitHub repository, in the script *ddp_centralized_ray.py (https://oreil.ly/eoqx3)*.

Setup

Let's start by reviewing the communication setup. The world-size is the number of processes to start. When you run this example, you'll specify this on the command line with the --world-size argument. As in the previous example, each process gets assigned a rank from the range [0, world_size). However, unlike in the previous exercise, each process in this example runs the training process. To allow for this to happen, a process group is initialized using dist.init_process_group, which leverages the gloo backend. This is shown in the following snippet from *ddp_centralized_ray.py (https://oreil.ly/GwZrb)* (lines 83–92):

```
dist.init_process_group(
    backend="gloo",
    rank=rank,
    world_size=world_size,
    init_method=f"tcp://{master_address}:{master_port}",
)

_run_trainer(rank, world_size)
dist.destroy_process_group()
```

Note that between initialization and destruction of the process group is the invocation of the training process, via a call to _run_trainer. This method internally invokes _run_training_loop, which implements a standard local training loop:

```
optimizer = optim.SGD(model.parameters(), lr=0.05,)
for epoch in range(2):
    train_loader = get_loader(rank, world_size)
    for i, (data, target) in enumerate(train_loader):
        optimizer.zero_grad()
        output = model(data)
        loss = F.nll_loss(output, target)
        if i % 5 == 0:
            print(f"Rank {rank} {epoch=} training batch {i} loss {loss.item()}")

        loss.backward()
        optimizer.step()
```

If you compare this with the training loop used in the previous exercise (lines 125–135 in *rpc_centralized.py* (*https://oreil.ly/NEFAr*)), you will note the parameter updates are happening locally to each process. This is in line with the workflow illustrated in Figure 6-4 and discussed in "Subtypes of centralized DDL" on page 196 (the gradient-partitioned joint worker/server configuration).

The magic of gradient synchronization is enabled by using the DataParallel modules. The PyTorch ecosystem has several implementations for DataParallel, as you'll see in the following section. This example uses DistributedDataParallel to wrap the SimpleNetwork model. When this parallelized model is loaded by any process of the known process group with a recognized rank, gradient synchronization and reduction using all-reduce can successfully commence. Because the DataParallel wrapper takes care of these synchronizations, you will note that, unlike the previous example, this example does not make any explicit use of distributed optimizers.

Observations

To run this example, use the following command:

```
deep-learning-at-scale chapter_7 ddp-centralized train --world-size 1
```

You can inspect the involved processes and networking with the commands provided in the previous section (see "Observations" on page 132).

Communication patterns.   As discussed in Chapter 6, with asynchronous setups it's very challenging to achieve convergence. For this reason, both PyTorch and Tensor-Flow treat the synchronous centralized approach as a first-class citizen, while the asynchronous approach is supported only by low-level APIs. The high-level API torch.nn.parallel.DistributedDataParallel uses synchronous communication, making this exercise an example of centralized synchronous distributed training. The third exercise in this chapter demonstrates a toy example using decentralized asynchronous distributed training, but the remaining exercises in the book will mainly focus on synchronous techniques, due to their greater reliability.

Discussion

Running a single process takes about 936 steps at a batch size of 64, and the total estimated time for two epochs is about 25.1 s. Scaling to two workers (`--world-size 2`), you will see the total step count per worker cut in half, with the total time reduced somewhat to about 22.3 s. As you keep increasing the number of workers, you may note that scaling is not linear. This is because the toy problem is small enough that the overhead from provisioning multiple processes, collective communication, etc. overshadows any minor gains in speed. You may note that after a `world_size` of 3, any improvement training time plateaus.

As shown by the equivalent Ray example (*ddp_centralized_ray.py* (*https://oreil.ly/ OwrVW*)), the overhead from kits like Ray that start up faster than PyTorch's `multi processing` also overshadows the gain. This is just a reminder to consider whether you really need to scale (as discussed in Chapter 1).

The minimalist toy examples used here are merely intended to demonstrate concepts. Later in this chapter, you will be looking at more practical meaty exercises and exploring how to scale them out efficiently for larger datasets using data parallel techniques.

Hands-On Exercise #3: Decentralized Asynchronous Distributed Training

In this exercise you will explore how a decentralized distributed training can be configured for asynchronous updates. The theoretical concept behind this approach, as discussed in Chapter 6, is that each worker not only computes its own gradient computation flow but also performs the parameter update flow locally; the parameters are then globally updated for the group.

The source for this exercise is located in the *hogwild.py* script (*https://oreil.ly/77u5V*) in the GitHub repository. This example is a simplistic implementation of a decentralized asynchronous distributed training algorithm known as HogWild, which was introduced in 2011[1] and revised to increase resource efficiency in 2016.[2] The key

---

1 Niu, Feng, Benjamin Recht, Christopher Re, and Stephen J. Wright. 2011. "HOGWILD!: A Lock-Free Approach to Parallelizing Stochastic Gradient Descent." arXiv, November 11, 2011. *https://arxiv.org/abs/ 1106.5730.*

2 Zhang, Huan, Cho-Jui Hsieh, and Venkatesh Akella. 2016. "HogWild++: A New Mechanism for Decentralized Asynchronous Stochastic Gradient Descent." In *2016 IEEE 16th International Conference on Data Mining (ICDM)*, 629–38. *https://doi.org/10.1109/ICDM.2016.0074.*

principle of this algorithm is to remove the locking required for synchronization of gradients and instead leverage shared memory across workers, enabling them to update the parameters independently, asynchronously, and in a lock-free fashion.

An important consideration with this implementation is that most multicore computation devices today are NUMA-based (as discussed in Chapter 3), meaning that they can have different performance characteristics for memory in the address space of a processor. As the shared memory requirement grows, the likelihood of being impacted by these varying performance characteristics increases, resulting in suboptimal performance. The revised version of this algorithm, HogWild++, considers NUMA architectures to leverage shared memory more effectively. In this toy example, however, you will be using the original HogWild algorithm.

Setup

Building on the previous exercises, in this example you will continue to use the `SimpleNetwork`. Like the first exercise, it uses the subsetting approach (see lines 63–77 in *hogwild.py* (*https://oreil.ly/8SuXi*)) to partition the dataset. The training loop (lines 87–97) is a standard single-process training loop that does not use the `torch.distributed` package.

The key enabler in this exercise is the use of `torch.nn.Module.share_memory` (i.e., `model.share_memory`), which moves the model onto the shared memory—specifically, the resource created on */dev/shm* (which is managed by the resource tracker, discussed in "Inspecting involved processes" on page 234). This allows all processes of this pool to use the same model and update it according to the results of their local loop, governed by their respective subset of the data. The relevant code snippet is in lines 110–118 (*https://oreil.ly/LxDY-*) of the *hogwild.py* script.

 /dev/shm is a temporary file storage filesystem (*tmpfs*) that stores data on RAM.

Observations

This example can be executed using the following command:

```
deep-learning-at-scale chapter_7 hogwild train --world-size 4
```

You can inspect the involved processes and networking with the commands provided in "Observations" on page 132.

Communication patterns. An important advantage of this method is reduced communication overhead. Given that all processes simply update the shared copy of the model, communication between workers is not required in this case.

Discussion

When you run this example, you will note that it runs a lot faster than the previous two examples, with a total elapsed time of 19 s. The lock-free asynchronous same-copy update approach used here, however, poses a risk of overwrites as well as convergence issues, as described in "Asynchronous decentralized DDL" on page 204. While the use of shared memory simplifies the implementation of single-node homogeneous device scale-out of training, this approach limits the scale-out of multinode and heterogeneous device training (e.g., using accelerated devices). There are two reasons for this: the performance of distributed shared memory is limited, and shared memory implementations involving accelerated devices require careful management of the devices' buffered streams and synchronization of the communication handoff between the CPU and GPU in conjunction with the use of the host's shared memory (from */dev/sm*).[3] Caffe (*https://oreil.ly/flCbd*) provides an accelerated implementation for this training approach. Apache MXNnet (*https://oreil.ly/0_mVq*) is another training framework that provides an implementation for decentralized asynchronous techniques.

So far in this chapter, you've looked at various simple examples to explore different aspects of distributed data parallel techniques. As mentioned earlier, the rest of the chapter will focus on synchronous centralized data parallel training, because this technique is more stable and better explored both from an engineering and an algorithmic viewpoint. In the following section, you will read about three popular data parallel strategies: data parallel (DP), distributed data parallel (DDP), and Zero Redundancy Optimizer–powered data parallelism (ZeRO-DP).

We'll follow this up with a more complex practical example using DDP, looking at it from the perspective of performance efficiency. You will then extend this exercise to leverage ZeRO-DP. By then, you will have a comprehensive understanding of how to scale out training using data parallel techniques. To conclude the chapter, you'll read about some tricks and techniques you can use to make your data pipelines faster and explore an exercise to practice this. Now, let's dive into a comparison of centralized synchronous data parallel techniques.

---

3 Noel, Cyprien, and Simon Osindero. 2014. "Dogwild! – Distributed Hogwild for CPU & GPU." *https:// web.stanford.edu/~rezab/nips2014workshop/submits/dogwild.pdf*.

Centralized Synchronous Data Parallel Strategies

The landscape of model development frameworks is rich and growing. Table 7-1 describes the support some of the popular frameworks used in distributed model training offer for different training modes. As you may note, very few frameworks (e.g., Caffe2) provide integrated support for synchronous/asynchronous decentralized training. Most of the well-established frameworks, like PyTorch and TensorFlow, provide APIs and modules to implement both synchronous and asynchronous versions of centralized and decentralized scale-out of model development. However, they tend to gravitate toward (and provide more extensive and integrated support for) a particular approach. Both PyTorch and TensorFlow, for example, provide first-class support for the synchronous centralized gradient-partitioned joint worker/server configuration, while providing extension endpoints and low-level APIs to realize other modes. With that in mind, and given the stability and reliability of this mode, this is the approach we'll concentrate on. As this book primarily focuses on PyTorch and its ecosystem, this section will focus on those APIs; however, the concepts discussed here may be relevant to other frameworks too.

Table 7-1. Summary of support for different training modes offered by popular distributed training frameworks (compiled August 2023)

Framework	Communication		Optimization flow		Sharding supported	Backends supported
	Sync	Async	Decentralized	Centralized		
PyTorch	Yes	Yes	Yes	Yes	Yes (recently added via Fully Sharded Data Parallel)	tcp, nccl, gloo off the shelf; mpi requires recompilation
Horovod	Yes	No	No	Yes	No	mpi
DeepSpeed	Yes	No	Yes	Yes	Yes	nccl, mpi requires recompilation
FairScale	Yes	No	Yes	Yes	Yes	tcp, nccl, gloo off the shelf; mpi requires recompilation
PaddlePaddle	Yes	Yes	No	No		nccl
TensorFlow	Yes	Yes	Yes	Yes	No	nccl
Apache MXNet	Yes	Yes	No	Yes		
Caffe2	Yes		Yes			
Microsoft Cognitive Toolkit (CNTK)	No	Yes (bounded async)	Yes	Yes		

Conceptually, the DP, DDP, and ZeRO-DP strategies mentioned in the previous section all assume that each worker is independently consuming a unique partition of the data. With this assumption, the implementations of these strategies transparently account for the effective batch size (i.e., the batch size is linearly scaled by the number of workers). As a part of handling the scaled-up batch size, assuming the synchronous centralized gradient-partitioned joint worker/server training mode is used, these implementations also account for replicating the model on each worker at the beginning of the forward pass and conducting an independent forward pass on each worker, followed by gradient synchronization during the backward pass. This process is then repeated for the next iteration with a reset of the module due to replication at the beginning of the forward pass.

An interesting implication of this algorithm is that it results in the loss of any local updates made to the model (`torch.nn.Module`). To address this, these implementations guarantee that the replica on the leader worker will have its parameters and buffers sharing storage with the worker module synchronized. This is required because some modules, like `BatchNorm` (*https://oreil.ly/Yuziz*), are not stateless; they keep batch statistics and require register buffers to keep the tensors. Now, let's discuss the differences between some of the implementations of the different data parallel strategies.

Data Parallel (DP)

DP is limited in its ability to scale because it's designed for single-node training. The upper bound of scalability is thus defined by vertical scaling of the node. By limiting itself to a single node, `torch.nn.DataParallel` is able to take ownership of partitioning the dataset itself. This is one key difference between DP and other strategies: all the other strategies offload this responsibility to the data pipelines (see "Data Partitioning" on page 229).

The `DataParallel` module leverages multithreading for scale-out of workers. This is an interesting implementation detail that should be considered carefully in deciding whether this is a suitable strategy for your use case or not. Because of the use of multithreading, any Pythonic logic will be limited by the GIL. As discussed in Chapter 3, multithreading is more effective for I/O-intensive workloads and less so for compute-intensive scale-out. Given that most of the computation side of PyTorch is written in C++, the GIL overhead is managed to some extent; however, it does limit the ability and peak performance of the `DataParallel` implementation.

In cases where model input pipelines are computationally intensive (e.g., requiring intensive preprocessing and/or augmentation of the data), due to the GIL, the DP approach may underperform. This may be manageable by decoupling the compute-intensive part of the workload and creating a serialized, cached version of the preprocessed dataset, but the overhead involved in such decoupling must be considered as well.

Distributed Data Parallel (DDP)

DDP is an implementation of the distributed package of PyTorch that can scale out across multiple nodes. The key implementation detail of this module (`torch.nn.par allel.DistributedDataParallel`) is the use of multiprocessing to scale workers. This means each worker in DDP is a dedicated process. As a result, this implementation is more performant and also more stable than `DataParallel`, although this comes at the expense of slightly slower startup (as a result of multiprocessing's slow start). Generally, DDP is at least three times faster than DP.

Unlike DP, DDP does not broadcast parameters to workers at the beginning of each iteration. Instead, DDP uses the all-reduce collective communication pattern to synchronize gradients and expects each worker to independently apply the same gradients to its replica. As a result of this approach, all the processes have similar parameters. Register buffers (i.e., other non-parameter attributes) of the model are broadcasted from the leader to the other workers on every iteration.

Unlike DP, DDP does not take responsibility for partitioning your data per worker. This is expected to be managed by you via your model input pipeline, as discussed in "Data Partitioning" on page 229. As in Hands-On Exercise #2 earlier in this chapter, you will need to ensure your data is partitioned or an appropriate sampler is used in your `DataLoaders`.

Devil in the details

`DataLoaders` (*https://oreil.ly/TE5do*), as you may recall, use Python multiprocessing to scale out the process of loading batches of samples from your dataset. This is required to ensure that your extremely fast computational devices are continually fed data, so they're utilized effectively. `fork`, `forkserver`, and `spawn` are three methods that can be used to launch a multiprocessing fleet (see the Python docs (*https://oreil.ly/i68dp*) for further information). By default, the `DataLoaders` use `fork`, as it is less intensive and a good fit for general use; however, it is susceptible to deadlocks because of its inheritance model.

When you use `fork`, you end up with multiple workers, each of which owns its own `DataLoader` that starts another pool of data-loading workers. That's quite a lot of fanout processes, suggesting why using a `fork` start can be dangerous. Because of limitations of `fork`, the `nccl` and `gloo` backends don't support it. Thus, when using DDP, it's best to ensure that your start method is configured to be either `spawn` or `fork server`. You can do this using the `multiprocessing_context=torch.multiprocess ing.get_context("forkserver")` (or `"spawn"`) argument to `DataLoader` if `num_worker` is > 0.

The multiprocessing approach of DDP gives it significant leverage over DP. TensorFlow is a purely multithreaded framework and thus, unlike PyTorch, does not have MP strategies to scale out DP.

Overall, if configured correctly, DDP is well adapted to both horizontal and vertical scale-out. However, the upper bound of scalability of this technique, as discussed earlier, is defined by the memory per worker, as each worker keeps a replica of the model. Scaling out using low-memory devices when the model specification has a large footprint can be challenging.

Horovod is another framework that uses DDP with the gloo backend and leverages MPI for collective communication.[4] With the increased popularity of the NVIDIA and the nccl backend, DDP with nccl is more commonly used these days.

Distributed Data Parallel 2 (DDP2)

DDP2 is a more recent strategy that combines DP and DDP, such that the workers on each node use DP while synchronization across the nodes is done via DDP. This strategy can be very effective for workloads where DP scales sufficiently well horizontally but is limited vertically. Because of the multithreading approach, which is a lightweight parallelization technique that shares the same processing context, DP has the advantage of reduced communication overhead. However, as discussed previously, if your pipeline or workload is compute-intensive on the Python side, DDP may still perform better.

DDP2 is supported by PyTorch Lightning (*https://oreil.ly/I-ovz*).

Zero Redundancy Optimizer–Powered Data Parallelism (ZeRO-DP)

DDP offers considerable scaling capabilities and is widely used. However, with this technique, each worker holds a copy of the model and the optimizer states in its memory. Thus, only the remaining memory is available to scale out batch size. This redundant memory consumption is a very inefficient approach, especially as the number of parameters scales and the optimizers continue to store higher-order moments.

---

4 Sergeev, Alexander, and Mike Del Balso. 2018. "Horovod: Fast and Easy Distributed Deep Learning in TensorFlow." arXiv, February 21, 2018. *https://arxiv.org/abs/1802.05799*.

Not all of these model states are actually required all of the time. Zero Redundancy Optimizer (ZeRO), [5] a technique developed by Microsoft, explored how to further scale out training by minimizing the redundancies. ZeRO-DP proposes to not only partition the data, but also the responsibility of managing the model states. With this approach, even though each worker computes and stores the entire computation graph locally, the workers only retain their respective parts of the optimizer states and gradients. At the end of each iteration, the all-gather communication paradigm is used to obtain the latest parameters from across all the workers. As a result, each of the N workers takes responsibility for managing $1/N$ of the parameters, despite computing the entire graph.

ZeRO-DP is particularly beneficial when it's used in conjunction with mixed-precision training, where redundant copies of the model states (both fp32 and fp16, as discussed in Chapter 4) are stored. ZeRO also leverages CPU offloading techniques to achieve further efficiency improvements.

ZeRO-DP proposes three optimization stages that can be applied cumulatively to partition the optimizer states, gradients, and parameters. For the purposes of this chapter, we're concerned with the first two:

ZeRO-1

> In ZeRO-1, in addition to partitioning the data, the optimizer states are also partitioned across the workers. That is, the optimizer states are divided into N equal partitions, such that each worker stores and updates only the optimizer states corresponding to its own partition. These updates are then communicated to the other workers at the end of each iteration through an all-gather operation. This enables a 4x reduction in the memory requirements for each worker, without increasing the communication overhead.

ZeRO-2

> In ZeRO-2, the gradients are additionally partitioned across the workers, with each worker responsible for updating only its partition. As in ZeRO-1, collective communication is leveraged for accessing the gradients of remote workers. Gradient synchronization is done via the reduce-scatter algorithm. ZeRO-2 is able to provide 8x greater memory efficiency than standard DP techniques for the same communication overhead.

You will read more about ZeRO in Chapter 9.

---

5 Rajbhandari, Samyam, Jeff Rasley, Olatunji Ruwase, and Yuxiong He. 2020. "ZeRO: Memory Optimizations Toward Training Trillion Parameter Models." arXiv, May 13, 2020. *https://arxiv.org/abs/1910.02054.*

In this section, you developed a deeper understanding of various data parallel strategies. As you saw in Table 7-1, there are several frameworks and tools that provide these implementation techniques. In the following section, we'll discuss fault-tolerant training.

Fault-Tolerant Training

Reliability is heavily discussed in this book (in Chapter 1 and elsewhere) because of its importance when running at scale. Most integrated implementations of centralized synchronous data parallel techniques are not fault-tolerant by themselves. The initiative to provide more fault-tolerant training commenced with TorchElastic (*https://oreil.ly/j7-rs*), incorporated into PyTorch 1.9 as the Torch Distributed Elastic (TDE) (*https://oreil.ly/HS1qb*) module. The initial entry point for Elastic Launch, `torch.distributed.launch`, has since evolved to its superset, `torchrun`. Functionally these two are equivalent, albeit used differently: the former through Python module invocation (e.g., `python -m torch.distributed.launch <your_python_train ing_script_with_trailing_arguments>`) and the latter as a CLI command wrapper (`torchrun <your_python_training_script_with_trailing_arguments>`).

To offer fault tolerance, TDE needs to handle scale-down (worker failure) and scale-up (failed workers being replaced by new workers) and coordinate peer discovery with active workers in the run. This peer discovery synchronization combined with collective communication (as discussed in Chapter 5) is termed *rendezvous* in TDE. The implementation for rendezvous is realized by using a distributed key/value store backend, a.k.a. the rendezvous backend, that maintains a registry of active workers. The default backend for rendezvous is C10d, which uses TCP; however, support for etcd (*https://etcd.io/*), a highly consistent, reliable, scalable, and fault-tolerant store (using TCP/gRPC) is also provided. As a result of these capabilities, rendezvous provides consistent knowledge of "active" workers across the fleet to manage collective communication effectively.

One advantage of TDE is that your training script requires no changes to be run in a fault-tolerant manner, besides ensuring two specific best practice measurements are met:

Do not overwrite environment variables specific to distributed training.
  To facilitate peer discovery and fault-tolerant coordination, TDE manages rank assignment to workers internally, injecting environment-specific details like rank and world size (`LOCAL_RANK` and `WORLD_SIZE`) into the workers directly. For this reason, when using TDE, you should not set/reset these environment variables.

Implement graceful recovery best practices.

Graceful recovery is an important part of fault tolerance. While most of the heavy lifting is already done by TDE, you should ensure that your training script saves checkpoints and that your workers start by loading checkpoints, so workers that are restarting or newly joining are (re)starting the training from the last known checkpoint.

To use torchrun, you wrap your main training script with the torchrun module, which requires additional rendezvous parameters. An example of this is shown here:

```
python -m torch.distributed.launch
        --nnodes=2
        --nproc_per_node=2
        --rdzv_id=chapter_7_torchrun
        --rdzv_backend=etcd
        --rdzv_endpoint=<etcd_host>:<etcd_port>
        chapter_7/complete_ddp.py train
```

The more recent TorchX (*https://oreil.ly/rFKLa*) launcher comes with scheduling capabilities so distributed jobs can be deployed more seamlessly using workload management tools such as Slurm, Ray, and Kubernetes (discussed in Chapter 5). TorchX enables distributed training via its dist.ddp module, which leverages TorchElastic under the hood. Other infrastructure and environment configurations (e.g., container images) can be configured inline with the torchx command or optionally separated into a configuration file, *.torchxconfig*. Here's a sample torchx command:

```
torchx run --scheduler kubernetes dist.ddp -j 2x2 --script
chapter_7/complete_ddp.py train
```

When using PyTorch Lightning, TDE can be enabled by using the TorchElastic plug-in configured on the trainer; e.g., Trainer(plugins=[TorchElasticEnviron ment(...)].

Hands-On Exercise #4: Scene Parsing with DDP

In the previous three toy exercises, you explored building blocks for distributed data parallel training. In this exercise, we'll revisit the SceneParse150 dataset used in Hands-On Exercise #2 from Chapter 4. The source code for this example can be found in the complete_ddp.py script (*https://oreil.ly/0NK2a*) in the book's GitHub repository.

Figure 7-1 shows the objective of this exercise: multiclass semantic segmentation. As this example illustrates, the image is segmented and parsed into different regions (house, tree, sky grass, etc.) per the 150 classes (*https://oreil.ly/0NEdK*) defined in the dataset. You'll use a model based on the U-Net architecture with an EfficientNet encoder, as in Chapter 4. In this exercise, you will just focus on scaling out the training.

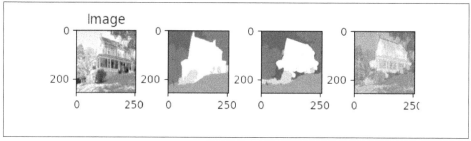

Figure 7-1. A sample image from the SceneParse150 dataset, with ground truth, model output, and overlay of model's output (from left to right)

Setup

As in Chapter 4, you will use PyTorch Lightning, which provides high-level APIs for PyTorch capabilities across its ecosystem and simplifies the infrastructure integration. Structurally, this code is very similar to the Chapter 4 example. You may also note that there is no special handling required for dataset partitioning in this case. This is because Lightning transparently applies `DistributedSampler` to the standard PyTorch `DataLoaders` if it detects distributed training mode. Another advantage of Lightning, as discussed earlier in this chapter, is that it can make other samplers, like `WeightedSampler`, distributed.

Observations

To execute the code for this example, run the following command:

```
deep-learning-at-scale chapter_7 ddp train
```

Again, you can inspect the involved processes with the command provided in the discussion of hands-on example #1, earlier in this chapter. Unlike in the previous implementations, however, now you'll only have as many processes as you have GPUs. This is because your main process is used for the first device and other processes are started for additional devices. This is a better configuration, utilizing resources more effectively.

The key change between this code and the code from Chapter 4 is the use of `strat egy="ddp"` in the `lightning.Trainer` API. This enables the use of the DDP strategy discussed in the previous section. Also note the use of `sync_dist=True` in the `Vision SegmentationModule` used in this exercise. This is required to ensure metrics are synchronized across devices; however, it should be used sparingly because of the communication overhead it can cause. This example uses it only for validation and testing and skips logging for training.

The following sections discuss the observations upon running this sample on two NVIDIA V100 GPUs with 32 GB VRAM/DRAM. The maximum number of samples per GPU for this device is about 85.

Baseline. When this example is run with one GPU, you will note that overall there are 238 steps/iterations required per epoch. The estimated time for this run is about 18 min 43 s at an average of 4.72 s per iteration.

If your system has more than one GPU, the example code will try to bind to all GPUs because `devices="auto"` is used in the `lightning.Trainer` API. You might want to control the visibility of the GPUs for your run by using NVIDIA's explicit environment variable, `CUDA_VISIBLE_DEVICES`, if you want only one to be visible:

```
CUDA_VISIBLE_DEVICES=0 deep-learning-at-scale chapter_7 ddp train
```

Alternatively, you can use the `--devices` argument to control the number of visible devices, as shown here:

```
deep-learning-at-scale chapter_7 ddp train --devices 0
```

Multi-GPU training. When you run this example with two GPUs, you will notice that the number of steps has been reduced to 119, leading to a total estimated elapsed time of about 10 min 24 sec. The step time is now 5.25 s per iteration; however, this is across two GPUs, so it's 5.25 s per 85 * 2 samples.

While you have scaled out your training by partitioning across GPUs, your scaling is not linear. Ideally, your step time would have remained consistent at 4.72 s per iteration, as per the previous example. As shown in Figure 7-2, this is because your data pipeline is not fast enough to fully utilize the scaled-out compute resources of two GPUs. We'll revisit this issue in Hands-On Exercise #6 later in this chapter, where you'll see how to improve the pipeline to achieve about the same iteration rate even at a scaled-out configuration.

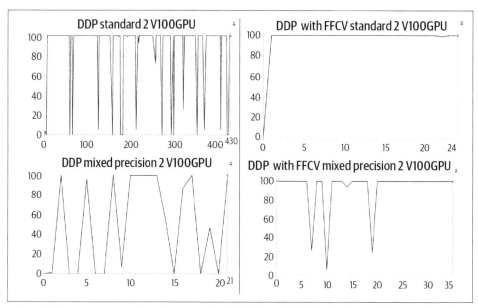

Figure 7-2. GPU utilization with standard DDP and DDP mixed precision, with and without FFCV (discussed in Hands-On Exercise #6)

Multinode. Because of the power wall, with vertical scaling your level of parallelism will be limited to a maximum of about eight GPUs. To scale further, you will need to use multiple nodes. With multinode training, the MASTER_PORT, MASTER_ADDR, WORLD_SIZE, and RANK (as discussed in Chapter 5 and at the beginning of this chapter) become important. MASTER_PORT, MASTER_ADDR is the address of the chosen leader, and all nodes should have access to this TCP endpoint before multinode training begins.

To enable multinode training, the networking is important. Provisioning of the same environment and runtime across nodes is also crucial. Use of Docker can greatly simplify provisioning of exactly the same environment; a Dockerfile (*https://oreil.ly/ blAtV*) that you can use for this book's examples is provided in the GitHub repository.

On the application side, the only change required is use of the num_nodes argument in the lightning.Trainer API. The num_nodes and devices arguments are used to infer the world_size and rank for each worker. It's just the MASTER_PORT and MAS TER_ADDR that require explicit configuration via environment variables. To start your multinode training, simply run the following command on each node, with the appropriate MASTER_PORT and MASTER_ADDR settings:

```
MASTER_PORT=<xxx> MASTER_ADDR=<yyy> deep-learning-at-scale chapter_7 ddp train
    -nodes 2
```

As discussed in Chapter 5, the management of this run across the nodes can be automated using workload management tools like Slurm, Kubernetes, etc.

Mixed-precision training.   As discussed in Chapter 4, use of reduced precision can provide further efficiencies, allowing you to increase the batch size. Mixed precision is heavily leveraged in ZeRO and other sharded techniques to more efficiently scale out training. Before diving into a sharded exercise, let's set a mixed-precision baseline with DDP. To do this yourself, use the following command:

```
deep-learning-at-scale chapter_7 ddp train --precision 16-mixed --batch-size 105
```

With mixed precision (specifically, `16-mixed`) you can use a batch size of 105 images per GPU, resulting in a total of 97 steps across both the GPUs. At a step time of 6.40 s per iteration, this results in an estimated total elapsed time of about 10 min 20 s. In this case there isn't much of a gain, because GPU utilization is worse than what you had in the two-GPU full-precision run (see Figure 7-2). This is because the data pipeline now needs to be faster to keep up with 105 * 2 samples every step. This is your throttle point. Without this bottleneck, you would have seen at least a 23% gain in performance in this case.

Hands-On Exercise #5: Distributed Sharded DDP (ZeRO)

In the previous exercises in this chapter, you explored various aspects of data parallel scale-out. This exercise will demonstrate the sharded data parallel technique discussed in "Zero Redundancy Optimizer–Powered Data Parallelism (ZeRO-DP)" on page 244, using Microsoft's DeepSpeed (*https://oreil.ly/uJd5w*). DeepSpeed bundles multiple CPU offloading and mixed-precision tricks in addition to ZeRO-1 and ZeRO-2. For this reason, in this exercise we'll look at ZeRO-1 and ZeRO-2 in conjunction with mixed precision.

Besides ZeRO, there are a handful of other implementations of sharded techniques you might want to consider, including Fair-Scale (*https://oreil.ly/czrpO*) from Facebook, which was originally designed for model parallelism in conjunction with data parallelism as a hybrid distributed training technique.

The source code for this example is located in the *sharded_ddp.py* script (*https://oreil.ly/GDSA3*) in the GitHub repository.

Setup

This exercise builds on the code and problem from the previous Hands-On Exercise (#4). The code is exactly the same as for the previous example, except for the use of the `strategy` argument to the `lightning.Trainer` API. Additionally, this exercise uses `DeepSpeedUNetSegmentationModule`, which extends the previous `VisionSegmen` `tationModule` module to customize the optimizer function to be DeepSpeed-specific when ZeRO-2 with CPU offload capability is used. DeepSpeed integration of Lightning is currently in beta state.

Runtime configuration. The runtime setup required for DeepSpeed is very involved, requiring various dependencies including an MPI library and the NVIDIA CUDA toolkit, matching the version packaged in your choice of PyTorch install. The full recipe is included in the Dockerfile (*https://oreil.ly/peXgk*) available in the GitHub repository; it installs `mpi4py`, `libopenmpi-dev`, and CUDA from NVIDIA, as well as DeepSpeed.

Observations

To run this example with the ZeRO-1 optimizer, partitioning the optimizer state across the two GPUs, use the following command:

```
deep-learning-at-scale chapter_7 sharded-ddp train --precision 16-mixed
--strategy deepspeed_stage_1
```

If you run this on the same two V100 GPUs used in the previous exercise, you will note that for the same number of steps (97), the step time is now 1.72 s per iteration, with a total elapsed time of 2 min 47 s. This is a significant performance boost from the previous ~10 min.

You may also note that the logger indicates the partitioning between the two workers:

```
Rank: 0 partition count
 and sizes[(4782502, False)]
Rank: 1 partition count
 and sizes[(4782502, False)]
```

To run it with the ZeRO-2 optimizer (sharding both gradients and optimizer states), use this command:

```
deep-learning-at-scale chapter_7 sharded-ddp train --precision 16-mixed
--strategy deepspeed_stage_2_offload
```

You should now see a step time of 1.09 s per iteration, leading to a total elapsed time of 2 min 10 s for 119 steps. (Note, however, that if using DeepSpeed without mixed precision, your mileage may vary.)

Discussion

You have now explored various implementations to realize scaling out your training using data parallel techniques. One of common challenges faced when scaling out training in this way is being throttled by the throughput of your data pipelines. This was evident in exercise #4. In the following section, we'll review some concepts and dive into considerations of building an efficient data pipeline.

Building Efficient Pipelines

Your data pipeline (a.k.a. the model input pipeline) is efficient if it can scale to the number of workers you are using for distributed data parallel training while minimizing any bottlenecks or resource wastage. For instance, in exercise #4, when you scaled out your training to use two GPUs, your estimated total elapsed time dropped from 18 min to 10 min. In that example, adding in mixed precision didn't have much effect, despite allowing for larger batch sizes and hence fewer steps. The reason for the lack of a performance boost was evident from the GPU utilization metrics (Figure 7-2), which indicated longer periods of idleness.

This section introduces some of the key considerations to keep in mind for writing efficient data pipelines.

Dataset Format

Chapter 3 discussed in detail the importance of using the right data type for the purpose. It also looked at the challenges of transferring data between the CPU and GPU and the bandwidth limitations that one may face. The less data you have to load onto the GPU, the faster your processes will be. That's why ensuring you're using the optimal data type and format is crucial to building efficient data pipelines.

The trade-off to serialize and deserialize data, as discussed in Chapter 5, can also be significant. Binary formats (e.g., protobufs) are generally faster to load but may not guarantee space efficiency. Compression techniques like gzip, zstd, LZMA, Snappy, LZO, Brotli, etc. are often used to achieve space efficiency. Table 7-2 lists some commonly used storage formats and their pros and cons, which should be considered carefully in the context of compression/decompression expense, I/O implications, and data types. Apache Arrow/Feather is promising, while Parquet is well established.

Table 7-2. Pros and cons of some of the popularly used data formats for training datasets

Popular storage formats	Pros	Cons
Pickle	Very fast	Can cause compatibility issues across Python versions Space-inefficient
Apache Arrow/Feather	Very fast (*https://oreil.ly/AKgXm*) Supports compression, including Snappy, gzip, LZO, and Brotli Mainly designed for ephemeral access, so very good for cache or intermediate processing	Not suitable for long-term data storage needs (e.g., data lakes)
Parquet	Fastest binary storage format, de facto choice for data lakes Supports compression, including Snappy, which is known to be fast	Partial reading is not allowed; entire record needs to be loaded Does not support appending to a record

Popular storage formats	Pros	Cons
HDF5	Relatively fast binary storage format Supports compression, including gzip and zstd; extendable for other techniques like LZMA Can allow access to slices of data without reading entire record Supports appending	Has been reported to be susceptible to data corruption (*https://oreil.ly/tPVTA*)
JSON	Simple format for structured data	Creates verbose and large file
GZIP/tar.gz	Very open-ended, suitable for any data files Average compression capabilities	Provides limited compression options

A general tendency practitioners have is to create many small, modular files. This results in a significant I/O burden, creating read bottlenecks when workers are scaled. Using fewer larger partitioned files can significantly reduce the burden on the system. This is another consideration to keep in mind when choosing your dataset format.

Local Versus Remote

Co-locality of data with regard to compute provides I/O efficiencies, as discussed in Chapter 3. Wherever possible, the use of faster drives like NVMe stores is hugely beneficial in scaling out training for large data volumes, as faster I/O is required. However, your data might be large enough that bringing it down for local access is infeasible or expensive. As discussed in "Working with Remote Datasets" on page 231, data pipelines can be defined to read directly from remote data stores, even though local reads are a more common approach. One additional consideration when using a remote dataset could be caching to implement a look-ahead strategy. This is a clever trick to mask the network latency due to required remote access/ download.

Staging

If your pipeline is intensive, staging it can be a helpful alternative. Breaking your pipeline into offline and online parts allows you to detach the intensive workload into a preprocessing step (i.e., cache/preload, then transform). You can then produce an intermediate format appropriate for use in low-latency, high-throughput model input pipelines, as discussed in "Dataset Format" on page 253.

In addition, if the logic of which record will be needed next is known (which may be the case, depending on the sampling technique used), then use of caching or pre-fetching techniques can provide further efficiency in your online pipelines. These techniques mask the latency of slow storage.

Threads Versus Processes: Scaling Your Pipelines

As discussed in "Devil in the details" on page 243, which data loading mode (`spawn`, `forkserver`, or `fork`) works best for you will depend on your choice of data parallel technique and the compute intensity of your data pipeline.

If your pipeline is doing custom things using threads or process pools underneath, be wary of deadlock issues—mixing threads and processes can lead to unpleasant results. The use of threads instead of processes removes the need for interprocess communication (shared memory, for instance) and reduces memory consumption; however, if your pipeline is compute-intensive, then using processes may be necessary.

Memory Tricks

Using shared memory (*/dev/smh*) and memory pinning, as discussed in Chapter 3, can provide significant efficiencies in your pipeline. Memory pinning is more relevant in the case of accelerated training, as pinning inhibits the memory paging of OS kernels so that they can be used for DMA/RDMA to speed up data transfer between the CPU and GPU and vice versa.

Data Augmentations: CPU Versus GPU

Data augmentation is a big part of data pipelines. Where you perform these operations can be an important consideration, as you may have augmentations that are vectorized operations and thus could more efficiently be done on a GPU than on a CPU. While most popular augmentation libraries, like `imgaug` (*https://oreil.ly/TVRgD*) and Albumentations (*https://oreil.ly/73GBG*), have CPU-only operators, libraries like Kornia offer GPU operators for a range of augmentations.

One interesting example to discuss is resizing. Say you have a 256x256 image that you need to resize to 1,024x1,024. Performing this operation on the CPU and then loading the image onto the GPU means you'll be loading 4x more data from the CPU to the GPU. Instead, you could load the 256x256 image onto the GPU and resize it there, saving you the overhead of increased data transfer over limited bandwidth.

JIT Acceleration

Python is slow. JIT compiler libraries such as Numba translate a subset of Python and NumPy code into fast machine code. These optimizations can provide a significant uplift if your code is Numba-compliant.

You've now looked at several considerations for creating more efficient data pipelines. Next, we'll explore how you can apply these considerations through a practical exercise.

Hands-On Exercise #6: Pipeline Efficiency with FFCV

In this exercise, you will use a library known as Fast Forward Computer Vision (FFCV). FFCV leverages many of the concepts discussed in the previous sections, including selecting a suitable format, JIT compilation, caching, prefetching, using intermediate formats for efficiency, and more.

The source code for this example is in the *efficient_ffcv_ddp.py* script (*https://oreil.ly/ yph6A*) in the GitHub repository.

Setup

In this example, you will continue to build on the same code and problem as in the previous two exercises. Now, however, executing the code is a two-step process:

1. Create the intermediate data format. FFCV has its own format, known as Benton. It integrates easily with a PyTorch `Dataset` (or any iterator providing samples and labels) and iterates through it to create the transformed Benton format of your dataset. In this example, you will create two different Benton files for training and validation. The source behind the conversion, located in lines 90–102 of the script (*https://oreil.ly/p1Pc0*), makes use of FFCV's `DatasetWriter` and creates `TorchTensorField` representations of the images and labels. To perform this step, use the following command:

   ```
   deep-learning-at-scale chapter_7 efficient-ddp data-to-beton
   ```

2. Align your pipeline to the new dataset. Now that you have created the Benton files, you will need your `DataLoader` to start using them. You will note that this exercise uses the `FFCVSceneParsingModule`, which leverages the FFCV `Loader` instead of PyTorch `DataLoaders`. The `distributed = 1` setting is required to apply `DistributedSampler`; without this, all workers will see the same samples. Besides this change, the remaining code is exactly the same as in exercise #4. You can run the example for multi-GPU and multi-GPU mixed-precision training using the following two commands:

   ```
   deep-learning-at-scale chapter_7 efficient-ddp train
   ```

   ```
   deep-learning-at-scale chapter_7 efficient-ddp train --precision 16-mixed
   --batch-size 105
   ```

Runtime configuration. The runtime setup required for FFCV is very involved, requiring various dependencies including OpenCV, an accelerated JPEG library (`libjpeg-turbo`), a series of encoding and compression libraries, Numba, CuPy, and the NVIDIA CUDA toolkit, matching the version packaged in your choice of PyTorch install. The full recipe is included in the Dockerfile (*https://oreil.ly/pnf7d*) available in the code repository.

Observations

When you run this example, you will note that the ~10 min elapsed time with two GPUs has now dropped to 7 min 48 s, with a step time of about 4.07 s per iteration. You may also note that your GPU utilization is looking much better than before, as shown in Figure 7-2. Likewise, the mixed-precision run that was previously taking ~10 min is now taking 8 min 14 s, at a step time of 5.10 s per iteration. In this exercise, you extended vanilla DDP to develop a more efficient pipeline and noted a ~2 min reduction in per-epoch training time. The performance gain can be further improved by augmenting these pipeline efficiency tricks with DeepSpeed, as was done in exercise #5.

As shown in Figure 7-2, your GPU utilization increased after applying the pipeline efficiency tricks discussed in this section. You may note that with mixed precision, even with all the tricks you have used, you're occasionally seeing a drop in utilization with FFCV. This is just a reminder that the battle between efficiency and scale is a progressive work.

Summary

In this practical chapter, you started with foundational exercises to implement various distributed data parallel techniques, exploring the use of centralized parameter servers, decentralized asynchronous data parallelism, and the more reliable synchronous centralized joint server/worker approach. You then took a deep dive into various strategies to implement the latter approach, and compared and contrasted them. Next, you revisited the SceneParsing150 example from Chapter 4, scaling it using DDP and then extending that further using ZeRO-based sharding techniques. Since efficiency and reliability are crucial to successful scaling, you also learned about fault-tolerant training and explored the nuances of developing efficient pipelines, following that up with a practical exercise.

In the next two chapters, you will explore and practice some additional distributed deep learning techniques, including model, pipeline, tensor, and hybrid parallelism.

## CHAPTER 8

Scaling Beyond Data Parallelism: Model, Pipeline, Tensor, and Hybrid Parallelism

You have read about several concepts and techniques related to distributed training in the previous chapters of this book. Chapter 6 laid out the fundamentals of distributed model training and discussed the possible dimensions of scaling, while Chapter 7 provided practical knowledge to scale based on the data dimension.

As you learned in Chapter 3, a task can typically be parallelized in two ways: by applying the same set of instructions on different data (SIMD) or by decomposing the set of instructions such that different parts of the algorithm can be performed at the same time on different data (MIMD). Data parallel model training is akin to SIMD, whereas the other forms of parallelism that you will read about in this chapter are akin to MIMD.

Scaling model training using data parallel techniques is often considered "weak" because you are scaling only horizontally, using just one of many possible dimensions of scale (i.e., data). Your overall scalability is limited by the number of parallel workers you can have, the ability of each worker to fit your model in its available memory, and the maximum effective batch size you can have before scaling law fails (for your case), producing diminishing returns. For most scenarios, weak scaling might be sufficient. However, if the limitations are causing you problems, you will need to look beyond data parallelism and explore more advanced vertical scaling techniques that scale your training workload over the other dimensions mentioned in Chapter 6: the model, hyperparameters, and tensors (or a combination thereof).

Vertical scaling in the context of deep learning is not a new concept; it has existed since AlexNet (2012).[1] Krizhevsky et al. split their 60M-parameter model (consisting of two branches with five convolution layers, a max pooling layer, and two fully connected layers, each followed by a final fully connected layer and a softmax layer, as shown in Figure 8-1) to train an ImageNet classifier on two GTX 580 3 GB GPUs. Training took about six days to converge. Today, more than a decade on, distributed training has been conducted for models with as many as 540B parameters on over 50,000 accelerators, while still achieving near linear scaling.[2]

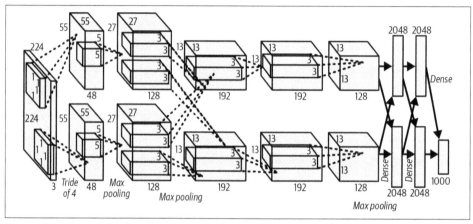

Figure 8-1. One of the first known implementations of vertical scaling: AlexNet

The objective of this chapter is to provide a fundamental understanding of various paradigms of vertical scaling and introduce the evolving trends in this area. You will learn about the considerations for scaling your training workload beyond the data dimension (i.e., model layers, tensors/parameters) and the pros and cons of the various approaches. You will also learn about hybrid parallelism, where scaling is performed along more than one dimension to achieve 2D or 3D training parallelism.

To provide you with practical exposure, this chapter includes hands-on exercises demonstrating the implementation of different vertical scaling paradigms. You will also learn about decision frameworks to choose the most appropriate training paradigm for your use case. We'll continue our exploration of these topics in the

1 Krizhevsky, Alex, Ilya Sutskever, and Geoffrey E. Hinton. 2012. "ImageNet Classification with Deep Convolutional Neural Networks." In *Advances in Neural Information Processing Systems (NIPS 2012)* 25, no. 2. *https:// papers.nips.cc/paper_files/paper/2012/file/c399862d3b9d6b76c8436e924a68c45b-Paper.pdf*.

2 Anantharaman, Rajesh. 2023. "Google Cloud Demonstrates the World's Largest Distributed Training Job for Large Language Models Across 50000+ TPU v5e Chips." Google Cloud blog, November 9, 2023. *https:// cloud.google.com/blog/products/compute/the-worlds-largest-distributed-llm-training-job-on-tpu-v5e*.

following chapter, which provides additional practical experience with these distributed training paradigms.

Questions to Ask Before Scaling Vertically

As discussed in Chapter 3, the memory of accelerator chips is limited due to the power wall. As a result, requiring vertical scaling is not uncommon. When scaling vertically, your objective is to increase the ability of your training system to hold larger models that otherwise will not fit on your accelerator(s), while maintaining computational efficiency. To achieve this aim, you split your model's layers or parameters/tensors across the available workers, creating a scaling pattern that from the model's vantage point is analogous to vertical scaling (adding more resources to existing components). This is in contrast to data parallel techniques, where your model is replicated across all the workers (a paradigm closely aligned with horizontal scaling).

Scaling model training vertically is an intricate process whose success rate varies on a case-by-case basis, warranting careful deliberation to justify its need. This section lays out some of the questions you should consider before venturing down this path. Vertical scaling is particularly complex, and no scaling effort is free or cheap. As always, the golden rule is "if it ain't broke, don't fix it." So, before deciding to implement any of the techniques discussed in this chapter, ask yourself:

Do we need it?
> The need to vertically scale your training rests on the premise of having very high memory requirements—more than what's available in the workers you can source. The accelerators used during training should have enough VRAM to load your model parameters and a batch of data, and to store the computed feature maps (during the forward pass) and gradients (during the backward pass), optimizer states, metrics and losses, and other intermediary cached values.
>
> For instance, the NVIDIA GeForce GTX 1080 Ti has 11 GB of GPU VRAM. If you take the example of GPT-2 (discussed in hands-on exercise #1 in Chapter 4), the 1.5B-parameter model itself at full precision would require 6 GB of VRAM, leaving less than 50% of the device's VRAM available to load the rest of the training state. This will lead to OOM errors during training. OOM errors are a good indicator of the need for vertical scaling.
>
> A good rule of thumb for measuring your needs is to profile your memory requirements (as discussed in Chapters 2 and 4); tune your workload for batch size, precision, etc.; and ascertain there are no leaks, undesired graph growth, or memory fragmentation issues that are amplifying your memory needs. For instance, training with a very large volume of data and computing a wide array of training metrics will amplify your memory usage. In such cases, omitting

training metrics while keeping validation metrics is a good trick to save on memory use. You should also explore whether you're detaching unneeded objects from your model graph and clearing metric state, as these are common causes of memory leaks or growth. GPU fragmentation is another cause of memory growth that exhibits when large chunks of memory is allocated, leaving many small (possibly insufficient) chunks. Configurations like `max_split_size_mb` can be used to manage fragmentation. However, making the split size too small may lead to suboptimal performance. If your memory requirements are still higher than what's available, then you are going to need to scale beyond data parallelism.

Are we ready?

Even if you do need to scale vertically, that doesn't mean you're ready to do so. If you have not been working with more than one GPU, then you will need to review the necessary considerations for scaling your workload beyond a single GPU (discussed at length in 5, 6, and 7). Vertical scaling requires much higher communication bandwidth than horizontal scaling, so this must be taken into consideration when setting up a cluster/compute for vertical scaling. In horizontal scaling (i.e., with data parallel techniques), each worker holds a full model replica and conducts independent training on chunks of the data, and the gradients are then synchronized across the workers. The communication between workers is thus centered around gradient synchronization, so the communication overhead is relatively low. With vertical scaling, in addition to gradients, the activations/feature maps, parameters, etc. will need to be communicated across the workers, putting further pressure on the network fabric and communication backbone. Vertical scale-out is not only harder to achieve but also provides varying performance characteristics given the number of workers.

Can we do without it?

As discussed previously, your memory requirements will drive whether you need to scale vertically. Those requirements scale with batch size, which determines the amount of memory needed to store a batch of data, prefetch/cache data (if those techniques are used), and store the feature maps/activations. Adjusting the batch size is therefore a useful exercise. It's important to triple-check whether you can achieve your goals without vertical scaling techniques, which (as mentioned previously) are often challenging to implement and can have unpredictable results in dynamic resource environments. Having said that, if you can't even fit a batch size of 1 on the GPU, then it's quite clear that you are going to need to explore other techniques than data parallelism.

It's important to note that freezing the graph and fine-tuning techniques such as those you'll read about in Chapters 11 and 12 can further reduce your memory requirements, as gradient computation and backpropagation can be constrained to a few selected layers. Techniques like mixed-precision training (discussed in

Chapter 4) or memory offloading, as implemented in ZeRO-1 and -2 (discussed in Chapter 7), should be explored if possible. These techniques are much simpler and more practical to implement than scaling training through the model and parameter/tensor dimensions.

In summary, before you decide to scale vertically, go through the following checklist to be sure that it's absolutely unavoidable:

1. Can you fit a batch size of 1 on your GPU?

2. Will any of the memory tricks discussed in Chapter 4, including use of mixed precision to reduce your memory footprint, allow you to fit a batch size of at least 1 on your GPU?

3. Will any of the techniques discussed in Chapters 11 and 12 help to reduce your memory footprint and enable you to fit a batch size of at least 1 on your GPU?

If the answer to all of these questions is no, then vertical scaling is unavoidable.

What negative effects should we expect?
Vertical scaling techniques are devised as a workaround for the power wall that limits the memory capacity of a GPU. This workaround allows you to scale out your memory capacity horizontally (across multiple devices); however, it results in increased latency, meaning the time it takes to complete each learning step will be longer. This is due to the increased communication across the dispersed devices and the resulting high interdependence within your computation graph.

When can vertical scaling be regressive?
If you are unable to manage multiple GPUs or orchestrate your workload on a fleet of devices, or if you have an inferior interconnection between the workers, vertical scaling is likely to have a regressive impact.

You are also likely to see regressive (compute) performance characteristics if your largish model consists of many small layers. Vertical scaling techniques hide the overhead via interleaving, a trick that works more effectively with larger layers. The partitioning of smaller layers is suboptimal, as the splits become too fine-grained to allow interleaved computation to mask the communication overhead. We'll explore this issue further in "Data Flow and Communications in Vertical Scaling" on page 271.

Now that you have been warned, let's dive into the details of vertical scaling.

Theoretical Foundations of Vertical Scaling

In Chapter 6, you read about the theoretical foundations of distributed deep learning and explored the partitioning dimensions and the data flows in centralized and decentralized distributed training. As discussed in Chapter 7, the parallelization is done over the input (data) dimensions under the assumption that the entire model and its state, including parameters, gradients, etc., can be independently held in each worker's memory. This assumption greatly simplifies the communication paradigm (discussed in Chapter 5) required for the workers and the leader to complete the training flow.

However, as discussed in Chapter 3, the memory growth of accelerators has not been keeping up with the growing demand for memory of deep learning models. This is especially evident in the context of large language models (LLMs), which have seen an explosion in parameter growth with wider adoption of Transformer-based architectures. For instance, GPT-3, a 175B-parameter model, requires 350 GB memory, and BERT, an early Transformer decoder-based model, has 340M parameters and requires 640 MB memory. PaLM, an LLM that has been competing with humans on various professional exams and passing them with above average scores,[3] has 540B parameters. However, due to the power wall, the current maximum memory on a single GPU is less than 100 GB. This challenge is a result of the misalignment between Moore's law and the scaling law of deep learning models (discussed in Chapter 1 and illustrated here in Figure 8-2) and underscores the need for scalability beyond data parallelism.

---

3 Singhal, Karen, Shekoofeh Azizi, Tao Tu, S. Sara Mahdavi, Jason Wei, Hyung Won Chung, Nathan Scales, et al. 2023. "Large Language Models Encode Clinical Knowledge." *Nature* 620: 172–180. *https://www.nature.com/articles/s41586-023-06291-2*.

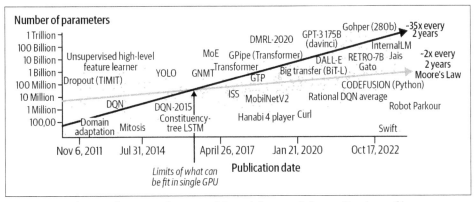

Figure 8-2. The misalignment between Moore's law and the scaling law of language models (based on data from https://oreil.ly/AAt-a)

Revisiting the Dimensions of Scaling

The solution to this challenge is to slice the model across a set of workers over the dimensions that are increasing the memory requirements. As discussed in Chapter 6, there are four possible dimensions of scaling: *data*, *hyperparameters*, *model* (the computation graph, a.k.a. network), and *tensors* (i.e., learnable and non-learnable parameters). In the context of accelerating model training, hyperparameters is an orthogonal dimension that only aids in choosing the optimal configuration for the most statistically efficient model. Hyperparameter optimization will be discussed further in Chapter 11, and we considered the data dimension in depth in the previous chapter. Here, we will primarily focus on the other two dimensions that can be scaled to realize distributed training: the model and tensors. We'll also discuss hybrid approaches that combine scaling along two or three of these dimensions (model, tensors, and data).

Let's take a toy example and work our way through splitting the model to achieve model and tensor parallelism. So far in this book, you have practiced classification, segmentation, and text generation problems. Now, we'll switch focus and look at recommendation solutions. DeepFM[4] is a deep learning model initially proposed for click-through rate prediction that is widely used in recommendation engines. Tik-Tok's recommendation engine is built on a similar architecture. DeepFM has two embedding layers, one sparse and one dense, to capture the feature embedding of the provided input vector. In DeepFM, the dense embedding is reduced twofold by factorization and feature reduction with linear layers. These reduced features are fused by

---

4 Guo, Huifeng, Ruiming Tang, Yunming Ye, Zhenguo Li, and Xiuqiang He. 2017. "DeepFM: A Factorization-Machine Based Neural Network for CTR Prediction." arXiv, March 13, 2017. *https://arxiv.org/abs/1703.04247.*

summation (a.k.a. residual connections) into a sparse embedding before a sigmoid activation is applied to obtain the recommendation. The model architecture is shown in Figure 8-3.

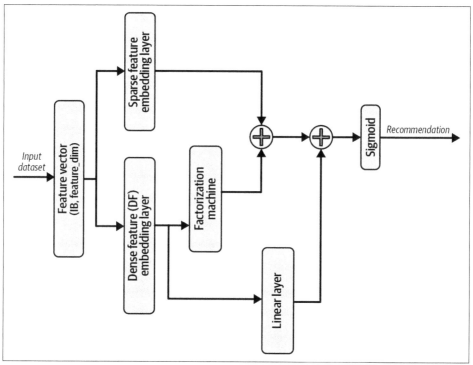

Figure 8-3. The architecture of DeepFM

Implementing tensor parallelism

The challenge with embedding-based models is that the embedding layers grow linearly to the size of the feature vector. If the depth of the dense layers is high, dense embedding layers can have significant memory requirements. Hypothetically speaking, if you were struggling to fit the DeepFM model on one GPU, then you might consider splitting the dense embedding layer into two sublayers and gathering the output before proceeding to the next layer. This is an example of tensor parallelism, because now the layer data (i.e., tensors/parameters) is split across worker(s), as shown in Figure 8-4.

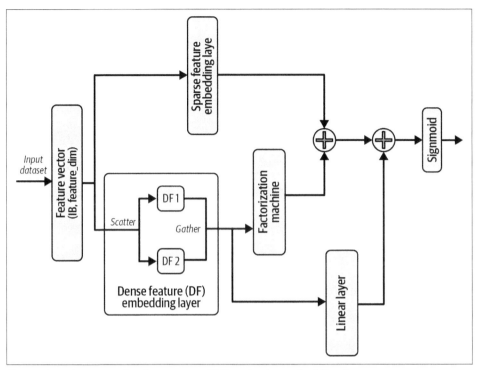

Figure 8-4. An example of tensor parallelism in the embedding layer

In this case, you have selectively partitioned only one layer. You can also partition the entire model along a given axis, such that every layer of the model is equally divided and distributed over the workers. This style of partitioning is user-friendly, but it may not be the most optimal implementation as smaller layers may become too fine-grained to hide the communication latency.

The ability to slice tensors opens up the possibility of converting more challenging MIMD-based operations into much more scalable SIMD operations. GShard identifies the tensor dot operation followed by an all-reduce to be a SIMD-compliant operation set.[5] This operation set is heavily used in most computationally expensive networks, such as Transformer or mixture of experts architectures. If this sequence of operations can be combined as a single instruction, then each slice (row and column) of the matrices being operated upon can be dynamically extracted and the computations can be performed in parallel instead of individually, treating them as a MIMD

---

5 Lepikhin, Dmitry, HyoukJoong Lee, Yuanzhong Xu, Dehao Chen, Orhan Firat, Yanping Huang, Maxim Krikun, Noam Shazeer, and Zhifeng Chen. 2020. "GShard: Scaling Giant Models with Conditional Computation and Automatic Sharding." arXiv, June 30, 2020. *https://arxiv.org/abs/2006.16668.*

operation, as shown in Figure 8-5. With this trick, GShard is able to selectively scale these types of networks.

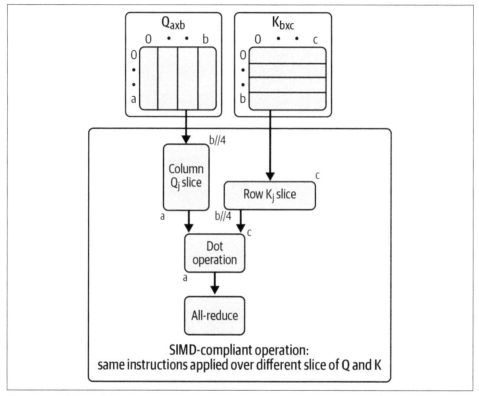

Figure 8-5. Transforming MIMD computation into SIMD, as proposed in GShard

Implementing model parallelism

Staying with the example of DeepFM, if you can fit the dense feature embedding layer on one GPU but not the entire model and all of the state, one option might be to place this layer, the factorization machine, and the linear layer on that device and have the sparse feature embedding layer on another device, where the rest of the computations are performed. This is an example of *model parallelism*, where the model is split layerwise, maintaining the integrity of the tensors/parameters. This approach is illustrated in Figure 8-6, with the solid and dashed lines representing parts 1 and 2, respectively. Part 2 will have smaller memory requirements as it has a smaller embedding dimension (n x 1) and a less memory-intensive sigmoid layer. In part 1, the dense embedding has higher dimensionality (n x m) that's only reduced after the last linear layer in this part.

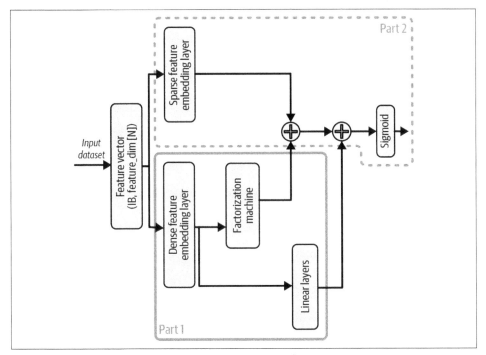

Figure 8-6. Example of model parallel partitioning of DeepFM

Let's assume that part 1 is placed on device 1 and part 2 is placed on device 2. An advantage of this approach is that the computational needs for part 1 and part 2 are different, meaning you could potentially explore using heterogeneous devices with, say, varying VRAM and compute capacity for the two parts.

An alternative approach, shown in Figure 8-7, would be to slice the model such that only the dense layer sits on device 1 and the rest of the computation is performed on device 2. In this case, device 1 only produces one output that's received by device 2 (unlike in the previous case, where two linear outputs are expected from part 1, resulting in wait time while the two sequential sum operations are computed). In other words, with the configuration in Figure 8-6 the outbound communication volume from device 1 to device 2 will be a lot smaller than with the configuration in Figure 8-7.

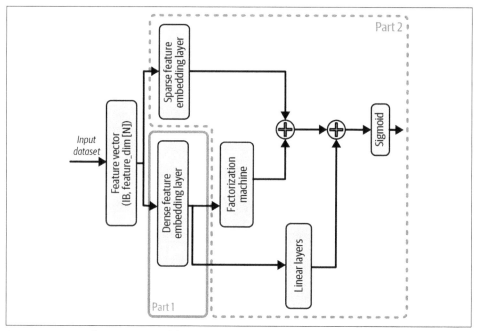

Figure 8-7. An alternative model parallel splitting

Choosing a scaling dimension

Here are some key points to remember when considering which dimension to scale on:

- When scaling vertically (i.e., beyond data parallelism), it is very important to understand your model's computation graph and its memory and compute requirements.

- The most optimal partitioning of your model is guided by the topology of your computing resources (the number of nodes and devices, types of devices, network interconnect, etc.).

- Heterogeneous computation with mixed types of accelerators is possible with model parallelism, on a case-by-case basis. However, it's challenging with tensor parallelism, because with this approach each split has the same compute capability requirements for effective operations (as the same operator(s) of the computation graph are split vertically).

Operators' Perspective of Parallelism Dimensions

This section has discussed scaling over dimensions of models involved in a full training loop (data, model, and tensors). At the heart of these computations are the operators that comprise your model graph. Another useful way to group the dimensions of scaling, therefore, is from the operators' perspective. There are two forms of operator parallelism to consider:[6]

Intraoperator parallelism

> In intraoperator parallelism, the same operator is applied in parallel to multiple inputs in a pure implementation of SIMD. Examples include splitting the input data along the batch dimension (i.e., data parallel techniques) or splitting the tensors along any of the other dimensions (i.e., tensor parallel techniques).

Interoperator parallelism

> Interoperator parallelism splits the computation graph such that each operator can operate in parallel as independently as possible. Model parallelism and its more efficient implementation, pipeline parallelism, are examples of interoperator parallelism.

Operator parallelism is a useful concept to keep in mind as you go deeper into vertical scaling.

Data Flow and Communications in Vertical Scaling

Let's now review the implications of vertical partitioning on the data flow of your model/computation graph. The traditional data flow for the toy example discussed previously is shown in Figure 8-8. Here, the loss is computed based on the ideal recommendation/truth and the recommended item and the computed gradients then backpropagate through the entire network.

---

6 Zheng, Lianmin, Zhuohan Li, Hao Zhang, Yonghao Zhuang, Zhifeng Chen, Yanping Huang, Yida Wang, et al. 2022. "Alpa: Automating Inter- and Intra-Operator Parallelism for Distributed Deep Learning." arXiv, June 28, 2022. *https://arxiv.org/abs/2201.12023*.

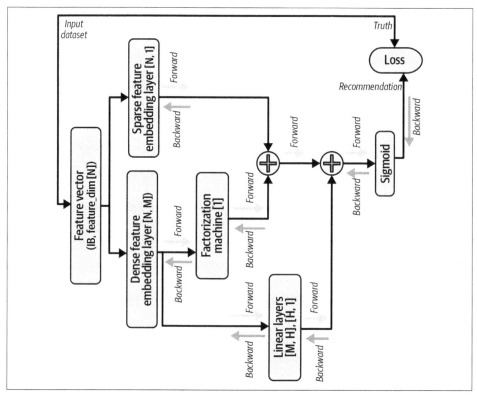

Figure 8-8. Standard data flow as observed in our example DeepFM model

As discussed in Chapters 6 and 7, with data parallelism, each worker conducts the forward pass independently on its own model replica. The gradients from all the workers are then synchronized across the workers using the all-reduce communication paradigm. This is followed by a totally independent backward pass over the worker's replica. The luxury of this total independence is forgone in vertical scaling because both the forward and backward passes now require communication between workers for requesting input or sending output (the feature maps/activations), as well as sharing gradients for their respective steps. Thus, with vertical scaling approaches such as model and tensor parallelism, the workers are highly interdependent.

Continuing with this example, let's now explore these dependencies in the context of tensor and model parallelism.

Tensor parallelism

As shown in Figure 8-9, in our example the dense feature layer is split into two parts, DF1 and DF2, making this intraoperator parallel. Note the use of the scatter communication pattern to handle the distribution of feature input to chunked dense layers and gather to consolidate the activations for upcoming layers. Besides this, the flow of the forward and backward passes remains unchanged.

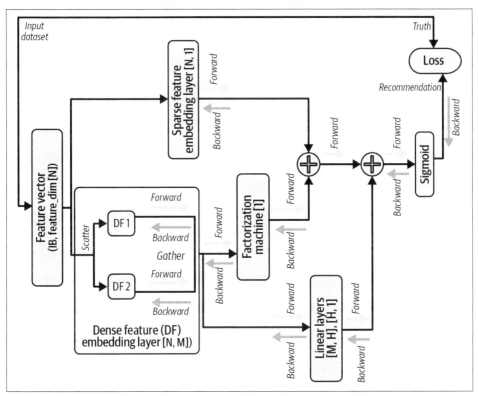

Figure 8-9. The data flow in the tensor parallel implementation of DeepFM

An interesting observation to make here is that now the data is flowing through the devices following the topology in which our model/graph was distributed. Tensors are multidimensional. How you partition them for tensor parallelism has implications on communication patterns. To handle a wide variety of partitioning needs, tensor partitioning is achievable in three unique patterns:

Row parallel
> With row parallelism, the tensor is split through the row axis. As shown in the lower part of Figure 8-10, the row-wise split requires scatter and all-reduce communication to consolidate the results across the devices/workers.

Column parallel

With column parallelism, the tensor is split through the column axis. As shown in the upper part of Figure 8-10, the column-wise split requires broadcast and all-gather communication to consolidate the results across the devices/workers.

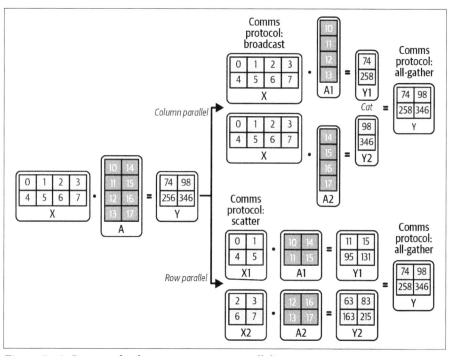

Figure 8-10. Row- and column-wise tensor parallelism

Pairwise parallel

Pairwise parallelism is used when column and row operations are applied in pairs, in that order. In this case, by default the required communication is the sum of what is needed for both column and row parallelism; i.e., *broadcast→gather→scatter→reduce*. However, as shown in Figure 8-11, the gather and scatter steps are unnecessary and are completely avoidable here. Pairwise parallelism implements this efficiency trick and simplifies the usage. This optimization was proposed as a part of Megatron-LM[7] and is known as *sequence parallelism*.

---

7 Korthikanti, Vijay, Jared Casper, Sangkug Lym, Lawrence McAfee, Michael Andersch, Mohammad Shoeybi, and Bryan Catanzaro. 2022. "Reducing Activation Recomputation in Large Transformer Models." arXiv, May 10, 2022. *https://arxiv.org/abs/2205.05198*.

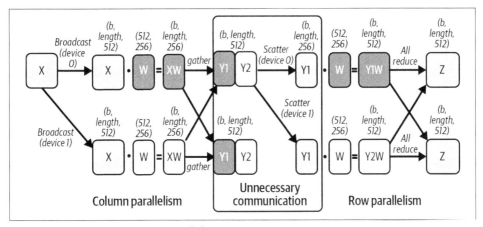

Figure 8-11. Pairwise tensor parallelism

Sequence parallelism is a special case that is possible only when column and row operations are paired in exactly this order; it's not achievable when row–row, column–column, or row–column operations are paired. The naive pairwise parallelism implemented in earlier Megatron-LM implementations[8] had a 4x greater communication expense. Megatron-LM is a really good example of incremental manual layerwise engineering to efficiently scale language models.

Model parallelism

While tensor parallelism requires additional communication expense to gather and collate model state information, model parallelism simply follows the topology in which the graph/model is distributed over the devices. Let's explore the data flow for the case illustrated earlier, in Figure 8-7.

As shown in Figure 8-12, the input feature vector will flow through both the sparse and dense embedding layers. Thus, the input feature vector will need to be loaded onto both of the devices. Following this, device/worker 1 will compute the feature embedding and send it over to device 2, which is responsible for executing part 2. The sparse embedding computation here is independent of the dense embedding computation, so device 2 can execute this task in parallel. However, for further computation, it will have to wait until it receives the dense feature embedding from device 1. Device 2 will then be able to perform the rest of the computations, leading to loss computation. The gradient propagation will follow the same route, tracing the graph by leveraging the connectivity between devices 1 and 2.

---

8 Shoeybi, Mohammad Mostofa Patwary, Raul Puri, Patrick LeGresley, Jared Casper, and Bryan Catanzaro. 2020. "Megatron-LM: Training Multi-Billion Parameter Language Models Using Model Parallelism." arXiv, March 13, 2020. *https://arxiv.org/abs/1909.08053*.

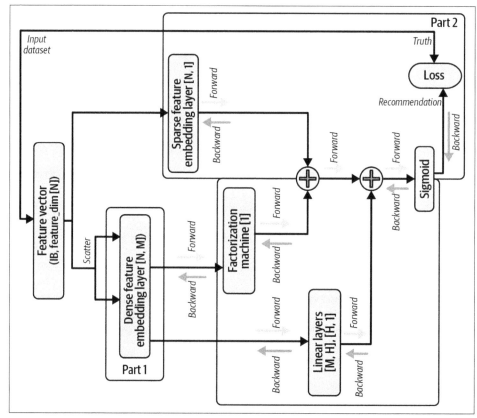

Figure 8-12. The data flow in the tensor parallel implementation of DeepFM

Pipeline parallelism: An evolution of model parallelism

Interlayer parallelism, as observed in model parallel scenarios, is typically very inefficient. As discussed previously, when the computational flow is overlaid over the
device topology, the inefficiencies introduced by the time each worker spends waiting
to receive input from the previous device become evident. Figure 8-13(b) demonstrates this challenge, showing how the graph effectively still executes sequentially
despite having the capacity to execute in parallel. Pipeline parallelism encapsulates a
series of technologies, starting with Google's GPipe, that seek to minimize this idle
time, as shown in Figure 8-13(c).

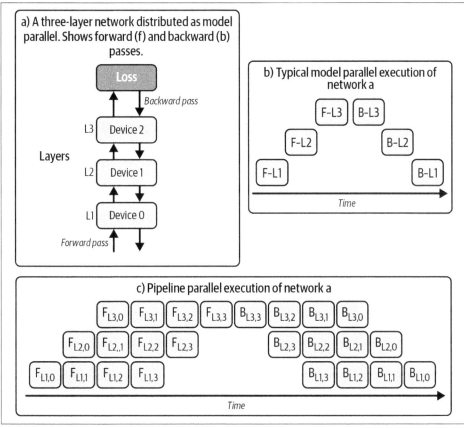

Figure 8-13. An illustration of how pipeline parallelism overcomes the main shortcoming of model parallelism by reducing the amount of idle time

GPipe. GPipe proposed pipelining in model parallel implementations by further splitting of batches of training data into mini-batches that can be processed in parallel to hide or minimize the wait time.[9] The advantage of this approach is only realized, however, when the batches are large (i.e., when splitting them further is still beneficial) and the model is partitioned coarsely (to avoid too small layers, as they will cause communication overhead).

---

9 Huang, Yanping, Youlong Cheng, Ankur Bapna, Orhan Firat, Mia Xu Chen, Dehao Chen, HyoukJoong Lee, et al. 2019. "GPipe: Efficient Training of Giant Neural Networks Using Pipeline Parallelism." arXiv, July 25, 2019. *https://arxiv.org/abs/1811.06965*.

GPipe sparked a series of explorations resulting in techniques such as PipeDream, Chimera, and DAPPLE, with the goal of realizing more efficient model parallelism via pipelining/interleaving. We'll take a look at PipeDream next; DAPPLE and Chimera will be discussed in the following section on hybrid parallelism.

PipeDream. Microsoft's PipeDream is an extension of GPipe where workers begin the backward pass as soon as they've finished the forward pass on their respective initial mini-batches.[10] GPipe is a synchronous pipeline, where backward passes start only after all workers have completed the forward pass on their mini-batches. PipeDream—also known as 1F1B, for 1 (mini-batch) forward, 1 backward—on the other hand, is asynchronous.

PipeDream achieves compute efficiency via more interleaved computations but introduces challenges with regard to managing weight updates. This is because, as shown in Figure 8-16 in the following section, after the first backward pass the pipeline is always updating, leaving no time to conduct weight synchronization and flushes. To manage this challenge PipeDream keeps multiple versions of weights, making this implementation highly memory-inefficient. The trade-off between memory and computation is really evident here, and in similar approaches.

A subsequent revision of PipeDream, known as PipeDream-2BW,[11] utilizes gradient accumulation heavily but stores only two versions of the weights (hence the name, for *double-buffered weight updates*) to manage the memory blowout. Another variant introduced at the same time, known as PipeDream-Flush, seeks to improve on 2BW by introducing pipeline flushes and thus keeping only one copy of the weights in memory. The cost asynchronicity on statistical performance is perhaps the reason why PipeDream is not widely used.

Hybrid parallelism

As discussed earlier, hybrid parallelism describes approaches where scaling is applied along two or more dimensions simultaneously. There are two subtypes of hybrid parallelism, 2D and 3D.

2D hybrid parallelism. Pairwise combination of the three dimensions that we are considering in this chapter to scale model training creates three paradigms of 2D hybrid scaling: data/model, model/tensor, and data/tensor. Let's return to the DeepFM

---

10 Harlap, Aaron, Deepak Narayanan, Amar Phanishayee, Vivek Seshadri, Nikhil Devanur, Greg Ganger, and Phil Gibbons. 2018. "PipeDream: Fast and Efficient Pipeline Parallel DNN Training." arXiv, June 8, 2018. *https://arxiv.org/abs/1806.03377*.

11 Narayanan, Deepak, Amar Phanishayee, Kaiyu Shi, Xie Chen, and Matei Zaharia. 2021. "Memory-Efficient Pipeline-Parallel DNN Training." arXiv, July 22, 2021. *https://arxiv.org/abs/2006.09503*.

example from earlier in this chapter. Hypothetically speaking, if your dense embedding is twice the capacity of a single GPU, then you are likely to need three devices: two for the tensor parallel split of the dense embedding and a third for the rest of the network. This is an example of 2D parallelism where both tensor and model parallel techniques are used in tandem. This is shown in Figure 8-14, where parts 1a and 1b are placed on devices 1 and 2, respectively, and part 2 is placed on device 3. Here, devices 1 and 2 form a unit analogous to part 1 in the model parallel case we looked at earlier (Figure 8-12), except now the computations are performed in a distributed fashion.

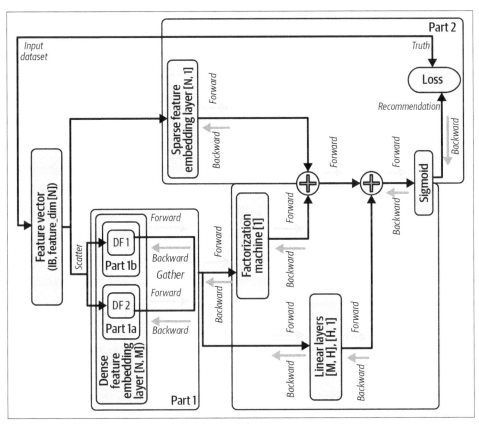

Figure 8-14. Model/tensor 2D hybrid parallelism

Likewise, you could envisage the implementations required for data/model and data/tensor parallelism. For instance, if your model were split over two devices in a tensor parallel pattern, then scaling out to another two devices would allow you to replicate your two-device architecture over another two, allowing the possibility of implementing data parallelism over these two groups of devices.

A common pattern for 2D hybrid parallelism, to minimize the remote communication, is vertical partitioning (tensor/model) within the host devices and data parallelism across the host.[12]

DAPPLE and Chimera are two implementations of 2D hybrid parallelism that specifically apply pipeline (model) parallelism in conjunction with data parallelism.[13] Both are synchronous implementations. DAPPLE focuses on profiling and planning to choose the most optimal split. Chimera, on the other hand, combines two pipelines from different directions (forward and backward, known in Chimera as the *down* and *up* pipelines, respectively). Figure 8-15 shows how this works for four-mini-batch training of a four-stage pipeline. The fact that the mini-batches all contain unique data allows the pipeline execution to be more hybridized for data and model parallelism.

The execution pipeline and memory use of this implementation is shown in Figure 8-16, along with a comparison with other related techniques like GPipe, Pipe-Dream, and DAPPLE. As you can see, the idle time is minimized with Chimera while memory usage remains on par with GPipe.

---

12 Shoeybi et al., "Megatron-LM," *https://arxiv.org/abs/1909.08053*.

13 Fan, Shiqing, Yi Rong, Chen Meng, Zongyan Cao, Siyu Wang, Zhen Zheng, Chuan Wu, et al. 2020. "DAP-PLE: A Pipelined Data Parallel Approach for Training Large Models." arXiv, July 2, 2020. *https://arxiv.org/abs/2007.01045*; Li, Shigang, and Torsten Hoefler. 2022. "Chimera: Efficiently Training Large-Scale Neural Networks with Bidirectional Pipelines." arXiv, February 25, 2022. *https://arxiv.org/abs/2107.06925*.

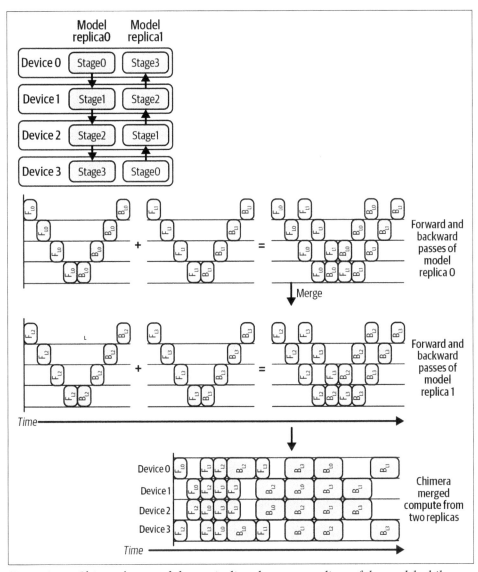

Figure 8-15. Chimera's up and down pipelines keep two replicas of the model while computing forward and backward passes simultaneously[14]

---

14 Li, Shigang and Torsten Hoefler, "Chimera: Efficiently Training Large-Scale Neural Networks with Bidirectional Pipelines," https://arxiv.org/abs/2107.06925

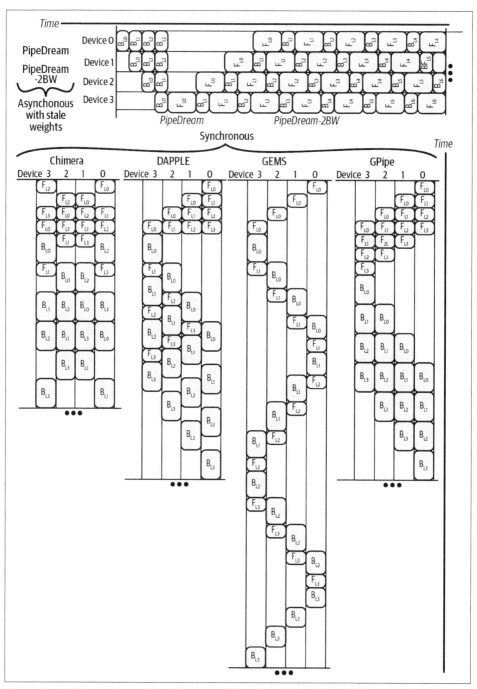

Figure 8-16. Comparison of pipeline parallel and 2D hybrid parallel approaches (based on analysis conducted by PipeDream; adapted from Li and Torsten, 2022)

3D hybrid parallelism. In the case of 3D hybrid parallelism, model, tensor, and data parallel techniques are combined. This approach is much harder to realize and thus not widely used. Let's take our toy example and explore a basic implementation of 3D parallelism. If you had six devices, they could be mapped in a topology such that there are two of the groups of three devices described at the beginning of the previous section (two for the tensor parallel split of the dense embedding plus one for the rest of the network). This replication will enable data parallel training, adding data parallelism to the 2D model/tensor parallelism achieved with a single group of three devices. The gradient synchronization between these two groups will follow the flow of data parallel semantics, as discussed in Chapter 7.

Effectively, you now have two replicas of your partitioned model running across six devices, with the model partitioned across two vertical dimensions. This is an example of 3D hybrid parallelism, illustrated in Figure 8-17.

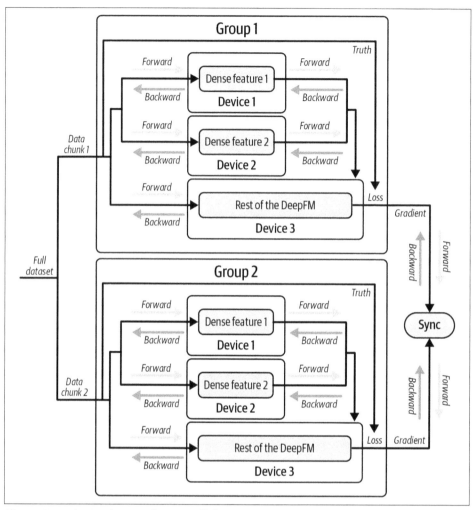

Figure 8-17. A simulation of 3D parallelism on our toy DeepFM example

Basic Building Blocks for Scaling Beyond DP

The previous section provided a theoretical understanding of vertically scaling model training. In this section, I'll introduce some of the practical considerations and building blocks required to implement vertical scaling.

PyTorch Primitives for Vertical Scaling

The evolution of the PyTorch ecosystem to support vertical scaling has been very organic. Many tools and frameworks (like DeepSpeed, FairScale, Megatron, DeepFM, GShard, GPipe, PipeDream, Chimera, and DAPPLE) have emerged over the last few years, but consistent, user-friendly interfaces in PyTorch have evolved more slowly. With PyTorch 2.0, the focus has shifted to providing much simpler APIs for vertical scaling. In this section, you will read about the native PyTorch primitives that are available and how they facilitate scale. Please note that at the time of writing of this book these APIs are actively being iterated, so some changes might have been made to the interfaces by the time you're reading this chapter.

Device mesh: Mapping model architecture to physical devices

As discussed earlier, in vertical scaling, the devices form a custom topology suited to scaling your model. This topology is often dictated by the engineer, given the considerations required in splitting and chunking your model.

`torch.distributed._tensor.DeviceMesh` is the primitive/API available in PyTorch to define the topology of devices that you wish to apply. Taking the example of Figure 8-17, you would define your mesh as `DeviceMesh("cuda", [[[0, 1], 2], [[3, 4], 5]])`. This would first split the devices into two groups for data parallelism (i.e., devices 0, 1, 2 and 3, 4, 5). The second dimension split, for model parallelism, is given by the pairs [0, 1] and 2 and [3, 4] and 5. Lastly, the third dimension split, for tensor parallelism, is given by [0, 1] and [3, 4]. This indicates the devices across which the dense layer will be split in each group.

Distributed tensors: Tensors with sharding and replication

Distributed tensors (`torch.distributed._tensor.DTensor`) are another primitive that extends tensors' capabilities for distributed features such as sharding or replicating and saving/loading tensors over multiple devices/workers. The `DTensor` API (*https://oreil.ly/XjPPF*) supersedes `ShardedTensor`, providing greater flexibility and capabilities similar to TensorFlow's `DTensor` (*https://oreil.ly/MwnPz*), Google's GSPMD, and OneFlow's global tensors.[15]

Sharding and replication are two complementary operations required to split the tensor over devices and replicate from one device to others, respectively.

Sharding and replication examples. The following is an example snippet for sharding with `DTensor`:

```
import torch
from torch.distributed._tensor import DTensor, DeviceMesh, Shard,
```

15 Xu, Yuanzhong, HyoukJoong Lee, Dehao Chen, Blake Hechtman, Yanping Huang, Rahul Joshi, Maxim Krikun, et al. 2021. "GSPMD: General and Scalable Parallelization for ML Computation Graphs." arXiv, December 23, 2021. *https://arxiv.org/abs/2105.04663*; Yuan, Jinhui, Xinqi Li, Cheng Cheng, Juncheng Liu, Ran Guo,
Shenghang Cai, Chi Yao, et al. 2022. "OneFlow: Redesign the Distributed Deep Learning Framework from
Scratch." arXiv, April 19, 2022. *https://arxiv.org/abs/2110.15032*.

```
                distribute_tensor

device_mesh = DeviceMesh("cuda", [0, 1, 2, 3])
rowwise_chunking=[Shard(0)] # shard along 0th dim, analogous to row-wise chunking
ginormous_tensor = torch.randn(888, 12)
dtensor = distribute_tensor(ginormous_tensor, device_mesh=device_mesh,
                            placements=rowwise_chunking)
```

Here, the 888x12-dimension tensor is sharded over four devices along the 0th dimension. As a result, the created distributed tensor will be split over these four devices row-wise. To switch the row-wise sharding to column, all you need to do is change [Shard(0)] to [Shard(1)].

The following is an example of replication:

```
replication_placement = [Replicate()]
replicated_tensor = distribute_tensor(ginormous_tensor, device_mesh=device_mesh,
                            placements=replication_placement)
```

Partial tensors. To distribute a tensor across workers, one can either shard and replicate or shard partially. In this case, the tensor has the same shape across devices, but only has partial values on each device. Partial tensors are created using the _Partial placement specification and are used internally by default.

Logical tensors: Representation without materialization

Logical tensors were created in acknowledgment of the use case of having a tensor or model logically represented without concrete values actually loaded (i.e., materialized). Meta and fake tensors are two such representations.

Meta tensors. The core premise of vertical scaling is that the data is too big to be loaded on one device and needs to be split. This challenge is more commonly faced on accelerators, where memory capacity per device is limited and manyfold smaller than on a CPU (on the order of GB versus TB). The need to pseudoload tensorial data is realized by the MetaTensor abstraction in PyTorch.

The meta tensor introduces a specialized logical device (tensor.device="meta") upon which tensor metadata (e.g., shape, size) can be loaded, without loading the actual tensor data. An example of creating a meta tensor is torch.randn(100000, 100000, device="meta"). Pseudomodels can be defined too: e.g., torch.nn.Lin ear(100000, 100000, device="meta"). The following section will present a practical use of meta tensors.

Because meta tensors are pseudotensors, they present challenges in materializing the tensors upon use. Fake tensors were designed to handle this challenge.

Fake tensors. The fake tensor is the successor of the meta tensor: it leverages meta devices but also can be materialized (i.e., evaluated to realize the true values of the tensor). Fake tensors are explicitly designed for lazy loading, with initialization deferred (*https://oreil.ly/3gIxN*) until the data is needed. Prior to this, all tensorial loading was eager (i.e., they were loaded right away).

Fake tensors leverage context manager closure to transparently handle the execution in fake or real mode. `FakeTensorMode` is the context for fake execution, and `FakeTensor` is the API for creating a fake tensor. If you'd like to see how this transparent execution can happen, there's a toy example in the book's code repository, in the script *fake_tensor_demo.py* (*https://oreil.ly/36I6d*). This example defines a simple regression model, `AModel`, which is then executed in the `FakeTensorMode` context.

Fake tensors are used extensively by PyTorch 2.x to trace through the graph, allowing it to extract and save information for IR conversions without actually running any operators on real tensors. Fake tensors can also be very useful for detecting data structure–related errors, such as shape or size mismatches, and for estimating configurations like batch sizes for the available compute resources.

Working with Larger Models

Traditionally, the model is first loaded on the host CPU/RAM, then transferred to a GPU via CUDA streams. The first challenge when loading a large model is therefore loading it onto the host itself. To contextualize this challenge, let's take the example of BLOOM, the 176B-parameter LLM by Meta AI and BigScience, which requires 1.4 TB of RAM. Irrespective of how many nodes and how many devices you have accumulated in your cluster, if your host has less than 1.4 TB of RAM (e.g., a DGX1 at 512 GB), then you will face challenges in loading this model.

Logical tensors, as discussed in the previous section, can be used to circumvent this challenge. With the help of a logical tensor that presents semantically consistent information about your model, you can load the model with either no initialization (using meta tensors) or deferred initialization (using fake tensors). In either case, you have a logical model represented on the host, while the loading of data/tensors is chunked and handled sequentially on the respective devices. The memory hierarchy (discussed in Chapter 3) can be useful in this case, as you can shard your model checkpoints into chunks and load the model data into the host's RAM one chunk at a time, transferring it to the appropriate device as per the device map/mesh and clearing the RAM by offloading that chunk to create space for the next chunk.

In summary, here are the steps you can follow to load very large model in memory:

1. Create your logical model without any materialization (i.e., with no true values assigned), say using fake tensors.

2. Plan your model partitioning and associated device mapping (which layer is going to which device, etc.).

3. Obtain your model weights from wherever they are persisted (e.g., checkpoint files).

4. Load these weights into the logical model you have created (i.e., materialize the tensors).

5. Transfer the materialized data to the appropriate device.

6. Repeat until all the chunks have been loaded.

Distributed Checkpointing: Saving the Partitioned Model

As discussed in Chapter 7, with data parallelism saving or checkpointing the model is managed by the leader worker. In this case, because each worker has an identical replica of the model, this step is a lot simpler.

In the case of a vertically scaled model, each worker trains a different slice of your model. Hence, a more sophisticated implementation is required to checkpoint the model weights. Most frameworks support saving sharded model checkpoints and provide APIs to reconcile all the shards into a single file if needed. DeepSpeed, for instance, follows this approach.

Approaches like Fully Sharded Data Parallel (FSDP), discussed in more detail in Chapter 9, use streaming to share weights with the leader for saving the partitioned model. PyTorch 1.x implementations of FSDP followed this streaming pattern with `FullStateDictConfig`; however, this approach has been deprecated in favor of a sharded weights file in PyTorch 2.x, enabled via Distributed Checkpointing (DCP) (*https://oreil.ly/7BOjj*). A sample snippet is shown here, where `my_vertically_paral lelized_model` is a model that's configured for `SHARDED_STATE_DICT`. Following this, the `dict` is saved in a checkpoint directory:

```
fsdp.set_state_dict_type(
    my_vertically_parallelized_model,
    StateDictType.SHARDED_STATE_DICT,
)
state_dict = {
    "model": my_vertically_parallelized_model.state_dict(),
}
distributed_checkpoint.save_state_dict(
    state_dict=state_dict,
    storage_writer=DCP.FileSystemWriter(CHECKPOINT_DIR),
)
```

The DCP API `load_state_dict` is then used for loading the sharded model. Unfortunately, these APIs are not transparently used by the `save/load` APIs of vanilla PyTorch but are offered under the `torch.distributed` module (`torch.distributed.checkpoint`).

Summary

In this chapter, you learned about a series of techniques to scale out your model training beyond the data dimension and to vertically slice it along the model and tensor dimensions. You learned what questions to consider when you're beginning to explore vertical scaling, and you explored the technical foundations for these techniques. You read about the implementation of model and tensor parallelism and the evolution of pipeline parallelism, and you considered 2D and 3D implementations of hybrid parallelism. You concluded the chapter by learning about some foundational building blocks used in vertical scaling.

The following chapter is an extension of this discussion of vertical scaling. In Chapter 9, to realize these techniques, you will practice scaling out the DeepFM recommendation model using model, tensor, pipeline, and hybrid parallelism. You'll also review some popular frameworks that are reducing the complexity involved in vertical scaling and try out a more automated implementation of hybrid parallelism.

## CHAPTER 9

Gaining Practical Expertise with Scaling Across All Dimensions

Chapter 8 discussed the theoretical concepts and foundational knowledge you need to scale model training beyond data parallelism, exploring techniques for model, pipeline, tensor, and hybrid parallelism. This chapter continues that discussion and provides practical experience with using these distributed training paradigms. You will also review some tools and libraries that are useful in vertical scaling and further explore DeepSpeed (introduced in Hands-On Exercise #5 in Chapter 7) through a vertical scaling lens. At the end of the chapter, you'll find a practical exercise to achieve more automated multidimensional hybrid training using DeepSpeed.

Hands-On Exercises: Model, Tensor, Pipeline, and Hybrid Parallelism

In this series of Hands-On Exercises, you will build a recommendation engine for movies. You will be leveraging the DeepFM model to explore simplistic implementations of vertical scaling. Please note that in order to make the implementations simpler and easier to follow, the use of monitoring and profiling tools has largely been omitted from these exercises. However, the tools and software discussed in Chapters 4 and 7 are equally applicable and useful for profiling and benchmarking model, pipeline, and hybrid parallel programs too.

The Dataset

The movie recommender will be based on the MovieLens dataset (*https://oreil.ly/-R2ZR*), open sourced by GroupLens Research. This dataset has two parts: the ratings of the movies by users and the movie metadata (title, genre, etc.). You'll be exporting users, movie titles, and movie genres as the features to provide recommendations for users.

The data module used in these exercises is defined as `MovieLensDataset` and can be found in the *deepfm.py* script (line 154) (*https://oreil.ly/oz-R6*) in the GitHub repository.

Since movies can belong to multiple genres (e.g., a family movie can also be a comedy), this is a multilabel classification task, and the genres are one-hot encoded. In this recommendation engine, you will directly model users and movies, meaning the size of the feature vector for the dataset will grow as more users, movies, and genres are added. This will provide a good basis for vertical scaling: as the number of users increases you will eventually run into the power wall for your device, requiring vertical splitting of your model. Please note, however, that this is not the ideal approach for implementing a recommendation engine!

> This is only a toy example of a recommendation engine to demonstrate vertical scaling. This example in its current form will have to be retrained for every new user or movie. Recommendation engines for industrial settings would be implemented differently to easily adapt to growing numbers of users or movies. To build more scalable recommendation engines, you may want to decouple the user from the input features and instead leverage features of "user behaviors" (deduced from the user's present or past sessions). This will also be a more robust solution because it can adapt to individuals' varying moods.

Hands-On Exercise #1: Baseline DeepFM

Let's first develop a baseline model, based on the architecture shown in Figure 8-3 in "Revisiting the Dimensions of Scaling" on page 265. You can find the code for this model (`DeepFactorizationMachineModel`) in the *deepfm.py* script (*https://oreil.ly/4AGz5*) in the book's code repository. You will note that in this module the dense embedding layer is called `embedding` and the sparse embedding layer is called `linear`. The obtained dense embedding is passed to the factorization machine, `fm`, and also to the `mlp` layer. The activations from these layers are cumulatively added to the sparse linear features before a sigmoid function is applied to obtain recommendations.

In the same file, you will also find an alternative implementation of the model, `Deep FactorizationMachineModelV2`, with a different composition. This implementation abstracts the processing of sparse features into the `LinearFMHead` module, which is combined with the dense embedding from the `embedding` layer to build the exact same network. However, `DeepFactorizationMachineModelV2` has only two layers, in a closer alignment to Figure 8-7 from the previous chapter, and it can be partitioned such that each of the two layers is placed on a different device in the case of two-worker model parallel scaling. Such considerations during model composition are important and will be discussed further in the following sections.

Training

In this set of exercises, native PyTorch training loops will be used (instead of higher-level wrappers or frameworks such as Lightning, DeepSpeed, etc.) to demonstrate the fundamental concepts.

The code for baseline training is located in the *torch_baseline_deepfm.py* script (*https://oreil.ly/2M1BU*) in the GitHub repository. In this exercise, DeepFactoriza tionMachineModel is used along with MovieLensModule, a LightningDataModule wrapper for MovieLensDataset. The training loop, shown here, is pretty standard, using binary_cross_entropy as the loss function:

```
for epoch in range(max_epochs):
    running_loss = 0.0
    for i, (x, y) in enumerate(datamodule.train_dataloader()):
        optimizer.zero_grad()

        outputs = model(x)
        y = y.to(outputs.device)
        loss = torch.nn.functional.binary_cross_entropy(outputs, y.float())
        mse = mean_squared_error(outputs, y)
        loss.backward()
        optimizer.step()

        running_loss += loss.item()
        if i % 100 == (99):
            print("[%d, %5d] loss: %.3f" % (epoch + 1, i + 1,
                                            running_loss / 100))
            running_loss = 0.0
```

Observations

To run this baseline on a single device, you can use the following command:

```
deep-learning-at-scale chapter_9 pt-baseline-deepfm train
```

You will find that it takes approximately 1 min 22 s to complete 10 epochs of training of this 177K-parameter model on an NVIDIA V100 GPU.

Next, we'll explore the basic implementations of splitting this model and observe the challenges encountered while doing so.

Hands-On Exercise #2: Model Parallel DeepFM

In this section, you'll build on the previous exercise and develop an implementation using model parallelism, as discussed in "Implementing model parallelism" on page 268 and illustrated in Figure 8-6.

Implementation details

To implement model parallelism, you want to break the stack of layers into small independent units, with each unit deployed on a unique device. The code for this exercise is located in the *torch_model_parallel_deepfm.py* script (*https://oreil.ly/Qw6CH*) in the book's code repository. Looking at the code for the `ParallelDeepFactorizationMachineModel` defined within this file, you will note that this module is aware of the number of GPUs, defined by the variable `num_gpus`. It's this input that provides the module with the device IDs:

```python
class ParallelDeepFactorizationMachineModel(torch.nn.Module):
    def __init__(
        self,
        in_features: List[int],
        num_gpus: int = 2,
        hidden_features: int = 16,
        dropout_rate: float = 0.2,
    ):
        super().__init__()

        if not (torch.cuda.is_available() and torch.cuda.device_count()
                != num_gpus):
            raise ValueError("Must have two NVIDIA GPU.")

        self.devices = [torch.device(f"cuda:{i}") for i in range(num_gpus)]

        self.embedding = FeaturesEmbedding(in_features, hidden_features).to(
            device=self.devices[0]
        )
        self.linear = LinearFeatureEmbedding(in_features).to(
            device=self.devices[1]
        )

        self.fm = FactorizationMachine().to(device=self.devices[1])

        self.deep_fm_embedding_size = len(in_features) * hidden_features
        self.mlp = MLP(
            embedding_size=self.deep_fm_embedding_size,
            hidden_features=hidden_features,
            dropout_rate=dropout_rate,
        ).to(device=self.devices[1])
        self.sigmoid = torch.nn.Sigmoid().to(device=self.devices[1])
```

You will also note that the layers are explicitly transferred to each of the devices, such that the dense embedding layer is placed on device 0 while the rest of the layers are explicitly moved to device 1. As a result of this explicit mapping, your ParallelDeep FactorizationMachineModel is now running over two devices.

Because of this split, your implementation of forward is tied to these devices too:

```
def forward(self, x):
    embeddings = self.embedding(x.to(self.devices[0]))
    linear_features = self.linear(x.to(self.devices[1]))

    embeddings = embeddings.to(self.devices[1])

    linear_features += self.fm(embeddings)
    linear_features += self.mlp(
        embeddings.view(-1, self.deep_fm_embedding_size))
    return self.sigmoid(linear_features.squeeze(1))
```

The module now explicitly transfers x to both device 0 and device 1, while the output of the dense embedding layer is explicitly moved to device 1 from device 0, where it was computed. The final recommended output—i.e., the result of the sigmoid function—will be on device 1 and will then have to be moved to the CPU for use.

Note that this is a very crude implementation of model parallelism. You will need two GPUs on the same host to run this example.

Observations

To execute the code for this example, run the following command:

```
deep-learning-at-scale chapter_9 pt-mp-deepfm train
```

Both of your GPUs will be used in the training. You should find that model convergence tracks along similarly to the baseline, running just a bit slower at 1 min 29 s. This is an indication that you are incurring the expense of distribution overhead—that is, the number of data onloading/offloading operations has been amplified. Having said that, the training dynamics are about the same in both cases (i.e., the validation loss and metrics are on par).

One issue with this implementation is that there is no clear separation of infrastructure (device topology) and logic (computation graph/model). The module code is intertwined with the device logic, making it extremely challenging to further scale out this implementation to, say, four devices. You could simplify the module by rearranging it to match the DeepFactorizationMachineModelV2 implementation discussed in the previous section, as shown in the following code snippet:

```
class ParallelDeepFactorizationMachineModelV2(torch.nn.Module):
    def __init__(
        self,
        in_features: List[int],
```

```
        num_gpus: int = 2,
        hidden_features: int = 16,
        dropout_rate: float = 0.2,
    ):
        super().__init__()

        if not (torch.cuda.is_available() and torch.cuda.device_count()
                != num_gpus):
            raise ValueError("Must have two NVIDIA GPU.")

        self.devices = [torch.device(f"cuda:{i}") for i in range(num_gpus)]

        self.embedding = FeaturesEmbedding(
            in_features, hidden_features).to(device=self.devices[0])

        self.linear = LinearFMHead(
            in_features=in_features,
            hidden_features=hidden_features,
            dropout_rate=dropout_rate,
        ).to(device=self.devices[1])

    def forward(self, x):
        embeddings = self.embedding(x.to(self.devices[0]))
        linear_features = self.linear(
            x.to(self.devices[1]), embeddings.to(self.devices[1]))
        return linear_features
```

In this case, your modules are compiled closely to the expected device topology for easier splitting. However, the loss of flexibility and ability to scale is evident in both implementations. In the following exercise, you'll extend this example to realize pipeline parallelism.

Hands-On Exercise #3: Pipeline Parallel DeepFM

In Chapter 8, you read about two techniques for implementing pipeline parallelism: GPipe and PipeDream. In this exercise, you will be implementing a naive version of GPipe-based pipeline parallelism on the DeepFM model

Implementation details

The code for this exercise is located in the *torch_pipeline_deepfm.py* script (*https://oreil.ly/zptCj*) in the GitHub repository. The PipeDeepFactorizationMachineModel module used in this exercise extends the ParallelDeepFactorizationMachineModel from the previous example. The forward method of this module splits the batch data (mini-batches) into chunks (micro-batches) and accumulates them in memory until the batch is exhausted. The definition for this method is as follows:

```
def forward(self, x: torch.Tensor):
    micro_outputs = []
    for xs in iter(x.split(self.micro_batch_chunks, dim=0)):
```

```
        micro_outputs.append(super().forward(xs))
    return torch.cat(micro_outputs)
```

Once the forward pass is completed, the backward pass commences, simulating the GPipe pipelines.

Observations

Run the following command to execute the code for this example:

```
deep-learning-at-scale chapter_9 pt-pipe-deepfm train
```

You'll note that the training takes a whopping 24 min to complete, as compared to just over 1 min previously. There are two reasons for this inefficiency: the model itself is very small, and the original batch size was quite small (240). Chunking this into eight parts makes the micro-batches too small to be effective. Next, we'll look at an alternative implementation of this approach using RPC.

Hands-On Exercise #4: Pipeline Parallel DeepFM with RPC

In this exercise, you will explore the implementation of pipeline parallelism over RPC. You will notice a lot of similarity between this example and the first Hands-On Exercise from Chapter 7, which also used RCP.

Implementation details

The code for this exercise is located in the *rpc_torch_pipeline_deepfm.py* (*https:// oreil.ly/A7hVG*) script in the GitHub repository. As mentioned previously, the implementation is very similar to exercise #1 in Chapter 7. Each worker is tied to a GPU device via a dedicated process. The communication between the workers happens via the torchpipe backend, which is initialized as follows:

```
rpc.init_rpc(
    "leaders" if rank == leaders_rank else f"trainer_{rank}",
    rank=rank,
    world_size=world_size,
    backend=rpc.BackendType.TENSORPIPE,
    rpc_backend_options=rpc_backend_options,
)
```

As in any RPC example, DistributedOptimizer is used in this case. Remote references are also used to wrap the model parameters, to allow RPC-based access of parameters on remote servers. The model splitting is conducted exactly as in the previous model parallel exercise, placing the dense embedding layer and the linear head on unique devices.

The pipeline parallelism is realized via the nuanced implementation in the main module, RPCDeepFactorizationMachineModel, which wires them up as shown in Figure 8-7. The forward method splits the batch data (mini-batches) into chunks (micro-batches). _forward_micro is called for each chunk to compute the forward pass chunkwise. The definitions for these two methods are shown here:

```
def forward(self, x: torch.Tensor) -> torch.Tensor:
    micro_outputs = []
    for xs in iter(x.split(self.micro_batch_chunks, dim=0)):
        micro_outputs.append(self._forward_micro(xs))
    # return torch.cat(torch.futures.wait_all(micro_outputs))
    return torch.cat(micro_outputs)

def _forward_micro(self, x: RRef) -> torch.Tensor:
    xs_rref = RRef(x)
    embeddings = self.embedding.remote().forward(xs_rref)
    # result = self.linear_head.rpc_async().forward(xs_rref, embeddings)
    result = self.linear_head.rpc_sync().forward(xs_rref, embeddings)
    return result
```

Once the forward pass is completed, the backward pass commences, simulating the GPipe pipelines.

Observations

To execute the code for this example, run the following command:

```
deep-learning-at-scale chapter_9 rpc-pt-pipeline-deepfm train
```

In this exercise, you extended the model parallel implementation from exercise #2 to realize pipeline parallelism. You will note that training is slow compared to the baseline run, taking 52 minutes. While the performance characteristics of these methods depend heavily on infrastructure and compute capacity, as this example illustrates, for the same configuration RCP methods tend to be slower than the standard approach demonstrated in exercise #3.

In this case, the cost of implementing pipeline parallelism is clearly seen because this toy example is not big enough to justify the need for scaling vertically in this way. If this model were too big to fit on one GPU, that would justify splitting it over two (or more) devices, but with a small model the added cost of the communication overhead would be too high for this to be feasible. With a bigger, more computationally intensive model, these numbers, albeit slow, would appear more practical.

 PyTorch also implements an easy wrapper for pipeline parallelism via the torch.distributed.pipeline.sync.Pipe module; however, at the time of writing it is still in an experimental state. You can find a translation of this example code to a Pipe wrapper in the *rpc_torch_exp_pipeline_deepfm.py* script (*https://oreil.ly/ixvjB*) in the GitHub repository.

Hands-On Exercise #5: Tensor Parallel DeepFM

In this exercise you will explore how to partition your model across the tensor dimension, as discussed in "Implementing tensor parallelism" on page 266.

Implementation details

At the time of writing of these exercises, PyTorch's Tensor Parallelism APIs (*https:// oreil.ly/1owi7*) were still experimental and could not support scaling the DeepFM model as discussed in Chapter 8. For tensor parallelism, the model has to be purely sequential and not branched, as the DeepFM model is. As a result, in this exercise, you will have a simplified recommendation model with one embedding layer and a very simple linear head for recommendations (RecoHead).

The code for this exercise is located in the *torch_tensor_deepfm.py* script (*https:// oreil.ly/oQp-l*) in the GitHub repository. You will note that the EmbeddingLayer and RecoHead are bundled sequentially into the model via the Sequential wrapper:

```
model = torch.nn.Sequential(EmbeddingLayer(), RecoHead()).to(rank_device)
```

You will also note the use of device_mesh, as defined by DeviceMesh("cuda", torch.arange(0, world_size)).

To parallelize, the wrapper parallelize_module is called, which wraps the model in pairwise fashion over the device topology:

```
model = parallelize_module(
    model,
    device_mesh=device_mesh,
    parallelize_plan=PairwiseParallel(),)
```

Note the use of the tp_mesh_dim parameter in the _run_trainer method to specify the axis on which to partition the model tensorially. The rest of the training code remains unchanged. In essence, in this exercise, you have opted to split your model over the 0th (row) dimension, such that all of the parameters will be distributed over the available devices.

Observations

To run this exercise, use the following command:

```
deep-learning-at-scale chapter_9 pt-tensor-deepfm train --use-pairwise-parallel
```

In this example, you have to explicitly partition each layer (embedding and linear head) over the two devices you have in training. These layers, however, are already small.

You may note that even though your model is now much simpler (for example, it does not have the sparse embedding layer), it's still taking longer to complete the

---

training than the baseline run. This is because the model is now much too small to hide the communication latency or to show any benefits from vertical scaling.

Hands-On Exercise #6: Hybrid Parallel DeepFM

In this exercise, you will extend the previous exercise to implement 2D parallelism by scaling additionally along the data dimension. You will need at least two GPU devices for splitting the tensors along the row (0th) dimension, and another two to replicate the model for data parallelism.

Implementation details

You will use the same example from exercise #5, with the EmbeddingLayer and Reco Head. The code for this exercise is located in the torch_tensor_fsdp_deepfm.py script (*https://oreil.ly/59BYp*) in the GitHub repository.

In this implementation, you combine FSDP (discussed in "FSDP" on page 305) with tensor parallelism to achieve 2D parallelism. Note the use of DistributedSampler, as discussed in Chapter 7, for enabling data partitioning:

```
dp_train_loader = to_parallel_data_loader(
    datamodule.train, batch_size, dp_rank, dist.get_world_size()
)
```

where to_parallel_data_loader wraps the dataset with the sampler to create a distributed loader:

```
def to_parallel_data_loader(dataset, batch_size, rank, world_size):
    sampler = torch.utils.data.distributed.DistributedSampler(
        dataset, num_replicas=world_size - 1, rank=rank
    )
    return torch.utils.data.DataLoader(
        dataset,
        sampler=sampler,
        batch_size=batch_size,
    )
```

Also notice the wrapping of the parallelized model in the FSDP API, as follows:

```
model = parallelize_module(
    model,
    device_mesh=device_mesh,
    parallelize_plan=PairwiseParallel(),
    tp_mesh_dim=1, # Take the col dim of device for tensor parallelism
)

dp_pg = device_mesh.get_dim_groups()[0] # Data parallel dim is row of
                                        # the device mesh
model = FSDP(model, process_group=dp_pg)
```

With these changes, you have converted your tensor parallel model into a hybrid 2D parallel model.

Observations

To run this exercise, use the following command:

```
deep-learning-at-scale chapter_9 pt-tensor-ddp-deepfm train
```

Tools and Libraries for Vertical Scaling

So far in this and the previous chapter, you have learned about the fundamentals of vertical scaling and explored toy examples. You may have noted the level of reengineering required to support vertical scaling and how infeasible it can get should your device layout change upon inference, for example. For these reasons, the adaptability of vertical scaling is limited. Ideally, the model partitioning would happen transparently to the user's code, automatically using the available devices. There are a limited set of tools that provide automation to this degree when it comes to vertical scaling. In this section, we'll review the tools available to support this type of scaling and conduct a more practical exercise demonstrating hybrid scaling.

OneFlow (*https://oreil.ly/8bqW3*), FairScale (*https://oreil.ly/5Rxuv*), and DeepSpeed (*https://oreil.ly/wB0fw*) are three popular frameworks in the PyTorch ecosystem that provide a variety of options for vertical scaling. PyTorch 2.x is also rapidly moving toward support for vertical scaling through the native `torch.distributed` APIs, drawing inspiration from the previously mentioned frameworks. Named to match FairScale's API, PyTorch's package for vertical scaling is known as FSDP. FSDP is being rolled out incrementally and still offers many features in experimental/beta state. We'll take a look at all of these in this section.

OneFlow

OneFlow[1] reinvents the communication paradigm with the clear goal of providing completely decentralized scheduling of parallelized workloads. The communication model adopted by OneFlow is based on the actor model, where each worker has an actor, or agent, and the agents communicate with each other via messages, offering decoupled communication.

---

1 Yuan, Jinhui, Xinqi Li, Cheng Cheng, Juncheng Liu, Ran Guo, Shenghang Cai, Chi Yao, et al. 2022. OneFlow: Redesign the Distributed Deep Learning Framework from Scratch. arXiv, April 19, 2022. *https://arxiv.org/abs/2110.15032.*

Another interesting feature of OneFlow is its global tensors that naturally support distribution, with the `split` and `broadcast` APIs providing sharding and replication capabilities. PyTorch's `DTensor` primitive, discussed in "Distributed tensors: Tensors with sharding and replication" on page 285, was inspired by OneFlow's implementation.

FairScale

FairScale is a library from Meta that enables scaling beyond data parallelism by sharding the model over the workers following a user-specified auto-wrapping policy. The FSDP implementation in PyTorch, discussed in "FSDP" on page 305, is an iteration of the FairScale parallelization paradigm.

DeepSpeed

DeepSpeed incorporates a number of tricks to optimize memory management. You read a little about this library in Chapter 7 and explored its application in data parallel scaling using the first two ZeRO-DP optimization stages (ZeRO-1 and ZeRO-2). The third stage, ZeRO-3, partitions not only the optimizer states (OS) and gradients (G), but also the model's parameters (P), distributing them across the workers.[2] This is a specialized implementation of vertical scaling, and it massively reduces the per-device memory requirements for model states.

Let's take a look at how this works. If your model has Ψ parameters (the model size), then the gradient size (assuming full training and no parameter freezing) will be the same. If K is a multiplier of Ψ that captures various optimizer states (e.g., variance), then all combined your minimum memory requirement will be $(2 + K) * \Psi$. Depending on your precision (4 for `fp32`, 2 for `fp16`), applying the byte multiplier will give you the total memory required to run your baseline model: $(2 + K) * \Psi * 4$ bytes, for example. Because of how ZeRO-1 shards optimizer states, it reduces the required memory to $(2 + K / N_d) * \Psi$, where N_d is the scale/degree of data parallelism. With ZeRO-2, where both OS and G are sharded, the effective memory requirement is further reduced to $(1 + (1 + K) / N_d) * \Psi$. In ZeRO-3, which additionally shards the parameters themselves (P), the memory requirement comes down to $((2 + K) / N_d) * \Psi$. These reductions are shown visually in Figure 9-1.

---

2 Rajbhandari, Samyam, Jeff Rasley, Olatunji Ruwase, and Yuxiong He. 2020. "ZeRO: Memory Optimizations Toward Training Trillion Parameter Models." arXiv, May 13, 2020. *https://arxiv.org/abs/1910.02054*.

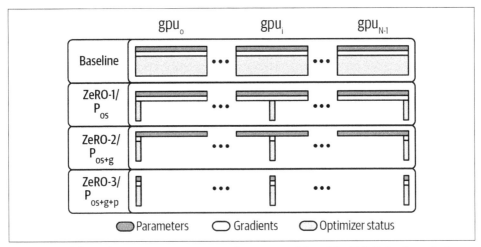

Figure 9-1. The reduction in memory requirements achieved by ZeRO-1, -2, and -3 (adapted from Rajbhandari et al., 2020)

ZeRO-Infinity, an update to ZeRO-3 introduced in 2021 and also available through DeepSpeed, makes this sharding automatic, requiring no changes to the model or the user code.[3] ZeRO-Infinity implements five techniques to provide vertical scale that make it possible to train a 32T-parameter model on 32 NVIDIA V100 DGX-2s (i.e., a total of 512 GPUs)—50x larger than the size of model that can be trained on the same devices using 3D hybrid parallelism. These techniques are:

- The *infinity offload engine*, to efficiently leverage the heterogeneous memory hierarchy by simultaneously exploiting GPU, CPU, and NVMe memory
- *Memory-centric tiling*, to support the execution of massive operations without requiring model parallelism
- *Bandwidth-centric partitioning*, to capitalize on the memory bandwidth available across all parallel devices
- *Overlap-centric design*, to enable efficient interleaving of communication and computations (reducing wait time)
- *Automated parameter sharing*, to provide an easy interface to vertically scale models without refactoring the code

As shown on the left side of Figure 9-2, the model states mainly comprise P, G, and OS values. For a two-layer model (layer 0 and layer 1), we can designate these P0, P1,

---

3 Rajbhandari, Samyam, Olatunji Ruwase, Jeff Rasley, Shaden Smith, and Yuxiong He. 2021. ZeRO-Infinity: Breaking the GPU Memory Wall for Extreme Scale Deep Learning. arXiv, April 16, 2021. *https:// arxiv.org/abs/2104.07857.*

G0, G1, and OS0, OS1, respectively. When this model is shared over four GPUs with N_d of 4, then each device, as shown on the right in Figure 9-2, gets its own respective shard of the model (M0…3). This figure shows the data movement of the infinity off-load engine over the forward and backward passes and how P, G, and OS are partitioned and sharded across the network during training. You will note that the host keeps all these states but exchanges P and G with the devices. As discussed in the previous section, the total volume of data moved in this case is $1/N_d$, which is further reduced to 1 at collection via all-to-one operations.

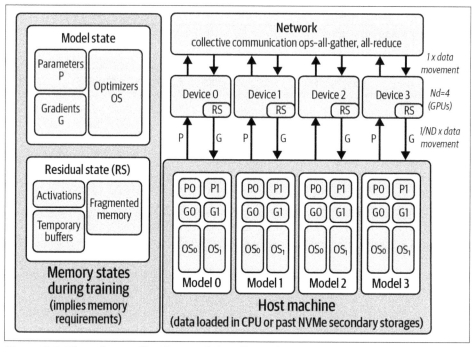

Figure 9-2. The infinity offload engine's handling of memory and data

Recently, DeepSpeed has added three more efficiency tricks via another update, called ZeRO++.[4] In ZeRO++, the focus has shifted to block quantization (discussed in "The effect of precision on gradients" on page 139). To build on this, a new quantized gradient averaging technique has been proposed that's more aligned with all-to-all communication than reduce-scatter (used in vertically scaled training). This new gradient averaging trick preserves accuracy but also achieves communication efficiency as a result of low-precision communication.

---

4 Wang, Guanhua, Heyang Qin, Sam Ade Jacobs, Connor Holmes, Samyam Rajbhandari, Olatunji Ruwase, Feng Yan, Lei Yang, and Yuxiong He. 2023. "ZeRO++: Extremely Efficient Collective Communication for Giant Model Training." arXiv, June 16, 2023. *https://arxiv.org/abs/2306.10209.*

FSDP

FSDP is an evolving implementation in native PyTorch for scaling beyond data parallelism. The vision the PyTorch community has for FSDP is to provide a single interface that enables vertical scaling and allows larger models to fit in memory, and that is as easy to use as the DDP techniques that are available today. The aim is to provide APIs that can seamlessly transition between DP, ZeRO-1 and -2, and FSDP (closely aligned to ZeRO-3/FairScale).

Automatic wrapping—i.e., the ability to automatically discover which parameters to partition—is the key to FSDP. The `torch.distributed.fsdp` module and its specific abstractions, such as `FullyShardedDataParallel`, `CPUOffload`, `wrap`, and `default_auto_wrap_policy`, are designed with the same principles in mind. For example, wrapping your model in `FullyShardedDataParallel` (i.e., `FullySharded DataParallel(model)`) will create a sharded model, whereas with `DataParal lel(model)` you would have created a replicated model. The rest of the operations and API calls for training, in theory, will remain just the same, enabling seamless transitions and scaling. In the case of FSDP, the module wrapper takes care of moving data to the right devices, greatly simplifying user code.

FSDP makes heavy use of two features of PyTorch: `nn.Module` (its structure, hooks), and overriding `nn.Module.forward`. The former lets FSDP reason about ownership of parameters and memory and make assumptions about where to find the parameters it needs to modify (shard). The latter provides a mechanism for FSDP to run special code just before and just after running key parts of the model, such as the `forward` function.

Overview and Comparison

A side-by-side comparison of these key libraries for vertical scaling is shown in Table 9-1. Of course, this is not an exhaustive list; as mentioned earlier, the evolution in this area has been quite organic, and covering all the available tools in this chapter would not be possible. A few other noteworthy libraries are FlexFlow, Alpa, and PaddlePaddle:

FlexFlow
> In contrast to DeepSpeed's auto-partitioning and FSDP's auto-wrapping logic, FlexFlow[5] conducts a Monte Carlo simulation to determine a suitable partitioning of the model and data, taking the device topology into consideration. While

---

5 Jia, Zhihao, Matei Zaharia, and Alex Aiken. 2018. "Beyond Data and Model Parallelism for Deep Neural Networks." arXiv, July 14, 2018. *https://arxiv.org/abs/1807.05358*.

FlexFlow's implementation is different than the frameworks discussed previously, at its core it is still a realization of model, tensor, and data parallelism.

Alpa

Alpa proposed the intra- and interoperator parallelism discussed in Chapter 8 to enable more seamless distributed training.[6] It follows a similar approach to Flex-Flow but relies on dynamic programming to deduce the effective scaling by focusing only on operator-based parallelization (instead of worrying about three dimensions: model, data, and tensors).

PaddlePaddle

PaddlePaddle[7] enables a resource-aware scale-out of the training workload, capturing a global cost model and facilitating planning for the right choice of parallelism to conduct all modes of distributed training discussed so far.

Table 9-1 focuses on just the four tools discussed in the previous sections, as these are the most widely used at the time of writing.

Table 9-1. Comparison of widely used tools for vertical scaling

	FSDP	DeepSpeed	FairScale	OneFlow
Fully automatic vertical scaling	To some extent (through auto-wrapping logic, but requires code changes and rethinking of model architecture)	Yes	To some extent (through auto-wrapping logic, but requires code changes and rethinking of model architecture)	No
Distributed tensors	Yes (available but not enforced)	No	No	Yes
Communication strategy	Collective comms (NCCL)	Collective comms (NCCL)	Collective comms (NCCL)	Actor model
Scheduling strategy	Centralized	Centralized	Centralized	Decentralized
Advanced mixed precision (support for low-precision collective comms and weights sync)	Yes	Yes	Yes	

6 Zheng, Lianmin, Zhuohan Li, Hao Zhang, Yonghao Zhuang, Zhifeng Chen, Yanping Huang, Yida Wang, et al. 2022. "Alpa: Automating Inter- and Intra-Operator Parallelism for Distributed Deep Learning." arXiv, June 28, 2022. *https://arxiv.org/abs/2201.12023*.

7 Ao, Yulong, Zhihua Wu, Dianhai Yu, Weibao Gong, Zhiqing Kui, Minxu Zhang, Zilingfeng Ye, et al. 2021. "End-to-End Adaptive Distributed Training on PaddlePaddle." arXiv, December 6, 2021. *https://arxiv.org/abs/2112.02752*.

	FSDP	DeepSpeed	FairScale	OneFlow
Activation checkpointing	Yes	Yes, but not automatic (requires changes to model)	Yes, but not automatic (requires changes to model)	Yes
Offloading	CPU	CPU or disk/ persistent storage	CPU	CPU
Distributed checkpointing	Yes	Yes	Yes (but requires nontrivial involvement)	
Experimental	Yes	No	No	No

None of these frameworks support auto-tuning or simulated assessment of best splitting strategies. In the next section, we'll wrap up our discussion of vertical scaling with a practical example of automatic scaling with DeepSpeed.

Hands-On Exercise #7: Automatic Vertical Scaling with DeepSpeed

The ability to partition models more seamlessly is a great enabler of vertical scaling. In this short exercise, you will extend the DeepSpeed exercise from Chapter 7 (see "Hands-On Exercise #5: Distributed Sharded DDP (ZeRO)" on page 251) to include ZeRO-3 training, to realize automatic vertical partitioning.

The code for this example is located in the *zero3_hybrid.py* script (*https://oreil.ly/ A9x5i*) in the GitHub repository. The only code change you will need to make to the example from Chapter 7 to retrofit it for vertical scaling is changing the strategy to deepspeed_stage_3_offload, as shown here:

```
trainer = PLTrainer(
    accelerator="auto",
    devices=devices if devices else "auto",
    num_nodes=nodes,
    max_epochs=max_epochs,
    precision=precision,
    callbacks=[..],
    logger=[...],
    strategy="deepspeed_stage_3_offload",
    log_every_n_steps=3,
)
```

Observations

To run this example, use the following command:

```
deep-learning-at-scale chapter_9 zero3 train
```

With this simple change, you are able to scale out your training along both the data and tensor dimensions, achieving 2D parallelism. You will note a reduction of more than 50% in VRAM memory usage, leaving more space for a larger model or batch size. You should now be able to use a batch size of 75 at full precision when training on two V100 GPUs, whereas with data parallelism only you would start to see OOM errors at a batch size of 40.

To leverage ZeRO++, you can use four additional configurations (shown here in bold):

```
{
    "zero_optimization": {
        "stage": 3,
        "reduce_bucket_size": 10000000,
        "reduce_scatter": true,

        "zero_quantized_weights": true,
        "zero_hpz_partition_size": 16,
        "zero_quantized_gradients": true,

        "contiguous_gradients": true,
        "overlap_comm": true
    }
}
```

These could, in theory, be enabled using DeepSpeedStrategy initialization (i.e., strategy=DeepSpeedStrategy(config=deepspeed_config)), but ZeRO++ is not yet fully supported in Lightning.

Summary

In this chapter, you practiced various techniques to scale out your model training beyond the data dimension and slice it vertically along the model and tensor dimensions. In a series of hands-on examples, you scaled out a simple recommendation model to achieve model, tensor, pipeline, and hybrid parallelism. To round out the chapter, you reviewed some of the popular frameworks that are simplifying the complexity involved in vertical scaling. Lastly, you practiced a more automated scale-out using DeepSpeed.

This chapter concludes the distributed training aspect of our discussion of scaling deep learning at scale. In the following chapter, you will learn some tricks and techniques for scaling deep learning efficiently.

## PART III

Extreme Scaling

This section delves into the aspects of scaling deep learning models to effectively handle vast amounts of data. It starts by emphasizing a data-centric approach, offering techniques to maximize data utilization and optimize data pipelines through sampling and selection methods. This section also focuses on scaling experiments, providing insights into effective experiment planning and management for improved model performance. Additionally, it explores efficient fine-tuning of large models using low-rank techniques and introduces the conceptual framework of foundation models, summarizing their significance in the evolving deep learning landscape.

## CHAPTER 10

Data-Centric Scaling

Parts I and II of this book discussed hardware, software, and algorithmic techniques to scale your model development–related workload. Part III focuses on data, design, processes, and other application-specific considerations needed to scale effectively. As discussed in Chapters 1 and 2, data has been fueling the success of deep learning for over two decades, and there is a long-held belief that increasing the size of the training dataset will continue to improve model performance.[1] It has been said that data is the oil of the 21st century, and much like oil, data possesses characteristics that can fuel innovation—when used and prepared with care. This is a real challenge, as has been confirmed by the 2023 State of AI Infrastructure Survey,[2] which ranks data among the top three biggest development challenges faced by organizations (along with infrastructure and compute). According to this survey, two out of five AI-practicing organizations identify data as the biggest issue in AI development.

The importance of data curation is evident from the success of ChatGPT (*https:// oreil.ly/iFIdd*), which has become a highly influential model largely due to the careful use of a set of data curation techniques to ensure the quality of the results. This example is especially relevant because ChatGPT mainly reimplemented the neural network innovations already proposed by InstructGPT (*https://oreil.ly/EQawP*), with extensive innovation in terms of data application strategies.

---

1 Sun, Chen, Abhinav Shrivastava, Saurabh Singh, and Abhinav Gupta. 2017. "Revisiting Unreasonable Effectiveness of Data in Deep Learning Era." arXiv, August 4, 2017. *https://arxiv.org/abs/1707.02968*; Hestness, Joel, Sharan Narang, Newsha Ardalani, Gregory Diamos, Heewoo Jun, Hassan Kianinejad, Md. Mostofa Ali Patwary, Yang Yang, and Yanqi Zhou. 2017. "Deep Learning Scaling Is Predictable, Empirically." arXiv, December 1, 2017. *https://arxiv.org/abs/1712.00409*.

2 Run:ai. 2023. "The 2023 State of AI Infrastructure Survey." *https://pages.run.ai/hubfs/PDFs/2023%20State %20of%20AI%20Infrastructure%20Survey.pdf*.

In this chapter, you will learn about how to "care" for your data and curate it for your model development purposes. You will read about the characteristics of data and the implications they have on scaling your model. You'll also explore various tricks and techniques, such as augmentation, sampling, and compression, that you can use to navigate the challenges that the seven Vs of data—*volume, velocity, variety, veracity, validity, volatility,* and *value*—bring to your deep learning workload.[3]

The Seven Vs of Data Through a Deep Learning Lens

Let's start with an overview of the seven Vs of data and the challenges they pose in scaling deep learning models:

1. *Volume* defines the size of your data. The volume is influenced by the format and throughput of your data and pipelines. Data volume poses unique challenges at both ends of the spectrum: too little data may require the use of techniques to synthetically grow the dataset, while too much data may require the use of volume reduction logic. Data distribution is a common challenge with data that often gets amplified when volume is scaled, leading to some unpleasant issues such as class imbalance (for multitask learning).

2. *Velocity* defines how frequently the data is coming into your store. Higher velocity requires careful management to incrementally ingest the incoming data but opens up the possibility of the application of continual and active learning techniques.

3. *Variety* is associated with how diversified and generalized your data is. If you go back to the roof classification example discussed in Chapter 1, does your data represent all types of roofs in the world?

4. *Veracity* pertains to how accurate and factual your data is for what it represents. For example, data extracted from social media may have very low veracity as opposed to data extracted from well-regulated systems like trading charts. Veracity can be associated with how noisy your data is.

5. *Validity* defines how suitable your data is for your modeling purposes. Does the data capture the problem domain well enough to expect a model to learn from it? Can you learn to perform the tasks you desire your model to do, from batches of this dataset? (From a deep learning perspective, veracity and validity are similar, but veracity is more commonly associated with source data whereas validity is more associated with ground truths, or labels.)

---

3 Khan, M. Ali-ud-din, Muhammad Fahim Uddin, and Navarun Gupta. 2014. "Seven V's of Big Data: Understanding Big Data to Extract Value." In *Proceedings of the 2014 Zone 1 Conference of the American Society for Engineering Education*, 1–5. *https://doi.org/10.1109/ASEEZone1.2014.6820689.*

6. *Volatility* is associated with the retention period of your data. It is typically more important in domains where personal information is captured, like ecommerce. A low retention period may require one to extract features, remove identifying information, and store the features instead of the data itself. Feature engineering, extraction, and compression techniques can be used to manage such challenges.

7. *Value* captures the usefulness of the data and its importance in learning.

Volume, velocity, and volatility influence data procurement, ingestion, and data systems under the data engineering discipline. These topics are too broad in themselves to be captured sufficiently in this chapter. We will focus on volume in the context of challenges of scale in developing models, and we'll look at validity, variety, veracity, value, and volume in the context of data quality. Volatility and velocity will also be discussed in the context of a data engine (a concept introduced in Chapter 1) and continual learning.

The Scaling Law of Data

The learned parameters of the model are a lossy distilled representation of the training data. What is the likelihood of obtaining a better representation by scaling your data? As discussed in "Evolving Deep Learning Trends" on page 16, it is not just the rapid growth in computing capabilities but also the growth in available training data that has been fueling the progress of deep learning. The effectiveness of data in deep learning has also been associated with a power law. It has been theorized that the performance of the model increases logarithmically as the size of the training dataset increases.[4] This scaling law association of data volume with the model's performance has been empirically proven across many specialized domains, such as machine translation, language modeling, image classification, and speech recognition.[5] As illustrated in Figure 10-1, as the data volume increases, the validation error of the model drops.

4 Sun et al., "Revisiting Unreasonable Effectiveness of Data in Deep Learning Era," *https://arxiv.org/abs/1707.02968*.

5 Hestness et al., "Deep Learning Scaling Is Predictable, Empirically," *https://arxiv.org/abs/1712.00409*.

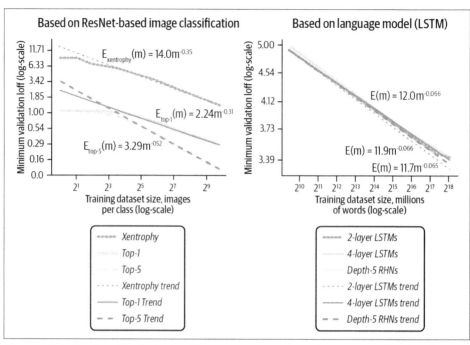

Figure 10-1. Empirically derived evidence to support the existence of scaling law for data

Theoretically, the power law of data is given as $\epsilon(m) = \alpha m \beta_g$, where ε is the error in generalization (often measured by validation loss), m is the number of samples in the training set, α is a constant (associated with the problem), and β_g is the scaling exponent defining the steepness of the learning curve (associated with the question of whether the model can perform better if the training data is scaled). Interestingly, even though the literature suggested β_g to be 0.5 or 1, empirically, β_g was estimated to be between −0.07 and −0.35.[6] Regardless of the numbers, the power law of data holds. This is shown in Figure 10-2.

---

6 Hestness et al., "Deep Learning Scaling Is Predictable, Empirically," *https://arxiv.org/abs/1712.00409*.

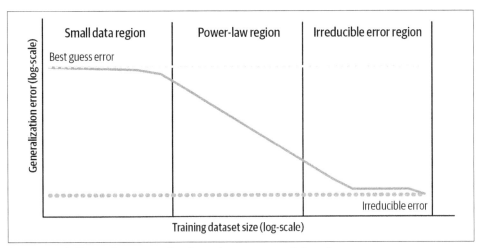

Figure 10-2. Power law curve for data size versus model performance

As shown in Figure 10-2, a model trained with a small dataset starts by making random guesses, with a high rate of error. Performance rapidly gets better as dataset size increases, eventually converging into the irreducible error region. Imperfect data is considered a key challenge in breaking through to irreducible error, causing imperfect generalization despite scaling. Your data can be imperfect due to problems with variety, veracity, validity, and value.

In the last few years, the emphasis has therefore shifted from scale to quality, highlighting the importance of having a high quantity of data that is of high quality. Advocates like Andrew Ng have been rallying behind this through data-centric AI efforts (*https://oreil.ly/XUTk0*). From being the dark horse of deep learning for a long time, data-focused techniques and tricks have now begun driving model excellence.

In the following section, I will discuss five of the seven Vs as they influence data quality. The remaining two Vs, volatility and velocity, will be discussed later in the chapter.

Human vision systems also optimize for a high quantity of high-quality data. We are equipped with very efficient systems that use high-resolution (foveal) and low-resolution (peripheral) vision in conjunction with rapid (saccadic) eye movements to see through the noise and focus only on "valuable" pieces of information, effectively filtering out the vast majority of data our vision system consumes. Although it's been shown that the deep learning models, to some extent, can not only cope with noise but also fill in the knowledge gaps,[7] there is a limit to this ability. Too much noise or gaps that are too large will lead to tricky model instability situations, such as exploding or imploding (a.k.a. vanishing) gradients. This is why AI/ML systems require careful curation of data and planning around data systems, to ensure that a high quantity of high-quality data is obtained.

Data Quality

In the context of deep learning, data quality can be defined as fitness for use—i.e., the degree to which the features of the data are useful to learn the task without causing confusion. When choosing a dataset, you are typically looking for relevancy, accuracy, consistency, completeness, validity, and uniqueness. These are also the characteristics of a high-quality dataset, and they are directly influenced by five of the seven Vs discussed previously. More specifically:

1. *Relevancy* captures how closely the data represents the problem domain. It is associated with the *validity* of the data. Lack of relevancy may mean challenges in achieving convergence and thereby model performance.

2. *Accuracy* captures the correctness of the dataset and is directly related to the *veracity* of the data.

3. *Consistency* tests whether similar data points obtained from diverse sources are in agreement. Both accuracy and consistency are directly related to *veracity*.

4. *Completeness* captures whether the data fully represents the problem domain and is associated with *variety*.

5. *Uniqueness* captures the diversity in the data without any redundancy, enabling optimization of *volume* and *value*.

The following sections will discuss the Vs associated with data quality in more detail.

---

7 He, Kaiming, Xinlei Chen, Saining Xie, Yanghao Li, Piotr Dollár, and Ross Girshick. 2021. "Masked Autoencoders Are Scalable Vision Learners." arXiv, December 19, 2021. *https://arxiv.org/abs/2111.06377*.

Validity

Of the Vs associated with data quality, validity is central and should directly be driven by the key development consideration of a *well-defined problem* (discussed in Chapter 1). Conducting sanity tests is a good way to check the validity of your data for the purpose. The *me test* is my own personal approach that I find quite helpful in the context of deep learning tasks. In a me test, I look through the dataset to test whether I can learn the task myself. I presume the model is likely to achieve a higher rate of accuracy if the data passes this test than if it doesn't—surely, the model can do better! This approach is not scalable, as there are only so many samples you can scan, but it provides a really good early indication of whether you have the right dataset for the task.

To address the validity aspects of your data, going to the source of the data and appropriately validating it as a part of a labeling or procurement protocol is often useful.

Variety

Variety is achieved by building a feature-rich dataset to capture all aspects of the problem in order to achieve diversity and generalization. Procurement of data is important here; you may want to ensure the representativeness of the data demographic (e.g., age, sex, personality) or consider obtaining data from different sources. To build feature-rich, varied datasets, you can draw inspiration from Gestalt theory, which explains how people perceive signals as organized patterns using the following key factors for pattern detection (see Figure 10-3). These principles are quite useful in curating high-quality datasets for deep learning as well because of their benefit in pattern detection:

- *Proximity* is defined as a tendency to perceive objects or shapes that are close to one another as forming a group. Proximity highlights the need for closely related samples. In a language context, an expression can be represented in many different ways, and having sentences that are proximal (e.g., "I love that book" and "I loved the book you gave me last week") in your dataset can be a helpful way of introducing variety.

- *Closure* is the tendency to see complete figures/forms even if what is present in the image is incomplete. Masked autoencoders (MAEs) recently demonstrated that Transformers can infer missing patches, confirming that closure indeed is possible in deep learning.[8] Closure is also an actively used technique in unsupervised learning techniques and can be a means of introducing variety in the

---

8 He et al., "Masked Autoencoders Are Scalable Vision Learners," *https://arxiv.org/abs/2111.06377*.

dataset. Random masking, random patch, and token drops are popular augmentation techniques that are used today that aligns with increasing variety through closure.

- *Similarity* is defined as the tendency to group objects by their physical resemblance (shape, pattern, color, etc.). Taking the previous example, the word "book" can be represented with various synonyms to describe the same object (e.g., paperback, textbook, manual, volume, etc.).

- *Good Gestalt* is the tendency to group items if a regular, simple, and orderly pattern can be formed. Increasing variety by having samples that show multiple instances of objects aligns with good gestalt. Likewise, variety of objects of similar category is useful to target better representation learning.

- *Continuity* is the tendency to perceive each object as a single continuous object.

- *Past experience* is the tendency to categorize objects according to previous experience. Past experience is quite central in model development as samples are repeatedly shown to the model for learning through repeating epochs. Having variety as a result of change in location, various background, and surrounding are helpful for better representation learning.

- *Symmetry* is the tendency to see objects as symmetrical and forming around a center point. Symmetry simplifies pattern recognition. This is also the reason why objects with well-defined shapes are much easier to train for (e.g., segmentation of balls, tables, roofs, etc. is simpler than segmentation of irregularly defined objects like trees, plants, etc.).

- *Common fate* is the tendency to associate similar movements as part of a common motion.

Much like with volume, too little or too much variety can pose challenges in modeling. You may have to curate your dataset to prune out-of-scope data or generate a synthetic dataset to create variety. Additionally, your dataset may be skewed toward some aspects of your problem more than others—a so-called *imbalance problem*. These challenges become a lot more evident when your task is modeled on a real dataset. In the following sections, we'll dive into these challenges and explore some techniques to address them.

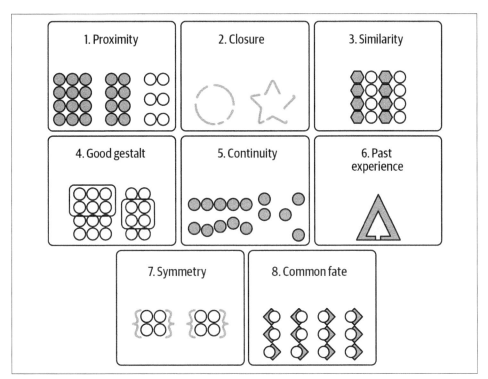

Figure 10-3. Gestalt theory presented pictorially

Handling too much variety

Ensuring your dataset is fit for purpose is always a good first step. Removing outliers and out-of-domain samples is part of this process. In this section, you will read about a few techniques and explore a practical exercise to prune your dataset.

Heuristic-based pruning. Taking the example of the roof identification problem from Chapter 1, if your task is to predict the presence of roofs in satellite images of Sydney, even if you have access to global satellite images, limiting your samples to images of Australian roofs can be a good approach. It can save you from having to deal with the challenges you might face in modeling sod roofs, for example, as this type of roof is not found in Australia. Knowledge of your data sources should drive a lot of these heuristics and rules to filter out data that may not fit your problem domain. In general, bounded tests on your data (e.g., range, constraints tests, and other similar analyses) should guide the heuristics for filtering.

Algorithmic outlier pruning. Another approach to identifying unwarranted variety is to use outlier detection algorithms. These algorithms can identify samples that lie outside the distribution of the rest of your data. Several algorithms exist, ranging from unsupervised techniques that explore features of the sample and identify the tail end of the distribution for outlier detection to semi-supervised techniques that leverage training datasets to find novel/interesting cases and even supervised techniques that simply build a binary classifier for outliers.

One such algorithm is Unsupervised Outlier Detection Using Empirical Cumulative Distribution Functions, a.k.a. ECOD.[9] ECOD leverages the fact that outliers are often the "rare events" that appear at the tails of a distribution and uses nonparametric approaches to estimate the underlying distribution of the input data by computing the empirical cumulative distribution. In the following section, you'll conduct a brief exercise to explore how ECOD can be helpful to identify outlier samples in a dataset.

Hands-on exercise #1: Outlier detection.   In this exercise, you will be using the Python Outlier Detection (PyOD) library (*https://oreil.ly/-hXy4*) over the SceneParse150 dataset that you used in 4 and 7. The code for this example is available in the *outlier_detection.py* script (*https://oreil.ly/-CLwc*) in the code repository and can be executed as follows:

```
deep-learning-at-scale chapter_10 od detect
```

The following is the key snippet that drives the outlier detection, where ECOD is the unsupervised classifier that predicts whether a sample is an outlier or not and assigns a continuous score to represent the extent of "outlierness":

```
# ECOD unsupervised classifier to identify outliers based on guesstimated
# outlier contamination of 0.1%
clf = ECOD(contamination=0.001, n_jobs=num_workers)
clf.fit(x)
# score assigned to the sample - the higher the score, the higher the risk
# of it being an outlier
print(clf.decision_scores_)
# 1/0 per sample to indicate if corresponding index sample is an outlier or not
print(clf.labels_)
```

You may have noticed that the images in the SceneParse150 dataset are colorful and vibrant. If you look at the results, you will note that the samples with the highest outlier scores tend to be night/dark shots, with the exception of a picture of snowy mountains. The sample with the highest score, recorded as *outlier_score_histogram.jpg* in the *.tmp/output/chapter_10/* directory, is of a sea/river cave, looking outward to the open waters (see Figure 10-4). This is indeed a rare sample for this dataset.

---

9 Li, Zheng, Yue Zhao, Xiyang Hu, Nicola Botta, Cezar Ionescu, and George H. Chen. 2022. "ECOD: Unsupervised Outlier Detection Using Empirical Cumulative Distribution Functions." arXiv, August 25, 2022. *https://arxiv.org/abs/2201.00382*.

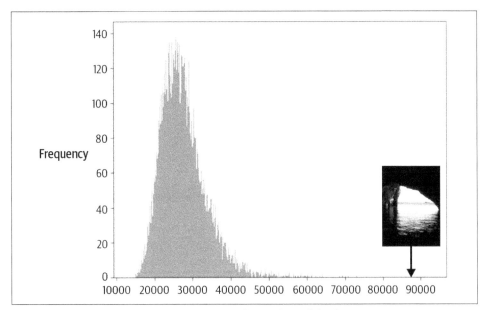

Figure 10-4. Histogram of outlier scores and sample with highest score

Scaling outlier detection. To scale outlier detection, techniques like Scalable Unsupervised Outlier Detection (SUOD) can be applied.[10] SUOD can combine multiple outlier algorithms, such as ECOD, Local Outlier Factor (LOF), or variational autoencoders (VAEs), and average the results to make more balanced decisions on outliers. This approach can be helpful to avoid bias in outlier selection.

Handling too-low variety

Often, obtaining varied samples at source is either too expensive or impossible. In such cases, a popular option is to use a technique known as *data augmentation* that leverages the ability to model desired effects as mathematical functions $f(x)$ to transform a sample x into its variants x''. With the proliferation of generative AI, using synthetic data generated from a stochastic function such as a proxy model is another option for increasing the richness and variety of the dataset.

---

10 Zhao, Yue, Xiyang Hu, Cheng Cheng, Cong Wang, Changlin Wan, Wen Wang, Jianing Yang, et al. 2021. "SUOD: Accelerating Large-Scale Unsupervised Heterogeneous Outlier Detection." arXiv, March 5, 2021. *https://arxiv.org/abs/2003.05731*.

Data augmentation. Data augmentation is a mature strategy for increasing variety in the dataset by artificially adding variations and richness in the features via transformation functions $f(x)$. These techniques aim to increase the volume and diversity of the data, lowering the risk of overfitting, while keeping the distribution about the same. Applying random runtime augmentation during gradient steps is also an effective technique to reduce overfitting.

The suite of augmentation techniques varies per domain. In computer vision datasets, for example, geometric augmentations such as affine transformation, shear, and other distortions have been actively used to generate variety, in addition to pixel intensity–based augmentations such as color shuffle, blurring, sharpness, contrast, jitter, noise injection, and more nuanced techniques like adding snow, rain, or sand splatter patterns.[11]

Cutout[12] is an interesting augmentation implementation that randomly drops patches of signals from a source, much as dropout randomly drops signals from neurons. Albumentations, imgaug, and Kornia are three popular libraries for this purpose; Kornia supports augmentation on the GPU, whereas most other libraries are CPU-only.

In natural language processing (NLP) datasets, augmentations can be achieved by replacing words with related words or similar phrases. Another technique that is sometimes used to account for common spelling mistakes and increase robustness against such errors is omitting frequently mistaken letters from words. Adding adversarial noise upon training using data augmentation is another great application to ensure the robustness of your model.

> For a hands-on example of data augmentation, see the *augmentation_example.ipynb* notebook (*https://oreil.ly/PUPe0*) in the code repository. This small example uses Kornia to generate variants of the same sample. Results are included in the notebook.

---

11 Mumuni, Alhassan G., and Fuseini Mumuni. 2022. "Data Augmentation: A Comprehensive Survey of Modern Approaches." *Array* 16: 100258. *https://www.sciencedirect.com/science/article/pii/S2590005622000911.*

12 DeVries, Terrance, and Graham W. Taylor. 2017. "Improved Regularization of Convolutional Neural Networks with Cutout." arXiv, November 29, 2017. *https://arxiv.org/abs/1708.04552.*

Advanced data augmentation. In their very interesting paper "A Data-Augmentation Is Worth a Thousand Samples," Randall Balestriero et al.[13] estimate that about 1,000 augmentations may be needed before the model correctly estimates the information encoded by the augmentation techniques. This indicates the scale at which samples can be exploited to increase the variety of your dataset. Let's take a look at some of the advanced augmentation techniques that have been proposed:

Soft labels

Augmentation is not limited to the samples themselves; labels can also be augmented. Commonly, the labels used in supervised training are defined by categorical outcomes—for example, 1 or 0 for binary classification, class encodings for multiclass problems, or one-hot-encoded binary vectors for multilabel problems. These so-called *hard labels* are assumed to represent the ground truth, which can be problematic when the quality of the predicted labels is poor (leading to overconfidence). A softer alternative, known as *soft labels*, also exists that seeks to represent labels as having a certain confidence level. For example, a soft label could be used to express 70% confidence that a blurb has a negative connotation by giving the text a 0.7 label for negative sentiment instead of a discrete 1. The benefit soft labels provide is accurate reflection of confidence in the given labels. As a result of this increased dimensionality, use of soft labels can increase the variety and richness in your dataset. Soft labels often end up being more qualitative and can act as regularizers as well (more on this in "Value via regularization" on page 345).

Mixup

Most of the augmentation techniques discussed so far operated on individual samples. Mixup is a niche data augmentation technique that applies transformations across samples.[14] In mixup, two samples x_i and x_j are linearly merged using a coefficient (β) randomly sampled from a beta distribution (with values ranging from [0, 1]). The corresponding labels (y_i and y_j) for these samples are also merged following the same distribution. The equations for merging can be represented as follows, with the results shown in Figure 10-5:

$$x^{'} = \beta_i x_i + (1 - \beta) x_j$$
$$y^{'} = \beta_i y_i + (1 - \beta) y_j$$

---

13 Balestriero, Randall, Ishan Misra, and Yann LeCun. 2022. "A Data-Augmentation Is Worth a Thousand Samples: Exact Quantification from Analytical Augmented Sample Moments." arXiv, February 16, 2022. *https://arxiv.org/abs/2202.08325*.

14 Zhang, Hongyi, Moustapha Cisse, Yann N. Dauphin, and David Lopez-Paz. 2018. "mixup: Beyond Empirical Risk Minimization." arXiv, April 27, 2018. *https://arxiv.org/abs/1710.09412*.

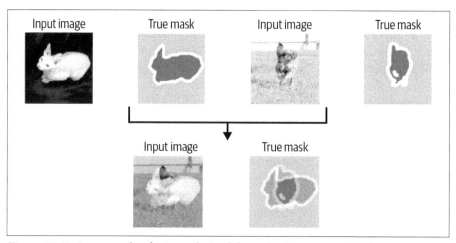

Figure 10-5. An example of mixup derived from the SceneParse150 dataset

It may seem counterintuitive, but mixup has shown to increase generalizability and reduce overfitting of noisy samples.[15] Not only that, but it can also be seen as a volume reduction technique where you combine a fraction of your dataset by merging some samples with others.

A demonstration of a naive implementation of mixup is available in the example repository, in the *augmentation_example.ipynb* notebook (*https://oreil.ly/Kma-M*). In this Jupyter notebook you will see how two samples are merged together to create mixup augmentation.

CutMix

CutMix is a combination of Cutout and inter-sample stitch wherein random crops from the source are patched onto a randomly selected target image.[16] A hybrid of mixup and CutMix could be an interesting implementation.

Automated augmentation. The usefulness of augmentation for increasing generalizability and reducing overfitting is universally recognized. Choosing optimal augmentation techniques is not always straightforward, though, as the feedback cycle is quite expensive. Most of the time, intuitive assessment of the problem provides a good basis for identifying effective augmentation techniques. The "me test" discussed

---

15 Zhang et al., "mixup: Beyond Empirical Risk Minimization," *https://arxiv.org/abs/1710.09412*.

16 Yun, Sangdoo, Dongyoon Han, Seong Joon Oh, Sanghyuk Chun, Junsuk Choe, and Youngjoon Yoo. 2019. "CutMix: Regularization Strategy to Train Strong Classifiers with Localizable Features." arXiv, August 7, 2019. *https://arxiv.org/abs/1905.04899*.

previously can help with this. However, this approach is neither scalable nor robust as your option space will be biased and limited, increasing the risk of unexplored opportunities when it comes to optimal and effective use of augmentation.

AutoAugment[17] is a technique that uses reinforcement learning to navigate the search space of potential augmentation strategies and evaluate the probability and magnitude of each operation in order to propose the most optimal augmentation. The workflow for AutoAugment is shown in Figure 10-6.

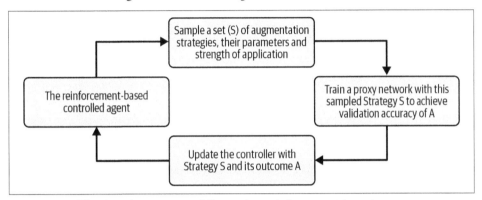

Figure 10-6. The AutoAugment workflow using reinforcement learning

Because of the use of reinforcement learning, the search process can take up a lot of GPU time. To minimize this, it's common to run the workflow on a smaller proxy task, but this raises questions about the transferability of the results. In an effort to make the process more palatable, a variant called RandAugment[18] sought to optimize the time taken to navigate the parameter space while removing the need for a proxy by reducing the size of the search space itself. Further efforts to make these automated augmentation techniques more effective include approaches such as TrivialAugment (*https://oreil.ly/MEMen*) and AugMix (*https://oreil.ly/Pn1gx*). These techniques, however, are mainly used in classification tasks, and the obtained results are not transferable across datasets.

Synthetic data generation. Data augmentation is useful when you have sufficient samples to augment, but that isn't always the case. For example, if you needed a sample for "a koala swimming in the Antarctic," finding one might be nearly impossible. However, such a sample can be generated with reasonable accuracy using more

---

17 Cubuk, Ekin D., Barret Zoph, Dandelion Mane, Vijay Vasudevan, and Quoc V. Le. 2019. "AutoAugment: Learning Augmentation Policies from Data." arXiv, April 11, 2019. *https://arxiv.org/abs/1805.09501*.

18 Cubuk, Ekin D., Barret Zoph, Jonathon Shlens, and Quoc V. Le. 2019. "RandAugment: Practical Automated Data Augmentation with a Reduced Search Space." arXiv, November 14, 2019. *https://arxiv.org/abs/1909.13719*.

recent generative AI techniques like diffusion or generative adversarial network (GAN)-based models.

An excellent example of synthetic data for training is Wayve's multimodal GAIA-1 (Generative AI for Autonomy) for autonomous driving. GAIA-1 produces synthetic videos of possible future events based on text, image, and driving action inputs. It's a powerful source for teaching autonomous vehicles a model of the world, offering numerous possible sequences of events rather than being biased toward one specific consequence.[19] Another example is Stability AI's Large Video Dataset (LVD), consisting of 580 million video clip/caption pairs—effectively 212 years' worth of video content—which was synthetically generated using the CoCa and V-BLIP models.[20]

Caution must be taken with such approaches, however, to ensure that the quality of the generated samples is acceptable. Depending on your objectives, you may find generative AI produces samples that are somewhat ridiculous, such as a koala that appears to be swimming in the ocean but has dry fur. Wayve gets around this by preceding the generation with a conceptual world model, but also in its case finer features like fingers, hands, and wet fur, where generative AI struggles the most, are less important details, making this perhaps a more feasible approach.

Using another model as a source for data generation, which one can argue is actually "distillation done the hard way," is an increasingly common technique. Alpaca, a fine-tuned LLaMA 7B model, was trained on a 52K-sample instruction-following dataset obtained from OpenAI's text-davinci-003 (an improved version of InstructGPT), per the training flow shown in Figure 10-7.[21] Likewise, tools like OpenAI Gym and Unreal Engine can be great sources of synthetic data generated from simulated environments.

19 Hu, Anthony, Lloyd Russell, Hudson Yeo, Zak Murez, George Fedoseev, Alex Kendall, Jamie Shotton, and Gianluca Corrado. 2023. "GAIA-1: A Generative World Model for Autonomous Driving." arXiv, September 29, 2023. *https://arxiv.org/abs/2309.17080*.

20 Blattmann, Andreas, Tim Dockhorn, Sumith Kulal, Daniel Mendelevitch, Maciej Kilian, Dominik Lorenz, Yam Levi, et al. 2023. "Stable Video Diffusion: Scaling Latent Video Diffusion Models to Large Datasets." arXiv, November 25, 2023. *https://arxiv.org/abs/2311.15127*.

21 Taori, Rohan, Ishaan Gulrajani, Tianyi Zhang, Yann Dubois, Xuechen Li, Carlos Guestrin, Percy Liang, and Tatsunori B. Hashimoto. 2023. "Alpaca: A Strong, Replicable Instruction-Following Model." *https://crfm.stan ford.edu/2023/03/13/alpaca.html*.

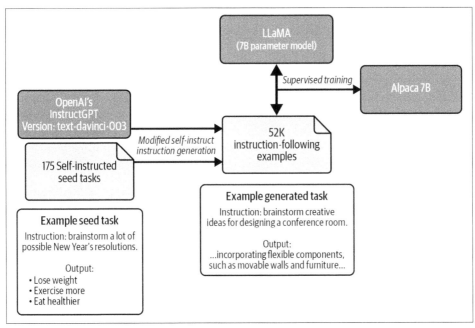

Figure 10-7. Alpaca sourced its training data from OpenAI's GPT model (adapted from Taori et al., 2023)

Synthetic data is best used in moderation, as the implications are still being explored. Some investigations indicate progressive worsening of model's generalizability as use of synthetic data is increased.[22]

Handling imbalance

Often when your dataset is varied and voluminous and your problem domain is multifaceted (multiclass, multilabel, or multitask), you may find yourself facing imbalance challenges. This is because the real world is imbalanced—some things happen more often than others. For example, some medical conditions, such as adenoid cystic carcinoma, are so rare that they have an annual incidence of just three or four cases per million people. Developing models that can accurately predict this type of cancer amongst other types that are much more prevalent can be very challenging, for two reasons: there may be very few signals to learn from for such low-prevalence conditions, and the gradients for these conditions can quickly vanish and be overpowered by those for other cancers that you are trying to model. To handle these

---

22 Alemohammad, Sina, Josue Casco-Rodriguez, Lorenzo Luzi, Ahmed Imtiaz Humayun, Hossein Babaei, Daniel LeJeune, Ali Siahkoohi, and Richard G. Baraniuk. 2023. "Self-Consuming Generative Models Go MAD." arXiv, July 4, 2023. *https://arxiv.org/abs/2307.01850.*

challenges, you can use sampling and loss tricks to increase the signal and appropriately leverage the gradients. Let's take a look at these two methods.

Sampling.   As discussed earlier, specialized sampling for your mini-batches may allow you to oversample the less frequently occurring classes in order to create consistent signals for all the classes. Oversampling for low-prevalence classes and undersampling for high-prevalence classes are the two approaches that one can balance to create more uniform signals in batches for all classes. In these cases, because the samples for less-prevalent classes are overused, increased use of random runtime augmentations can reduce overfitting.

 Reservoir sampling algorithms take a different approach, choosing a simple random sample from the population. This is a useful technique for datasets where the size is unknown.

Chapter 7 mentioned the `WeightedRandomSampler`, which assigns weights to indicate the importance of samples in drawing batches. This sampler works well for imbalanced multiclass datasets. In multilabel settings, however, where co-occurrences of subgroups of the classes may not be known, it provides little assistance. In such cases, depending on the distribution and type of data, simply amplifying the weights of low-prevalence classes can help increase the signals. Things get more difficult as the number of classes increases, though, as most samplers only account for classes individually, while in multilabel tasks you are really sampling for classes that co-occur.

A particular challenge with highly skewed multilabel datasets can be very low co-occurrence of low-prevalence findings. This means oversampling for some findings will implicitly undersample other non-occurring findings, because the batch size is limited. For example, suppose your batch size is 10 and there are 150 classes in your dataset, with 60% of classes rated as low prevalence. If at most 10 of these classes co-occur, then however you sample, every batch draw at the best of times will only draw signals for 100 classes, and the remaining classes will have to take a back seat. Techniques like hierarchical or per-class sampling try to get around this problem by having each batch draw samples from a different set of classes. Another technique, known as label powerset, creates weighted samples based on all the possible unique class combinations.[23]

23 Bogatinovski, Jasmin, Ljupčo Todorovski, Sašo Džeroski, and Dragi Kocev. 2021. "Comprehensive Comparative Study of Multi-Label Classification Methods." arXiv, February 16, 2021. *https://arxiv.org/abs/2102.07113*.

There is also a suite of sampling tricks, such as SMOTE and Multilabel SMOTE (MLSMOTE),[24] that leverage a technique known as "synthetic minority oversampling" where synthetic instances of minority classes are created to increase their representation in the dataset. SMOTE has been combined with Tomek Links to undersample high-prevalence classes based on nearest neighbor statistics.[25] REMEDIAL-HwR (REsampling MultilabEl datasets by Decoupling highly ImbALanced Labels Hybridization with Resampling) is another technique that specifically accounts for classes in multilabel settings that may or may not co-occur.[26]

Let's use the SceneParse150 dataset again to explore how these sampling tricks can aid in amplifying signals for multilabel scenarios. I'll follow this up with a simulated example of ML-SMOTE.

Hands-on exercise #2: Handling imbalance in a multilabel dataset. Scene parsing is a multiclass segmentation problem, but at image level it is a multilabel challenge. In this exercise, you will create a derived multilabel classification dataset using the SceneParse150 dataset, which consists of 151 classes. The example code for this exercise is located in the *weighted_sampler.ipynb* notebook (*https://oreil.ly/pBoUi*) in the book's GitHub repository.

In this example, a `SceneParsingStatsDataset` abstraction is created that captures the class statistics. The function `summarize_batches` simulates the epochs and captures the class distribution per mini-batch. As shown in Figure 10-8, the dataset is highly skewed toward the first 30 classes.

24 Charte, Francisco, Antonio J. Rivera, María J. del Jesus, and Francisco Herrera. 2015. "MLSMOTE: Approaching Imbalanced Multilabel Learning Through Synthetic Instance Generation." *Knowledge-Based Systems* 89: 383–97. *https://doi.org/10.1016/j.knosys.2015.07.019*.

25 Viadinugroho, Raden Aurelius Andhika. 2021. "Imbalanced Classification in Python: SMOTE-Tomek Links Method." Towards Data Science, April 18, 2021. *https://towardsdatascience.com/imbalanced-classification-in-python-smote-tomek-links-method-6e48dfe69bbc*.

26 Charte, Francisco, Antonio J. Rivera, María J. del Jesus, and Francisco Herrera. 2019. "REMEDIAL-HwR: Tackling Multilabel Imbalance Through Label Decoupling and Data Resampling Hybridization." *Neurocomputing* 326–27: 110–22. *https://doi.org/10.1016/j.neucom.2017.01.118*.

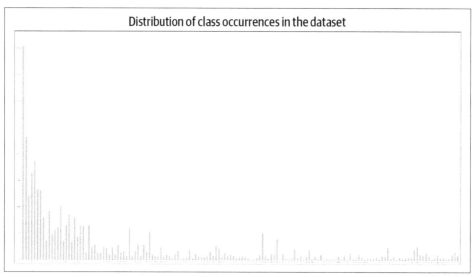

Figure 10-8. Distribution of classes in the SceneParse150 dataset

In this example, four samplers are compared to increased signals for low-prevalence findings:

- A standard `RandomSampler`
- A `WeightedRandomSampler` that derives weightings using class frequency
- An amplified version of `WeightedRandomSampler` that assigns higher class weightings to low-prevalence classes
- A `PowerSet` sampler that uses class co-occurrences to balance the holistic class distribution

You may note, from the analysis in the notebook, a step change in low-prevalence class signals (like class 106) across batches when `WeightedRandomSampler` is used (see Figure 10-9). The signals for these rare classes are further improved with amplified `WeightedRandomSampler`. You might also note that while `PowerSet` amplifies signals for most findings from the long tail of low-prevalence findings, it adopts a more balanced approach. This is expected, because the amplification when using `PowerSet` is not independent class-wise but rather is determined by combinations of classes that occur rarely. This logic should drive analysis of what may work best for your use case.

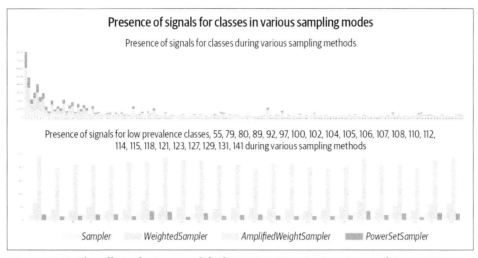

Figure 10-9. The effect of using amplified `WeightedRandomSampler` *and* `PowerSet` *sampling to increase the frequency of low-prevalence classes*

The second part of the exercise in this notebook contains a simulation of MLSMOTE that first subsamples based on labels to create a candidate list of cases to draw from, then uses the nearest neighbor technique to further filter the sample sets to create feature-rich samples.

Loss tricks. Weighted loss functions (e.g., `binary_cross_entropy_with_logits`) with class (`weight`) and positive (`pos_weight`) weighting are commonly used in scenarios with class imbalances to better manage the gradients. Binary cross entropy with these weighting options is useful for imbalanced datasets, because it can assign higher penalties for misclassifications of minority classes. Focal loss is a variant of binary cross entropy that downweights the loss assigned to well-classified classes to allow gradients for other (poorly classified) classes to have an effect.[27] Tversky loss—based on the Tversky similarity index, a generalization of the Dice similarity coefficient and F_β scores—is another useful loss trick for an imbalanced dataset.[28] In practice, all these loss functions can be combined together, creating a customized composite loss.

27 Lin, Tsung-Yi, Priya Goyal, Ross Girshick, Kaiming He, and Piotr Dollár. 2018. "Focal Loss for Dense Object Detection." arXiv, February 7, 2018. *https://arxiv.org/abs/1708.02002*.

28 Salehi, Seyed Sadegh Mohseni, Deniz Erdogmus, and Ali Gholipour. 2017. "Tversky Loss Function for Image Segmentation Using 3D Fully Convolutional Deep Networks." arXiv, June 18, 2017. *https://arxiv.org/abs/1706.05721*.

Some more recently introduced loss tricks, such as vector scaled (VS) loss,[29] apply temperature scaling (per class scale factor) of classwise logits along with logit shift. On the more extreme end, techniques like AutoBalance[30] use an inner training loop along with an outer validation loop to automatically tune loss hyperparameters. Both these projects are open source, with their code available on GitHub.

 As mentioned earlier, when facing imbalances in your dataset, you may have to leverage either sampling or loss tricks like the ones discussed here. If the imbalances are extreme, you may find combining both loss and sampling tricks helpful to accelerate the learning.

Veracity

> Learning exists in the context of data, yet notions of confidence typically focus on model predictions, not label quality.
>
> —Curtis G. Northcutt et al.[31]

As discussed earlier, consistency and accuracy are crucial aspects of a veracious dataset. The model is only as good as the data!

The test of veracity can be applied on both the samples and the labels (ground truth). For samples, this may be based on whether certain features are present (e.g., if the image is crisp, not blurry, or if the text blurb is structurally and grammatically correct). We'll talk more about the veracity of samples in the following section, in the context of value. Most of this section will be dedicated to the veracity of labels.

Reasons for error in labels

The process of labeling is human-centered, requiring searching for the object of interest and applying prior knowledge and heuristics to decide on the appropriate label. Yet, "to err is human!" Labeling error exists due to a range of systemic and human issues, from tooling/software bugs to knowledge gaps and innate cognitive and perceptual biases. The larger your labeling workforce and the more complex your problem domain, the higher the risk of label noise. The challenge when it comes to scaling your data for deep learning is that noise, if present, will increase too. For

---

29 Kini, Ganesh Ramachandra, Orestis Paraskevas, Samet Oymak, and Christos Thrampoulidis. 2021. "Label-Imbalanced and Group-Sensitive Classification Under Overparameterization." arXiv, November 8, 2021. *https://arxiv.org/abs/2103.01550.*

30 Li, Mingchen, Xuechen Zhang, Christos Thrampoulidis, Jiasi Chen, and Samet Oymak. 2022. "AutoBalance: Optimized Loss Functions for Imbalanced Data." arXiv, January 4, 2022. *https://arxiv.org/abs/2201.01212.*

31 Northcutt, Curtiss G., Lu Jiang, and Isaac L. Chuang. 2022. "Confident Learning: Estimating Uncertainty in Dataset Labels." arXiv, August 22, 2022. *https://arxiv.org/abs/1911.00068.*

---

reference, one study found that 10 of the most popular, specifically curated training datasets used in deep learning exhibit an average labeling error of 3.3%; the ImageNet dataset, for instance, was found to have an error rate in its validation set of over 6%.[32]

In object detection scenarios, more information (e.g., bounding boxes, masks, key points) is required during labeling. To provide this additional information, drawing methods are often used in annotation. As a result, labeling is not only more involved but also becomes slightly subjective (for example, there may be variations in the placement of bounding boxes, whether or not a buffer is included around the object, etc.), increasing the risk of labeling error. Rebecca Crowley et al. provide a detailed analysis of reasons why an object of interest may be missed when searching in a scene, or why a wrong final decision on labeling may be made.[33] The following key biases can greatly influence errors in labels but are extremely hard to eliminate:

Search satisficing
> The tendency to call off a search once something has been found, leading to premature stopping, thus increasing the chance of missing annotations. This mainly applies to scenarios where more than one annotation is needed, such as multilabel or segmentation annotation tasks. For example, both a dog and a pen might be included in an image, but the labeler might only annotate it for the dog and not take the time to look further and annotate the pen.

Overconfidence and underconfidence
> Over- or underestimation of the accuracy of one's "feeling of knowing."

Availability
> If prevalence of an object is either very high or very low, this can lead to an implicit bias resulting in false positive or false negative labels, respectively. For instance, adenoid cystic carcinoma, discussed earlier, is highly likely to be missed because it's not a common type of cancer.

Anchoring/confirmation bias
> When a labeler preempts the labeling task and seeks data to support the preemptive decision. For example, if they believe they have a cancer case, they may explicitly look for cancer-like formations. This bias is error-prone.

---

32 Northcutt, Curtiss G., Anish Athalye, and Jonas Mueller. 2021. "Pervasive Label Errors in Test Sets Destabilize Machine Learning Benchmarks." arXiv, November 7, 2021. *https://arxiv.org/abs/2103.14749.*

33 Crowley, Rebecca S., Elizabeth Legowski, Olga Medvedeva, Kayse Reitmeyer, Eugene Tseytlin, Melissa Castine, Drazen Jukic, and Claudia Mello-Thoms. 2013. "Automated Detection of Heuristics and Biases Among Pathologists in a Computer-Based System." *Advances in Health Sciences Education: Theory and Practice* 18(3): 343–63. *https://doi.org/10.1007/s10459-012-9374-z.*

Gambler's fallacy
> This describes how, when labelers encounter a repeated pattern of similar objects, they are likely to deviate and favor an outcome that breaks that pattern.

In addition to these, *cognitive overload* is also a common reason for errors in labels.

Approaches to labeling

At scale, the labeling process requires maturity so it can adapt to the challenges discussed in the previous section. Various modes have emerged to manage noise in labels. These include:

Label once
> Each sample is labeled only once, by exactly one labeler.

Consensus labeling
> Each sample is labeled by multiple labelers, and a consensus algorithm is applied to determine the most popular labels.

Pre-labeling (auto-labeling)
> Labelers are provided with suggested labels and only tune/adjust the labels.

Relabeling (iterative labeling)
> Labels assigned by one labeler undergo an iterative cycle of purification where another view is taken into account to increase the quality of the labels.

Hybrid
> The previous techniques are combined to create purpose-specific labeling approaches.

These modes are not one size fits all, but are often curated to meet your problem needs. Next, we'll discuss some tricks and techniques that you can use to increase the veracity of your dataset, depending on the labeling mode you use.

Techniques to increase veracity/decrease noise

Feedback is crucial in improving the veracity of your dataset (both the data itself and the labels). It's been shown that between noisy samples and noisy labels, noisy labels often pose more problems in training.[34] The more signal you can get on the accuracy of the labels, the better equipped you are to manage the noise. Let's consider some of the approaches you can take.

---

34 Toneva, Mariya, Alessandro Sordoni, Remi Tachet des Combes, Adam Trischler, Yoshua Bengio, and Geoffrey J. Gordon. 2019. "An Empirical Study of Example Forgetting During Deep Neural Network Learning." arXiv, November 15, 2019. *https://arxiv.org/abs/1812.05159.*

Using heuristics to identify noise.   Using the data gathered from problem definition, discussed in Chapter 1, bounded datasets can be created to eliminate noise. For example, you might eliminate emails from an email dataset that don't follow certain patterns. As these heuristics are very problem-specific, analysis of the problem domain should drive their development. Tools like Snorkel (*https://oreil.ly/iedED*) can be very handy for this purpose.

Using inter-label information, such as ontology.   You may find that your classes implicitly define rules that can be followed to identify poor labels. If you take the example of identifying roofing materials discussed in Chapter 1, if a pixel is an annotated "metal roof" it should not also be annotated "concrete roof," because these two classes are exclusive. Using composition, associativity, and exclusivity in your classes, if possible, can be very helpful in finding poor labels. My project "Leveraging Domain Knowledge for Deep Learning Based Computer Vision" (*https://oreil.ly/NLJoi*) goes into the details of such techniques.

Continuous feedback.   Some organizations have the luxury of a continuous source of ground truth information; Tesla, for example, gets this information from various automobile sensors. In those instances auto-labeling (*https://oreil.ly/lqa7c*) is a popular choice, with human labeling employed only selectively. If your model is mature enough, using the model in the labeling process (termed "model-in-the-loop") can be quite helpful in creating more useful labels by focusing on where the model may disagree with labelers and/or the model may not be very confident in its predictions. The model can also be used in pre-labeling scenarios, such that labelers only have to review and make corrections instead of annotating from scratch. Data obtained from these correction/review labeling processes is a great source of feedback for model improvements.

Similar approaches can be observed in all settings where the same sample is labeled more than once to identify disagreement areas. The disagreement may highlight the need for better training on how to label, better definition of the classes, or penalties for poor labeling. This can not only provide a powerful continual learning loop, but also provide statistics about the sources of errors. Feedback can be extended and applied in many ways. For instance, Reinforcement Learning from Human Feedback (RHLF), the key technique behind the success of ChatGPT, relies on feedback from human users.

Handling disagreements from multiple annotators.   It's both good and bad when you have multiple labels for the same sample that disagree—good because you have feedback on the sources of noise, and bad because you now have noise in the dataset that needs handling. A common approach for disagreement resolution is to use the outcome of a consensus majority voting mechanism as a source of truth. A related concept is the soft labeling technique discussed in "Handling too-low variety" on page

321, where labels are assigned a confidence level. In some cases, if one has ratings of the accuracy of labelers from independent benchmarking, soft labels can be derived by using the weighted mean to prioritize superior labelers.

Algorithmic approaches like Dawid and Skene's[35] that use the expectation–maximization (EM) algorithm to estimate true labels are popular in crowdsourced labeling regimes to arrive at an estimated true label from multiple annotators. Variants such as Fast Dawid-Skene and a hybrid approach that combines the Dawid-Skene algorithm and majority voting are also used.[36]

Identifying noisy samples by loss gradients. The desired training objective is a continual decrease in loss over the course of an epoch. You may find there are some samples in your dataset for which the loss does not decrease or gradually increases. If your model is on the right track, this can be a very effective technique to find samples that are either very hard to train for or simply have incorrect labels. Andrej Karpathy (*https://oreil.ly/W6Wg6*) famously emphasized this by saying, "When you sort your dataset descending by loss you are guaranteed to find something unexpected, strange and helpful."

A similar concept is leveraged in techniques that use sample-wise accuracy over the course of training to calculate the "forgetting score," a measure of how often the model makes a misprediction on a given sample.[37] Again, this can help with the identification of noisy or difficult-to-classify samples. More recently, formulae for scores derived from sample-wise loss gradients have been proposed to identify samples for their usefulness in training.[38] In the following section, you will go through an exercise that illustrates this technique.

---

35 Dawid, A.P., and A.M. Skene. 1979. "Maximum Likelihood Estimation of Observer Error-Rates Using the EM Algorithm." *Journal of the Royal Statistical Society Series C-applied Statistics* 28: 20–28. *https://doi.org/10.2307/2346806*.

36 Sinha, Vaibhav B., Sukrut Rao, and Vineeth N Balasubramanian. 2018. "Fast Dawid-Skene: A Fast Vote Aggregation Scheme for Sentiment Classification." arXiv, September 7, 018. *https://arxiv.org/abs/1803.02781*.

37 Toneva et al., "An Empirical Study of Example Forgetting During Deep Neural Network Learning," *https://arxiv.org/abs/1812.05159*.

38 Paul, Mansheej, Surya Ganguli, and Gintare Karolina Dziugaite. 2023. "Deep Learning on a Data Diet: Finding Important Examples Early in Training." arXiv, March 28, 2023. *https://arxiv.org/abs/2107.07075*.

Hands-on exercise #3: Loss tricks to find noisy samples. In this exercise, you will use the MNIST code from Chapter 2 and extend it further. The code is located in the *data_diet.py* script (*https://oreil.ly/-iu7r*) in the GitHub repository and can be executed as follows:

```
deep-learning-at-scale chapter_10 data-diet train
```

The supporting visualization for this exercise can be created using the *vis.ipynb* notebook (*https://oreil.ly/af_tx*) in the code repository.

The key change in this exercise is the introduction of a sample ID, or index, in the IndexedMNISTDataModule and corresponding handling in the model wrapper, Index edMNISTModel. With this modification, the dataset now returns an index along with the image and label and the model handles it; otherwise, the implementations are the same as in the exercise in Chapter 2.

You may also note the use of two new callbacks, SampleWiseStatsLogger and Data DietLogger. SampleWiseStatsLogger captures the sample-wise loss over the course of training, and DataDietLogger captures the gradient scores. The Neural Tangents library (*https://oreil.ly/lhLHS*) from PyTorch is used to calculate the loss gradient score. The loss gradient norm is calculated by computing the reverse Jacobian of the sample-wise loss and applying normalization over it:

```
rev_jacobian_dict = torch.func.jacrev(sample_wise_loss_fn)(params, x, y)
flat_jacobian = torch.utils._pytree.tree_flatten(
    torch.utils._pytree.tree_map(torch.vmap(torch.ravel), rev_jacobian_dict)
)[0]
loss_grads = torch.concatenate(flat_jacobian, axis=1)
grad_score_per_sample = (
    torch.linalg.norm(loss_grads, axis=-1).detach().cpu().numpy().tolist()
)
```

After running the train command, you can use the *vis.ipynb* notebook to visualize the results. A side-by-side comparison of samples that were very easy to learn from, very easily forgotten, and very hard to train for is shown in Figure 10-10. As you can see, many of the samples that were identified as hard to learn from are quite ambiguous or malformed, as are some of the samples in the often forgotten category. These could, in practice, be sent for review and correction as needed.

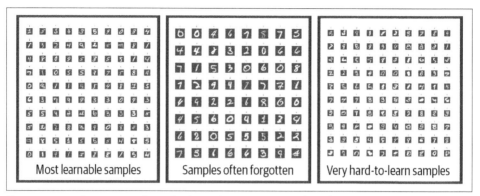

Figure 10-10. Summary of results from this exercise to identify noisy and difficult to learn from samples.

Using confident learning. Confident learning, an implementation of model-in-the-loop, is about using the output from one source of truth, the labelers, and testing it with the model.[39] This approach is based on the assumption that the label noise is class-conditional, depending only on the latent true class, not the data. Of course, this isn't always the case; for example, a leopard is likely to be mistakenly labeled as a jaguar irrespective of the background, whereas a dinghy is less likely to be mislabeled as a car if it's in water than if it's on land (in other words, in some cases data does influence outcome).

Still, this assumption can capture a large fraction of class confusion noise. In essence, confident learning estimates the joint class-conditional probabilities and tests these against the actual computed confident joint probabilities to single out samples where the estimates disagree by a given threshold/margin. The workflow for confident learning is shown in Figure 10-11. An implementation is available via the cleanlab library (*https://oreil.ly/-GhLl*), which automatically detects issues in machine learning datasets. Cleanlab also provides a confidence-based approach to identify segmentation error by approximating a soft minimum confidence region and comparing it with the mean confidence region.[40]

---

39 Lad, Vedang, and Jonas Mueller. 2023. "Estimating Label Quality and Errors in Semantic Segmentation Data via Any Model." arXiv, July 11, 2023. *https://arxiv.org/abs/2307.05080*.

40 Lad and Mueller, "Estimating Label Quality and Errors in Semantic Segmentation Data via Any Model," *https://arxiv.org/abs/2307.05080*.

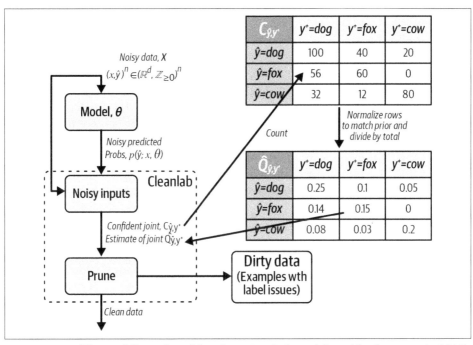

Figure 10-11. The workflow of confident learning (adapted from Northcutt et al., 2022)

The background behind confident learning is beyond the scope of this book, but if you're interested in reading more, I've written an article (*https://oreil.ly/TvWct*) about it that explains this in detail. You can also find an example that demonstrates the use of cleanlab in my GitHub repository (*https://oreil.ly/5BMi9*); the result identifies one of the samples, shown in Figure 10-12, as a potential mislabel.

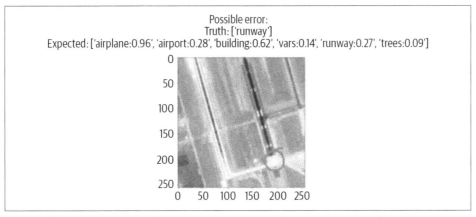

Figure 10-12. An example of a noisy sample detected using cleanlab where annotations for "airplane" and "airport" were missing

Summary of veracity tactics. In this section, you have explored several tricks to identify noise in your dataset to make it more accurate. Deep learning models are capable of handling noise to some degree. Sometimes, noise can even be an effective technique to fill in missing information. For example, if part of an image is missing, instead of padding the image with a fixed pixel value (say, 0 or 1), filling in the missing part using random noise can be an effective technique that avoids potential confusion with other objects that may have patches of black or white. It is more the systemic noise—too much noise that distorts the features and decision boundaries—that can collapse the model or increase the number of forgettable samples, making training less impactful.[41] Keeping some challenging and noisy samples in the dataset does not hurt the model's performance; indeed, it can only help.[33]

Value and Volume

Return on investment is a good metric to ascertain the value of samples in your dataset. As discussed in Chapter 1, you pay a hefty price for scaling up model training, part of which is producing large amounts of carbon emissions (e.g., 25 metric tons in the case of BLOOM). As you scale your data, the computation time per epoch increases, and so does your blood pressure as you await the outcome. The length of this wait is crucial for the model development experience, as a prolonged feedback cycle for training can be very expensive and slow down progress. Training times of more than a week can be a significant hindrance, but when performing rapid development having to wait even a few days can cause significant friction. If we know the value of samples, we can use that information to reduce the volume of training data (saving on compute and increasing the training rate) while ensuring the data remains maximally useful and impactful by culling only less valuable or useless samples.

Core principles driving value

Here are some questions to think about when characterizing the value of your samples:

- How useful is this sample for your task?
- How impactful is this sample proving to be in your model development?
- Do you need this sample as much as others?
- What is the extent of redundancy in your dataset?

---

41 Toneva et al., "An Empirical Study of Example Forgetting During Deep Neural Network Learning," *https://arxiv.org/abs/1812.05159.*

The key consideration here is what added value the samples are offering you in exchange for their cost (both monetary and in terms of usability). Size matters, but high quality matters even more.

Techniques to improve efficiency and reduce size, like regularization, pruning, compression, knowledge distillation, and leveraging phenomena such as catastrophic forgetting, have been extensively explored on the model side. With the proliferation of data-centric AI, these approaches are increasingly being applied on data as well. Table 10-1 summarizes the aim of such techniques from both a model-centric and a data-centric perspective.

Table 10-1. Model-centric and data-centric perspectives on techniques useful in estimating and improving the value of samples

Technique	Model-centric aim	Data-centric aim
Pruning	Eliminate low-magnitude weights to reduce the data size and computational overhead.	Omit samples that don't offer much value in generalization or learning from the training regime.
Compression	Reduce the data size and computational overhead. Comprises a broad range of techniques, including quantization, wherein some amount of information loss is expected.	Reduce dataset size without compromising on generalization.
Distillation	Extract a learned representation from a more complex model to use in a smaller model.	Extract knowledge present in the larger dataset into a smaller synthesized set.
Maximizing learning (leveraging loss/objective function)	Leverage the loss function (the objective function used in learning) to maximize the training objective.	Leverage the loss function to find important/useful samples or to find similar samples to maximize training efficiency.
Regularization	Reduce overfitting. Includes techniques such as dropout and batch normalization.	Reduce overfitting. Includes techniques such as data augmentation, mixup, and label smoothing.

We'll explore several of these techniques in greater depth in the following sections.

Volume reduction via compression and pruning

Compression and pruning are useful tricks for volume reduction. We talked about compression in Chapter 7 (see "Dataset Format" on page 253), and I discussed some pruning tricks in "Handling too much variety" on page 319. Pruning is a good way to eliminate data that doesn't contribute much to the accuracy of the model, keeping only the high-value data. Some samples may consistently not be useful in training, whereas other samples' usefulness may be subject to the model's design and parameters. If you have to run extensive computations to find the subset of data that's most optimal for your case, that approach will be useful only if you can either reuse this filtered dataset often or filter the samples early in the training. Otherwise, the cost outweighs the benefit.

Volume reduction via dimensionality reduction

Dimensionality reduction techniques like principal component analysis (PCA), uniform manifold approximation and projection (UMAP), t-distributed stochastic neighbor embedding (t-SNE), and autoencoders are useful when working with very high-dimensional data. These techniques can be used to prune or compress your dataset to a lower dimension. t-SNE and UMAP both use gradient descent for arriving at the optimal embeddings, but UMAP is known to preserve more of the global structure and is algorithmically faster. All the techniques mentioned here are based on gradient descent; they can be used in the context of labels but also can be applied directly on the source data to reduce the dimensionality.

Volume reduction via approximation

The concept of approximating a larger dataset (known as the *full set*) through a smaller subset (referred to as the *core set* or *coreset*) has been used in classical machine learning and is also applicable in deep learning. Here are some of the key challenges when aiming to reduce volume by approximating the full set:

- How to approximate is *not well defined*. Some approaches are more commonly used than others. Generally speaking, you either approximate the features of your data or approximate the decision boundaries.

- The process of approximation *must be fast*—faster than your main training and convergence thereof. Otherwise, this exercise may not be justified, unless perhaps if the obtained coreset is reusable.

- Selecting the coreset is only half the story. The other key question is whether your model can *learn from it* equally as well.

- This approach is *not a one-size-fits-all* solution, unfortunately. You'll need to empirically evaluate whether this method is useful for your task and data.

With these challenges in mind, let's look at some coreset selection techniques:

Matching statistically
> Nonparametric methods like the Kolmogorov–Smirnov (KS) test that compare the similarity of two datasets can be iteratively applied to obtain the best approximating dataset. Likewise, parametric techniques like Jensen–Shannon divergence can be explored to measure the similarity (distribution-based) between two datasets.

Selection by proxy
> As mentioned earlier, the selection process must be fast to be useful. Often, faster learning algorithms are used as a proxy to estimate an approximately similar (i.e., closely representative) dataset. This approach leverages approximating decision boundaries and is common in classical machine learning—for example, naïve

Bayes might be used to approximate a coreset for a more computationally expensive technique such as decision trees. Similarly, in deep learning, a lightweight proxy model might be used as a proxy for selection of the coreset.[42]

Selection by gradient approximation

Deep learning is a gradient-based learning technique, so it's only fair to approximate the coreset by approximating the gradients. The challenge is that gradient computation (i.e., backpropagation) is the most computationally expensive part of the learning. Consequently, while this technique has the most potential to be effective, it can be very inefficient. On the plus side, since the gradient techniques focus on variance reduction, the coresets obtained through this technique can speed up convergence when used in training.

Coresets for Accelerating Incremental Gradient descent (CRAIG) is one example of this technique that seeks to filter out samples by estimating their weights, with the aim of minimizing the error in gradient approximation.[43] The challenge with estimating the coreset purely from the training dataset is that it may not generalize. This problem can get worse if your dataset has problems with imbalance or noise. Bi-level optimization techniques, a form of meta learning that selects the coreset using gradient estimates on the training set while also optimizing for effectiveness on the validation set to guarantee generalizability, have recently been proposed as well. Generalization-based Data Subset Selection for Efficient and Robust Learning (GLISTER) is an example of a gradient-based data selection technique that proposes bi-level optimization to select training data that maximizes the generalizability.[44]

Libraries like `cords` (*https://oreil.ly/K0OVX*) provide implementations for CRAIG and GLISTER and have hands-on examples for such techniques to obtain the coreset.

Reducing by sample importance

In "Techniques to increase veracity/decrease noise" on page 334, you read about using loss norms to identify noisy samples. In "Deep Learning on a Data Diet: Finding Important Examples Early in Training," Mansheej Paul et al. proposed a Gradient Normed (GraNd) score that's computed per training sample (x, y) at a

---

42 Coleman, Cody, Christopher Yeh, Stephen Mussmann, Baharan Mirzasoleiman, Peter Bailis, Percy Liang, Jure Leskovec, and Matei Zaharia. 2020. "Selection via Proxy: Efficient Data Selection for Deep Learning." arXiv, October 27, 2020. *https://arxiv.org/abs/1906.11829*.

43 Mirzasoleiman, Baharan, Jeff Bilmes, and Jure Leskovec. 2020. "Coresets for Data-Efficient Training of Machine Learning Models." arXiv, November 16, 2020. *https://arxiv.org/abs/1906.01827*.

44 Killamsetty, Krishnateja, Durga Sivasubramanian, Ganesh Ramakrishnan, and Rishabh Iyer. 2021. "GLISTER: Generalization Based Data Subset Selection for Efficient and Robust Learning." arXiv, June 11, 2021. *https://arxiv.org/abs/2012.10630*.

given time t by calculating the L2 norm of the gradient of loss (the Error L2-Norm, or EL2N).[45] The smaller the GraNd score is, the higher its influence on learning.

By calculating the GraNd score per sample averaged over multiple weight initializations, they found that this score correlated with forgetting scores. Using these averaged GraNd scores to select samples, they were able to prune 50% of the CIFAR-10 dataset without affecting accuracy. Applying the same technique to CIFAR-100, they showed that 25% of samples could be pruned with only a 1% drop in accuracy.

Volume reduction via distillation

Distillation is a commonly used technique to distill the knowledge obtained from a complex or larger corpus into a smaller or simpler one. In Chapter 11, you will read about distillation as a modeling technique, allowing a larger model's learned representation to be distilled down into a much smaller model without any significant drop in performance. Treating the larger model as a teacher and the smaller one as a student in the same training loop is a common approach to distillation.

Distillation has also been explored in the context of managing dataset size.[46] This technique is not a selection or filtering process; rather, the obtained coreset is a synthesized dataset that may not match the original samples. Conceptually, this technique is realized by:

- Assuming the network weights are a differentiable function of the synthetic training data
- Setting the training objective to optimize the pixel values of target synthesized/to-be-distilled images (in cases where samples are images)

When used on the MNIST dataset, this approach demonstrated that distillation can achieve compression at such a high rate that just one synthetic image per category might be sufficient to obtain a highly performant model.[47] More specifically, using this approach to distill the 60K training images in the MNIST digit dataset into only 10 synthetic images and using these to train a standard LeNet model yielded an

---

45 Mansheej et al., "Deep Learning on a Data Diet: Finding Important Examples Early in Training," *https://arxiv.org/abs/2107.07075*.

46 Zhao, Bo, and Hakan Bilen. 2021. "Dataset Condensation with Differentiable Siamese Augmentation." arXiv, *https://arxiv.org/abs/2102.08259*; Wang, Tongzhou, Jun-Yan Zhu, Antonio Torralba, and Alexei A. Efros. 2018. "Dataset Distillation." arXiv, June 10, 2021. *https://arxiv.org/abs/1811.10959*.

47 Wang et al., "Dataset Distillation," *https://arxiv.org/abs/1811.10959*.

accuracy rate of 94%, compared to 99% when using the full set. Figure 10-13 shows how distillation produces images in different feature spaces.

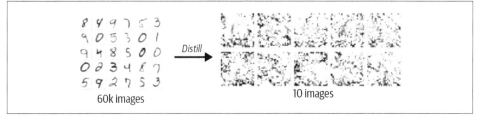

Figure 10-13. The result of distilling 60K MNIST samples into 10 samples[48]

Another distillation technique is Kernel Inducing Points (KIP), which follows similar principles but leverages kernel ridge regression methods for approximations.[49] (In the technique discussed previously, the approximation is obtained using the same model.) KIP has the advantageous ability to distill labels without changing the source. Distillation using Siamese networks is another related approach where the coreset is synthesized.[50]

Value via regularization

You have read about several techniques to effectively manage the volume of your dataset when scaling your training data. This is important because as the size of the dataset increases, the risk of challenges such as imbalances and overfitting also increases. You read about techniques for dealing with the first problem in "Handling imbalance" on page 327. Data regularization methods, as outlined in Table 10-1, are used to reduce overfitting and are orthogonal to model-based regularization techniques (such as dropout).

As discussed previously, data augmentation techniques like mixup and Cutout can also act as regularizers. Another popular approach to regularize your data is label smoothing.[51] With this technique, a small amount of noise is injected in the ground truths via a marginal value of epsilon (ε). While this approach may seem counterintuitive, much like dropout, empirically it has proven its benefit in both reducing

---

48 Wang et al., "Dataset Distillation," *https://arxiv.org/abs/1811.10959.*

49 Nguyen, Timothy, Zhourong Chen, and Jaehoon Lee. 2021. "Dataset Meta-Learning from Kernel Ridge-Regression." arXiv, March 22, 2021, *https://arxiv.org/abs/2011.00050.*

50 Zhao and Bilen, "Dataset Condensation with Differentiable Siamese Augmentation," *https://arxiv.org/abs/2102.08259.*

51 Szegedy, Christian, Vincent Vanhoucke, Sergey Ioffe, Jonathon Shlens, and Zbigniew Wojna. 2015. "Rethinking the Inception Architecture for Computer Vision." arXiv, December 11, 2015. *https://arxiv.org/abs/1512.00567.*

overfitting and increasing generalization.[52] The following equation is a smoothing formula that applies a marginal value (ε) when the true label is found (i.e., $i == k$) but assigns a fixed value (ε/K) when the label is false:

$$Q_i = \begin{cases} 1 - \epsilon \text{ if } i = k \\ \frac{\epsilon}{K} \text{ otherwise, where } K \text{ is number of classes} \end{cases}$$

The use of smoothing, because of its magnitude, does not introduce noticeable changes in the labels. This is in contrast to mixup, which uses similar motivations but visibly changes the labels.

The Data Engine and Continual Learning

As discussed via the seven Vs, scaling data is not just a matter of volume but is also done to account for various needs related to operations and performance efficiencies. If your operations are at a level of maturity where a continual stream of new data is coming through, then incorporating the concepts discussed in the previous section becomes crucial to ensuring you are effectively using your labeling workforce and capitalizing on the data corpus available to you. The techniques you've learned about here can be helpful to ensure that you:

- Effectively sample data for labeling operations, to minimize labeling expenses.
- Effectively measure the labeling outcome to manage noise and to handle at-scale data challenges such as class imbalances.
- Effectively utilize the data corpus to select useful samples for training, to keep training expenses minimized while maximizing the generalizability and robustness of your model.

These aims can be achieved more effectively if data procurement, labeling, and model operations are well integrated into a unified system (your *data engine*, as discussed in Chapter 1) to allow continual learning. An example of such integration is shown in Figure 10-14.

---

52 He, Tong, Zhi Zhang, Hang Zhang, Zhongyue Zhang, Junyuan Xie, and Mu Li. 2018. "Bag of Tricks for Image Classification with Convolutional Neural Networks." arXiv, December 5, 2018. *https://arxiv.org/abs/1812.01187*.

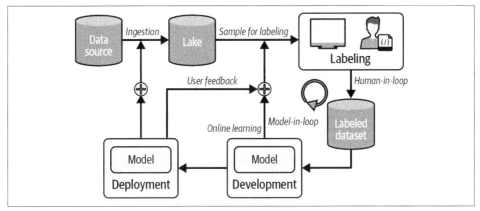

Figure 10-14. The data flow in a unified system integrating the data engine and model development

In this section, we'll briefly consider the last two of the seven Vs discussed at the beginning of this chapter, volatility and velocity, in the context of procuring and managing data at scale.

Volatility

We live in an ever-evolving world where commonly held definitions and perceptions of things change over time. To give one example, Figure 10-15 demonstrates how our perception of the concept of "car" has changed over the last two centuries. Such volatility is also evident in language. For instance, in the 1300s–1400s the word "nice" meant silly, foolish, or ignorant. By the 1500s, the meaning had completely changed to mean meticulous, attentive, or sharp. More recently (from about the 1800s) it shifted again, now being taken to mean agreeable and pleasant. Changes in representation like these can cause shifts in a model's domain knowledge. Continuously updating models with newer knowledge as part of continual learning is a good approach to scale temporally.

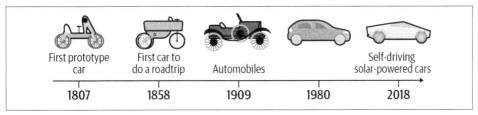

Figure 10-15. Changing conceptions of "car" over the last two centuries

Velocity

Effective and efficient labeling plays an essential role in managing the velocity of data in the context of veracity, value, and variety. In addition to the techniques discussed in "Approaches to labeling" on page 334, online/active learning is quite useful in the implementation of data engines and continual learning. With this approach, which you'll read about in the following chapter, the training process proactively asks for labels for specific data. CRAIG and GLISTER, two techniques discussed earlier in this chapter, can also be used in such online learning operations to reduce labeling expense by removing noise and optimizing labeling.

Summary

In this chapter you explored the seven Vs of data—volume, velocity, variety, veracity, validity, volatility, and value—and their importance in developing good models. You read about the power law of data and the positive influence scaled-up data volumes have had on scaling of model development and model generalizability, then you explored several challenges relating to variety, veracity, validity, and value that surface when data volumes are increased. You also read about the evolving trend toward high quality of high-quantity data, departing from the earlier focus purely on increased volume. You explored several tricks and techniques to manage the quality, volume, and variety of your dataset and learned about the importance of maintaining the value of your samples. You also completed various practical exercises to tackle these challenges head on.

In the next chapter you will read about experiment planning and review a set of techniques to scale your experiments.

## CHAPTER 11

Scaling Experiments: Effective Planning and Management

Plans are worthless, but planning is everything.
—Dwight D. Eisenhower

In this chapter, you will learn how to plan and manage scaling your training workload in an iterative and efficient manner by making informed choices along the way. The chapter is divided into two main sections, "Planning for Experiments and Execution" on page 351 and "Techniques to Scale Your Experiments" on page 357.

The first of these sections focuses on the problem framing side of things and discusses how to plan your experiments to incrementally build up capabilities while keeping the entropy to a minimum. This section also provides some guiding principles on setting up projects and environment and system configurations to support smoother iterative development. You will learn about some tooling for versioning and card/summary systems to facilitate fluid iteration.

The following section dives into a set of deep learning techniques that are helpful in setting the direction and roadmap for experiment planning for iterative improvement of your model. In this section, you will learn about various approaches that are useful in accelerating model development, such as hyperparameter optimization, AutoML, transfer learning, meta learning, contrastive learning, and mixture of experts. Practical exercises demonstrating the use of some of these techniques are provided in "Hands-On Exercises" on page 382.

We'll start by briefly considering the iterative nature of model development, then dive into planning to scale experimentations.

Model Development Is Iterative

The process of model development is highly entropic and iterative. The stochasticity and opacity of deep learning (discussed in Chapter 2) makes planning for model development much more complex than traditional software development. The high entropy of model development comes from the nondeterminism and the lack of upfront clarity about success. As a result, iteration proves to be quite helpful.

Deep learning is also iterative by design: the training steps (forward and backward passes) are repeated in each epoch, the epochs are repeated in experiments that validate the feasibility and usefulness of a technique, and the experiments are repeated to make improvements for each feature or capability that is introduced. Changes to a model's features and capabilities thus represent only the tip of the iceberg, as illustrated in Figure 11-1, and when planning to scale your experiments you need to take into account the entire process, with all the complexity that's hidden underneath.

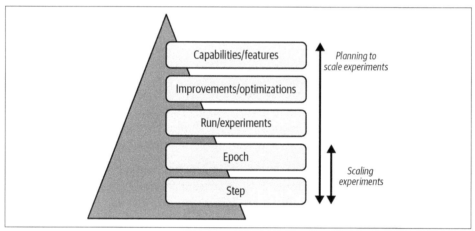

Figure 11-1. The iterative process of model development—introducing a new feature is just the tip of the iceberg!

Albert Einstein famously said, "No amount of experimentation can ever prove me right; a single experiment can prove me wrong." Due to the high entropy of development, pragmatic planning and designing to identify suitable techniques will still leave you with many open questions, variables, and techniques to explore. Thus, navigating to the tip of the iceberg is often a process of elimination and rejection. Iterating and focusing on one change at a time streamlines development by avoiding confusion caused by compounding effects.

With that in mind, let's dive into planning for experimentation.

Planning for Experiments and Execution

As discussed in Chapter 1, the first step of any modeling undertaking is *framing the problem*—i.e., outlining exactly what you are trying to achieve. Planning plays a crucial role in optimizing effort and avoiding mistakes, especially in highly entropic fields such as deep learning model development. It's vital that you know the constraints and scope of the objective to develop a plan for achieving it. To get you started, this section presents six tips for planning effectively.

Simplify the Complex

Rome was not built in a day! Breaking down the modeling task into smaller piecemeal problems not only simplifies the problem but also allows for incremental improvement. Taking the roof identification example from Chapter 1, if your task is to create outlines of buildings in satellite images, this could be broken down as follows:

1. Determine whether or not the image contains a roof (classification).
2. Localize where roofs are in the image (semantic segmentation).
3. Identify instances of roofs (instance segmentation).
4. Produce key points or geometry vectors (polygons, etc.) to create outlines of the roofs.

In this example, tasks 1–3 are relatively straightforward because there are few unknowns. So, you might even decide to frame this as a two-step process:

1. Perform instance segmentation of images containing roofs.
2. Produce key points or geometry vectors to create outlines of the roofs.

However, if the problem were a lot more complex and there were a large number of unknowns, you might want to simplify it and build your model incrementally. For instance, if your task were to count the number of tiles per roofing tile variety (e.g., specific types of concrete tiles, such as Horizon, Tudor, Atura, etc.), you would have more unknowns. Factors like the resolution of the images would become quite important, as the textures of the tiles might provide the most useful information for detecting and identifying tiles by their subtypes. At a ground sampling distance (GSD) of ~1 m per pixel, would you have enough signals to detect the textures of the tiles? In such a case, if the model failed to delineate between the tile types, attempting to debug the failure of instance detection/segmentation would be harder because of the additional components and logic involved. Attempting to skip steps might mask the underlying problem and make the task very challenging to implement and debug.

For our original roof identification problem, the approach of iterating over steps 1–4 is analogous to bottom-up model development. A top-down approach, on the other hand, would be directly tackling creating building outlines and stepping down from there as challenges arise. In general, a bottom-up approach can be more rewarding as you start to see success and make data-driven decisions, but it does require more development effort as staging requires more time and auxiliary development. A top-down approach can work well for well-established problems, but when faced with unknowns, this approach can accrue a lot of complexities and create development friction, leading to time estimate blowouts that can be discouraging.

Fast Iteration for Fast Feedback

The fringe benefit of an iterative and incremental approach is a fast iteration and feedback loop. This allows you to be data-driven as you make informed practical choices based on the outcomes of your preceding iterations and your future plans.

In the roof tile example, incrementally building from step 1 will allow you to confirm what resolution of images you need to get useful signals to be able to identify and count instances of different subtypes of tiles (and indeed, whether it's possible to classify tile subtypes this way). In this case, you may start with just a feature encoder and a classifier head. Success in step 1 drives you to step 2, where you can replace the classifier head with a decoder followed by a segmentation head. In turn, success in this step informs that you can effectively segment tile types and distinguish between them. You could then build up incrementally from here, adding modules for region proposals (e.g., with bipartite matching) to learn to segregate instances.

By taking this incremental approach, you resolve quite a few of the unknowns along the way. Hypothetically speaking, you might not have enough signals to see the tile boundaries, so instance segmentation might fail. In this case, using a data-driven approach, you might decide to fall back to using another approximation technique to identify instances of different subtypes of tiles. For example, each subtype has a well-defined size, so knowing the size and total segmentation area can guide the instance count.

Decoupled Iterations

Model development, as you have seen in previous chapters and their respective hands-on exercises, is an integration of various components including data, data pipelines, evaluation methodology, and the model itself as a learnable algorithm. All of these components offer useful capabilities worthy of reuse. For instance, data pipelines can be quite handy to integrate with visual tools to debug and diagnose issues in your data. Evaluation components can also be very useful to diagnose data quality issues. Developing these as independently abstracted modules with appropriate software engineering principles (e.g., SOLID (*https://oreil.ly/qlese*)) can significantly reduce the entropy of iteration.

Feasibility Testing

As discussed in Chapter 10, data is critical fuel for the modeling process. Aside from good software practices for testing your code and verifying your data, you may find keeping a synthetic dataset (sometimes called a smoke dataset) for use in end-to-end sanity testing of your system helpful.

Having a smoke dataset that you know is easily modeled can be crucial if your modeling task is nuanced and complex. Such data can be particularly helpful in debugging stochastic challenges (like no convergence, model collapse, etc.), to quickly identify whether the problem is due to bugs in your system or learning dynamics challenges. In the roof tile identification example, for instance, you could simulate much simpler, clearer tiles by generating random square patches of different colors/tones and try to overfit your model on this to confirm that it is at least learning, even if not generalizing. This is such a simple problem that the system should start to show convergence, or at least overfit to your samples. If not, you know your implementation has issues. Tricks like this can minimize entropy by providing fast, impactful feedback without you having to comb through your system and codebase looking for bugs in the logic, data flow, or learning dynamics.

Developing and Scaling a Minimal Viable Solution

To ascertain whether your base task is achievable and learnable—that is, that you are fighting the right battle—you can derive an initial baseline from your training dataset using conditional probabilities. This should reflect the expected performance of a random, no-skill model (*https://oreil.ly/dJmCe*), and your first minimal viable solution should supersede this random baseline.

Once you have proven your first prototype—i.e., shown that it performs better than random guessing—your challenge becomes shooting for the North Star. At this point, your iterations become more about adding features and capabilities or boosting the statistical performance of the model (i.e., improving metrics of success such as perplexity, accuracy, precision, etc.). Measuring success is much easier if you have a baseline to compare your results to, whether in terms of statistical or computational performance. Again, this enables you to make data-driven decisions regarding whether to keep or discard new features and capabilities.

Setting Up for Iterative Execution

Machine learning systems are always at risk of accumulating technical debt,[1] underscoring the importance of carefully managing dependencies, considering the configuration, and enforcing separation of concerns. When it comes to planning and executing your experiments, you need to think about not only your system itself but also its integrations with all downstream and upstream components, including data stores, the deployment environment, etc.

Project setup can be thought of as the orchestration of all the parts of the end-to-end system, encompassing integrations with external systems and data stores, development tooling, environment management, configuration management, and continuous delivery for deep learning. A full discussion of all of these points, crucial as they are, is beyond the scope of this book. In this section, we'll specifically consider planning for experimentation, with a focus on development tooling, environment management, and configuration management. Resources such as Chip Huyen's book *Designing Machine Learning Systems* (*https://oreil.ly/YkjVP*)[2] and Danilo Sato et al.'s article "Continuous Delivery for Machine Learning"[3] may be useful when planning for integration.

Planning for experiment execution entails thinking about development tools, the runtime environment, and your ability to track and manage inputs and outputs (e.g., configuration, data, and model performance metrics, as well as the computational requirements to capture all the data needed to iterate and improve). Here are some things to bear in mind when planning experiments:

Fixed runtime

Reproducibility, reliability, and repeatability—the three Rs—are very helpful concepts to keep in mind during development. Lacking any of these elements can cause significant slowdowns in development and pose challenges in debugging (say, if you can't reproduce or re-create the scenario/issue reliably). Dependency management tools like `pip`, `pip-tools`, Poetry, Conda, and Mamba are popular in Python environments; however, the ability to reliably freeze a Python environment is best guaranteed by the use of `pip-freeze` or Docker-based container environments.

---

1 Sculley, D., Gary Holt, Daniel Golovin, Eugene Davydov, Todd Phillips, Dietmar Ebner, Vinay Chaudhary, et al. 2015. "Hidden Technical Debt in Machine Learning Systems." In *Proceedings of the 28th International Conference on Neural Information Processing Systems (NIPS '15)*, vol. 2, 2503–11. *https://www.research gate.net/publication/319769912_Hidden_Technical_Debt_in_Machine_Learning_Systems*.

2 Huyen, Chip. 2022. *Designing Machine Learning Systems*. Sebastopol, CA: O'Reilly Media.

3 Sato, Danilo, Arif Wider, and Christoph Windheuser. 2019. "Continuous Delivery for Machine Learning." *https://martinfowler.com/articles/cd4ml.html*.

Project as application

Having a well-defined project structure is equally as important as fixing the runtime, especially when you are scaling. A well-structured project paves the way for clear abstractions and separation of concerns—important characteristics to have when iterating across dimensions (data, code, algorithms, configurations, etc.). Having automation testing increases the rate of useful experimentation, as you are less likely to run into failed experiments due to bugs. It's useful to incorporate testing frameworks like `pytest` to create unit/integration and smoke tests, especially when iterating rapidly. Much like the "goodput" metric[4] mentioned in Chapter 6, I advocate for "goodput" metrics to minimize compute and effort wastage.

Configuration

A large part of experimenting is exploring different sets of configurations (learning rates, weight decay, etc.). Building experiment components such that they are easily configurable and trackable allows for fluid and rapid iteration. Using a hierarchical configuration management tool like Hydra (*https://oreil.ly/9Xz2i*) in conjunction with libraries like Pydantic (*https://pydantic.dev*) for data validation can be quite beneficial to improve the experimentation experience and minimize the risk of configuration errors. If Hydra seems like a big investment, a more lightweight alternative like OmegaConf (*https://oreil.ly/Mashj*) (the library Hydra is based on) can be an effective choice as well. `fvcore` (*https://oreil.ly/jv6cM*) is another popular lightweight tool for hierarchical configuration, used extensively in Detectron2 (a popular library for vision-related deep learning models). While APIs like `argparse` are handy, managing them can get out of hand very quickly as modeling configurations are not only hierarchical but connected, much like the DAGs that your models represent.

Experiment tracking

In earlier chapters of this book (e.g., Chapter 2), you used the experiment tracking tool Aim to track and visualize the outcomes of your runs. There are several other tools, such as Weights & Biases, Comet, and ClearML, that provide similar capabilities; for a comparison, see Patrycja Jenker's and Kilian Kluge's post on the neptune.ai MLOps Blog.[5]

---

4 Qiao, Aurick, Sang Keun Choe, Suhas Jayaram Subramanya, Willie Neiswanger, Qirong Ho, Hao Zhang, Gregory R. Ganger, and Eric P. Xing. 2020. "Pollux: Co-Adaptive Cluster Scheduling for Goodput-Optimized Deep Learning." arXiv, August 27, 2020. *https://arxiv.org/abs/2008.12260*.

5 Kluge, Kilian and Patrycja Jenkner. 2023. "15 Best Tools for ML Experiment Tracking and Management." MLOps Blog, December 19, 2023. *https://neptune.ai/blog/best-ml-experiment-tracking-tools*.

Versioning and lineage

Full system traceability is a crucial part of debugging and making data-driven decisions. When you're developing an opaque system, as in the case of deep learning, using end-to-end tracking tools like Data Version Control (DVC and DVC Studio), Pachyderm, and ClearML can be quite advantageous.

Releases and reporting

Iterative improvements require capturing the complete specifications of each iteration, not just from a model performance viewpoint but from a full system viewpoint. In other words, for full system benchmarks you'll want to measure and track the specifications of the data, the model, and the computational requirements. Card concepts such as model and data cards[6] are useful in providing a bird's-eye view of every iteration; they're similar to release notes but they record the details of their respective runs.

Figure 11-2 shows a workflow—an abstract mind map—for experiment planning. The process starts with a well-defined problem (as discussed in Chapter 1), and you progress from there to curating the data and generating and validating the model.

In Chapter 10, you learned about different techniques to navigate data-related processes, including data curation, preprocessing, and automated techniques like AutoAugment and coreset selection. This section focused on experiment planning, including both top-down and bottom-up approaches, and iterating effectively. In the following section, you'll dive into the parts of the workflow (circled in Figure 11-2) that pertain to model generation and evaluation and read about various techniques and tricks you can use to scale up your iterations once you have arrived at your minimal viable solution.

---

6 Mitchell, Margaret, Simone Wu, Andrew Zaldivar, Parker Barnes, Lucy Vasserman, Ben Hutchinson, Elena Spitzer, Inioluwa Deborah Raji, and Timnit Gebru. 2019. "Model Cards for Model Reporting." arXiv, January 1, 2019. *https://arxiv.org/abs/1810.03993*; Pushkarna, Mahima, Andrew Zaldivar, and Oddur Kjartansson. 2022. "Data Cards: Purposeful and Transparent Dataset Documentation for Responsible AI." arXiv, April 3, 2022. *https://arxiv.org/abs/2204.01075*.

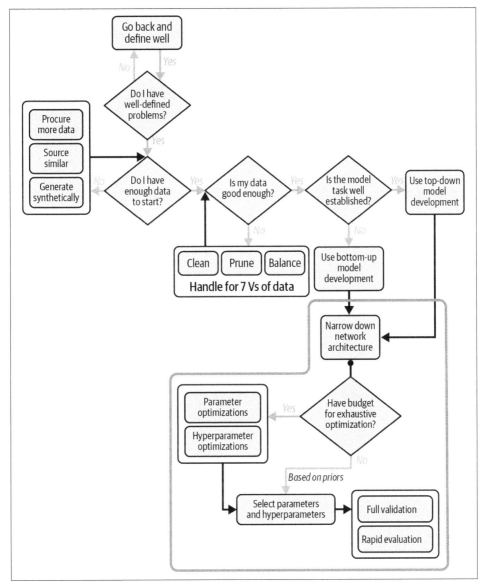

Figure 11-2. Mind map of model development and planning

Techniques to Scale Your Experiments

This section introduces various techniques you can use to improve your model's per-formance. Its aim is to provide a broad perspective, so you can plan the most suitable directions for your experiments and decide how best to scale up your model improvement iterations given the resources at your disposal. We'll look at techniques for accelerating model convergence, accelerating learning via optimization and automation, accelerating by increasing expertise, and learning with scarce supervision.

Accelerating Model Convergence

The longer it takes to accept or reject an attempted experiment, the slower the iteration will be. Rapid iteration is only possible when convergence is fast. In this section, we'll look at two techniques for expediting convergence that are often helpful in accelerating learning and improving performance: transfer learning and knowledge distillation.

Using transfer learning

Transfer learning[7] is a widely adopted technique where a model's prior learning is repurposed to learn another task, with the goal of speeding up convergence. For example, if a model already knows how to tell roofs apart from other things that appear in satellite images, then it will be much faster for it to learn to distinguish roof tile types. The benefits of this approach in neural networks were established as early as the connectionist era (the mid-1970s), and these hold true for deep learning as well.

In a practical sense, using transfer learning is the same as starting from a well-known set of weights rather than random initializations like Xavier, except now you use weights from a previously trained model. Figure 11-3 shows the acceleration in convergence that can be achieved with this technique.

 One caution with transfer learning is the negative effect that may occur if the origin domain of the source model (from which learning is being transferred) does not overlap with the target domain.

7 Tan, Chuanqi, Fuchun Sun, Tao Kong, Wenchang Zhang, Chao Yang, and Chunfang Liu. 2018. "A Survey on Deep Transfer Learning." arXiv, August 6, 2018. *https://arxiv.org/abs/1808.01974*.

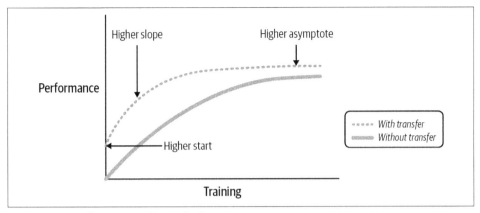

Figure 11-3. Advantages of transfer learning

Transfer learning is further specialized into three modes, retraining, fine tuning, and pretraining, which are defined in the following subsections.

Retraining.   In retraining, you start with your target model graph and the weights of another source model. You essentially copy over all the weights from the source model, then begin training using your updated target model and data. The entire model is trained end to end, and you are not bound by the techniques (e.g., optimizations) used in the source model.

Using retraining has no implications on your computing resources; the only change is that you're starting training from a known point instead of using random initializations.

Fine tuning.   In fine tuning, you again start with your target model graph and the weights of another source model, copying them over into the target model. However, in addition, you also "freeze" a subset of the layers of your target model (using `Module.requires_grad=False`) so that their parameters are not updated during backpropagation.

In this case, all the layers you freeze are essentially just acting as non-learnable feature generator layers where features are produced as per the learning of the source model. This approach can provide significant compute and memory efficiencies, because you don't have to compute gradients for the frozen layers.

This approach is very helpful where there is a significant overlap between the source and target models, as it can accelerate iteration and development. Specialized fine-tuning techniques like Reinforcement Learning from Human Feedback (RHLF), mentioned in Chapter 10, are increasingly being used to achieve specific outcomes such as alignment and are shown to work well even with small quantities of high-quality data.[8]

Pretraining. Pretraining is another variant of transfer learning where the source model is first explicitly trained on a larger dataset (typically related to the target domain) using unsupervised techniques and then reused as the target model for the main task. The premise for this approach is to accelerate learning and convergence by starting with good domain knowledge, learned from the source dataset. OpenAI's Contrastive Language-Image Pre-training (CLIP) is a good example of this pretraining paradigm.[9] In CLIP, two encoders (one for images and one for text) are trained using pairwise samples consisting of images and their associated captions, with a contrastive loss objective. In this case, image features are learned from text through contrastive learning (see "Contrastive learning" on page 381).

Such image/text paired training not only enables the association of words (e.g., "apple") with their corresponding visual features, but also ensures that variations of the features (e.g., green versus red, cut versus whole, "apple" versus "apples") are incorporated in learned representations. It can even distinguish the fruit apple from expressions such as "my daughter, the apple of my eye." Masked autoencoder–based techniques,[10] where parts of images or text are randomly masked and the model is tasked to predict mask content to guide the feature learning, can also be used in pretraining.

For a practical exercise using transfer learning, see "Hands-On Exercise #1: Transfer Learning" on page 383.

Knowledge distillation

In Chapter 10, you learned about distillation in the context of dataset compression and extracting useful information into a smaller coreset. Knowledge distillation in models is a related concept, where the knowledge of an expert (teacher) is extracted into a much smaller "capacity" model known as a student. The student model is generally a simpler (pruned) or quantized version of the same architecture as the expert, or it may be a completely different but smaller architecture or even the same model as the expert.

---

8 Zhou, Chunting, Pengfei Liu, Puxin Xu, Srini Iyer, Jiao Sun, Yuning Mao, Xuezhe Ma, et al. 2023. "LIMA: Less Is More for Alignment." arXiv, May 18, 2023. *https://arxiv.org/abs/2305.11206*.

9 Radford, Alec, Jong Wook Kim, Chris Hallacy, Aditya Ramesh, Gabriel Goh, Sandhini Agarwal, Girish Sastry, et al. 2021. "Learning Transferable Visual Models from Natural Language Supervision." arXiv, February 26, 2021. *https://arxiv.org/abs/2103.00020*.

10 He, Kaiming, Xinlei Chen, Saining Xie, Yanghao Li, Piotr Dollár, and Ross Girshick. 2021. "Masked Autoencoders Are Scalable Vision Learners." arXiv, December 19, 2021. *https://arxiv.org/abs/2111.06377*.

The motivation behind distillation is threefold: reusability (of learnings), efficiency (faster training cycles), and faster convergence. Online, offline, and self distillation are the three principal modes of knowledge distillation. In the online mode, the teacher and student are trained together in the same training cycle, but they follow different optimization schedules. In the offline mode, the teacher is pretrained and simply used as an advisor during a training loop created for the student. With self-distillation, the teacher and student are the same model.

The distillation process, illustrated in Figure 11-4, is divided into three categories: response-based distillation, feature-based distillation, and relation-based distillation.

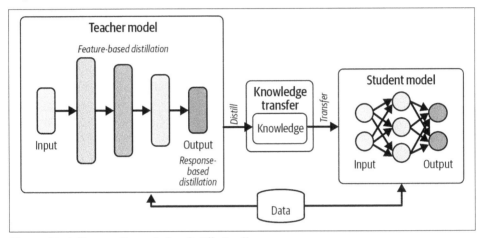

Figure 11-4. Types of knowledge distillation[11]

Let's take a look at the objectives of each:

Response-based distillation

    Response-based distillation focuses on extracting learning from the teacher by defining the objective as not only producing accurate labels, but also producing output close to the teacher's. Because of this focus, the objective function for distillation, commonly known as the *distillation loss*, is derived from the logits of the teacher. This concept originated from Hinton et al.'s work[12] where they defined temperature scaling (i.e., scaling the logits by a factor τ) to handle soft targets (a.k.a. soft labels, discussed in Chapter 10).

11 Gou, Jianping, Baosheng Yu, Stephen John Maybank, and Dacheng Tao. 2021. "Knowledge Distillation: A Survey." arXiv, May 20, 2021. *https://arxiv.org/abs/2006.05525*.

12 Hinton, Geoffrey, Oriol Vinyals, and Jeff Dean. 2015. "Distilling the Knowledge in a Neural Network." arXiv, March 9, 2015. *https://arxiv.org/abs/1503.02531*.

See "Hands-On Exercise #3: Knowledge Distillation" on page 384 for a specific implementation of response-based offline distillation training.

Feature-based distillation

Feature-based distillation attempts to keep the student's features closely aligned to the teacher's features. Feature alignments are generally derived from activation maps, feature representations, or the parameter distribution and are commonly implemented by distance metrics such as L1/L2 norm. For more details, see Jianping Gou et al.'s survey of knowledge distillation techniques.[13]

Relation-based distillation

Both feature- and response-based distillation focus on singular aspects (features and output, respectively), without accounting for interdependencies between the layers or the features extracted by these layers. Relation-based distillation exists to bridge this gap: the aim is to extract pairwise knowledge from the teacher in the form of relationships between the input and output and distill that to the student model. This is often implemented using complex distance measures, such as earth mover's (Wasserstein) distance, Huber loss, angle-wise loss, etc., that measure the notion of "relations" between the input/output pairs of layers.

 Researchers from Facebook and Inria explored distillation with no labels (DINO) in a self-supervised setting.[14] DINO is similar to online distillation, except the teacher is updated with an exponential moving average of the student's parameters, so they learn from each other's logits when shown the same data following extensive data augmentations. This technique is an example of response-based distillation, similar to the hands-on exercise later in this chapter, and thus it also leverages temperature scaling in loss computation.

Accelerating Learning Via Optimization and Automation

This section presents a selection of automation techniques that can help you scale out your model improvement efforts. You will learn about the use of hyperparameter optimization, AutoML, and Daydream to explore the evolving landscape of efficient scaling through automation and simulation.

---

13 Gou et al., "Knowledge Distillation," *https://arxiv.org/abs/2006.05525*.

14 Caron, Mathilde, Hugo Touvron, Ishan Misra, Hervé Jégou, Julien Mairal, Piotr Bojanowski, and Armand Joulin. 2021. "Emerging Properties in Self-Supervised Vision Transformers." arXiv, May 24, 2021. *https://arxiv.org/abs/2104.14294*.

Hyperparameter optimization

Hyperparameters are the configuration settings of your model that can be tuned to improve its ability to generalize. Commonly, the hyperparameters are chosen based on similar or original experiments (as reported in the papers describing this work) and adjusted intuitively to suit the task at hand. This process often requires a lot of trial and error, so optimization techniques are frequently used to scale up navigation of the hyperparameter search space.

As discussed in Chapter 6, hyperparameters are one of the dimensions suitable for horizontally scaling model development because of the complete independence across sets of parameters. Conceptually, you create a study that defines sets of hyperparameters to explore. Then, for each set of hyperparameters, you run experiments (often called *trials*). Based on the outcome of the trials, you choose the most optimal set of hyperparameters. Figure 11-5 illustrates how this process works in a distributed setting for horizontal scale-out.

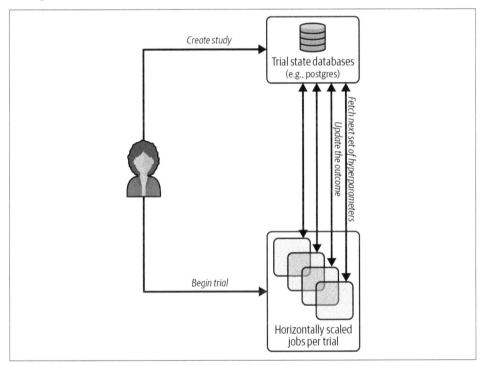

Figure 11-5. Hyperparameter tuning at scale

Using your intuition and knowledge of deep learning to limit the search space prior to performing hyperparameter optimization allows you to better manage your time and computation budget. For instance, if your batch size is large, using too-small learning rates may not be effective. Hence, you may want to adjust the learning rate search space to reflect this.

Outside of this "intuitive" knowledge, grid search and random search are two popularly used techniques for hyperparameter selection. Random search is generally more effective, due to the naiveness of grid search. A quasi-Monte Carlo–based approach also exists that extends random search by more efficiently sampling the hyperparameter set.[15] Tree-Structured Parzen Estimation (TSPE) is another technique that uses Bayesian estimation to prioritize a set of hyperparameters that are likely to be more successful given the known prior trials.[16]

In general, you want your model and selection techniques to be less sensitive to hyperparameters because searching for more effective hyperparameters is a computationally intensive and minimally rewarding task. Similar to the concept of early stopping in model training, stopping criteria are commonly applied in hyperparameter optimization studies. These algorithms do not stop the trials (that's achieved by early stopping) but rather prune the set of hyperparameters that are deemed less promising.

Aside from simple statistics-based pruning techniques that rely on thresholds, medians, and percentiles, more advanced approaches exist. Hyperband, for example, is a bandit-based technique that applies successive halving, a divide and conquer approach, to navigate the search space; it can prune the search space very efficiently, providing up to a 30x speedup compared to popular Bayesian optimization algorithms.[17] TSPE combined with Hyperband pruning works well in general.

Optuna, Ray, BoTorch, and Hyperopt are some of the widely used libraries for hyperparameter tuning. See "Hands-On Exercise #2: Hyperparameter Optimization" on page 383 for a practice workout on hyperparameter tuning using Optuna.

AutoML

Figure 11-6 shows another perspective of the model development workflow shown originally in Figure 11-2. This figure depicts the end-to-end model development process by grouping the steps into categories of *data curation* (data procurement, cleaning, filtering, and selection), *data preprocessing* (data augmentation, sampling, and

---

15 Bergstra, James, and Yoshua Bengio. 2012. "Random Search for Hyper-Parameter Optimization." *Journal of Machine Learning Research* 13(10): 281–305. *https://jmlr.org/papers/v13/bergstra12a.html*.

16 Watanabe, Shuhei. 2023. "Tree-Structured Parzen Estimator: Understanding Its Algorithm Components and Their Roles for Better Empirical Performance." arXiv, May 26, 2023. *https://arxiv.org/abs/2304.11127*.

17 Li, Lisha, Kevin Jamieson, Giulia DeSalvo, Afshin Rostamizadeh, and Ameet Talwalkar. 2018. "Hyperband: A Novel Bandit-Based Approach to Hyperparameter Optimization." arXiv, June 18, 2018. *https://arxiv.org/abs/1603.06560*.

feature engineering), *model generation*, and *model validation*. The ambitious target of automating this entire process to arrive at the most optimal model is termed *AutoML* (for *Auto*mated *M*achine *L*earning). A lot of work is going on to make this a viable option. At present, your benefit from this technique will be dependent on your use case.

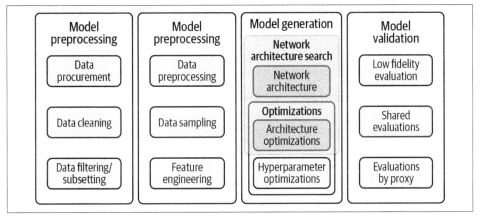

Figure 11-6. Scope of AutoML

The workflow of AutoML is also implemented using a directed acyclic graph, except this DAG is process-level and integrates across infrastructure and processes, unlike model DAGs, which mainly show the operations applied to data as it flows through the model. Most public cloud providers (discussed in Chapter 5) offer integrated solutions for AutoML, with varying degrees of features. Other open source tools, like AutoGluon (*https://oreil.ly/r5uDI*) and Auto-PyTorch (*https://oreil.ly/-jF75*), provide useful capabilities for AutoML via Pythonic APIs.

You already read about some data curation and preprocessing-related automation techniques in Chapter 10 (e.g., AutoAugment, coreset selection). In this section, we'll focus on model generation and validation in the context of AutoML. The model development process has two phases:

Architecture search
In this phase, you narrow down the search space for model architecture selection and select the most suitable architecture.

Optimization
In this phase, you optimize your selected architecture for the best-performing parameter and hyperparameter set.

Neural architecture search.   The previous section discussed techniques for hyperparameter optimization, so here we will mainly cover architecture search and parameter optimization. These two phases can be automated with an approach known as *neural* *architecture search* (NAS).[18] However, this can be an expensive operation. For instance, with Zoph et al.'s NASNet, performing an architecture search using the CIFAR-10 classification task on NVIDIA P100s took 2,000 GPU-hours, and the authors report that with a previous version of NAS (and less-performant K40s) it took a whopping 22,400 GPU-hours.[19] More recent work, such as that by Chen et al.,[20] has massively reduced this cost, with TE-NAS (training-free neural architecture search) completing the same task on a single GTX 1080 Ti GPU in just 0.5 hours. Still, broadly speaking, the compute requirements for NAS are huge; consequently, it's not a widely used technique, and when it is used the search space is typically first heuristically and intuitively pruned to manage the cost.

There are four known patterns for architecture search: entire structure, block-based, hierarchical, and morphism-based. Examples of architecture optimization methods include reinforcement learning, evolutionary algorithms, and gradient descent–based and surrogate model–based optimization.[21]

An *entire structure* search,[22] as the name suggests, is exhaustive and is parameterized by the number of layers and possible types of layer (these can include rudimentary layers like convolution and pooling, or commonly known blocks/modules like dilated convolution, Squeeze-and-Excitation, and Transformer encoder blocks). Commonly, the deeper the model, the better its generalizability; however, greater depth makes entire structure–based searches extremely computationally expensive.

Figure 11-7 illustrates this architecture search approach. In these examples, two possible outcomes are shown (including the configurations of the layers; i.e., kernel size), one purely sequential and one including residual connections. The search will also explore many other possible options to choose the most optimal one.

18 Zoph, Barret, and Quoc V. Le. 2017. "Neural Architecture Search with Reinforcement Learning." arXiv, February 15, 2017. *https://arxiv.org/abs/1611.01578*.

19 Zoph, Barret, Vijay Vasudevan, Jonathon Shlens, and Quoc V. Le. 2017. "Learning Transferable Architectures for Scalable Image Recognition." arXiv, April 11, 2018. *https://arxiv.org/abs/1707.07012*.

20 Chen, Wuyang, Xinyu Gong, and Zhangyang Wang. 2021. "Neural Architecture Search on ImageNet in Four GPU Hours: A Theoretically Inspired Perspective." arXiv, March 16, 2021. *https://arxiv.org/abs/2102.11535*.

21 Zoph and Le, "Neural Architecture Search with Reinforcement Learning," *https://arxiv.org/abs/1611.01578*; Zhu, Hui, Zhulin An, Chuanguang Yang, Kaiqiang Xu, Erhu Zhao, and Yongjun Xu. 2019. "EENA: Efficient Evolution of Neural Architecture." arXiv, August 27, 2019. *https://arxiv.org/abs/1905.07320*; He, Chaoyang, Haishan Ye, Li Shen, and Tong Zhang. 2020. "MiLeNAS: Efficient Neural Architecture Search via Mixed-Level Reformulation." arXiv, March 27, 2020. *https://arxiv.org/abs/2003.12238*; Liu, Chenxi, Barret Zoph, Maxim Neumann, Jonathon Shlens, Wei Hua, Li-Jia Li, Li Fei-Fei, et al. 2018. "Progressive Neural Architecture Search." arXiv, July 26, 2018. *https://arxiv.org/abs/1712.00559*.

22 Zoph and Le, "Neural Architecture Search with Reinforcement Learning," *https://arxiv.org/abs/1611.01578*.

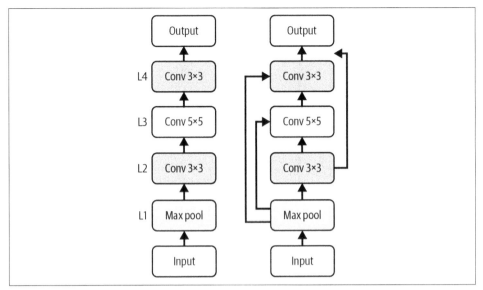

Figure 11-7. Two examples of the outcome of entire structure search on a four-layer (L1..4) network comprising convolution and pooling layers

In contrast, *block-based* searches look for the optimal configuration of blocks that are repeated in a network. This approach, first proposed as NASNet,[23] is analogous to many popular hand-designed networks, such as the ResNet and Inception families of networks. An example of block-based search is shown in Figure 11-8. In this example, instead of the entire graph, only different implementations of blocks ("normal blocks" and "reduction blocks," convolutional blocks that return either a feature map of the same dimension as their input or a feature map with lower dimensionality) are searched. The complexity is reduced by limiting the searches to blocks only; however, any foreseeable optimizations from the macro assembly of the full network are not explored.

---

23 Zoph et al., "Learning Transferable Architectures for Scalable Image Recognition," *https://arxiv.org/abs/ 1707.07012*

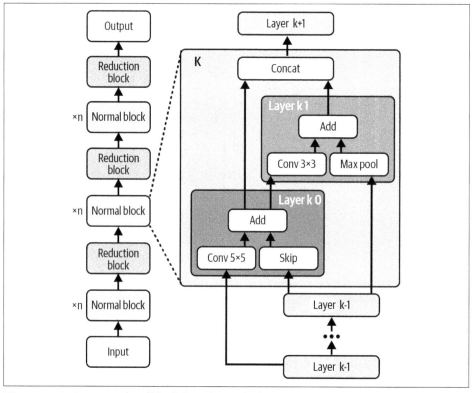

Figure 11-8. An example of block-based search showing a network composed of n normal blocks and one reduction block stacked sequentially

Hierarchical search, as proposed in MnasNet,[24] aimed to mitigate this shortcoming by introducing levels of optimization. An example of hierarchical search is shown in Figure 11-9. Unlike entire structure searches, the results from both block and hierarchical searches are transferable and reusable, allowing the possibility of searching on a smaller proxy dataset for greater efficiency.

---

24 Tan, Mingxing, Bo Chen, Ruoming Pang, Vijay Vasudevan, Mark Sandler, Andrew Howard, and Quoc V. Le. 2019. "MnasNet: Platform-Aware Neural Architecture Search for Mobile." arXiv, May 29, 2019. arXiv, May 29, 2019. *https://arxiv.org/abs/1807.11626v3*.

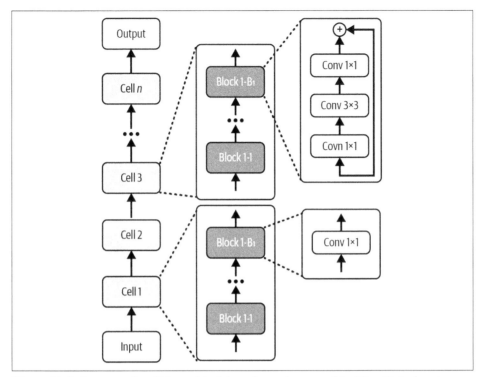

Figure 11-9. An example of hierarchical-based search, as used in MnasNet, showing leveled searching for architecture (in this example, each block of a given cell is of the same architecture, but the architecture differs between cells)

Inspired by reusability, *morphism-based* searches morph already successful architectures, altering their depth or width to obtain an even more efficient variant. An example of morphism search is shown in Figure 11-10. The architecture of EfficientNet, a highly popular and widely used encoder (which you used in Chapter 4's scene parsing exercise) was derived via morphism-based searching.[25]

---

25 Tan, Mingxing, and Quoc V. Le. 2019. "EfficientNet: Rethinking Model Scaling for Convolutional Neural Networks." arXiv, May 28, 2019. *https://arxiv.org/abs/1905.11946*.

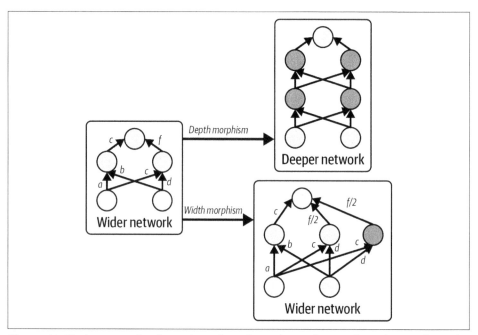

Figure 11-10. An example of morphism-based searching, showing how the topology of a network is morphed to achieve a more optimal configuration

Model validation. Once the network architecture has been decided upon, as shown in Figure 11-6, the model needs to be validated. In principle, validation is simply model evaluation. However, conducting a full evaluation as part of the automation pipeline can be expensive. As a result, lightweight evaluation approaches are often adopted. Some examples of lightweight evaluation methods are:

Low-fidelity evaluation
    Low-fidelity evaluation is about reducing the complexity of validation. Approaches like reducing sample dimensionality by reducing the input (e.g., image) size or conducting validation on a subset of the input data are often used, either independently or in combination.

Shared evaluation
    Another way to speed up validation is by reusing previously explored and validated searches. For example, the Transfer Neural AutoML method[26] is able to speed up automation significantly by sharing weights with smaller networks and

---

26 Wong, Catherine, Neil Houlsby, Yifeng Lu, and Andrea Gesmundo. 2019. "Transfer Learning with Neural AutoML." arXiv, January 28, 2019. *https://arxiv.org/abs/1803.02780*.

leveraging their validation performance as a reward to update the controller for the task at hand.

Evaluation by proxy

With this approach, the model/architecture selection and evaluation is done using a proxy dataset that is much smaller but representative of the problem space. We discussed selection by proxy in "Volume reduction via approximation" on page 342.

Short-circuit evaluation

Short-circuiting optimization and evaluation in early stages of convergence is also an effective technique to manage computation budget.

Simulating optimization behavior with Daydream

As discussed earlier, efficiency becomes critical when you scale up. Throughout this book, you have read about several techniques to achieve efficiencies, including mixed-precision training, use of a coreset, and *n*-bit optimizations (e.g., 8-bit optimization via `bitsandbytes`), discussed in Chapters 4 and 10. However, simply exploring which of these techniques may lead to fruitful results can itself be expensive.

Daydream,[27] part of Microsoft's Project Fiddle (*https://oreil.ly/-kFzW*), pursues the idea of simulating your workload in an effort to provide a quick turnaround in identifying the most helpful techniques in scaling and efficiency. It achieves this by tracking dependencies at the GPU kernel level, mapping tasks to network layers, and modeling diverse neural network optimizations. Table 11-1 shows two categories of optimizations aimed at by Daydream alongside possible strategies that it can explore. Most of the techniques mentioned in this table have already been discussed in previous chapters.

Table 11-1. Examples of Daydream optimization goals and strategies explored to meet them

Optimization	Strategy
Improving hardware utilization in single-worker settings	Increasing mini-batch size by reducing memory footprint (see "Memory Tricks for Efficiency" on page 142)
	Reducing precision (automatic mixed precision)
	Fusing kernels/layers (e.g., FusedAdam, XLA)
	Improving low-level kernel implementation (e.g., BatchNorm reconstruction[a], tensor compression)

---

27 Zhu, Hongyu, Amar Phanishayee, and Gennady Pekhimenko. 2020. "Daydream: Accurately Estimating the Efficacy of Optimizations for DNN Training." arXiv, June 5, 2020. *https://arxiv.org/abs/2006.03318*.

Optimization	Strategy
Lowering communication overhead in distributed training	Reducing communication workloads (deep gradient compression)
	Improving communication efficiency by interleaving

[a] Jung, Wonkyung, Daejin Jung, and Byeongho Kim, Sunjung Lee, Wonjong Rhee, and Jung Ho Ahn. 2019. "Restructuring Batch Normalization to Accelerate CNN Training." arXiv, March 1, 2019. *https://arxiv.org/abs/1807.01702*.

Figure 11-11 shows a simulation conducted by Daydream. It first constructs a dependency graph using the CUDA Profiling Tools Interface (CUPTI) for kernel-level measurements, then maps the graph to network usage to extrapolate the implications of adjusting the required network bandwidth by estimating the bandwidth required during all-reduce operations. These simulations inform the techniques useful in achieving overall efficiency.

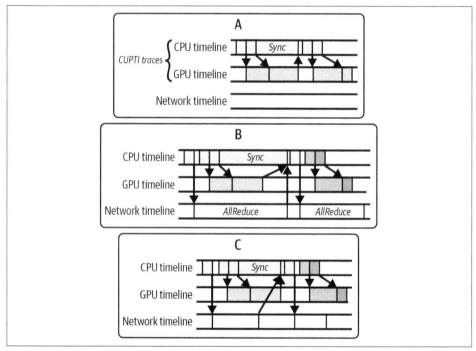

Figure 11-11. An example of Daydream simulation (adapted from Zhu et al., 2020)

Accelerating Learning by Increasing Expertise

In this section, you will learn about techniques to iteratively scale the model's expertise. We'll look at continuous learning, meta-learning, curriculum learning, and mixture of experts–based approaches.

Continuous learning

As the name implies, continuous learning (a.k.a. continual learning) is a training paradigm where learning continues for an indefinite period of time. There are three modes of continuous learning:

Offline

Offline continuous learning captures the use case where versions of a model with similar abilities are trained, deployed, and continually iterated on, following continuous integration and deployment strategies. Feedback captured while the current version of the model is deployed and in use is then repurposed to further retrain/fine tune it to improve its performance and abilities. Implementing offline continuous learning is not just an MLOps challenge but also a data engine and algorithmic challenge. Amassing data indefinitely requires careful management of data systems, with the seven Vs discussed in Chapter 10 in mind.

Without programs in place to efficiently select useful samples, the cost of model development can grow quite rapidly, with a corresponding drop in ROI. One way to increase training efficiency in offline continuous learning scenarios is to just fine tune on the delta dataset (i.e., data accumulated since the last release). However, if these smaller datasets are not representative (i.e., generalized), algorithmic challenges such as catastrophic forgetting,[28] may cause deterioration in model performance. To mitigate these challenges, techniques to obtain representative sets, as discussed in "Volume reduction via approximation" on page 342, may be used in combination with the delta set.

Online

Online continuous learning, a.k.a. online learning, is a concept borrowed from classical ML wherein the model is continuously updated while in use for inference. Because of intensive resource needs during backpropagation, online continuous learning has not been as popular in deep learning as in classical ML. Having said that, there are use cases, particularly in the recommendation domain, where this approach has been quite successful. One such example is ByteDance's Monolith,[29] a recommendation engine based on deep factorization

---

28 Kaushik, Prakhar, Alex Gain, Adam Kortylewski, and Alan Yuille. 2021. "Understanding Catastrophic Forgetting and Remembering in Continual Learning with Optimal Relevance Mapping." arXiv, February 22, 2021. *https://arxiv.org/abs/2102.11343*.

29 Liu, Zhuoran, Leqi Zou, Xuan Zou, Caihua Wang, Biao Zhang, Da Tang, Bolin Zhu, et al. 2022. "Monolith: Real Time Recommendation System with Collisionless Embedding Table." arXiv, September 27, 2022. *https://arxiv.org/abs/2209.07663*.

machines (DeepFM)[30] that uses online learning to leverage users' feedback. The architecture of Monolith, shown in Figure 11-12, consists of dedicated processes for training and inference, with an interface between the two processes for parameter synchronization (from training to inference).

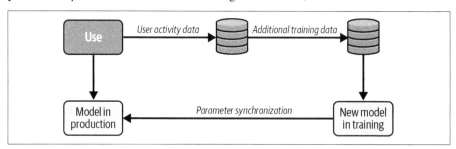

Figure 11-12. The architecture of the Monolith online recommendation engine

Active

Active learning can be seen as a middle ground between online and offline learning. In active learning, instead of labeling the entire incoming corpus of data, for purposes of efficiency the labeling is performed only on the samples identified as most useful in learning. Techniques like CRAIG and GLISTER, described in Chapter 10, are used for selecting samples in an active learning loop.

Learning to learn via meta-learning

One of the challenges of continuous learning is adapting to the growing demand to support new concepts (i.e., develop your model's abilities). For instance, if you were continually releasing improved versions of the roofing tile counting model discussed earlier in the chapter, then you would find yourself continually scaling your model's output to capture newer variants (concepts) of roof materials and tile types. While continuous improvement with existing concepts is a challenge (as discussed previously) in itself, you also have to dedicate efforts to procuring new data and labeling and processing it before you can incorporate these new concepts into your release. This is neither efficient nor a sign of an intelligent system.

Biological systems (human and animal) can efficiently reuse their existing knowledge to learn new concepts fairly quickly. The initial premise that machines can do this too

---

30 Guo, Huifeng, Ruiming Tang, Yunming Ye, Zhenguo Li, and Xiuqiang He. 2017. "DeepFM: A Factorization-Machine Based Neural Network for CTR Prediction." arXiv, March 13, 2017. *https://arxiv.org/abs/1703.04247.*

has been proven via Bayesian statistics[31] and has since expanded into the field of *meta-learning*, or learning to learn. Meta-learning applies to all subdomains of deep learning where the objective is to learn new concepts quickly; for example, learning new classes in supervised learning or adapting to new environments in reinforcement learning.

Meta-learning is similar to fine tuning (discussed in "Using transfer learning" on page 358), except in meta-learning you either have no labels at all (known as zero-shot learning) or very few labels (known as few-shot learning), whereas in fine tuning you have a much larger sample size to tune with. This section will focus mainly on few-shot learning; zero-shot learning is an inference-time technique and its exploration is left as an exercise for the reader. Few-shot/meta-learning techniques can be broadly classified into three categories, each requiring a small number of samples of new classes (called the *support set*) to fine tune the model to predict those classes:

Metric-based

Metric-based meta-learning is inspired by nearest neighbor techniques, where the distance between two samples in an embedded space is used to approximate the output for new classes/concepts. Siamese neural networks are often used for metric-based learning. With this approach, as shown in Figure 11-13, feature embeddings are extracted from a target and support set and then a distance calculation (e.g., L1 distance) is performed, leading to a binary output that can be used to determine whether the support sample is the same as the target.[32]

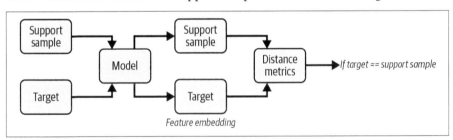

Figure 11-13. Metric-based meta-learning

31 Lake, Brenden M., Ruslan Salakhutdinov, and Joshua B. Tenenbaum. 2015. "Human-Level Concept Learning Through Probabilistic Program Induction." *Science* 350, no. 6266: 1332–1338. *https://doi.org/10.1126/science.aab3050*.

32 Malhotra, Abhiraj. 2023. "Single-Shot Image Recognition Using Siamese Neural Networks." In *Proceedings of the 2023 3rd International Conference on Advance Computing and Innovative Technologies in Engineering (ICACITE)*, 2550–53. *https://doi.org/10.1109/ICACITE57410.2023.10182466*.

Prototypical networks (protonets)[33] are a more advanced implementation of metric-based meta-learning where an embedding function is used to encode each input in the support set into an N-dimensional feature vector. Using the labels in the support set, an average feature vector for each class c is obtained. These vectors represent the prototypes that are used to approximate how close any sample is to the classes.

Memory-based

Memory-based meta-learning does not approximate based on feature vectors; rather, models based on these techniques have a specialized structure that enables learning rapidly in just a few steps. Meta Networks (MetaNet)[34] and memory-augmented neural networks (MANNs)[35] are good examples of memory-based learning; however, these networks are still in the early stages of research and development and are not yet widely used.

Optimization-based

One challenge with deep learning or any gradient-based approximation technique is that it works better for larger sample sizes. Techniques like model-agnostic meta-learning (MAML) and its more optimized version Reptile have explored adapting the traditional deep learning optimization procedure to few-shot learning.[36] MAML is a bi-level optimization process where the inner loop optimizes for the support set, updating the model parameters, while the outer loop evaluates the gradients for the loss with respect to the original parameters. Consequently, MAML requires second-order gradient computation, making it highly compute-intensive. Reptile introduces approximation and omits the second-order terms in this optimization process, making it a more adaptable option.

For a practical exercise demonstrating meta-learning techniques, see "Hands-On Exercise #6: Meta-Learning" on page 389. Few-shot learning is also applied in context as a training-free, inference-only adaptation technique that's more applicable in the scope of foundation models (discussed in Chapter 13).

---

33 Snell, Jake, Kevin Swersky, and Richard S. Zemel. 2017. "Prototypical Networks for Few-Shot Learning." arXiv, June 19, 2017. *https://arxiv.org/abs/1703.05175*.

34 Munkhdalai, Tsendsuren, and Hong Yu. 2017. "Meta Networks." arXiv, June 8, 2017. *https://arxiv.org/abs/1703.00837*.

35 Santoro, Adam, Sergey Bartunov, Matthew Botvinick, Daan Wierstra, and Timothy Lillicrap. 2016. "One-Shot Learning with Memory-Augmented Neural Networks." arXiv, May 19, 2016. *https://arxiv.org/abs/1605.06065*.

36 Finn, Chelsea, Pieter Abbeel, and Sergey Levine. 2017. "Model-Agnostic Meta-Learning for Fast Adaptation of Deep Networks." arXiv, July 18, 2017. *https://arxiv.org/abs/1703.03400*; Nichol, Alex, Joshua Achiam, and John Schulman. 2018. "On First-Order Meta-Learning Algorithms." arXiv, October 22, 2018. *https://arxiv.org/abs/1803.02999*.

Curriculum learning

Curriculum learning is inspired by the fundamental principle of effective learning: start simple and build up complexity gradually.[37] Most biological learning follows this principle. At a coarse level, curriculum learning can be observed in two modes:

Data-based

> In data-based curriculum learning, you rank your data on a scale of easy to hard to learn from and define a data sampling strategy that samples simple samples first and increments the complexity during later phases of the training. The techniques discussed in "Handling imbalance" on page 327 can be helpful to stratify samples in this way.

Model-based

> In model-based curriculum learning, the complexity is derived from the model architecture/layers. Use of progressive layer dropout (for Transformer-based models) is a good example of model-based curriculum learning.[38]

Model-based curriculum learning is not as widely explored as data-based curriculum learning, so this section will mainly focus on the former. In effect, this is a collection of data sampling and selection tricks that are used in conjunction with the learning schedule to progressively guide the learning. Curriculum learning has also been used in stabilizing training of large language models by slowly increasing sequence length via sequence length warmup.[39]

One interesting variant of curriculum learning is known as self-paced learning, where sample complexity is derived from the model's performance itself (meaning categorization of samples will vary as the model progresses through the learning stages). Leveraging approaches discussed in Chapter 10, such as selection by gradient approximation, importance, or loss (see "Volume reduction via approximation" on page 342), can be quite useful. Self-paced curriculum learning[40] can also be adopted in automated learning regimes, as discussed in "AutoML" on page 364.

---

37 Bengio, Yoshua, Jérôme Louradour, Ronan Collobert, and Jason Weston. 2009. "Curriculum Learning." In *Proceedings of the 26th Annual International Conference on Machine Learning (ICML '09)*, 41–48. *https:// doi.org/10.1145/1553374.1553380*.

38 Zhang, Minjia, and Yuxiong He. 2020. "Accelerating Training of Transformer-Based Language Models with Progressive Layer Dropping." arXiv, October 26, 2020. *https://arxiv.org/abs/2010.13369*.

39 Li, Conglong, Minjia Zhang, and Yuxiong He. 2022. "The Stability-Efficiency Dilemma: Investigating Sequence Length Warmup for Training GPT Models." arXiv, October 16, 2022. *https://arxiv.org/abs/ 2108.06084*.

40 Guo, Yong, Yaofo Chen, Yin Zheng, Peilin Zhao, Jian Chen, Junzhou Huang, and Mingkui Tan. 2020. "Breaking the Curse of Space Explosion: Towards Efficient NAS with Curriculum Search." arXiv, August 5, 2020. *https://arxiv.org/abs/2007.07197*.

Mixture of experts

In Part II of this book, you learned about scaling out your model development using a variety of approaches, such as data parallelism and model parallelism. These techniques help you obtain a scaled-up model that's been trained to perform your task. As discussed in Chapter 6, if your task is complex, you might want to explore developing multiple models for the same task. This is a special type of scale-out where horizontal scaling is performed along the model dimension. Each model is trained slightly differently, either with a different subset of the data or with different initial weights or configurations. The independently trained models (i.e., task experts) each contribute to the final outcome at a fixed rate, either equally or via weighted averaging, with the ensemble typically achieving better statistical performance than any of its independent parts.

The computational cost of ensembles increases linearly, as all experts need to be trained and inferred jointly. Mixture of experts (MoE)[41] is an alternative approach that aims to minimize the computational expense while maximizing the accuracy of the outputs. With MoE, n experts are trained jointly on different parts of the task, and a learnable gating module selects a fraction of the experts to process each sample of the batch. Each training sample is thus sent to a selected k experts among the available n experts. Because of the dynamic routing implemented by the gating module, the number of samples processed by each expert can vary and be less than the full batch size. This challenge, known as the *shrinking batch problem*, can be mitigated by leveraging data, model, or hybrid parallelism to scale out the batch size to be large enough to still be informative to experts.

MoE is in effect a single model wherein parts of the network are activated based on the gating logic. Chen et al.[42] explored how this approach improves neural network learning and whether there is a risk of the mixture model collapsing into a single model. They identified nonlinearity of the experts as a crucial property leading to more successful use of MoE. This can be seen in Figure 11-14, where the nonlinear experts result in more accurate and well-defined decision boundaries than their linear counterparts.

41 Shazeer, Noam, Azalia Mirhoseini, Krzysztof Maziarz, Andy Davis, Quoc Le, Geoffrey Hinton, and Jeff Dean. 2017. "Outrageously Large Neural Networks: The Sparsely-Gated Mixture-of-Experts Layer." arXiv, January 23, 2017. *https://arxiv.org/abs/1701.06538*.

42 Chen, Zixiang, Yihe Deng, Yue Wu, Quanquan Gu, and Yuanzhi Li. 2022. "Towards Understanding Mixture of Experts in Deep Learning." arXiv, August 4, 2022. *https://arxiv.org/abs/2208.02813*.

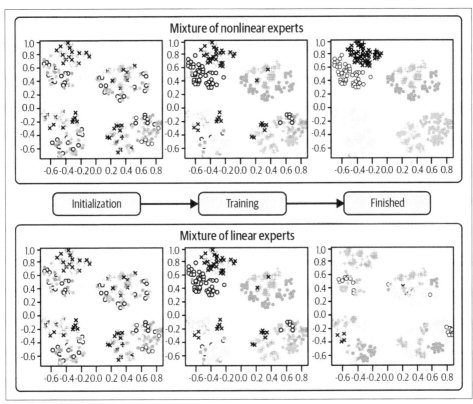

Figure 11-14. Nonlinear experts have better decision boundaries in MoE (adapted from Chen et al., 2022)

Stabilized training with MoE is a challenge considering that early in training "experts" are not "experts" yet, and the gating logic needs to be learned jointly. There is a risk of skewing toward a random expert, especially during the early phases of training. Limiting the maximal fraction of batches that can go to an expert can help build stability. This concept, termed the *capacity factor*, was introduced in the Switch Transformer,[43] which extends MoE concepts with top-k experts selection while ensuring each expert gets an appropriate distribution of samples. As a result of these tricks, a Switch Transformer model with 1.6T parameters has the same compute requirements as a 10B-parameter dense model.

43 Fedus, William, Barret Zoph, and Noam Shazeer. 2022. "Switch Transformers: Scaling to Trillion Parameter Models with Simple and Efficient Sparsity." arXiv, June 16, 2022. *https://arxiv.org/abs/2101.03961*.

In addition, frameworks like GShard and DeepSpeed, discussed in Chapters 8 and 9, can leverage the sparsity of MoE to provide further efficiencies.[44] GShard, for instance, can train 600B-parameter models using fewer compute resources than would be needed for a 100B-parameter dense model.

Riquelme et al. explored the use of sparse MoE in conjunction with Vision Transformers, where patches of images (see Figure 11-15) were suitably routed to dense experts following multihead attention.[45] In this work, known as V-MoE (*https://github.com/google-research/vmoe*), a technique known as Batch Prioritized Routing was used, where only important and useful patches were routed and the rest were dropped.

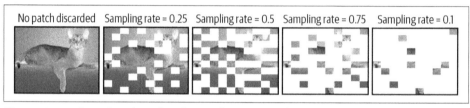

Figure 11-15. Samples of patches dropped as per Batch Prioritized Routing at different capacity (C) levels

For a practical example of using the MoE approach, see "Hands-On Exercise #4: Mixture of Experts" on page 386.

Learning with Scarce Supervision

Despite it being more successful and widely adopted than unsupervised learning, due to data procurement and labeling expenses, practicing supervised learning can be very expensive. This is true especially when you are building a custom model requiring highly specialized data. The path to more efficient and nuanced learning is learning from multiple sources and modalities, and infusing the knowledge across domains while requiring as little supervision as possible.

44 Lepikhin, Dmitry, HyoukJoong Lee, Yuanzhong Xu, Dehao Chen, Orhan Firat, Yanping Huang, Maxim Krikun, Noam Shazeer, and Zhifeng Chen. 2020. "GShard: Scaling Giant Models with Conditional Computation and Automatic Sharding." arXiv, June 30, 2020. *https://arxiv.org/abs/2006.16668*; Rajbhandari, Samyam, Conglong Li, Zhewei Yao, Minjia Zhang, Reza Yazdani Aminabadi, Ammar Ahmad Awan, Jeff Rasley, and Yuxiong He. 2022. "DeepSpeed-MoE: Advancing Mixture-of-Experts Inference and Training to Power Next-Generation AI Scale." arXiv, July 21, 2022. *https://arxiv.org/abs/2201.05596*.

45 Riquelme, Carlos, Joan Puigcerver, Basil Mustafa, Maxim Neumann, Rodolphe Jenatton, André Susano Pinto, Daniel Keysers, and Neil Houlsby. 2021. "Scaling Vision with Sparse Mixture of Experts." arXiv, June 10, 2021. *https://arxiv.org/abs/2106.05974*.

Self-supervised learning

As Yann LeCun argues in "A Path Towards Autonomous Machine Intelligence," the next phase of evolution in deep learning will come from joint learning of various specialized models trained with minimal supervision.[46] Self-supervised learning, approaches to which are extensively covered in Randall Balestriero et al.'s recipe-style "cookbook," forms a key part of this vision.[47] Self-supervision is still an active area of research, but it is increasingly used in two modes: learning from no labels, or supervised fine tuning of a self-supervised network (as discussed in "Pretraining" on page 360), where self-supervised training is conducted over a large corpus of data, followed by supervised fine tuning on a much smaller dataset.

With self-supervision, samples are augmented to obtain multiple variants. These variants of the same samples are then compared and contrasted to learn representative features. As discussed in "Handling too-low variety" on page 321, in a supervised context, research has shown that samples can be varied up to 1,000 times before the model learns enough from them that further augmentations are not helpful.[48] In self-supervised learning, however, augmentations play an even more important role in guiding attention to key features relevant for the task. Because of this approach of comparing and contrasting different pairs of samples, this technique is known as *contrastive learning*.

Contrastive learning

Contrastive learning is a special class of self-supervision. It's not just a data trick, but also a modeling trick. In this approach, different versions of a sample are shown to the model, and the model's objective is to ensure that the embedding it generates for these versions of the same data is very similar (e.g., using the cosine similarity index). A popular objective function in this context is Info Noise-Contrastive Estimation (InfoNCE).[49] The models/encoders trained using contrastive learning can be used on their own for use cases where feature embedding is required (e.g., search scenarios) or can be further extended (e.g., using a regression head for segmentation or classification tasks).

---

46 LeCun, Yann. 2022. "A Path Towards Autonomous Machine Intelligence." Version 0.9.2, 2022-06-27. *https://openreview.net/forum?id=BZ5a1r-kVsf*.

47 Balestriero, Randall, Mark Ibrahim, Vlad Sobal, Ari Morcos, Shashank Shekhar, Tom Goldstein, Florian Bordes, et al. 2023. "A Cookbook of Self-Supervised Learning." arXiv, June 28, 2023. *https://arxiv.org/abs/2304.12210*.

48 Balestriero, Randall, Ishan Misra, and Yann LeCun. 2022. "A Data-Augmentation Is Worth a Thousand Samples: Exact Quantification from Analytical Augmented Sample Moments." arXiv, February 16, 2022. *https://arxiv.org/abs/2202.08325*.

49 van den Oord, Aaron, Yazhe Li, and Oriol Vinyals. 2019. "Representation Learning with Contrastive Predictive Coding." arXiv, January 22, 2019. *https://arxiv.org/abs/1807.03748*.

SimCLR is an early framework for contrastive learning leveraging one modality of data per sample (e.g., either image or text).[50] The data flow for this is shown in Figure 11-16. CLIP, mentioned earlier in this chapter, expands this to leverage multimodal data; it extracts knowledge from both image and text inputs while also learning the interoperability between the two.[51] The data flow for this is also shown in Figure 11-16.

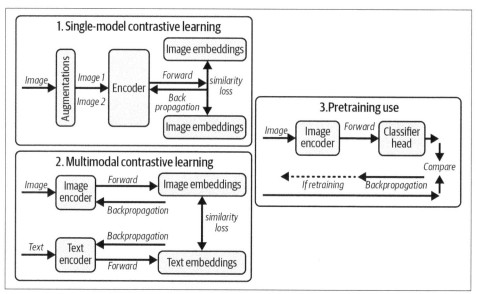

Figure 11-16. Contrastive learning: single-model, multimodal, and pretraining use cases

For a practical example demonstrating this technique, see "Hands-On Exercise #5: Contrastive Learning" on page 388.

Hands-On Exercises

In this section, you'll find six hands-on exercises to help you practice some of the techniques discussed in this chapter.

---

50 Chen, Ting, Simon Kornblith, Mohammad Norouzi, and Geoffrey Hinton. 2020. "A Simple Framework for Contrastive Learning of Visual Representations." arXiv, July 1, 2020. *https://arxiv.org/abs/2002.05709*.

51 Pushkarna et al., "Data Cards," *https://arxiv.org/abs/2204.01075*.

Hands-On Exercise #1: Transfer Learning

Transfer learning is a popular approach; in fact, you used it in the UNetSegmentation Model in the scene parsing example (hands-on exercise #2) in Chapter 4. The following snippet from the *chapter_4/vision_model.py* script (*https://oreil.ly/NV7ez*) shows that the encoder used from the timm module is actually loaded with pretrained weights (in this case, trained with the ImageNet dataset):

```python
class UNetSegmentationModel(torch.nn.Module):
    def __init__(
        self,
        in_channels: int = 3,
        depth: int = 5,
        decoder_channels: List[int] = (256, 128, 64, 32, 16),
        num_classes: int = 151,
    ):
        super().__init__()
        encoder = timm.create_model(
            "efficientnet_b2",
            pretrained=True,
            features_only=True,
            output_stride=32,
            in_chans=in_channels,
            out_indices=tuple(range(depth)),
        )
```

In this example, you transferred the encoder's ability to extract features from Image-Net to the SceneParse150 dataset.

Hands-On Exercise #2: Hyperparameter Optimization

In this exercise you will use Optuna (*https://optuna.org*) to extend the scene parsing exercise from Chapter 4 to practice hyperparameter tuning in a distributed setting.

The code for this exercise is located in the *hpo.py* script (*https://oreil.ly/sBkai*) in the GitHub repository. It requires a Postgres database, where trial stats will be stored. You can use Docker to create the database, with a command similar to the following:

```
docker run --name postgres -e POSTGRES_PASSWORD=postgres -p 5432:5432 -d postgres
```

To SSH into the container, use:

```
docker exec -it postgres bash
```

Then run the command psql -U postgres -W postgres to obtain a Postgres prompt, where you can create the database you need using the following command:

```
CREATE DATABASE study_db;
```

In the following code snippet, note the use of Postgres for storage:

```
study = optuna.create_study(
    sampler=optuna.samplers.TPESampler(),
    pruner=optuna.pruners.HyperbandPruner(),
    storage=
        f"postgresql://{study_db_user}:{study_db_pwd}@postgres:5432/{study_db}",
    study_name="scene-parsing",
)
```

This study (collection of trials) is then executed by calling the `optimize` API, which takes the `_optuna_objectives` function and the number of trials as arguments and conducts independent training for each trial:

```
study.optimize(_optuna_objectives, n_trials=2)
```

Once you've created the database, you can run the exercise using the following command:

```
deep-learning-at-scale chapter_11 hpo train
```

You can use Optuna Dashboard to visualize the trial progress by running the following command:

```
optuna-dashboard postgresql+psycopg2://postgres:postgres@hostname:5432/study_db
```

Hands-On Exercise #3: Knowledge Distillation

In this exercise, you will explore offline response-based distillation using the Fashion MNIST dataset (*https://oreil.ly/t2Vzb*). First, you will train an EfficientNet-B4, a 17.6M-parameter model, as a teacher for this image classification task. Then, you will distill its knowledge to a smaller EfficientNet-B0, a 4M-parameter model. The code for this exercise is available in the *distillation.py* script (*https://oreil.ly/l3rna*) in the example repository. You can use the following command to run this example; it will first train the teacher (the EfficientNet-B4 model), then it will begin training the EfficientNet-B0 model in offline mode:

```
deep-learning-at-scale chapter_11 distill train
```

Note the use of `TimmLightningModule` in the example code. This is a lightweight wrapper around Hugging Face's `timm` library (*https://oreil.ly/vMrJc*), which is trained with the Fashion MNIST dataset. The data-loading module for this is defined as `MNISTDataModule`. The distillation training occurs in the `DistillationLightning Module`. The key logic enabling distillation is shown here:

```
def forward(self, inputs):
    with torch.no_grad():
        teachers_logits = self.teacher_model(inputs)
        students_logits = self.model(inputs)
    return {"teachers_logits": teachers_logits,
            "students_logits": students_logits}

def _common_step(self, batch, batch_idx, key: str):
```

```
images, labels = batch
result_dict = self(images)
teachers_logits, students_logits = (
    result_dict["teachers_logits"],
    result_dict["students_logits"],
)
    predictions = students_logits.argmax(1)

distill_loss = self.distill_loss_fn(teachers_logits, students_logits)
student_loss = self.student_loss_fn(students_logits, labels.long())
loss = distill_loss + student_loss
```

Here, the teacher predicts in offline mode. Its logits are used to calculate the distillation loss, which contributes 50% of the loss, whereas the student's logits are used to calculate both cross-entropy loss and distillation loss. The student_loss_fn is simply cross-entropy loss; the distill_loss_fn is shown here:

```
class DistillationLoss(torch.nn.Module):
    def __init__(
        self,
        temperature: float = 0.5,
        num_classes: int = 10,
    ):
        super().__init__()
        self.temperature = temperature
        self.register_buffer(
            "weights", torch.Tensor([self.temperature**2] * num_classes)
        )

    def forward(self, student_logits: torch.Tensor,
                teacher_logits: torch.Tensor):
        teacher_probs = torch.nn.functional.softmax(
            teacher_logits / self.temperature, dim=0
        )
        kd_loss = torch.nn.functional.cross_entropy(
            student_logits / self.temperature, teacher_probs, self.weights
        )

        return kd_loss
```

The effective workflow used in this exercise is shown in Figure 11-17.

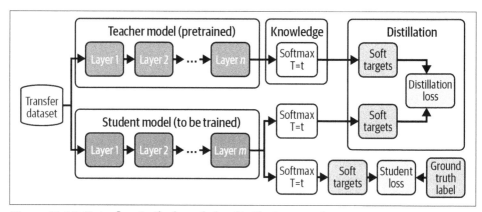

Figure 11-17. Data flow in the knowledge distillation exercise

As discussed in "Knowledge distillation" on page 360, the loss computed here is based on soft labels and is scaled with temperature scaling.

You will note that while the teacher trains for a full 15 epochs, achieving an F1 score of 0.76, the student, despite being smaller, is actually clocking a validation F1 score of ~0.9 after the third epoch. Here, the student's training comes to an early stop at the fifth epoch, where it achieves a test F1 score of 0.899.

To get a baseline for comparison, you can train just the student using the following command:

```
deep-learning-at-scale chapter_11 distill train-student-baseline
```

In this case, you will note that even at epoch 8 your validation F1 score is still only at ~0.7, and the training continues for a full 14 epochs, achieving the same F1 score as the teacher (0.76) on the test set. In conclusion, by using distillation you have not only reused the knowledge of the teacher model and sped up your training time, but also gained a significant statistical performance improvement.

Hands-On Exercise #4: Mixture of Experts

In this section, you will revisit MoE (discussed in "Mixture of experts" on page 378). First, you will look at a mock implementation of simple gating logic that selects the top two experts. Then, you'll look at another MoE implementation using the Deep-Speed library.

Mock MoE

The code for this example is located in the *moe.py* script (*https://oreil.ly/SUkdA*) in the code repository and can be executed using the following command:

```
deep-learning-at-scale chapter_11 moe run
```

Let's say you have an MoE model that has a gating module followed by a fake set of experts. The experts, conveniently defined in the module Experts, in this case are simple MLP layers with a LeakyReLU layer between them. The gating module, Top2ThresholdGating, has a capacity_factor of 1.5 and 2 for training and evaluation, respectively. This module applies the top-1 criterion to select a sequential nonoverlapping expert routing map for all samples in each batch. This routing tensor is then used in the forward call, as follows:

```
def forward(self, inputs, **kwargs):
    routing_tensor = self.gate(inputs)
    expert_inputs = torch.einsum(
        "bnd,bnec->ebcd", inputs, routing_tensor.bool().to(inputs)
    )

    # Now feed the expert inputs through the experts.
    orig_shape = expert_inputs.shape
    expert_inputs = expert_inputs.reshape(self.num_experts, -1,
                                          inputs.shape[-1])
    expert_outputs = self.experts(expert_inputs)
    expert_outputs = expert_outputs.reshape(*orig_shape)

    output = torch.einsum("ebcd,bnec->bnd", expert_outputs, routing_tensor)
    return output
```

You may note here that the input tensors are of dimension [batch, group_dimen sion, feature_dimension], whereas the routing_tensor has a shape of [batch, group_dimension, experts, capacity]. The experts' input is obtained by transforming the input per the routing map, which is then passed on to the respective experts. By this logic, two experts provide output per sample; however, the final output is obtained by transforming the output tensor according to the routing map.

DeepSpeed-MoE

In Chapters 7 and 8 discussed scaling model training using DeepSpeed-based ZeRO techniques. In this exercise, you will see how to extend your MoE model to support conditional computation using DeepSpeed-MoE so that you can leverage ZeRO for distributed training efficiency.

You'll be doing a side-by-side comparison of the model used in the MNIST exercise from Chapter 2 with a newer version extended with DeepSpeed-MoE. The code for the new version is in the *deepspeed_moe.py* script (*https://oreil.ly/pPfB5*) in the Git-Hub repository, whereas the code for its baseline counterpart is in the *mnist_moe_baseline.py* script (*https://oreil.ly/oBthW*). The architecture of the baseline model is exactly the same as the version you used in Chapter 2, while the updated model has an MoE layer stack right before the logits layer, as shown in the following snippet:

```
self.moe = deepspeed.moe.layer.MoE(
    hidden_size=hidden_size,
    expert=expert,
    num_experts=6,
    ep_size=2,
    use_residual=False,
    k=2,
    min_capacity=0,
    noisy_gate_policy="Jitter",
)
```

Here, six experts, each of which is an MLP (i.e., nn.Linear(hidden_size, hid den_size)), are added, with each sample only getting two experts' opinions at a time. You may also note the use of jitter to stabilize the learning.

To run this exercise, you will need one node with at least two GPUs. The results documented here are based on two V100 NVIDIA GPUs. You can run your baseline using the following command:

```
deep-learning-at-scale chapter_11 mnist-baseline train
```

You should obtain a test set accuracy of 0.97, with the test set loss sitting at about 0.08.

To run the MoE version, use the following command:

```
deepspeed \
    --num_nodes=1 \
    --num_gpus=2 \
    --bind_cores_to_rank \
    deep_learning_at_scale/chapter_11/mnist_deepspeed.py
```

The test set accuracy should be slightly higher, at about 0.973, with a loss of 0.10.

Hands-On Exercise #5: Contrastive Learning

In this example you will revisit contrastive learning, discussed in "Contrastive learning" on page 381. The code is available in the *contrastive_learning.py* script (*https://oreil.ly/Oaq29*) in the GitHub repository and can be executed as follows:

```
deep-learning-at-scale chapter_11 cl train
```

This exercise extends the MNIST exercise from Chapter 2. Here, you will omit the use of labels in the training process to simulate contrastive learning and use transforms to create augmented copies of the provided samples. ContrastiveTransforms applies random perspective changes and affine transformations and adds color jitter and Gaussian blur to create two versions of each input. These transforms were chosen to make sure the digit's integrity remains intact (which might not be the case if crop transforms were applied, for example).

Use of `ContrastiveTransforms` in the loader doubles the number of input images, turning each one into a pair. These paired images are used in the `NCELoss` function, which calculates the cosine similarity of the samples and scales it by a temperature factor, per the InfoNCE loss formulation.[52] On the model side, `MNISTModel` module has two submodules, `encoder` and `fc`, representing the feature encoder and a fake simulation of the classification head, respectively.

Upon running the exercise, you should see that both training and validation loss decrease, indicating that learning is taking place. Note that this is a toy example to demonstrate the role of augmentation and contrastive loss in self-supervised training. In this example, the MNIST classification labels are not used in learning.

Hands-On Exercise #6: Meta-Learning

Phillip Lippe has developed a very good hands-on exercise for meta-learning. You can find it in the University of Virginia's Deep Learning Tutorials (*https://oreil.ly/ c2Wno*).

Summary

In Parts I and II of this book, you learned various techniques for scaling model development and your training workload. A natural extension to this is understanding the nuances of how to control input and other parameters to get the most out of the data you have at hand. In Chapter 10, you read about the seven Vs of data and looked at different ways to maximize your investment in data in order to develop a high-performing model. The objective of this chapter was to arm you with a set of techniques and a mental model for experiment planning so you can start conducting experiments and incrementally adding value to your model through a series of iterations.

In this chapter, you read about the importance of planning your experiments and getting properly set up for iterative execution. You also read about some of the tools you can use to facilitate these processes. You then learned about four categories of techniques to accelerate model development iteration, with a focus on speeding up convergence, automation, increasing expertise, and iterating when labels are scarce. To extend your learning, this chapter also provided some practical exercises demonstrating several of these techniques.

---

52 van den Oord, "Representation Learning with Contrastive Predictive Coding," *https://arxiv.org/abs/ 1807.03748.*

## CHAPTER 12

Efficient Fine-Tuning of Large Models

As discussed in the preceding chapters of this book, the capacity of deep learning models is rapidly increasing. The scaling law of deep learning (discussed in Chapter 1) is still fuelling (over)parameterization, to the extent that human brain–scale models with hundreds of trillions of parameters have been built.[1] The general industry trend is departing from the battle-tested approach of developing small, purpose-built models for specific tasks to rapidly adapting large, general-purpose models to the task at hand, through the use of fine-tuning and meta-learning techniques like the ones discussed in Chapter 11. While this newer approach, which you will read more about in Chapter 13, may be more economical in terms of development cost, its efficacy is still relatively untested.

This shift is welcome because of its potential to minimize development time and reduce the time to production. However, in line with the "no free lunch" theorem, it comes with its own challenges—for example, when dealing with limited hardware resources. This chapter focuses on the approach of adapting a larger model for a specific task and extends the discussion of fine tuning from the previous chapter, introducing two new techniques: Low-Rank Adaptation (LoRA), which allows you to efficiently fine tune large models on limited-capacity hardware, and its quantized version, QLoRA, which provides further memory efficiencies by using mixed precision. This discussion will be supported by a practical exercise demonstrating the use of QLoRA on the 7B-parameter version of the LLaMA large language model.

---

1 Ma, Zixuan, Jiaao He, Jiezhong Qiu, Huanqi Cao, Yuanwei Wang, Zhenbo Sun, Liyan Zheng, et al. 2022. "BaGuaLu: Targeting Brain Scale Pretrained Models with Over 37 Million Cores." In *Proceedings of the 27th ACM SIGPLAN Symposium on Principles and Practice of Parallel Programming (PPoPP '22)*, 192–204. *https:// doi.org/10.1145/3503221.3508417*.

Review of Fine-Tuning Techniques

Before diving into low-rank adaptation methods, let's summarize the types of fine-tuning methods available today. All of these, with the exception of low-rank tuning, were discussed in Chapter 11. Revisiting them in the context of parameter-efficient tuning will help you appreciate the pros and cons of each one.

Standard Fine Tuning

In standard fine tuning (Figure 12-1), discussed in "Using transfer learning" on page 358, an already trained model with learned weights is trained again with a separate, more nuanced or customized dataset suitable for your task. In this case, the model architecture does not change at all but the parameter values are improved to adapt to new tasks. For instance, you might fine tune a general-purpose GPT model for the healthcare domain so it can be adapted for various tasks, such as patient history summarization.

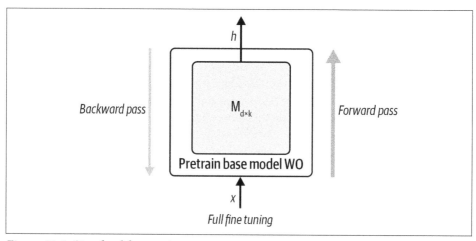

Figure 12-1. Standard fine tuning

Because the new model has the same number of parameters, standard fine tuning has the same compute requirements as the original model, although the data requirements may vary. Techniques like RLHF and other data-centric tricks mentioned in Chapter 10 can reduce the data volume requirements if high veracity and variety can be maintained in a smaller dataset. In addition, the training time and therefore the monetary cost of fine tuning is generally much lower than training from scratch, due to faster convergence. For example, while it took 53 days to train the purpose-built

50B-parameter finance model BloombergGPT,[2] at an estimated cost of about 2.7M, AI4Finance's FinGPT (*https://oreil.ly/Kvf12*) can be fine tuned much more quickly, for a cost of under 300.

The inference time compute cost of a standard fine-tuned model is also the same as the original model. However, this approach does not scale well to multitask environments where each task requires custom tuning, due to increased training and deployment burdens.

Meta-Learning (Zero-/Few-Shot Learning)

Meta-learning (Figure 12-2), as discussed in the previous chapter, either requires no labels or a small number of examples to adapt to the new domain. When explored in a training setting, the compute requirements for meta-learning are similar to those for standard fine tuning, except for the size of the dataset, which may be close to single digits. Meta-learning is also applied as an inference-only trick using large, general-purpose models where training is not needed and simple text instructions are sufficient for adaptation. This category of adaptation, popularly known as prompt engineering, is beyond the scope of this book.

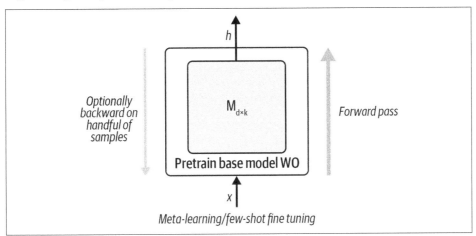

Figure 12-2. Meta-learning/few-shot fine tuning

Adapter-Based Fine Tuning

Adapter-based tuning (Figure 12-3) is a special type of fine tuning where custom layers/heads are appended at the end of the network. During training, these heads are

2 Wu, Shijie, Ozan Irsoy, Steven Lu, Vadim Dabravolski, Mark Dredze, Sebastian Gehrmann, Prabhanjan Kambadur, David Rosenberg, and Gideon Mann. 2023. "BloombergGPT: A Large Language Model for Finance." arXiv, December 21, 2023. *https://arxiv.org/abs/2303.17564.*

expected to adapt to the desired tasks, with the backbone of the network optionally trained in line with standard fine tuning. This kind of tuning is required when your task is too custom to adapt from a general-purpose model. For example, if you wanted to train a question answering model, you could use a general-purpose autoregressive language model as a backbone and attach a Q&A head to it. You could then either freeze the backbone or fully fine tune it to adapt the model for Q&A. Likewise, you could also adapt this general-purpose model for entity recognition tasks, for example. During training, your task-specific heads are learning to perform the desired task (e.g., Q&A) with your specialized dataset.

With this approach, if you perform standard fine tuning, the compute requirements are generally higher than those of the base model. However, if the backbone is frozen, the training time compute requirements can be a lot smaller. At inference time, the compute requirements increase with adaptation layers due to the extra computation required by the newly added head(s). This challenge increases with the complexity of the desired task (e.g., in multitask scenarios that may require more than one head).

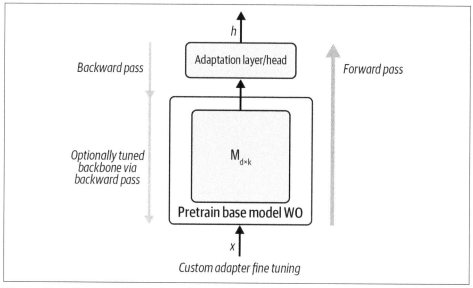

Figure 12-3. Custom adapter-based fine tuning

Low-Rank Tuning

Standard fine tuning of a large model is very expensive. Adding adaptation layers/ heads, as discussed in the previous section, increases the capacity of the model, but also increases the risk of overparameterization. The backbone can be frozen for efficiency, but in this case the risk of obtaining a suboptimal model increases. In other words, none of these techniques are befitting for large models. Low-rank tuning is a recent innovation that addresses some of these challenges. The rest of this chapter is focused on low-rank fine tuning of large models.

LoRA—Parameter-Efficient Fine Tuning

Low-rank tuning seeks to mitigate the previously described risks by selectively updating a subset of the base model's parameters. This partial update strategy minimizes the compute requirements of large models. Additionally, since the base model itself is being updated, the risk of overparameterization is mitigated.

Low-rank tuning was inspired by the finding that large pretrained models can learn efficiently in a smaller parameter space.[3] Mathematically, if the weight matrix of the pretrained model is given as W_0 and is of dimension $d \times k$, then its forward pass for input x will yield $h = W_0 x$. For low-rank tuning, a hyperparameter r (for rank) is chosen that is much smaller than the smallest dimension of the weight matrix (i.e., $\min(d, k)$) itself. The rank r defines the subset of parameters that will be updated during fine tuning, given by $\Delta W = BA$, where A and B are of dimensions $r \times k$ and $d \times r$ and are initialized with random Gaussian values and 0, respectively. Since $B = 0$ at the beginning of training, for $h = W_0 x$ the forward pass of the fine-tuned model yields the following:

$$
\begin{aligned}
h \quad &= W_0 x + \Delta W x \\
&= W_0 x + BAx
\end{aligned}
$$

Since r is very small, the fine tuning is happening in a decomposed low-rank matrix space with both A and B of rather small size. This is shown in Figure 12-4.

This allows for much faster training of large models on devices with a relatively small memory footprint. With LoRA, VRAM usage can be reduced by up to 3x.[4] In addition, LoRA offers easier adaptation for specialized multitask fine tuning. Due to the linear composability of the base pretrained model and low-rank matrices, deployment and inference are a lot easier to manage as well; the base model's output can be reused across multiple tasks as needed along with their respective low-compute-intensive LoRA weights. In the event that such composition is not required, the

3 Aghajanyan, Armen, Luke Zettlemoyer, and Sonal Gupta. 2020. "Intrinsic Dimensionality Explains the Effectiveness of Language Model Fine-Tuning." arXiv, December 22, 2020. *http://arxiv.org/abs/2012.13255*; Hu, Edward J., Yelong Shen, Phillip Wallis, Zeyuan Allen-Zhu, Yuanzhi Li, Shean Wang, Lu Wang, and Weizhu Chen. 2021. "LoRA: Low-Rank Adaptation of Large Language Models." arXiv, October 16, 2021. *http://arxiv.org/abs/2106.09685*.

4 Hu et al., "LoRA: Low-Rank Adaptation of Large Language Models," *http://arxiv.org/abs/2106.09685*.

weights $W_0 + BA$ can be fused and stored to remove any inference latency that might otherwise surface as a result of branch computation.

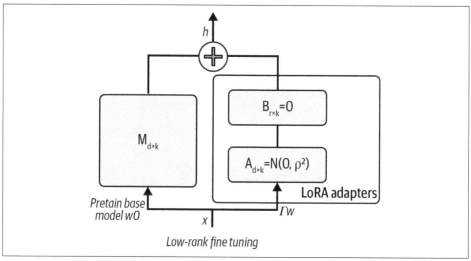

Figure 12-4. Low-rank adaptation fine tuning

Quantized LoRA (QLoRA)

As mentioned in the previous section, LoRA can reduce the memory requirements by up to 3x, increasing the possibility of fine tuning large models on consumer GPUs. If your target model is still too large for the memory at your disposal, then you will need to explore LoRA at reduced precision. Let's take the example of the LLaMA 65B model, which at half precision (`fp16`) requires 780 GB of VRAM. A third of that is still beyond the capacity available on commonly available consumer GPUs such as the 80 GB A100. Even the newer H200, offering 141 GB of memory, will fall short for this purpose.

Quantized LoRA[5] is an extension of the work by Timm Dettmers et al. that was discussed in "8-bit optimizers and quantization" on page 140. QLoRA defines a new 4-bit float format, 4-bit NormalFloat (`nf4`), that builds on the same concepts as the 8-bit quantile quantization discussed in Chapter 4. In addition, it implements *double quantization* by quantizing the quantization constants in order to save more memory. The third and last trick QLoRA uses is a CUDA trick: it utilizes Unified Virtual Addressing (discussed in Chapter 3) to introduce paging to offload unneeded memory onto the CPU to create more VRAM space on demand.

---

5 Dettmers, Tim, Artidoro Pagnoni, Ari Holtzman, and Luke Zettlemoyer. 2023. "QLoRA: Efficient Finetuning of Quantized LLMs." arXiv, May 23, 2023. *https://arxiv.org/abs/2305.14314*.

These three memory tricks are all combined with LoRA to achieve even more memory-efficient fine tuning, allowing LLaMA 65B to be trained on a GPU with a VRAM capacity of under 50 GB with no loss in performance. It's important to note, however, that this memory efficiency comes at the cost of some computation overhead due to all the quantization and dequantization steps, meaning training with QLoRA can be relatively slower than LoRA.

In the following section, you will explore an exercise that demonstrates how QLoRA can be used to fine tune large models.

Hands-on Exercise: QLoRA-Based Fine Tuning

LLaMA 2 7B is a 14 GB model typically saved in two chunks, one of ~10 GB and the other ~4 GB. Given the size of the model, it is typically used in half-precision (fp16) mode. In contrast, LLaMA 13B is a 27 GB (in fp16) model. In this exercise, you will be fine tuning the LLaMA 2 7B model on the bookcorpus dataset (*https://oreil.ly/ZQ1ff*) on a single 32 GB V100 node.

Implementation Details

The code for this exercise is located in the *qlora_llama_2.py* script (*https://oreil.ly/oAkWJ*) in the GitHub repository and can be executed by running the following command:

```
deep-learning-at-scale chapter_12 qlora train
```

In this example, you will use three libraries from Hugging Face: Transformers, Parameter Efficient Fine Tuning (PEFT), and Transformer Reinforcement Learning (TRL). You'll use Transformers to pull open source pretrained LLaMA models. PEFT provides implementations for various efficient fine-tuning techniques, including LoRA. TRL provides the SFTTrainer API that wraps an easy-to-use utility for fine tuning custom adapters.

You'll start by initializing the tokenizer, base LLaMA model, and bookcorpus dataset. Note the call out to BitsAndBytesConfig, which transparently uses the bitsandbytes library mentioned in Chapter 4, and the use of 4-bit nf4 format and double quantization:

```
quant_config = BitsAndBytesConfig(
    load_in_4bit=True,
    bnb_4bit_quant_type="nf4",
    bnb_4bit_compute_dtype=torch.float16,
    bnb_4bit_use_double_quant=True,
)
```

This example does not opt for CPU offloading. The configuration for LoRA is shown here:

```
peft_parameters = LoraConfig(lora_alpha=16, lora_dropout=0.1,
                             r=8, bias="none", task_type="CAUSAL_LM")
```

Here, `lora_alpha` is a hyperparameter used to derive the scaling coefficient to LoRA weights during fine tuning/the forward pass. The scale factor `f` is given by (`lora_alpha/r`) and applied to `W += (BAx) * f`. Popular values of `lora_alpha` and `r` are 16 and 8, respectively. LoRA has a dropout configuration to manage overfitting.

Besides these changes, the rest of the example's wiring is traditional. The `SFTTrainer` consumes the LoRA config and commences the fine tuning, allowing training of the 7B-parameter model to be fine tuned on a single 32 GB V100 node.

Inference

As discussed earlier, the low-rank fine tuning will produce only the adapter weights. These weights either need to be fused together prior to performing inference, or the forward pass is called separately on both the pretrained and adapter weights and the results are fused afterwards. Sebastian Raschka's excellent article "Finetuning LLMs with LoRA and QLoRA: Insights from Hundreds of Experiments"[6] goes into the details of weight merging and provides useful tips on choosing `r` and `lora_alpha`.

In this exercise, the inference logic follows the PEFT mechanism. First load the base model:

```
model = AutoModelForCausalLM.from_pretrained(
    config.base_model_name_or_path,
    device_map="auto",
    torch_dtype=torch.float16,
    low_cpu_mem_usage=True,
)
```

Then, we use the `PeftModel` API to load the adapter weights and fuse them into the base model, producing the final updated full weights:

```
# Load the LoRA adapters
model = PeftModel.from_pretrained(
    model,
    lora_model_fn,
    torch_dtype=torch.float16,
    device_map="auto",
)
```

---

6 Raschka, Sebastian. 2023. "Finetuning LLMs with LoRA and QLoRA: Insights from Hundreds of Experiments." Lightning AI blog. October 12, 2023. *https://lightning.ai/pages/community/lora-insights*. (*https://lightning.ai/pages/community/lora-insights/*)

To perform inference, we simply call the forward pass on the fused model using the `generate` API of the LLaMA model, as shown here:

```
text = "Without QLoRA fine tuning a large deep learning model can be daunting."
inputs = tokenizer(text, return_tensors="pt")
with torch.no_grad():
    text_gen = model.generate(
        **inputs,
        max_new_tokens=512,
        do_sample=True,
        penalty_alpha=0.6,
        top_k=5,
        pad_token_id=tokenizer.pad_token_id,
        eos_token_id=tokenizer.eos_token_id,
        repetition_penalty=1.1,
    )
    print(
        tokenizer.batch_decode(
            text_gen.detach().cpu().numpy(), skip_special_tokens=True
        )
    )
```

To run inference using the fine-tuned model, execute the following command, followed by training (as discussed in the previous section):

```
deep-learning-at-scale chapter_12 qlora inference
```

Exercise Summary

In this exercise, you trained a 7B-parameter model on a single 32 GB V100 node. At a batch size of 20, on this node the fine tuning will take about 6 hours. You will note no difference in inference latency, as your LoRA adapters are fused prior to inference (so, latency of LLaMA == latency of base LLaMA + adapter).

If you have access to a ~50 GB VRAM GPU, then you may want to check out fine tuning LLaMA 65B and see how QLoRA fares.

Summary

In this chapter you learned about a specialized fine tuning trick that will come in useful if you are working with large pretrained models that require custom adaptation for specialized tasks. Techniques like LoRA are increasingly valuable as we move closer and closer toward foundation models that are capable of performing a multitude of tasks (but that require fine tuning to perform accurately) being put into production and in the hands of users, where correctness is crucial.

With that said, the next and final chapter of this book will dive into the evolving landscape of foundation models.

## CHAPTER 13

Foundation Models

The loftier the building, the deeper must the foundation be laid.
—Thomas à Kempis

Extreme scaling of deep learning models in various dimensions (data, compute, capacity) has led to the development of general-purpose models that are capable of performing many different tasks without any explicit supervision. These evolutionary models often have generative and adaptive capabilities and are so effective across many tasks, ranging from basic perception and cognition to scene or text understanding and instruction following, that they are becoming increasingly central to applied AI.

In this chapter, you will learn about the fundamentals of these so-called foundation models and their evolution to date. You'll read about challenges involved in developing and adapting these models, explore how they are becoming multimodal, and review the groundbreaking architectures LLaVA, Flamingo, and BLIP-2.

What Are Foundation Models?

The term *foundation model* was coined by the Stanford Institute for Human-Centered Artificial Intelligence's Center for Research on Foundation Models to describe large-scale deep learning models that were trained on very large datasets and have the ability to perform well at many tasks without being explicitly (i.e., with full supervision) trained to do so.[1] These models are not only capable in their own unique

---

1 Bommasani, Rishi, Drew A. Hudson, Ehsan Adeli, Russ Altman, Simran Arora, Sydney von Arx, Michael S. Bernstein, et al. 2022. "On the Opportunities and Risks of Foundation Models." arXiv, July 12, 2022. *https://arxiv.org/abs/2108.07258v3*.

ways but, much like the foundations of a building, also provide a strong basis to extend and adapt to much more complex, purpose-specific tasks.

Two concepts associated with foundation models are emergence and homogenization. *Emergence* is associated with acquiring the ability to perform a task without being explicitly trained to do so. It's important to note that while emergence is a very broad concept, the foundation model's emerging abilities are limited to transfer of knowledge (learned from the training dataset).[2] On abstract reasoning and novel thinking tasks, these models exhibit abilities greatly inferior to biological intelligence.

Homogenization pertains to acquiring the ability to perform multiple tasks. The existence of both of these characteristics makes a model a "foundation model."

The Evolution of Foundation Models

It's interesting to note that the evolution of foundation models is essentially an example of extreme scaling. When deep learning models (deep networks) first emerged, they were simply neural networks at scale; i.e., with a very large number of layers (Figure 13-1). Similarly, foundation models are essentially deep learning models at scale. These models are typically highly parameterized (billions of parameters), trained with extremely large unlabeled datasets using distributed training techniques, and enabled by transfer learning and self-supervision. In terms of techniques and algorithms, most of what's required to develop a foundation model has already been discussed in the preceding chapters of this book.

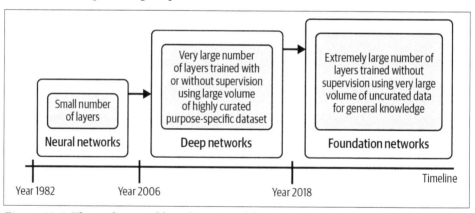

Figure 13-1. The evolution of foundation models

2 Mitchell, Melanie, Alessandro B. Palmarini, and Arseny Moskvichev. 2023. "Comparing Humans, GPT-4, and GPT-4V On Abstraction and Reasoning Tasks." arXiv, December 11, 2023. *https://arxiv.org/abs/2311.09247*.

The evolution of foundation models began following the introduction of the Transformer architecture by Vaswani et al. in 2017.[3] Two early Transformer-based architectures, the encoder-based Bidirectional Encoder Representations (BERT) and decoder-based Generative Pre-trained Transformer (GPT), exhibited both the emergence and homogenization desired in foundation models.[4] The evolution that started with these two language models continued in the NLP domain, with models such as RoBERTa, T5, GPT-2/3/3.5/4, Mistral, Mixtral, Google's PaLM-E, and Microsoft's Kosmos-1/2 emerging over the following years.

The key features these models share are scaling across multiple dimensions and self-supervision via masked language training. Their ability to take instructions and adapt to new tasks using zero-or few-shot learning, as discussed in Chapters 11 and 12, has enabled many applications in the text processing and analytics domain; they can easily be adapted to a variety of language-based tasks, such as question answering, instruction following, text summarization, and many more.

Early foundation models were predominantly large language models, for two reasons: the Transformer architecture was initially explored in the NLP domain, and language contains a huge amount of complex, compressed knowledge curated by humans, so general learning, as is needed in foundation models, is easily developed with language as the source of knowledge. However, the shift that started with NLP soon spread across other domains as well, such as computer vision and speech. The Segment Anything Model (SAM) and its newer variant, the Segment Everything Everywhere Model (SEEM), are examples of foundation models that can segment anything in an image given different types of prompts (e.g., text, boxes, points, etc.).[5] As expected from a foundation model, these are general models that may offer varying degrees of performance for specific domains and may need fine tuning to adapt to more nuanced use cases. Accordingly, SAM and its variants often require fine tuning to perform reasonably well on domain-specific tasks such as medical image segmentation.

---

3 Vaswani, Ashish, Noam Shazeer, Niki Parmar, Jakob Uszkoreit, Llion Jones, Aidan N. Gomez, Lukasz Kaiser, and Illia Polosukhin. 2017. "Attention Is All You Need." arXiv, December 6, 2017. *https://arxiv.org/abs/1706.03762v5*.

4 Devlin, Jacob, Ming-Wei Chang, Kenton Lee, and Kristina Toutanova. 2019. "BERT: Pre-Training of Deep Bidirectional Transformers for Language Understanding." arXiv, May 24, 2019. *https://arxiv.org/abs/1810.04805v2*; Radford, Alec, Karthik Narasimhan, Tim Salimans, and Ilya Sutskever. 2018. "Improving Language Understanding by Generative Pre-Training." *https://paperswithcode.com/paper/improving-language-understanding-by*.

5 Kirillov, Alexander, Eric Mintun, Nikhila Ravi, Hanzi Mao, Chloe Rolland, Laura Gustafson, Tete Xiao, et al. 2023. "Segment Anything." arXiv, April 5, 2023. *https://arxiv.org/abs/2304.02643*; Zou, Xueyan, Jianwei Yang, Hao Zhang, Feng Li, Linjie Li, Jianfeng Wang, Lijuan Wang, Jianfeng Gao, and Yong Jae Lee. 2023. "Segment Everything Everywhere All at Once." arXiv, July 11, 2023. *https://arxiv.org/abs/2304.06718*.

While most foundation models today are Transformer-based, alternative architectures are rapidly evolving to address the quadratic computation inefficiency of the Transformer architecture. These include the convolution-based Hyena hierarchy; state-space architectures like S4, H3, and Bidirectional Gated SSM (BiGS), which uses sequence routing without attention; single-headed gated attention architectures like MEGA; and Monarch Mixer, which seeks to replace the attention module of Transformers with unique diagonal matrices.[6]

Neural network architectures like Stable Diffusion, CLIP, and DALL-E that combine the knowledge expressed in language and images through self-supervision (using techniques such as contrastive learning, masking, etc.) are generative foundation models capable of producing impressive creative results given instructions/prompts (so-called generative AI).[7] The creative abilities of such models go beyond generating static images, too, to early-stage video curation and editing; Emu Video (*https://oreil.ly/DQJPw*) from Meta is a good example of such foundational abilities.

One of the challenges with generative AI is getting the consistency and correctness of fine features right. Take the example of "The Dog and the Boy" (*https://oreil.ly/AgljT*), the three-minute AI-assisted short film published by Netflix Japan; it demonstrates the impressive abilities of foundation models, but the creation required editing refinements post-AI generation.

6 Poli, Michael, Stefano Massaroli, Eric Nguyen, Daniel Y. Fu, Tri Dao, Stephen Baccus, Yoshua Bengio, Stefano Ermon, Christopher and Ré. 2023. "Hyena Hierarchy: Towards Larger Convolutional Language Models." arXiv, April 19, 2023. *https://arxiv.org/abs/2302.10866*; Gu, Albert, Karan Goel, Christopher and Ré. 2022. "Efficiently Modeling Long Sequences with Structured State Spaces." arXiv, August 5, 2022. *https://arxiv.org/abs/2111.00396v3*; Fu, Daniel Y., Tri Dao, Khaled K. Saab, Armin W. Thomas, Atri Rudra, Christopher and Ré. 2023. "Hungry Hungry Hippos: Towards Language Modeling with State Space Models." arXiv, April 29, 2023. *https://arxiv.org/abs/2212.14052v3*; Wang, Junxiong, Jing Nathan Yan, Albert Gu, and Alexander M. Rush. 2023. Pretraining Without Attention. arXiv, May 9, 2023. *https://arxiv.org/abs/2212.10544v2*; Ma, Xuezhe, Chunting Zhou, Xiang Kong, Junxian He, Liangke Gui, Graham Neubig, Jonathan May, and Luke Zettlemoyer. 2023. Mega: Moving Average Equipped Gated Attention. arXiv, January 28, 2023. *https://arxiv.org/abs/2209.10655v3*; Fu, Daniel Y., Simran Arora, Jessica Grogan, Isys Johnson, Sabri Eyuboglu, Armin W. Thomas, Benjamin Spector, et al. 2023. "Monarch Mixer: A Simple Sub-Quadratic GEMM-Based Architecture." arXiv, October 18, 2023. *https://arxiv.org/abs/2310.12109*.

7 Rombach, Robin, Andreas Blattmann, Dominik Lorenz, Patrick Esser, and Björn Ommer. 2022. "High-Resolution Image Synthesis with Latent Diffusion Models." arXiv, April 13, 2022. *https://arxiv.org/abs/2112.10752v2*; Radford, Alec, Jong Wook Kim, Chris Hallacy, Aditya Ramesh, Gabriel Goh, Sandhini Agarwal, Girish Sastry, et al. 2021. "Learning Transferable Visual Models from Natural Language Supervision." arXiv, February 26, 2021. *https://arxiv.org/abs/2103.00020*; Ramesh, Aditya, Mikhail Pavlov, Gabriel Goh, Scott Gray, Chelsea Voss, Alec Radford, Mark Chen, and Ilya Sutskever. 2021. "Zero-Shot Text-to-Image Generation." arXiv, February 26, 2021. *https://arxiv.org/abs/2102.12092*.

These innovations are influencing how audio streams are handled as well. For instance, Meta's SeamlessM4T[8] provides powerful capabilities covering about 100 languages in text and speech form. Though impressive, this is still a very small portion of the approximately 7,000 languages spoken around the world. The biggest challenge seems to be in acquiring a speech and text dataset suitable for training such a general multilingual model.

Figure 13-2 lists some of the key foundation models known today, along with the modalities of data they are trained with. You may note that while foundation models have penetrated other modalities beyond text/language, NLP remains a constant source to power the learning.

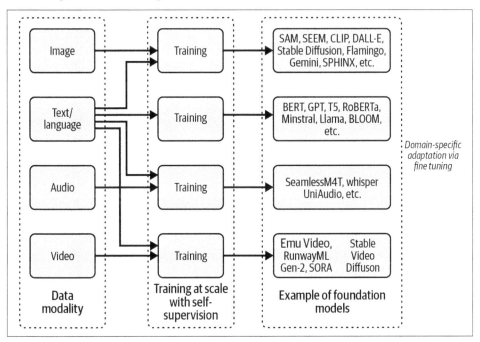

Figure 13-2. Examples of foundation models by data modality

As shown in this figure, most foundation models are multimodal, learning from more than one dataset modality. Having said that, most of these models can't handle true interleaved multimodal content as we humans do. For example, CLIP is a multimodal model that is trained on both images and text, but it handles the knowledge from these two modalities separately and cannot reason with intermixed text and

8 Barrault, Loïc, Yu-An Chung, Mariano Coria Meglioli, David Dale, Ning Dong, Mark Duppenthaler, Paul-Ambroise Duquenne, et al. 2023. "Seamless: Multilingual Expressive and Streaming Speech Translation." arXiv, December 8, 2023. *https://arxiv.org/abs/2312.05187.*

image content like you do. Techniques capable of achieving true multimodality (i.e., handling interleaved mixed content types) are still emerging. Models that attempt to mimic human perception in this way are known as *multimodal large language models* (MLLMs), or *large multimodal models* (LMMs)—terms that don't necessarily make clear the goal they are aiming for! In later parts of this chapter, you will read about a specific set of techniques widely used to develop foundation models. For a more comprehensive overview of the MLLM landscape, see Li et al.'s paper "Multimodal Foundation Models: From Specialists to General-Purpose Assistants."[9]

Now that you understand what foundation models are and where they came from, in the following section we'll briefly review some of the challenges involved in developing these models.

Challenges Involved in Developing Foundation Models

The training of a foundation model is complex, due the extensive scaling involved. Since the challenges of experiment planning, sourcing data, and training at scale have already been discussed in this book, this section will highlight challenges unique to foundation models. All the other issues discussed so far will implicitly apply, given the required scale.

Measurement Complexity

One of the biggest challenges in developing a foundation model is defining the right metrics to measure its performance and capabilities. The metrics and measurements that are available tend to get more accurate and specific the more specific the task/objective is. For instance, measuring error (e.g., mean squared error) in object counting in any given image is a much more relatable and reflective metric of the model's ability to perform the task than loss (e.g., contrastive loss) or even mean average precision or intersection over union, since the goal here is not segmentation correctness but counting. Conversely, the more abstract and general the model is, the more abstract the metrics and measurements become (e.g., perplexity as a metric for language ability). Such metrics are often more qualitative than quantitative, resulting in noisy measurements. For instance, using ratings (say, on a scale of 1–5) to measure the quality of generated text is very subjective. It would be very hard to achieve an unambiguous rating across many raters, let alone by measuring a model's ability based on one rater's grades.

---

9 Chunyuan Li, Zhe Gan, Zhengyuan Yang, Jianwei Yang, Linjie Li, Lijuan Wang, and Jianfeng Gao, "Multimodal Foundation Models: From Specialists to General-Purpose Assistants," arXiv, September 18, 2023, *https://arxiv.org/abs/2309.10020*.

Absence of labels can be a complicating factor. To address this, auxiliary tasks are often added to training objectives where possible (e.g., adding image captioning tasks to image-language pretraining).

Deployment Challenges

Foundation models pose unique challenges during deployment as well, for a few reasons. First, they are implicitly large models, and the cost is the same whether you use them to perform trivial tasks or complex ones. As a result, these models can increase the cost of your production system when applied for trivial yet high-demand use cases. Second, these are general models, and thus they require fine tuning for specialized tasks. Inference-time tuning methods like prompting or few-shot tuning require careful refinement and are more of an art than a science, so often these techniques are fragile. Although improvements have been made in this space with chain-of-thought and more refined reasoning strategies, the reality is such tuning requires careful curation of prompts inspired by understanding of the problem domain and of the model's abilities.

Propagation of Defects to All Downstream Models

The advantage that foundation models can accelerate specialized model development through adaptation comes at the cost of any defects and limitations in these models being inherited by all downstream adapted models. For instance, if the base model had a defect wherein upon receiving a specific prompt, it regurgitated training data,[10] then all downstream models would carry this defect as well, which could risk affecting the correctness and quality of their output in production.

Legal and Ethical Considerations

Foundation models are trained with very large corpora of data with minimal curation. In addition, training is self-supervised, so there is little control over what the model is learning. As a result of these factors, managing and controlling the dataset and the learning abilities of the model becomes very difficult. Ensuring that data used for training is obtained within legal and ethical bounds and that the model is safe and suitable to be deployed, adheres to social norms, and will be useful to users are significant challenges. Safety, ethical, and legal considerations are big, open questions that

---

10 Nasr, Milad, Nicholas Carlini, Jonathan Hayase, Matthew Jagielski, A. Feder Cooper, Daphne Ippolito, Christopher A. Choquette-Choo, et al. 2023. "Scalable Extraction of Training Data from (Production) Language Models." arXiv, November 28, 2023. *https://arxiv.org/abs/2311.17035*.

require significant research. At the moment, much of the alignment is ensured by human feedback and fine tuning. However, the limitations are widely known.[11]

Ensuring Consistency and Coherency

Foundation models must be consistent and coherent to be useful. This is currently an unsolved problem and an active area of research. An inference technique known as Woodpecker[12] shows promising results with MLLMs; it decomposes the original output into key concepts, formulates verification questions, validates the results, and uses this information to correct the original output as needed (see Figure 13-3).

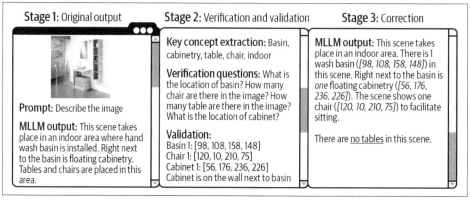

Figure 13-3. Model output correction as proposed by Woodpecker

Multimodal Large Language Models

You read about CLIP in Chapter 11 in the context of contrastive learning (see Figure 11-6 in "Contrastive learning" on page 381). Even though CLIP is a multimodal network, it is not a true multimodal language model in the sense discussed earlier (an MLLM). In this section, you will read about the specialized class of foundation models that are capable of handling intermixed multimodal content. At the time of writing, there are a very limited set of models that possess this ability; they include OpenAI's GPT-4, DeepMind's Flamingo, Google's Gemini, BLIP-2, LLaVA, Microsoft's Kosmos-G, and Shanghai AI Lab's SPHINX. Unfortunately, many of these models are closed source—that is, their details are not available publicly—but the field is rapidly evolving.

---

11 Wei, Alexander, Nika Haghtalab, and Jacob Steinhardt. 2023. "Jailbroken: How Does LLM Safety Training Fail?" arXiv, July 5, 2023. *https://arxiv.org/abs/2307.02483*.

12 Yin, Shukang, Chaoyou Fu, Sirui Zhao, Tong Xu, Hao Wang, Dianbo Sui, Yunhang Shen, Ke Li, Xing Sun, and Enhong Chen. 2023. "Woodpecker: Hallucination Correction for Multimodal Large Language Models." arXiv, October 24, 2023. *https://arxiv.org/abs/2310.16045*.

Currently, there are three known approaches to achieve this intermixing of different modalities: projection, gated cross-attention, and query-based encoding. Each of these approaches uses a pretrained language and vision encoder, mostly trained in the same way as CLIP (Figure 13-4).

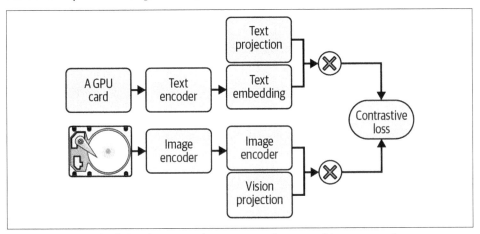

Figure 13-4. The high-level CLIP architecture, with text and image encoders

Projection

In the simplest approach, as proposed in the LLaVA architecture,[13] images are passed through a pretrained CLIP vision encoder to obtain a vision embedding that is then sent through a learnable projection layer to produce a fixed-size embedding. This fixed-size embedding is then appended to the text (or prompt) embedding before being passed through the network to obtain the final result, which is now based on the combined language and vision representation, as shown in Figure 13-5.

---

13 Liu, Haotian, Chunyuan Li, Qingyang Wu, and Yong Jae Lee. 2023. "Visual Instruction Tuning." arXiv, December 11, 2023. *https://arxiv.org/abs/2304.08485*.

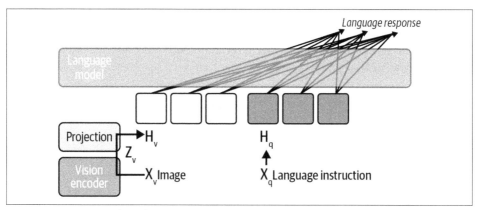

Figure 13-5. LLaVA-based intermixing with a projection layer

Shanghai AI Lab's SPHINX[14] also adopts this approach; its source code is available on GitHub (*https://oreil.ly/qn5Pj*).

Gated Cross-Attention

Flamingo proposed the use of gated cross-attention to realize the intermixing of modalities.[15] It uses CLIP's pretrained language and vision encoders such that the language output is conditioned on the visual embedding, allowing it to generate free-form content that considers features from images as well. Gated attention, as shown in Figure 13-6, attends to the vision embedding that's obtained from the vision encoder following a perceiver-based resampling. The perceiver resampler module enables attending to varying-sized vision embeddings and producing a fixed-sized embedding.

---

14 Lin, Ziyi, Chris Liu, Renrui Zhang, Peng Gao, Longtian Qiu, Han Xiao, Han Qiu, et al. 2023. "SPHINX: The Joint Mixing of Weights, Tasks, and Visual Embeddings for Multi-Modal Large Language Models." arXiv, November 13, 2023. *https://arxiv.org/abs/2311.07575*.

15 Alayrac, Jean-Baptiste, Jeff Donahue, Pauline Luc, Antoine Miech, Iain Barr, Yana Hasson, Karel Lenc, et al. 2022. "Flamingo: A Visual Language Model for Few-Shot Learning." arXiv, November 15, 2022. *https://arxiv.org/abs/2204.14198*.

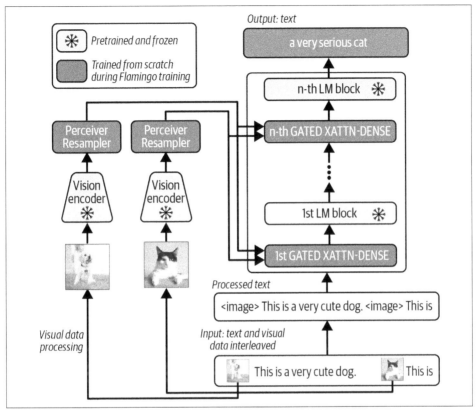

Figure 13-6. The high-level architecture of Flamingo (adapted from Alayrac et al., 2022)

Query-Based Encoding

Query-based encoding, the third approach to intermixing, uses a Querying Transformer (Q-Former) to obtain the joint embedding. The Q-Former is a Transformer-based module that acts as an information bottleneck between the image encoder and the language model, extracting visual features and passing on only the ones that are most useful for the given text/prompt to produce the output. To perform this extraction, it learns a set of queries (that is, the queries of Q-Former are learnable). This approach, illustrated in Figure 13-7, was proposed as part of Salesforce's BLIP-2.[16]

16 Li, Junnan, Dongxu Li, Silvio Savarese, and Steven Hoi. 2023. "BLIP-2: Bootstrapping Language-Image Pre-Training with Frozen Image Encoders and Large Language Models." arXiv, June 15, 2023. *https://arxiv.org/abs/2301.12597*.

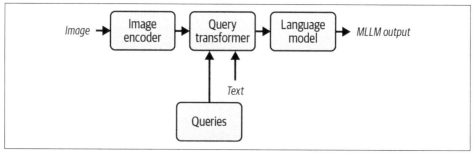

Figure 13-7. The high-level architecture of BLIP-2

Further Exploration

Additional resources you might want to explore to learn more about MLLMs include LAVIS (*https://oreil.ly/G8ayM*), LLaMA2-Accessory (*https://oreil.ly/BsAxX*), and Microsoft's UniLM (*https://oreil.ly/hUKE9*). The TorchScale library (*https://oreil.ly/BWvJr*) is also quite useful for more low-level implementations of foundation models. Newer architectures, such as Open AI's GPT-4 and Google's Gemini, are able to interleave multimodal content that goes beyond text and vision and also includes audio, etc.; however, specific architectural details of these models are not known.

Summary

In this chapter, you read about foundation models and their evolution. You also learned about some of the challenges involved in developing these models. As discussed earlier, unresolved concerns about ethics, safety, and consistency make their use quite tricky in decision-critical systems. Still, these models are powerful and are being used increasingly in less mission-critical fields, such as generative arts, where users have more controls for further refinement and tuning for correctness and consistency. With cross-modality reasoning now possible, this is an exciting area to watch.

Index

About the Author

Suneeta Mall is passionate about leveraging engineering, data, science, and machine learning to solve real-world challenges. With a Ph.D. in applied science and a strong background in computer science and engineering, Suneeta has amassed extensive experience in distributed, scalable computing and machine learning. Her previous stints include IBM Software Labs, Expedita, USyd, and Nearmap; currently, she leads the AI engineering division at harrison.ai, a clinician-led artificial intelligence medical technology company, where she works to address pressing healthcare issues. Apart from her work at harrison.ai, Suneeta is a firm believer in lifelong learning and knowledge sharing.

Colophon

The animal on the cover of *Deep Learning at Scale* is a beluga sturgeon (*Huso huso*). The animal is also referred to as a great sturgeon or beluga. This species of anadromous fish can be found primarily in the Caspian and Black Sea basins.

In general, a sturgeon has an elongated body, heterocercal tail, naked skin, and a series of scutes—thickened bony plates. What makes the beluga sturgeon stand out is its size. It is considered the third-most-massive living species of bony fish; it is the largest freshwater fish in the world; and it is known as one of the largest actively predatory fish. Records of beluga sturgeon being caught highlight the fish's huge size, with some fish weighing thousands of pounds. As of the current average, a caught beluga sturgeon is about 4 to 11 feet in length and weighs anywhere from 42 to 582 pounds. However, some have been known to measure much larger.

The fish's appearance changes over the course of its life. As a juvenile, a beluga sturgeon is slender with a narrow head and upward-pointing mouth. Its flanks are dark gray or black and its belly is white. As an adult, the beluga sturgeon has a massive head, with its mouth having gradually moved into a frontal position with a short snout. Its coloring is blue-gray or dark brown with silver or gray flanks, and the belly remains white. The most predominant feature of the beluga sturgeon as it continues to age, specifically in its elder years, is its huge mouth.

Much like the beluga sturgeon's appearance changes over the course of its life, the beluga sturgeon's diet also changes. As a juvenile, the animal feeds on benthic invertebrates. As an adult, the animal eats a wide range of large fish, which makes up 73% of its diet. Other food the beluga sturgeon eats includes mollusks, crustaceans, aquatic birds, and young seals.

The beluga sturgeon population, specifically the female fish, is heavily fished for its beluga caviar. Since 2005, the United States Fish and Wildlife Service has banned imports of beluga caviar and other beluga products. Over time, populations have been reduced due to overfishing and poaching, and the animal is currently considered critically endangered. Many of the animals on O'Reilly covers are endangered; all of them are important to the world.

The cover illustration is by Karen Montgomery, based on an antique engraving from *Lydekker's Royal Natural History*. The series design is by Edie Freedman, Ellie Volckhausen, and Karen Montgomery. The cover fonts are Gilroy Semibold and Guardian Sans. The text font is Adobe Minion Pro; the heading font is Adobe Myriad Condensed; and the code font is Dalton Maag's Ubuntu Mono.

O'REILLY®

Learn from experts.
Become one yourself.

Books | Live online courses
Instant answers | Virtual events
Videos | Interactive learning

Get started at oreilly.com.

Milton Keynes UK
Ingram Content Group UK Ltd.
UKHW020851220624
444461UK00001B/3